W9-AXX-037

The Illustrated History

SUPERHERO ★COMICS★

ALSO BY MIKE BENTON:

Horror Comics: The Illustrated History

The Comic Book in America: An Illustrated History

Comic Book Collecting for Fun and Profit

FORTHCOMING TITLES IN THE TAYLOR HISTORY OF COMICS:

Science Fiction Comics: The Illustrated History

Superhero Comics of the Golden Age: The Illustrated History

The Illustrated History

SUPERHERO COMICS

MIKE BENTON

Author of *The Comic Book in America*

TAYLOR PUBLISHING COMPANY

DALLAS, TEXAS

Published by
Taylor Publishing Company
1550 West Mockingbird Lane
Dallas, Texas 75235

Designed by David Timmons

Interior photography by
Austin Prints For Publication
Jeff Rowe, photographer

Library of Congress
Cataloging-in-Publication Data

Benton, Mike.
Superhero comics of the silver age : the illustrated history / Mike Benton.
p. cm. — (The Taylor history of comics ; 2)
Includes bibliographical references and index.
ISBN 0-87833-746-6 $24.95
1. Comic books, strips, etc.—United States—History and criticism. I. Title II. Series
PN6725.B385 1991
741.5'0973—dc20 91-18560
CIP

Printed in the United States of America

10 9 8 7 6 5 4 3 2 1

To the superheroes,
the heroes who dreamed them,
and everyone who has ever
dreamed about them . . .

The author gratefully acknowledges the help of the following people who have aided in the development of this book: Laura Benton, Jerry Bails, Mary Kelly, Max Lakin, Holly McGuire, Lou Mougin, Mike Tiefenbacher, and Carol Trammel.

Tales to Astonish #90, ©1966 *Marvel Entertainment Group, Inc.* Gil Kane.

CONTENTS

The Story

Amazing Fantasy #15 © *1962 Marvel Entertainment Group, Inc.* Steve Ditko. The first appearance of Spider-Man.

HEROES AND SUPERHEROES

"As Peter Parker, I was just a helpless, confused school kid! But as Spider-Man, things are gonna be a lot different!"

— *Amazing Spider-Man* #10

Superman #161 © *1963 DC Comics, Inc.* Curt Swan, George Klein.

It was the summer of 1963 and we had heroes.

We had our first astronauts—Virgil "Gus" Grissom, John Glenn, Walter Schirra, and Gordon Cooper—new heroes of the dawning Space Age. We had sports heroes like Roger Maris and Cassius Clay; Nobel Prize winners like Martin Luther King and John Steinbeck. Our president was a war hero, and we watched as he honored American heroes with the new Presidential Medal of Freedom.

Our leaders encouraged us to be heroic. It was a time of hope and optimism. Vietnam would not be on the front pages for a year. No one had even heard of Lee Harvey Oswald.

We had so many real-life heroes that we needed—demanded—more from our fictional heroes. We needed heroes larger than life, more powerful than ordinary men or women. We needed *superheroes*.

And we got them—aplenty—in our comic books.

Iron Man, Spider-Man, Wonder Woman, Green Lantern, the Fantastic Four, Flash, Supergirl, Hawkman, the Incredible Hulk, Aquaman, Ant-Man, Batman, Thor—dozens of costumed comic book heroes were all over the newsstands and magazine racks in the summer of 1963.

Ever since the 1940s, comic books have given us our most colorful and powerful heroes. Superman, Wonder Woman, Batman, Captain Marvel, Plastic Man, and others saw us through World War II and beyond. They were a part of the Golden Age of superhero comic books, which lasted until the end of the 1940s.

By the 1950s, however, most of these superheroes had disappeared. Green Lantern, Captain America, and the Human Torch, were replaced by western, war, romance, horror, and crime comics.

Then, in the late 1950s, the old heroes slowly returned. Some wore their old costumes; some had new uniforms and identities. By 1963, over a dozen superheroes from the Golden Age reappeared. And there were also new superheroes, from nearly every publisher, created especially to satisfy an ever-growing demand.

This Silver Age of Comics was a renaissance, a hearkening back to the Golden Age of superheroes. The best of the old heroes were resurrected and updated; new heroes burst forth in numbers not seen for twenty years. Comic book writers and comic book artists dazzled us with their creativity and imagination.

The superheroes were back.

UP IN THE SKY...

Blue Beetle #18 ©1955 Charlton Comics

"You nabbed a crook? Let me have the exclusive scoop, Superman! After all, I'm your pal!"

— *Superman's Pal Jimmy Olsen* #19

The superheroes were dying in the fading years of the 1940s. One by one they vanished. Captain America, Green Lantern, and the Blue Beetle were on the newsstands one month. The next month, they were gone.

As the 1940s ended, superhero comics were replaced by romance comics, western comics, crime comics, and horror comics. By the early 1950s, less than a dozen comic book superheroes could be found.

In the post-war years of the late 1940s and early 1950s, America was settling in for a decade of readjustment, grim introspection, and fearful preparation for a Cold War which had already begun. The time for nationalistic heroics and superheroes was over.

Crime comics and horror comics, with their antiheroes and nihilistic vision of society, were the most popular comic books in the early 1950s. They were read by millions of readers who found it easier to believe in Frankenstein's monster than in Billy Batson's alter ego, Captain Marvel.

In fact, Captain Marvel, the most popular superhero of the 1940s, was fighting for his life. Declining sales and an impending copyright lawsuit finally ended the entire line of Captain Marvel comics in 1953. The magic word "Shazam!" would no longer be whispered by wide-eyed readers.

It was the end of an era.

Not only were the superheroes dying, but the entire comic book industry was under a growing cloud of gloom and despair. A 1954 congressional investigation into the alleged ill effects of comic books upon children shook the industry. Parents and educators joined with opportunistic politicians and self-appointed moral guardians in a national anti-comic book campaign. Comic books were smeared, slammed, and nearly destroyed by a congressional subcommittee which accused them of contributing to juvenile delinquency and undermining the moral fiber of the nation's youth.

By the early 1950s, with the growing anti-comic book sentiment and troubles of the comic book publishers, it seemed unlikely that there would be any impetus for a rebirth of the superhero comic—at least from within the comic book industry itself.

Ironically, it would be television, that new and dreaded one-eyed competitor for the comic book audience, that would save the superheroes.

"Yes, it's Superman . . . strange visitor from another planet who came to Earth with powers and abilities far beyond those of mortal man. Superman, who can change the course of mighty rivers, bend steel in his bare hands. . . . "

The Adventures of Superman premiered on TV in 1951. He was "faster than a speeding bullet, more powerful than a locomotive," and his show was more popular than any other afternoon television show of the 1950s. Superman was alive and well in our living rooms, from 1953 to 1957, for a total of 104 episodes.

The Superman TV show was the brainchild of producer Robert Maxwell and DC Comics editor Whitney Ellsworth. Ellsworth knew that TV might turn out to be the comic book industry's biggest competition, and he wanted to get Superman on the small screen. It was up to Maxwell to find the person who could bring the comic book hero to life.

Walking along a beach, Maxwell saw a handsome movie actor wearing a pair of sunglasses. To Maxwell, the actor looked like Clark Kent in the glasses, and when he took them off, he looked like Superman. Maxwell had found his star: George Reeves.

Reeves would make Superman a household word not only in America but around the world. Ellsworth had been right. Television, a young and dynamic visual medium, was the perfect home for a superhero who was having trouble as a newsstand comic book.

Meanwhile, back at the corner newsstand, anxious comic book publishers were trying to figure out what new trick, new gimmick, or new approach would grab the readers' attention. The latest hot craze had been 3-D comic books; kids wore red-and-blue cellophane glasses and got eyestrain when they read them. That fad lasted for one year.

Stan Lee, the longtime editor at Marvel Comics, remembered that "every few years there was a new trend. We'd be very big in westerns and suddenly the western field would dry up . . . and we'd do romances or mysteries or funny animals . . . whatever."

In the volatile and competitive comic book market of 1953, publishers often relied on tips from distributors, industry gossip, and gut instinct in their search for new titles and new readers.

The Superman TV show was the talk of the trade. Increased sales of *Superman* comic books were being reported by newsstand agents. Martin Goodman, publisher of Marvel Comics, trend follower and trend maker par excellence, took notice.

Goodman, under the name of Timely Comics, had published some of the more memorable superhero comics of the 1940s—Captain America, Human Torch, and Sub-Mariner. Goodman's company would become even better known as Marvel Comics.

Like many other companies, Timely (or Marvel) Comics had retired its heroes in the late 1940s and was churning out war, romance, and horror comics. With the popularity of the new Superman TV show, Goodman thought perhaps it was time to bring the Marvel superheroes back.

In the pages of a late 1953 war/adventure comic book called *Young Men*, Captain

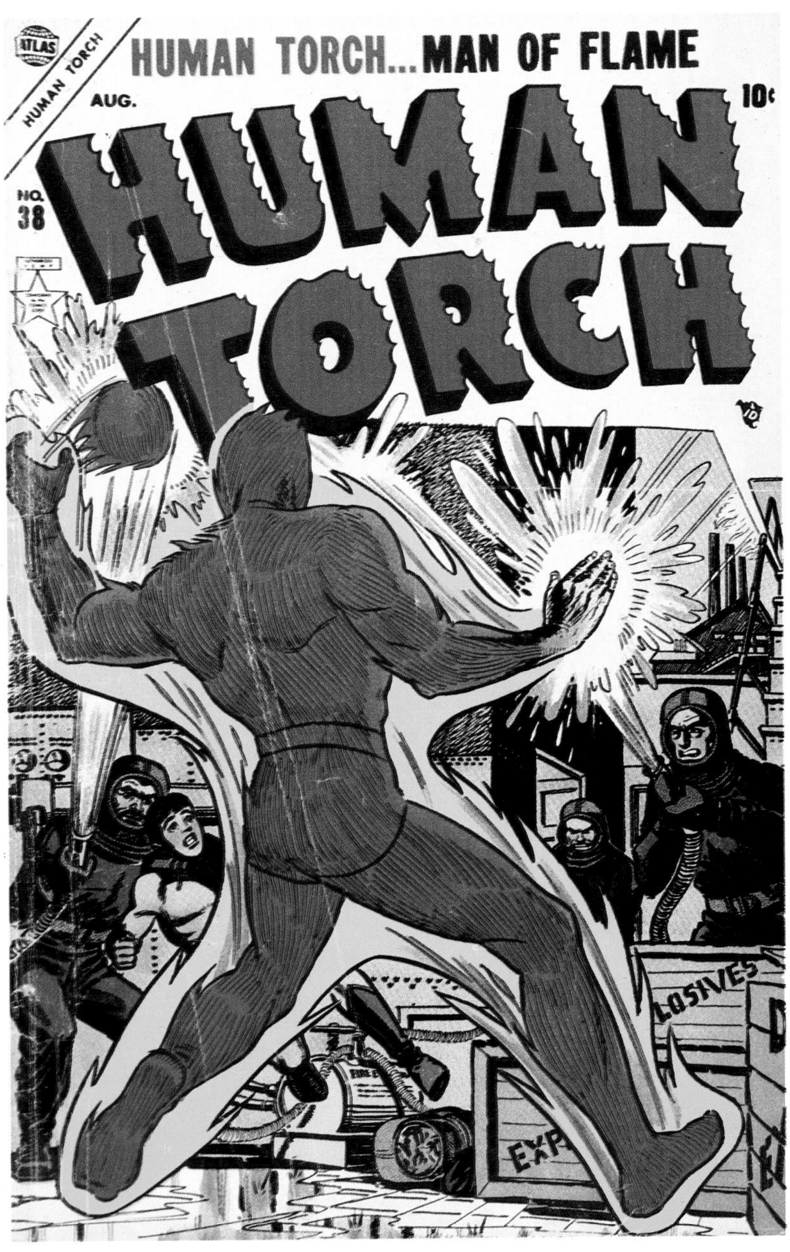

Human Torch #38
©1954 Marvel Entertainment Group, Inc.

Nature Boy #3 ©1956 *Charlton Comics*. John Buscema.

America, Human Torch, and Sub-Mariner returned. By the spring of 1954, each of the three heroes had books of his own.

The Sub-Mariner attracted the attention of television producer Frank Saverstein, who wanted to create a TV show about the underwater superhero. The popularity of the Superman television series was enough to convince Arthur Godfrey to back a pilot for a Sub-Mariner show, but negotiations ultimately fell through.

Still, there were three new superhero comic books on the newsstands in 1954: *Sub-Mariner, Human Torch,* and *Captain America.* It wasn't a tidal wave of superheroes—the three Marvel comics were almost lost in the over 650 comic titles that crowded the stands that year. Marvel alone was publishing dozens of other titles, like horror comics and romance comics, which were much more popular than Captain America or the Human Torch. A casual comic reader in 1954 would probably have overlooked the new Marvel superheroes on the crowded comic racks.

Strongman #3 ©1955 *Magazine Enterprises*. Bob Powell.

One person, however, did notice the resurrected superheroes. Joe Simon, who (along with Jack Kirby) had created Captain America for Marvel Comics in 1941, particularly scrutinized the new *Captain America* comic book. He was annoyed that his and Kirby's creation was being revived and reused without their permission or benefit. Simon's position as an early comic book creator was not unusual. Most comic book characters created by writers and artists in the 1940s became company properties with no benefits accruing to their creators.

Samson #13 ©1955 *Four Star Publications*

"We were bitter about not owning Captain America," Simon recalled when he and Jack Kirby saw their character brought back by Marvel in 1953. "We thought we would show them how to do Captain America again. Instead we did *Fighting American*. We thought they (Marvel) would take action against us, but they didn't."

Fighting American was the first new superhero series created for the 1950s, and the *Fighting American* showed his Cold War origins. He was an anti-communist crusader—"my country right or wrong." After the first superpatriotic issue in April 1954, there was a backlash in the media against the anti-communist tactics used by Senator Joseph McCarthy in his congressional investigation. The later issues of *Fighting American* still featured communist villains like Poison Ivan and Hotsky Trotsky but, as the names might suggest, the comic quickly became a parody of the patriotic superhero genre, or as artist Jack Kirby called it, "a satire on our condition."

Another longtime comic book professional, S.M. "Jerry" Iger, also took note of Marvel's reentry into the superhero field, as well as Simon and Kirby's *Fighting American*. Iger had started one of the first comic book studios in 1936. His art shop supplied comic book stories to early publishers such as Victor Fox. For Fox, Iger's studio created superheroes like the Blue Beetle, the Flame, the Green Mask, and Samson in the early 1940s.

Fox was out of business by now, and Iger's studio was producing art and stories for several small 1950s comic book publishers, including Robert Farrell who published comics under the name of Ajax-Farrell and Four-Star Publishing. Ever quick to spot and follow a trend, Iger offered to supply Farrell with new stories featuring the old Fox superheroes.

Together with editor and writer Ruth Roche in late 1954, Iger's shop turned out reprises of such 1940s superheroes as the *Flame, Phantom Lady*, and *Samson*.

At almost the same time, Martin Smith, the editor at Sterling Comics (a one-room comic book company with three titles), hired artist Mike Sekowsky to draw a new superhero for his line. *Captain Flash* appeared in the fall of 1954. His superpowers occurred as a result of radioactivity—a common trait of many superheroes later created in the 1960s.

By the beginning of 1955, there were almost a dozen new superhero titles, including the *Avenger, Strong Man, Blue Beetle*, and *Wonder Boy*.

The Superman TV show, along with the self-imitation of the comic book marketplace, had created a miniboom of 1950s superhero comics. Nearly all of these new titles, however, would die within a year—victims of a huge depression that crippled most of the industry by the mid-1950s.

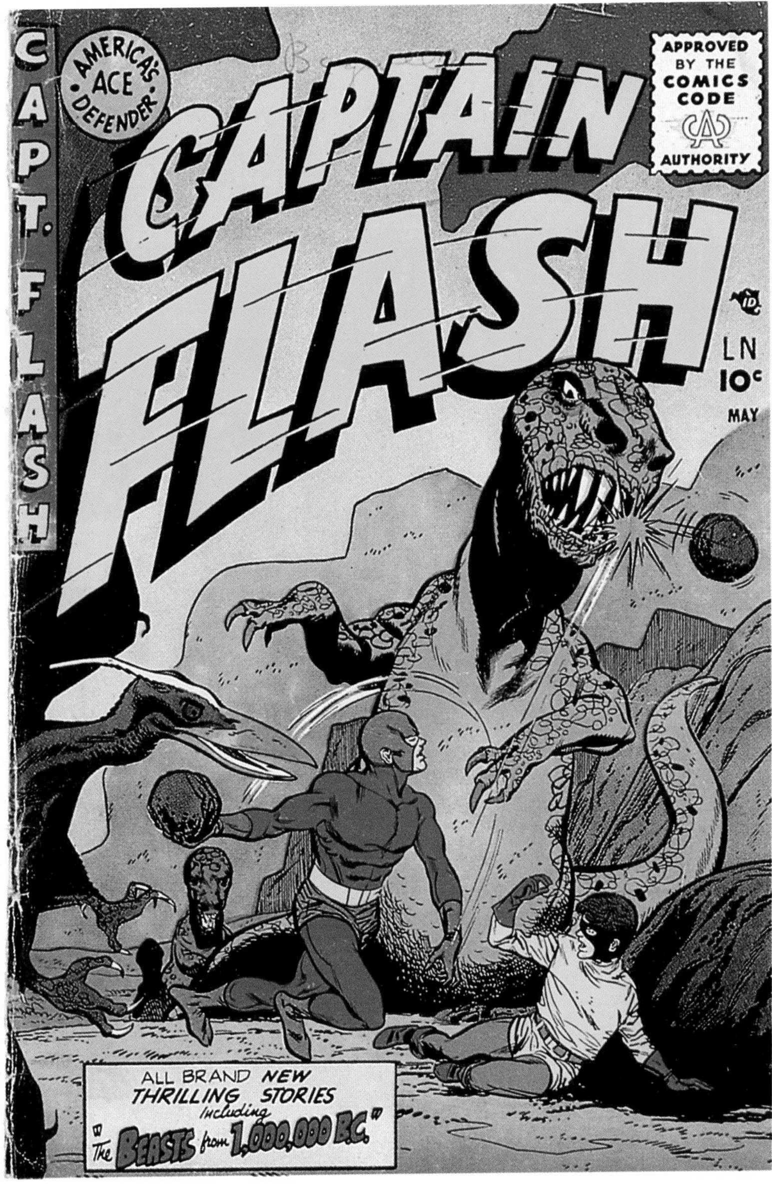

Captain Flash #3 ©1955 Sterling Comics. Mike Sekowsky, Mike Peppe.

There was one title, however, that survived. Of all the 1950s superhero comics, it was also the one most directly inspired by the success of the Superman television show. It was a comic book about Superman's friend, or, as it was titled in September 1954, *Superman's Pal Jimmy Olsen*.

Jimmy Olsen, cub reporter for *The Daily Planet*, first appeared in a starring role on the radio show in the 1940s. As portrayed by actor Jack Larsen on the TV show, Jimmy Olsen was the character whom young viewers could identify with. He was Superman's

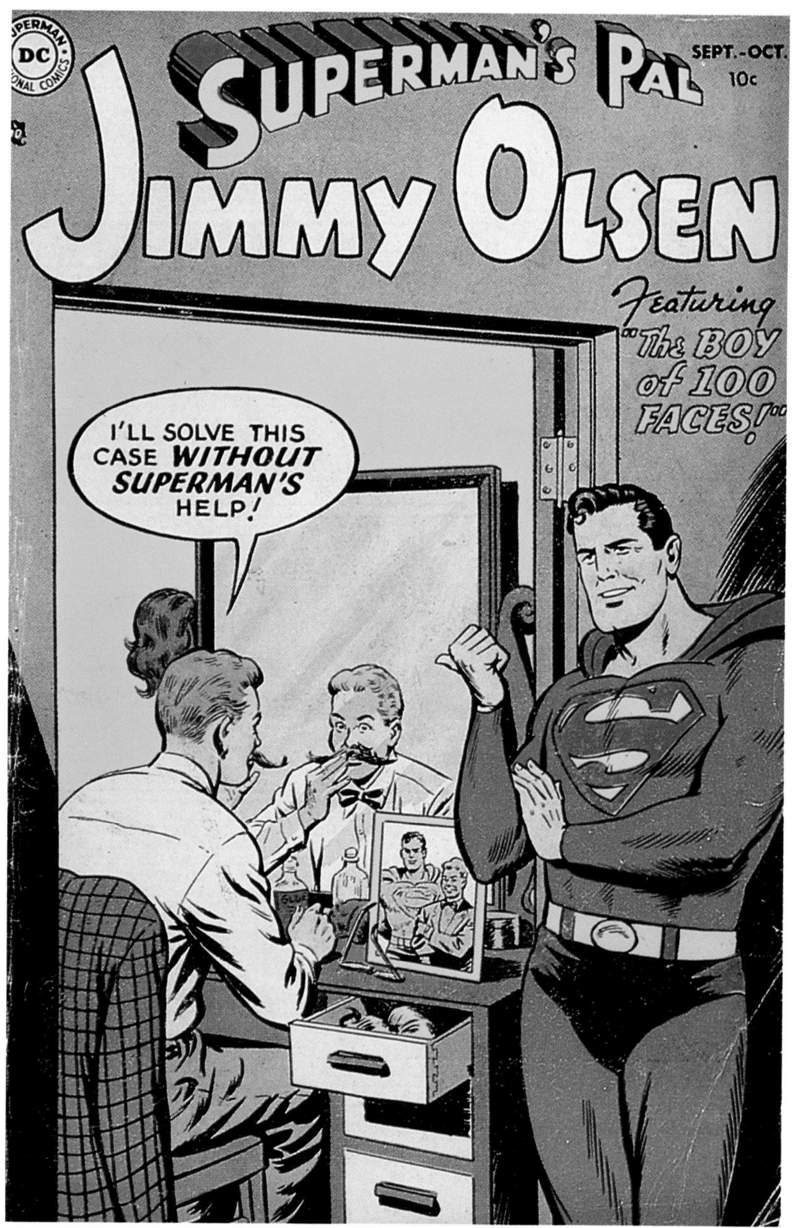

Superman's Pal Jimmy Olsen #1 ©1954 *DC Comics, Inc.* Curt Swan.

pal—the kid sidekick all good superheroes had since the days of Batman and Robin.

The idea for a Jimmy Olsen comic book got its start when Whitney Ellsworth at DC Comics brought Superman comic book editor Mort Weisinger over to the TV show to be its story editor. Weisinger recalled that on the way to Hollywood, he and Ellsworth "sat in a roomette on a train with a tape recorder and plotted about fifteen stories for the series."

Weisinger's job was to tone down the violence in the TV show and keep it more in character with the *Superman* comic books. Weisinger's approach to the TV show was much the same as it had been in his comic books: He emphasized the human interest side of Superman. Ellsworth remembered that he and Weisinger "made the crooks comic so we wouldn't frighten our audience. We'd have them running into each other, cracking their heads on the wall."

As a result of the less-violent approach, the characters of Clark, Lois, Jimmy, and editor Perry White grew in such importance that Superman sometimes appeared only in the last segment of the show.

As the TV show entered its third season, Weisinger knew the time was right to capitalize on its popularity. A comic book featuring Superman and one of the show's main characters, Jimmy Olsen, was a perfect way to reach a new audience which had grown up watching the television show.

Weisinger assigned artist Curt Swan the job of drawing the first issue of *Superman's Pal, Jimmy Olsen.* Swan recalled the influence that the TV show had on his art for the comic book: "I gave some thought to making Superman look more like George Reeves, the actor who played him on television. I had seen Reeves once on the set, briefly, on one of my trips to the coast. I began to study his features on the TV show, but finally decided that it would be pointless to copy him too literally, though I think I did get his profile a little bit from time to time."

Weisinger remembers that even with the success of the Superman TV show, it was still difficult to launch a new superhero-related comic book in the uncertain days of 1954.

"I created the *Jimmy Olsen* book over a lot of opposition," Weisinger recalled. "The management protested that the character wasn't strong enough and it'd never go. But I had a gut feeling—I had talked to the kids."

The kids were right. The *Jimmy Olsen* comic book was a success. At least as far as Superman and DC Comics was concerned, comic book superheroes were starting—slowly—to make a comeback.

THE AMAZING WORLD OF DC COMICS

"Maybe I can't change the future—but I may be able to *outwit* it!"

— *Flash* #116

Flash #114 ©1960 DC Comics, Inc. Carmine Infantino, Joe Giella.

It was an early summer day in 1956 in New York City. Inside an office building at 480 Lexington Avenue, several men in their late thirties and early forties were racking their brains to come up with an idea for a new comic book that would separate ten-year-olds from their dimes.

It was getting harder and harder for a comic book publisher to survive in the mid-1950s. Over a dozen comic book companies disappeared in 1955, and sales had plunged from the boom years of the 1940s and early 1950s. DC Comics was one of the largest and most successful surviving comic book companies, thanks in part to Superman and Batman. But now, even the editors at DC Comics that day in 1956 were struggling to find new titles and characters that kids would buy.

"What's selling? Did you get that report from the distributor yet? How were the sales on that first issue of that new comic book, what's it called—*Showcase*?"

"For a first issue, not bad. Not great, but not bad. Now, what we are we going to put in the fourth issue? We need a new feature."

"Okay, okay—let's see, we had a story about a bunch of firefighters in the first issue, and that animal adventure story in the second issue. What's in that third issue Bob Kanigher is writing?"

"The Frogmen."

"Frogmen—sounds like some weird hero, you know, like Batman, Aquaman, Frogman."

"They're deep-sea divers. Now come on, what's going in the next issue of *Showcase*? We need some kind of adventure story."

"You know, if you guys are looking for a new adventure feature, we could do some sort of hero. The Flash was always one of my favorite characters. Maybe we ought to take a crack at putting him out again."

"Yeah, it's been five, six years since the *Flash* came out! That's great! Now, who worked on the *Flash* in the 1940s? Who are we going to give this one to?"

All eyes turned toward Julius Schwartz, an editor at DC Comics since 1944. Schwartz had worked on many of the 1940s superhero titles—*Green Lantern*, *All-Star Comics*, and *All-Flash Comics*, among others.

"Julie, weren't you the editor on the *Flash*?"

Schwartz smiled. "Okay. I'm stuck with it. I'll give it a try. We'll bring back the Flash."

Schwartz returned to his desk, thinking about his new assignment. "For some reason," Schwartz recalled, "I decided not to revive the original Flash, but to do a new Flash with the same power, super-speed." For a new generation of 1950s readers,

Showcase #4 ©1956 *DC Comics, Inc.* Carmine Infantino, Joe Kubert.

Schwartz wanted this Flash to have "a new costume, new secret identity, new origin."

Schwartz's desk backed against the desk of editor and writer Robert Kanigher. Kanigher had written many superhero stories for titles that Schwartz had edited in the late 1940s, including the Flash. Kanigher was also an editor of *Showcase,* the title that the new Flash would appear in. He was a natural choice for writing the new origin story.

To draw the new Flash, Schwartz again looked for someone who had worked on the original 1940s *Flash* comic. Carmine Infantino, an artist on Schwartz's western and science fiction titles, was the last person to have drawn the Flash in his 1940s series. Infantino remembered that "I wasn't thrilled—I never liked doing the superhero stuff. But I said okay and we did it."

After drawing the first tryout issue of Flash for *Showcase* (September 1956), Infantino returned to work on a "Detective Chimp" story for *Adventures of Rex the Wonder Dog* and thought little else about superheroes.

The following year, however, he was asked to draw the Flash again for a second *Showcase* appearance (May 1957). And while this Flash issue sold better than the previous one, there was still no groundswell or outcry for more superhero comics. Most of the best-selling comics were still humor, romance, and western titles.

At about this time, editor Mort Weisinger returned from working on the Superman TV show. He wanted to capitalize on the show's popularity, and he suggested to DC Comics that it give Lois Lane (Superman's girlfriend) a chance at her own comic book, much as they had done with Jimmy Olsen three years earlier. Lois followed the Flash and appeared in the next two issues of *Showcase* (July and September 1957). The following spring, she received her own comic book, *Superman's Girlfriend Lois Lane* (April 1958). That same month, Weisinger, with writer Otto Binder,

Adventure Comics #275 ©1960 *DC Comics, Inc.* Curt Swan, Stan Kaye.

Green Lantern #3 ©1960 DC Comics, Inc. Gil Kane, Joe Giella.

introduced the Legion of Super-Heroes in a Superboy story in *Adventure Comics* (April 1958).

Also that spring, the Flash returned for two more tryout appearances in *Showcase* (March and May 1958). "Each one sold better than the other," remembered editor Julius Schwartz, "and we put out the Flash in his own magazine." The new *Flash* comic book appeared in the early spring of 1959.

With the rising interest in superheroes, Weisinger knew he and Schwartz were on to something good. Besides Superman, Weisinger also handled two other superheroes, Green Arrow and Aquaman, for *Adventure Comics*. Weisinger had originally dreamed up Aquaman and Green Arrow for DC Comics back in 1941. Now in 1959, he decided to "freshen" them up for new readers, much like what had already been done with the Flash. He gave Aquaman and Green Arrow new origins which seemed "schmaltzier and better. At the time we thought, who'd remember the old origins?"

To keep the Superman stories interesting—"from just becoming a fad!" Weisinger and writer Otto Binder created the first new female superhero in ten years. Supergirl made her debut in the May 1959 issue of *Action Comics*. That same year, Jerry Siegel, the original writer and cocreator of Superman, returned after a long absence to help Weisinger continue revamping the Man of Steel.

Wonder Woman, who first appeared in 1941, was also in line for an overhaul that year. Editor and writer Robert Kanigher rewrote her origin and assigned a new art team to create a more modern look to attract new readers. Although he considered Wonder Woman "an icon of the comics field," Kanigher knew it was necessary to introduce new characters and concepts to keep the long-running Wonder Woman fresh. The Amazon Princess got a Merman boyfriend and a family of siblings (Wonder Girl, Wonder Tot) in her new incarnation.

Yet another DC editor, Jack Schiff, also jumped on the superhero bandwagon in 1959. For *Tales of the Unexpected*, he began a series of adventures featuring the Space Ranger, a futuristic hero with a secret identity. Schiff's main superhero editorial charge, Batman, was also appearing in futuristic science fiction stories in his own magazine and in *Detective Comics* as well that year.

Julius Schwartz finished up the 1959 DC superhero sweepstakes by reviving Green Lantern, another 1940s superhero, for *Showcase* (October 1959). Like the new Flash, Green Lantern was a modernized version of his old namesake. The character had a new costume, a new identity, and a new origin that was heavily influenced by writer John Broome's proclivity for science fiction plots involving alien civilizations. Broome would write many of the 1960s Green Lantern and Flash stories for Schwartz.

Schwartz's other chief superhero writer was veteran comic book author Gardner Fox. Fox had written superhero stories for DC since 1939, creating such 1940s heroes as the Flash, Hawkman, Starman, Dr. Fate, and the Justice Society of America, a team of popular 1940s DC heroes.

Schwartz asked Fox to recreate the Justice Society in 1960 for new readers by using Batman, Superman, Wonder Woman, Aquaman, Martian Manhunter, and the new

Wonder Woman #155 ©1965 DC Comics, Inc. Ross Andru, Mike Esposito.

Brave and the Bold #29 ©1960 DC Comics, Inc. Mike Sekowsky, Murphy Anderson.

Flash and new Green Lantern. Fox and Schwartz christened their new team of superheroes the *Justice League of America* (October 1960). They arrived on the scene almost ten years after the demise of the old Justice Society of America in *All Star Comics*.

Next, Fox was asked to revive Hawkman, one of his 1940s characters, for *Brave and the Bold* comics. After writing three Hawkman issues, Fox then went on to help resurrect yet another 1940s superhero, the Atom. The "World's Smallest Hero" appeared in three issues of *Showcase* comics in late 1961.

The new DC superheroes (Flash, Green Lantern, Hawkman, and the Atom) were far different from their 1940s counterparts. Science fact—and fiction—dominated the stories and characters. Both the Atom and Flash were originally scientists (nuclear physicist and police chemist); indeed, it is their interest in science which was responsible for their becoming superheroes. Green Lantern's alter ego, Hal Jordan, works in the emerging high-tech aeronautical industry. Hawkman is a super-scientific policeman from an advanced alien civilization.

"I was the world's biggest science fiction fan," editor Julius Schwartz admits. Science fiction elements continually appeared in his superhero comics: time-travel, subatomic universes, alien races, robot duplicates, and parallel worlds. As Schwartz rightfully pointed out, "anything you can imagine, you can do with a superhero."

Writer Fox agreed. "Julie had no set rules; our attitude always was: Give'em what sells."

Actually, all of the DC superhero comics were selling. The *Justice League of America* was their best-selling new title in 1961. In comic books, the maxim has always been to do more of what works. Schwartz began looking for a way to get even more new DC heroes into the comics.

Hawkman #1 ©1964 DC Comics, Inc. Murphy Anderson.

Showcase #36 ©1962 DC Comics, Inc. Gil Kane, Murphy Anderson.

According to Gardner Fox, Schwartz told him during a plotting session in 1961: "I want a story with both Flashes." Schwartz was referring to both the original 1940s Flash comic book character, which Fox had written, and the recently resurrected 1960s Flash, who had a different costume, origin, and identity. If one Flash was selling, think how well two Flashes would do.

The problem was how to explain the existence of a 1940s Flash co-starring with a 1960s Flash. Schwartz insisted that the superhero stories maintain an internal logic and credibility. Somehow, the readers had to accept the fact that there could be both a 1940s Flash and a 1960s Flash.

Fox, himself a longtime science fiction fan and writer, came up with a solution: They would use parallel worlds, two earths existing simultaneously in different dimensions, each with its own Flash. "It was an old science fiction device," admitted Fox, and he called the parallel worlds "Earth-One" and "Earth-Two." The Flashes from each world would meet through a dimensional doorway in a story called "Flash of Two Worlds."

The Earth-One and Earth-Two concept literally gave Schwartz and his writers another world of superheroes. On Earth-Two, there would be all the DC superheroes from the 1940s, the members of the Justice Society of America. Earth-One would contain all the modern-day 1960s versions of these superheroes. The superheroes from both worlds would meet once a year in a regular team-up series in the pages of *Justice League of America*. By 1963, Schwartz and Fox had over a dozen superheroes cavorting about in a single story.

Flash #123 ©1961 DC Comics, Inc. Carmine Infantino, Joe Giella. Flash-One and Flash-Two.

Superman #123 ©1958 DC Comics, Inc. Curt Swan, Stan Kaye.

As popular as Schwartz's heroes were, however, it was editor Mort Weisinger's *Superman* which was still the top-selling superhero comic of the early 1960s. While Schwartz was busy reviving and unearthing as many heroes from the 1940s as he could find, Weisinger built an empire on a single superhero.

Superman was appearing in seven comics by 1958, all edited by Weisinger. Every five days, on the average, there was a new comic book on the newsstands starring Superman: *Action Comics* (with Superman and Supergirl), *Adventure Comics* (with Superboy), *Superman's Girlfriend Lois Lane, Superman's Pal Jimmy Olsen, World's Finest* (with Superman and Batman), *Superboy*, and, of course, *Superman*. Weisinger was responsible, in his words, for creating the "whole mythology which made Superman different from all the other bigshot bang-crash heroic characters."

Schwartz and Weisinger had been boyhood friends after meeting at a science fiction fan club in 1931. As young men, they became active in publishing science fiction in the late 1930s, Schwartz as a literary agent and Weisinger as an editor. By 1941, Weisinger was working for DC Comics, editing over 40 comic books, including Superman.

Showcase #9 ©1957 DC Comics, Inc. Al Plastino.

Schwartz joined his friend three years later as a story editor. He read his first comic books while riding over to his job interview at DC. Schwartz slipped easily into the superhero business. "I have a strong scientific interest, and basically comics are science-fiction minded. Let's face it, superheroes aren't regular characters."

Like Schwartz, Weisinger also depended heavily upon science fiction themes in his stories. Two of his main writers, Edmond Hamilton and Otto Binder, were accomplished science fiction authors as well as comic book writers. Hamilton had written science fiction potboilers for the pulp magazines since the 1920s. His scripts for the Superman comics, according to artist Wayne Boring "were no effort to draw. Always smooth. He wrote good pictures. I could always visualize his descriptions. His stories sang."

Schwartz and Weisinger each had his own stable of writers and artists who worked on his superhero comics, but both men shared a common background and editorial approach. Each insisted that his writers first plot a story with him before turning in a script. In this way, both men controlled the character, style, and content of the comics they edited.

Over a fifty-year period, Schwartz recalled that of all the thousands of stories he published, all but two of them were first plotted with him. Schwartz explained that "when a fellow plotted with me, it was accepted—there was no writing the story blind."

Weisinger also plotted nearly every story with his writers in legendary browbeating sessions which were "full of frequent, brutal, often cruel criticism," according to one scripter. Curt Swan, who drew hundreds of Superman stories for Weisinger, remembered that the man "definitely wanted to manipulate and keep that control. He would never relinquish that."

"People always accuse me of being an egomaniac as an editor because I always gave the writers my own plots," Weisinger recalled. "I did that for a reason. If I asked a

World's Finest #94 ©1958 DC Comics, Inc. Curt Swan, Stan Kaye.

writer to bring in four plots and I didn't like any of the four, then he's wasted all his time. The least I could do was to think of a plot for a writer and if he liked it, we'd kick it around and evolve a story. A writer knew he would never go away empty-handed."

Both editors also worked closely with their artists, telling them specifically what they wanted drawn on each cover. The cover sold the comic book, and often it was the most important decision an editor made.

Weisinger would often think of some outrageous cover idea that would grab a kid's attention: Superman turns into Superbaby and Lois Lane is pushing him in a baby carriage, or Superboy discovers his parents are evil robots, or Jimmy Olsen proposes marriage to Supergirl. From the dramatic cover idea, Weisinger and his writers would then try to dream up a story which could conceivably contain such a bizarre scene. As a result, many plots and stories were gimmick-driven and wrapped around the sensationalistic cover idea.

Schwartz also liked the idea of doing the cover first. He recalled that "one of the most successful *Batman* covers I did was Batman leaving Gotham City and the people were throwing eggs and tomatoes at him. He was in disgrace! We called the story, 'The Fallen Idol of Gotham City.' So we had to figure out a story of what Batman had done to warrant such a treatment."

Because of this approach, DC writer Arnold Drake remembered that "we always knew we could sell a story by giving them a helluva cover. Even if the book was full, they'd put the story in inventory."

The heavy emphasis on plot and cover ideas tended to make the superheroes themselves one-dimensional, like actors in a well-scripted play with carefully modulated char-

Batman #128 ©1960 DC Comics, Inc. Bob Kane, Shelly Moldoff.

World's Finest #94 ©1958 DC Comics, Inc. Dick Sprang, Stan Kaye.

The DC superhero comics of the 1960s have been accused of emphasizing a clever plot to the detriment of well-realized characterizations. Stan Lee, Marvel Comics' chief writer in the early 1960s, preferred to delve into the personalities of his characters, "but at DC," Lee observed, "the opposite is true. The way they build their stories, they'll spend most of their time saying, 'This will be the crime we'll have, and these will be the clues we plant, but nobody notices this last clue until the end when somebody spots it.' They spend most of their time thinking about that. And, to me, the characters are just one-dimensional."

For millions of other readers, however, the DC superheroes were exactly what they wanted in a comic book. The DC heroes were competent, attractive, and in control. They knew that a careful application of wit, intelligence, and righteously applied strength would solve any problem they would encounter in their well-ordered worlds.

In fact, it was that simplicity, that single-minded dedication to simply being heroic, that made the DC superheroes so attractive. The always carefully polished art and cleverly constructed stories presented readers with a world so rich with superheroes that it scarcely seemed any others could be needed.

For a reader with a dime in 1961, it was all that was needed to enter the Amazing World of DC Comics.

acterization. There was no space in the heavily plotted stories to explore the men and women behind the superhero costumes.

As writer Gardner Fox observed, "I always figured that there were so few pages available that I had to concentrate on plot and action. I always figured that was what my readers, who were mostly children and young teenagers, would want."

Mystery in Space #90 ©1964 DC Comics, Inc. Carmine Infantino, Murphy Anderson. Adam Strange.

THE MARVEL UNIVERSE

"The legend has come true! By the will of the gods, I am *alive*! I am *invincible*! I am—THOR!!!"

— *Journey Into Mystery* #83

Journey Into Mystery #88 ©1963 Marvel Entertainment Group, Inc. Jack Kirby, Steve Ditko.

Stan Lee, chief editor and writer of Marvel Comics, sat alone in his small office. It was 1957, and Lee was almost all that was left of a comic book company which had once employed hundreds of people during the 1940s.

Lee first came to Marvel Comics as a sixteen-year-old office boy in 1939. He later became editor and writer for most of Marvel's comics all through the 1940s and 1950s. During the boom years of comics, Lee kept three secretaries busy as he dictated scripts for hundreds of Marvel comics like *Captain America, Millie the Model, Rawhide Kid,* and *Ziggy Pig.*

Now, the bottom had fallen out. After almost a 15-year boom period, comic books were in a rapid decline by 1955. Distribution problems, bad publicity about comic books, and the new medium of television had all taken their toll on sales. In 1957 Stan Lee was the caretaker of just another one of the many dying comic book companies of the day.

"The comic book business hit rock bottom," Lee recalled. "My publisher said to me, 'Stan, we have to let the whole staff go. I'm just going to keep you, but I want you to fire everybody.' I said, 'I can't do it!' He said, 'You'd better,' and he went off to Florida, while I was given the job of firing more people than I could count."

One of those people let go in 1957 was freelance artist Don Heck, who worked for Marvel Comics for nearly 25 years.

"I was working exclusively for Marvel then," Heck recalled. "Yeah, it was straight through until May 1957. I remember going into the city, and I sent my wife up to the office at the time and said, 'Just pick up another job,' and she came down and said, 'There is none.' Which was a surprise."

Johnny Romita, another Marvel freelance artist, got the word to stop in the middle of a western story. Even longtime staff artist Bill Everett had left and was working for a greeting card company.

In 1957, Marvel Comics canceled more than two-thirds of its titles and subsisted on an inventory of existing stories for its surviving comics. The bad situation was made worse by a distribution foul-up which prevented Marvel's comics from appearing on the newsstands.

By 1958, sales were so bad that it appeared Stan Lee and Marvel Comics would soon be out of business.

At that time, Jack Kirby, an artist who had worked at Marvel Comics in the early 1940s, was seeking additional art assignments to supplement his other freelance work. He remembered walking into the office of Marvel editor Stan Lee in the summer of 1958:

"I came in and they were moving out the furniture, they were taking desks out—and I needed the work! I had a family and a house and all of a sudden Marvel is coming apart." Kirby recalled that he told Stan Lee "to stop moving the furniture out, and I'll see that the books make money. And I came up with a raft of new books and all these books began to make money."

Kirby's books always had the reputation of making money. As early as 1941, Kirby, along with partner Joe Simon, created Captain America for Marvel, or Timely Comics as it was known then. They also drew superhero comics for DC Comics in the early 1940s. In 1947, the two men created the first romance comic book and later worked to-

Tales to Astonish #55 ©*1964 Marvel Entertainment Group, Inc.* Jack Kirby, Sol Brodksy.

Tales of Suspense #45 ©*1963 Marvel Entertainment Group, Inc.* Jack Kirby, Don Heck.

gether on the *Fighting American* superhero comic in 1954.

Kirby was fresh from drawing the *Challengers of the Unknown* for DC Comics when he began working for Marvel Comics in 1958. The first new Marvel title with Kirby art was *Strange Worlds* (December 1958). The fantasy and science fiction comic also featured a cover by Kirby and a story by Steve Ditko, another artist who would be closely identified with the nascent Marvel Comics.

Business was picking up. Distribution problems had been ironed out, and Kirby's monster stories and covers were helping sales. Lee asked Don Heck to return in July 1958 to draw a "five-page space story" and also the cover for the first issue of another new Marvel comic, *Tales of Suspense* (January 1959). That same month, Kirby and Ditko drew stories for a second new Marvel comic, *Tales to Astonish* (January 1959).

For the next three years, Kirby turned out dozens of giant-monster stories for these and other Marvel science fiction comics, including *Strange Tales*, *Journey into Mystery*, and *Amazing Adventures*.

Kirby's monsters were huge, hulking, scaly creatures with unpronounceable names, like Zzutak, Vandoom, and Orrgo. Most of the stories involved radiation-spawned monsters or giant alien lizards from outer space. Frequently, the creatures were the results of scientific experiments gone wild, like "I Created Spoor—The Thing That Wouldn't Die!"

As silly as they sound, Kirby's monster stories grabbed readers with their dramatic visuals and dynamic layouts. As he said, "When I'm drawing a monster book, I'm giving you the real thing and you'll enjoy it."

By 1961, Marvel was in better shape but still a minor company, overshadowed by the two giants, DC Comics and Dell Publishing, and even behind family-owned Archie Comics and Harvey Comics.

Stan Lee recalled those days in the summer of 1961: "We were turning out monster magazines, and then one day my publisher found out that National Comics (DC) had a book called the *Justice League* that was selling

Strange Tales #126 ©*1964 Marvel Entertainment Group, Inc.* Steve Ditko.

reasonably well. Better than our monster books, at least. And he said, 'Hey, maybe there's still a market for superheroes; why don't you bring out a team like the Justice League? We could call it the Righteous League or something.' I worked for him and I was willing to put out a team of superheroes. But I figured I'll be damned if I'm just going to copy National. I said, 'We'll do a superhero team, but let's make it different.'"

The *Fantastic Four* appeared in late 1961, and they were certainly different. A teenager who burst into flames, a man who could stretch into any shape, an invisible girl, and a grotesque orange-colored and tumor-skinned "thing" were the *heroes* of what was to be billed "The World's Greatest Comic Magazine!"

The first thing that comic book readers noticed in 1961 was that the Fantastic Four did not act like the polished, restrained, and perfectly polite superheroes in other comic books.

"Ben, I'm sick and tired of your insults . . . of your complaining," the leader of the Fantastic Four thunders to his teammate. "I didn't purposely plan for our flight to fail!"

"And I'm sick of you . . . period," snarls Ben Grimm. "In fact, I'm gonna paste you right in that smug face of yours!"

Stan Lee recalled that he "really hated the way superheroes had been done previously—they were all perfect. To me, the most interesting story is when you care about the characters."

Jack Kirby, the artist of the *Fantastic Four*, was described by Lee as a "natural" choice to draw the comic since "Jack had probably drawn more superhero strips than any other artist and he was as good as they come."

Lee and Kirby made their readers care about the characters who made up the Fantastic Four. Readers become fascinated with Ben Grimm, The "Thing," or monsterlike hero of the Fantastic Four. He was a man trapped in the body of a monster. He had to hide under a trenchcoat just to walk the streets. He may have been powerful—a superhero—but he was also a tragic figure. "I'll never be human again! I'll live—and die—

Strange Tales #114 ©*1963 Marvel Entertainment Group, Inc.* Jack Kirby, Dick Ayers.

Fantastic Four #4 ©*1962 Marvel Entertainment Group, Inc.* Jack Kirby, Sol Brodsky.

just the way I am . . . an orange-skinned freak!"

The Human Torch, the youngest member of the group, was a hot-headed teenager whose superhero obligations often sidelined him from the normal 1960s teen rituals of dating and hot-rodding. "Of all the crummy luck," he tells his girlfriend Doris when he is summoned from their date by an emergency call from his teammates. Doris pouts: "This means another date ruined! Any girl who dates a so-called superhero should have her silly head examined!"

Mr. Fantastic and the Invisible Girl, the remaining pair of the Fantastic Four, also had a difficult time developing their own simmering personal relationship amidst the pressures of saving the world:

"Everything I do is for your own good," Mr. Fantastic tells Sue Storm, the Invisible Girl, "but you're too scatter-brained and emotional to realize it!"

"Oh, go polish a test tube or something!"

Lee recalled that he and the Marvel artists were trying "to get rid of the old clichés. Comics were too predictable. Why not accept the premise that the superhero has his superpower, and then keep everything else as realistic as possible? If I were a superhero, for example, wouldn't I still have romantic problems, financial problems, sinus attacks, and fits of insecurity? Wouldn't I be a little embarrassed about appearing in public in a costume? We decided to let our superheroes live in the real world."

The "real world" loved the new type of Marvel superhero. For the first time, Marvel Comics received fan letters from its readers. "The *Fantastic Four* is the most original, most exciting, most realistic, most surprising comic in the universe! We like the way the FF is always reading comic books in their stories—it shows their high mentality!"

The reader response to the *Fantastic Four* inspired Stan Lee and Jack Kirby to create yet another superhero who didn't look, act, or

Incredible Hulk #1 ©*1962 Marvel Entertainment Group, Inc.* Jack Kirby. First appearance of the Incredible Hulk.

sound like a superhero. The *Incredible Hulk* first appeared in early 1962 and he was more like a Frankenstein monster than a bona fide do-gooder.

"I don't need you! I don't need anybody! With my strength—my power—the world is mine!"

The Hulk was a rampaging, green-skinned brute. He wore no superhero costume. He was motivated more by survival than by altruism. He was created by a nuclear accident which transformed him from a rational scientist into a brutish monster. The Hulk was more in the tradition of *Dr. Jekyll and Mr. Hyde* than of *Batman* or *Superman*.

Three months after the Hulk appeared, Stan Lee got together with artist Steve Ditko to create the quintessential Marvel 1960s superhero. In a brilliant move, they made an ordinary teenager—Peter Parker—into an extraordinary superhero—Spider-Man.

Spider-Man made it possible for every teenager and would-be teenager to dream about what it would be like to *really* be a superhero. Peter Parker went to school, had money and girlfriend problems, and lived with his frail and elderly aunt. He also snuck out at night so he could fight crime and villains as the costumed superhero, Spider-Man.

The Spider-Man stories by Lee and Ditko became a continuing superhero soap opera. Readers became involved in the personal life of Peter Parker, as supporting characters were introduced and complex subplots unraveled. Marvel Comics successfully blended the elements of a good romance comic book story—strong characterization and on-the-sleeve emotion—into a costumed, action-packed fantasy.

"The Amazing Spider-Man! Able to climb walls . . . to fight, to run, to think better and faster than any two dozen men! Even those who hate me envy my powers! My powers! What a joke! I sometimes think they've proven to be nothing but a curse! I'd trade places with almost any normal man! At least then those I love wouldn't have to suffer for my secret!"

Stan Lee observed that "the best stories of all, whether in comic books, TV shows, movies, novels, or whatever, are the stories in which the characters seem to be real. You feel you know them, you understand them, you can relate to them."

Stan Lee, Jack Kirby, Steve Ditko, and the other Marvel artists and writers quickly created a half dozen more new superheroes that readers could relate to. In August 1962, Marvel Comics introduced Thor the Thunder God in *Journey into Mystery*. The next month marked the first appearance of Ant-Man in *Tales to Astonish*. The following month, the Human Torch received his own series in *Strange Tales*.

Amazing Spider-Man #3 ©*1963 Marvel Entertainment Group, Inc.* Steve Ditko.

Avengers #16 ©1964 Marvel Entertainment Group, Inc. Jack Kirby, Chic Stone.

The following year was marked by a frenzy of superhero creativity: Iron Man was introduced in *Tales of Suspense*, Dr. Strange was created for *Strange Tales*, Spider-Man received his own comic book, and two new teams of superheroes—the *Avengers* and the *X-Men*—were introduced simultaneously in September.

As Lee recalled, "the year 1963 was a bounteous bonanza for superheroes. At Marvel Comics we were grinding them out like popcorn and they seemed just as habit forming."

By the spring of 1964, all the Marvel superheroes were in place. Captain America, resurrected from the 1940s, was made a member of the *Avengers. Daredevil*, the last major Marvel 1960s superhero, also made his debut that spring.

In less than thirty months, the major superheroes and future foundation of the Marvel Comic empire had been created. Even more impressive, it had all been done through the creative direction of primarily two people—Stan Lee and Jack Kirby.

Many of the kernel ideas for the 1960s Marvel heroes were developed by Lee and Kirby in plotting sessions that took place in Lee's office or at a luncheonette down the street. Since that time, both men have recalled different accounts of how some of the Marvel superheroes were actually created.

For example, Kirby recalls that he came up with the name, *Fantastic Four*, for the first Marvel superhero comic book and also designed the characters of Mr. Fantastic, the Invisible Girl, the new Human Torch, and the Thing as well. Stan Lee has also stated that he thought of the name, and also described the four characters in "a detailed plot synopsis" for the first *Fantastic Four* story

X-Men #35 ©1967 Marvel Entertainment Group, Inc. Dan Adkins.

Daredevil #16 ©1966 Marvel Entertainment Group, Inc. John Romita, Frank Giacoia.

which he gave to Kirby.

Artist Don Heck remembered the discussions and visits that Kirby had with Lee when the new characters were being created. "Stan and he (Kirby) would get together, and they'd start discussing it together, that's the way it happened. Jack Kirby is the one who created most of the characters. Absolutely, no question. He's the one who was always in there, and he's the one who was developing all those characters. You may hear all different types of stories, though."

The confusion over the roles of Stan Lee and Jack Kirby in creating many of the 1960s Marvel superheroes probably came from the way in which the actual comic books were produced.

Most comic books are first written as a script, much like a movie or TV show, which contains not only dialogue but also directions to the artist on how to draw the story and interpret the characters. Until the early 1960s, Lee wrote finished scripts this way and then handed them to the artists who produced the completed artwork. Joe Sinnott, who had worked for Marvel since the early 1950s, recalled that his most vivid memory of Lee "is that he was always typing on these long yellow legal sheets, always working on the next story."

To meet the high production demands as essentially Marvel's one-man script department, Lee changed over from writing a full script for the artists to giving them a synopsis or a plot summary of the story.

Based upon Lee's synopsis, the artist drew the story and then gave it back to him (or another scripter) to write the dialogue and captions to accompany the finished artwork. In this way, the artist had a great deal of freedom in interpreting a story and often influenced its plotting, pacing, and even characterization—all things formerly controlled by the writer.

For some artists, like Kirby, Lee had to give little or no direction. Indeed, Kirby remembers that the usual way he worked with Lee was to tell him what he wanted to do with the story and the characters. According to Kirby, Lee always would say "great" and give him free rein to come up with the story for each issue. This loose working relationship and collaboration between the artist—Kirby—and the writer—Lee—sometimes made it difficult perhaps to ascertain who created what.

Kirby and the other artists would also

Daredevil #1 ©1964 Marvel Entertainment Group, Inc. Bill Everett. First appearance of Daredevil.

Journey Into Mystery #115 ©1965 Marvel Entertainment Group, Inc. Jack Kirby, Frank Giacoia. Thor the Thunder God or, as Stan Lee affectionately called him, "Old Goldilocks."

sometimes write suggested dialogue or explanatory notes to Lee and other writers on the edges of their artwork.

Although the "Marvel" way of drawing and writing a comic book gave the artist more creative control, it was also intimidating at first. Don Heck remembered when Stan Lee first handed him a synopsis instead of a full script in 1962: "I thought, 'Oh, my God! This'll never work!'"

Working from a synopsis, said Heck, usually meant that "Stan would give you the first three pages, tell you who the character was you were fighting, and give you the last couple of pages so you'd know how it ended. And in between you'd put about fifteen pages of stuff. You'd send the pages in, and then you'd see Stan put the dialogue to it, and it really worked out nice. It was a good combination, because he was great for looking at things, and being able to put stuff there."

As Stan Lee said, he was responsible for "actually putting the words in all their pink little mouths." And what words they were. Stan Lee introduced a form of tragicomedic writing to comics, packed with angst, wisecracks, and hip slang. Lee's superheroes often spoke in soliloquies and soul-searching monologues:

"Nobody can help me," rages Tony Stark, the Ironman. "Nobody can repair my damaged heart! Nobody can guarantee how much longer it will keep beating! Nobody can ever feel the the torment known by Iron Man! I must continue to live in a shadow world . . . spending half my days as the Golden Avenger, and the other half as Anthony Stark, the envy of a million men . . . but one of the unhappiest humans alive!!"

Although he wrote for several dozen heroes, Lee always kept them in character through their dialogue. "The well-written character is one who is always verbally true to form," Lee observed. "Every character must have his manner of speech, and the style and content of his delivery must be constant."

Ben Grimm, The Thing of the Fantastic Four, spoke with a wiseacre Bronx accent: "Sheeesh, me jumpy?! I wuz just practicing my isometric *panic* lessons! Ya shouldn't outta sneak upon a guy that way! It ain't *couth*!"

On the other hand, Thor the God of Thunder rarely cracked a smile as he delivered his lines: "Your cunning shall not save you now, evil one! Naught but naked power can stop the first-born of Odin! This time you have sealed your doom!"

Lee realized that the new superheroes were allowing him to write "the way I wanted to write. Up until this time, I was writing the way I felt the publisher wanted—and it was my job to please the publisher. So now I forgot about the publisher; I was off and running; I was going to have fun with my things. It came easy to me, because it's my own natural style."

Lee's working and writing style at Marvel in the 1960s also arose from the monthly necessity of turning out comic books in an assembly-line fashion:

"I would do the plotting very quickly in about an hour, then I would give the plot to the artist. So to me the writing came in when the artist would give me back the artwork and I put the copy in. And then of course, the artists would always add their own things above and beyond what I had told them in the plot. Jack Kirby, for example. He would change my original plot so much half the time I couldn't recognize it. Which was fine with me, it made it more interesting."

Most of the Marvel artists had an influence in the way that the stories were eventually written by Lee. "I would very often deviate from my own original plot because as I looked at the artwork and as I saw how the story was going, I'd often get the ideas that I hadn't had when I wrote the plot. So like as not, the stories would turn out to be quite a bit different than I had originally planned them. It was like doing a crossword puzzle when I was doing those things."

By allowing the artists to have an active role in the storytelling, Lee freed himself so he could exercise some creative control over all the Marvel comics. He began developing long-running storylines for the characters and titles. Subplots in one comic book might be continued in another title. Superheroes made guest appearances in each other's books. Villains and supporting characters in one comic book might suddenly become superheroes in another book. It was a dynamic and exciting approach to comics. Lee was no longer simply writing adventure stories for individual superheroes, he was weaving the fabric for an integrated mythology.

Lee did not realize that, at the time, he was breaking new ground. "I didn't even feel that the stories were that different; all I knew was that it was fun to make them continued, instead of each story existing in a world of its own. I got the idea that if they're going to be living in the real world, the characters might meet each other once in awhile. So we began to let Spider-Man meet the Fantastic Four in a story, or to have the Hulk passing by while something was happening to Iron Man. Of course, it was easy for me to control, since I was writing virtually all of them and could keep track of them. Also, I could keep them in the style I wanted. I was creating my own *universe*."

Yet Stan Lee's partner in building the Marvel Universe was artist Jack Kirby. While Lee wrote the majority of the 1960s Marvel superhero comics, Kirby drew a substantial portion of all the stories. Kirby was penciling at *least* 80 pages of art per month, sometimes more. In a period from 1963 to 1964, he was penciling five books (*Avengers*, *X-Men*, *Journey into Mystery*, *Fantastic Four*, and *Sgt. Fury*) plus occasional stories and layouts for other titles, as well as six to eight covers every month. Toss in the summer annuals, and at times, Kirby was drawing 120 or more pages each month.

During that time, Kirby worked in "a little dungeon basement" at his home. "I was alone in my studio everyday," Kirby recalled about his 1960s work. "I'd come in once or twice a month to the Marvel offices."

During his visits, Kirby would consult with writer and editor Stan Lee about what

Incredible Hulk #6 ©1963 Marvel Entertainment Group, Inc. Steve Ditko.

Fantastic Four #5 ©*1962 Marvel Entertainment Group, Inc.* Jack Kirby, Joe Sinnott.

would appear in next month's titles. Back in his studio, Kirby would let his imagination run rampant as he embellished, expanded, and created upon the plot ideas worked out with Lee.

"I was a penciller and a storyteller and I insisted on doing my own writing," Kirby recalled. "I always wrote my own story, no matter what it was. Nobody ever wrote a story for me. I created my own characters. I always did that. That was the point of comics for me. I created my own concepts and I enjoyed doing that."

According to his wife, "He never wrote the story ahead of time, he wrote while he was drawing. I never remember in all the years that Jack erased a panel." Kirby explained that when he drew a comic, "I never planned a story. I had to do it panel by panel because I had to think for each individual character."

Kirby's style was so successful that he often broke in new Marvel artists who were coming on board in the mid 1960s. For artists like John Romita and John Severin, Kirby would lay out their first stories so they could see what the Marvel style of storytelling was like.

By the mid- and late 1960s, other artists like Gene Colan, John Buscema, and Marie Severin were giving a helping hand to long-time stalwarts Kirby, Steve Ditko, and Don Heck.

Stan Lee was also getting some help in the writing department. In 1965, he hired Roy Thomas as an assistant editor and writer. Thomas recalled that when he "came in, Stan was writing virtually all of the main books. I began writing a couple of the books that Stan wanted to give up."

Thomas, a long-time comics fan and high school English teacher, broke into comic books with scripts for Charlton Comic's *Son of Vulcan* and *Blue Beetle*. His first work for Marvel Comics was for *Kid Colt Outlaw* and *Millie the Model*. He later took up the writing reins on the *Avengers, Daredevil, Dr. Strange, The Incredible Hulk,* and *Captain Marvel*. With Thomas's help, Lee was able to ease up on his writing and devote more attention to promoting the Marvel line of superheroes. He came up with an idea for a Marvel fan club—the Merry Marvel Marching Society, or the "MMMS" as it was known to the over 50,000 college students who joined in the first year.

Lee turned the letter columns in the comics into real fan pages. He gave out "No

Prizes" (an envelope with nothing in it) to readers who spotted errors in the comics. There were even special names and titles for diehard Marvel fans, like R.F.O. ("Real Frantic One—A Buyer of at least three Marvel Mags a Month") and K.O.F. ("Keeper of the Flame—One who recruits a newcomer to Marvel's Rollickin' Ranks"). Every Marvel reader was designated a "True Believer," and was often instructed by Lee to "Face Front!"

Each issue contained a Marvel Bullpen Bulletin page with features like "The Mighty Marvel Checklist" and "Stan's Soapbox," a forum for self-aggrandizing promotion and philosophizing. A typical banner on the December 1966 Bullpen Page read: "Earth-Shattering Essays, Eloquent Epithets, and Exaggerated Endorsements Which You Can Easily Live Without!"

Lee was making Marvel Comics more personalized, more human to its readers, just as he had humanized its superheroes. "I always felt that in the past comic books were so incredibly impersonal," Lee recalled. "You didn't know who wrote them, who drew them, there was no humor. There was no contact between the reader and the person writing or drawing the work. So I thought having credits would be fun, and that's why I gave the characters nicknames and had my Bullpen page where I had a column and would talk to the readers. I was trying to make the reader feel not just like a reader but like a friend—as if we're sharing sort of an in-joke."

Readers soon knew Lee as "Stan the Man" or "Ol' Smiley." He referred to the other Marvel artists ("The Bullpen") as "Jolly" Jack Kirby, "Sturdy" Steve Ditko, "Dashing" Don Heck, and "Jazzy" John Romita.

On the stories themselves, Lee would dream up new ways of putting in the artist and writer credits for each story, such as:

> Written by Stan Lee, The Monarch of the Marvel Age at the Pinnacle of His Power!
> Illustrated by Jack Kirby, The Prince of Pageantry at the Height of His Titanic Talent!
> Inked by Chic Stone, The Dean of Line Design at the Peak of His Prowess!
> Lettered by S. Rosen, The Sultan of Spelling at the Little Table in His Studio!

Oftentimes the credits would even have a punchline, of sorts:

> Written with the Mastery of Stan Lee,
> Illustrated with the Genius of Jack Kirby,
> Delineated with the Delicacy of Chic Stone,

Fantastic Four Annual #2 ©1964 *Marvel Entertainment Group, Inc.* Jack Kirby, Chic Stone.

Lettered with the India Ink of
Artie Simek.

The shameless and good-natured self-promotion paid off. Marvel readers were loyal readers, and they often read most of the company's superhero titles in order to stay fully apprised of the current state of the Marvel Universe and its inhabitants.

Sales soared, new titles were launched, and before the 1960s were over, Marvel Comics would be positioned to become the most popular producer of superhero comics.

Even with their worldwide success and fame, the Marvel offices and working conditions remained exceptionally modest and friendly all through the 1960s. Jim Shooter, who was to become chief editor at Marvel Comics in the late 1970s, recalled his first visit to the offices in the summer of 1969:

"Marvel in those days had only two real offices, Stan's and Sol Brodsky's. Sol was the production manager, which meant he handled anything Stan didn't want to, which meant anything technical, administrative, or financial. Sol's office looked like a combination production office/storeroom."

Shooter recalled that "the whole place had a cluttered, used feel. Everybody did everything. Loudly. Unabashedly. Frantically." Receptionists, art assistants, and even delivery boys were often sucked into impromptu plotting sessions by writers and artists.

In fact for a while in the 1960s, it seemed that everyone who ever *read* a Marvel comic book was similarly seduced, sucked in, and made a part of the Marvel Universe. Marvel Comics were read by people who would never otherwise read a comic book.

As Stan Lee explained, "By telling our tales on two levels—color, costumes, and exaggerated action for the kids; science fiction, satire, and sophisticated philosophy for the adults and near-adults—we've managed to expand the perimeters of our audience."

Comic books would never be the same again.

SUPER-DUPER HERO STUPOR

"It's zeroes for heroes, Batman!"

— *Batman* #186

Detective Comics #371
©1968 DC Comics, Inc.
Carmine Infantino,
Murphy Anderson.

'Nuff Said, True Believers.

It's 1965. A Saturday night at the Playboy Mansion. Hugh Hefner, publisher of *Playboy* magazine, prepares for another party.

Tonight there would be a screening in his private theater room of the 1949 movie serial *Batman and Robin*. Hefner hoped his friends would find the old Batman movie as unintentionally funny and nostalgic as he had.

They did. Hefner's hip party guests loved the *Batman*. It was so bad, it was good. It was "camp"; it was pop culture.

Hefner's lifelong interest in the comics was well known. His magazine had run an excerpt from a 1965 book *The Great Comic Book Heroes* by Jules Feiffer, which featured a nostalgic look at the superhero comic books of the 1940s.

Evidently a lot of people besides Feiffer, Hefner, and *Playboy* readers had fond memories of superheroes that year. *Time* magazine, in a 1965 article called "Batfans and Supermaniacs," took note of the rapidly growing popularity of superhero comic books and the crazy collectors who were paying big bucks for old Batman comic books.

Old Batman comic books were also attracting the attention of TV producer William Dozier. Dozier had heard about the Playboy screenings of the old 1940s Batman serial. On his way to the airport, he picked up the May 1965 issue of the *Batman* comic book off the newsstands. He read it. He remembered the 1950s Superman TV show. Wasn't it still being shown in syndication, even after a decade?

Wheels turned and clicked. Deals were made. Actors were found.

By the end of the year, Dozier produced what would be the most sensational TV show of 1966. It would be broadcast twice a week. It would start a pop culture craze. It would be fun—camp—and tongue-in-cheek. It would star Adam West and Burt Ward as Batman and Robin.

"Holy ratings! We're an overnight smash, Batman!"

The Batman TV show was a wild, goofy success. It started trends, fads, and fashions. There was a national dance craze, the Batusi, and even the Batman theme song ("*B-a-t*-mannnn! . . . *B-a-t*-mannnn! . . . ") became a Top 40 hit and junior high school chant.

It was Batmania. It was more. It was Super-Duper Heroitis. Already in the works was a Broadway musical production of Superman. Trend-following TV executives had pilots being shot for shows like the *Green Hornet*, *Captain Nice*, and *Mr. Terrific*.

Even the Saturday morning kiddie shows turned into a superhero cartoon battleground. From 1966 to 1968, kids could tune into the *Superman-Aquaman Show*, *Fantastic Four Show*, *Spider-Man Show*, *Superman-Batman Cartoon Hour*, *Super President*, and *Super Six* (with Granite Man, Magnet Man, Captain Wammy, and Super Bwoing).

The overwhelming reaction of a Bat-crazed media and superhero-loving population was not lost on the comic book industry. As early as 1965, every comic book publisher was already aware that superheroes were the fastest-growing segment of the market. Now with the Batman TV show in 1966 confirming what they already knew, publishers scrambled to bring out more and more superhero comics.

It seemed DC Comics could not print enough Batman comic books. In 1966 and 1967, *Batman* was the top-selling comic book—a first for the Caped Crusader. In fact, nine out of the top ten-selling comic books in 1967 featured a DC Comics superhero.

Batman #190 ©1967 DC Comics, Inc. Carmine Infantino, Joe Giella.

THUNDER Agents #1 © 1965 Tower Comics. Wally Wood.

The following year, Marvel Comics pumped out more new superhero titles in a four-month period than it had done for the entire previous six years. *Captain America, Sub-Mariner, Silver Surfer, Dr. Strange, Captain Marvel, Incredible Hulk,* and *Iron Man* appeared on the newsstands in the spring of 1968.

Besides DC and Marvel Comics, there were new (and old) comic book publishers rushing out new (and old) superhero comics for readers in the Bat-Years of 1966 to 1968.

Archie Comics, which had dabbled in superheroes since 1959 with the Fly and the Shield, brought back dozens of 1940s heroes for its new "Mighty Comics" line in the mid 1960s, which featured the *Mighty Crusaders.* The Archie superheroes were the most intentionally "camp" and exaggerated of the Batman TV era ("Howzabout a *knuckles* message, sweetie-pie?! No charge! Just use your super-villain credit card!").

An even more broad takeoff on superheroes was Milson Publishing's *Fatman the Human Flying Saucer.* The comic book's hero, a several-hundred-pound young man whose hobbies are bird-watching and eating ("Just a big fat birdbrain," sighs his dad), fought evil doers when he wasn't raiding the refrigerator.

Not all the new superheroes of the mid- and late 1960s were buffoons or clones of Adam West and Burt Ward. Tower Comics started a small but high-quality line of superheroes in 1965 with its *THUNDER Agents* comics. Wally Wood, an accomplished artist, created and packaged the THUNDER Agent superhero stories out of his small studio apartment. Dan Adkins, one of Wood's assistants then, recalled that "Wood was the editor and controlled the whole show . . . we worked 12 to 18 hours a day. His other assistants included Tim Battersby, Larry Ivie, Tony Coleman, and Ralph Reese. I guess Ralph was about fourteen years old at the time."

Over at Charlton Publishing, at about the same time, editor Dick Giordano was also bringing in new artists and writers to work on a growing line of superheroes: *Judomaster*, *Peacemaker*, *Blue Beetle*, and *Captain Atom*. Steve Ditko, who left Marvel Comics in 1966, worked on the last two superheroes, and also created the Question for Charlton's *Mysterious Suspense*.

Special War Series #4 ©1965 *Charlton Comics*. Frank McLaughlin.

It seemed that every comic book company was birthing superheroes in 1966 and 1967. The small American Comics Group came out with Magicman and Nemesis, two supernatural superheroes. Dell Comics made superheroes out of monsters like Frankenstein, Dracula, and Wolfman.

Harvey Comics also decided to add a string of superhero comics to their kiddie-comic empire of *Richie Rich*, *Little Dot*, and *Casper the Friendly Ghost*. In just one year, editor Joe Simon put together a Harvey Comics superhero lineup consisting of Jigsaw, Pirana, Spyman, Glowing Gladiator, Bee-Man, Magicmaster, Tiger Boy, and Jack Quick Frost.

Now there were more superheroes on the newsstands than anytime since the early 1940s. Just to trip through the alphabet, there was Aquaman, Batman, Captain America, Daredevil, Elasti-Girl, Fly Man, Green Lantern, Hawkman, Iron Man, Judomaster, Kid Flash, Lightning Lad, Magicman, NoMan, Owl, Plastic Man, Question, Raven, Silver Surfer, Thor, Ultra Boy, Vision, Wonder Woman, X-Men, Yellowjacket, and Zatanna.

It was too much of a good and bad thing. With so many superhero comics, there were bound to be some stinkers. Even the better ones became tainted by the hype and hoopla of the "pop" culture craze. Marvel Comics took to calling itself "Marvel Pop Art Productions" for a few months. DC Comics responded by running black-and-white "Go-Go Checks" across the top of all its covers. Longtime DC Comics writer Gardner Fox lamented that "camp was in style, so we tried to give the readers what they seemed to like, judging by the sales. We wrote what we were told to write; we didn't just write what we liked."

Ironically, it would be the departure of Gardner Fox and other longtime DC writers that would mark the beginning of the end of the 1960s Silver Age of Superheroes. In a disagreement with management in 1968, Gardner Fox, Bill Finger, Ed Herron, Arnold Drake, and Otto Binder quit writing for DC Comics. "We were all rather sad and bitter," Fox recalled years later. "Most of us had been at National (DC Comics) for 20 years or

Fly Man #33 © *1965 Archie Comics*. Paul Reinman.

Captain Atom #86 ©*1967 Charlton Comics*. Steve Ditko, Rocke Mastroserio.

Not Brand Echh #3 ©1967 Marvel Entertainment Group, Inc. Marie Severin.

more. Bill longer than any of us."

Bill Finger had been the principal author of the Batman legend. Otto Binder, along with Mort Weisinger, was responsible for most of the Superman mythos. Arnold Drake wrote the Doom Patrol and other superheroes. Ed Herron wrote for many of editor Jack Schiff's titles, while Gardner Fox wrote more superhero stories for editor Julius Schwartz than anyone else. Their departure, coupled with the loss of some longtime artists and editorial shuffling, pretty much destroyed all the original creative teams who worked on the DC Silver Age superheroes of the 1950s and 1960s.

At Marvel Comics, editor and writer Stan Lee had long since given up writing all the Marvel titles by the late 1960s. Other writers were coming in and, while many performed to both Stan Lee's and the readers' expectations, the effect was a gradual loss of a single guiding force in the Marvel Universe. By 1970, Jack Kirby would leave Marvel Comics: The heart and soul of the Fantastic Four, Captain America, and the Mighty Thor was gone. Two years later, Lee would also end much of his creative involvement with the storytelling.

As quickly as the boom, came the bust.

Superhero comics plummeted in popularity by the end of the 1960s. The Batman TV show zapped and powed its last in the spring of 1968. Comic book titles were cancelled and heroes vanished. By 1970, only Marvel and DC were publishing superhero comics.

The Silver Age of Superhero Comics had ended. . . .

Batman #156 ©DC Comics, Inc. Shelly Moldoff, Charles Paris.

Sputniks, Mutants, Commies, and Science Fairs

"He thinks his powers are greater than *ours,* huh? Well, they *ain't*! *Nothing's* more powerful than those cosmic rays that turned us into what we are!"

— *Fantastic Four* #3

Mystery in Space #64
©1960 DC Comics, Inc.
Carmine Infantino, Joe Giella. "The Radioactive Menace."

It was the coldest day of the Cold War. October 22, 1962. The United States threw up a naval blockade to prevent Soviet missiles from reaching Cuba.

As Soviet submarines approached a line of American ships, we glanced nervously over at our neighbor's fallout shelter. Nuclear annihilation never seemed more likely.

Kids that year practiced civil defense drills at school, ducking under desks or huddling in the school gymnasium as imaginary atomic bombs fell down.

Just that summer the family fallout shelter was used as a neighborhood clubhouse where comic books were traded and read. Along with the tinned meat, batteries, and water-purification tablets were stacks of *Superman, Batman,* and *Green Lantern* comic books—perfect reading for the holocaust.

Once before America had faced such desperate and uncertain times. In 1941, the terrifying specter and horrible reality of World War II was upon the land. American soldiers in European trenches and on Pacific islands read the adventures of *Superman* and *Captain America* in comic books from home.

Patriotic superheroes like the Shield fought villains like "the super-Nazi rat, the Son of the Hun." It was Captain Nazi versus Captain Marvel, Jr., and the Human Torch hurled fireballs at subhuman Japanese soldiers.

Some say the war ended on August 6, 1945—the day the first atomic bomb fell on Hiroshima. It was also the day the superheroes of the 1940s began a decline that culminated in nearly their demise by 1950. In a world after the A-Bomb, the Golden Age Superheroes of the 1940s seemed innocently quaint—humbled by the powers of our new super-science.

But now they were back. Post-atomic superheroes. New heroes like Spider-Man, the Fantastic Four, and the Incredible Hulk. New versions of the Golden Age heroes like the Flash, Green Lantern, and the Atom. Fallout shelter reading for troubled 1962 kids. A Silver Age of Superheroes for the Cold War generation.

In 1957, the Soviet Union launched the first satellite into space, Sputnik. America was mortified. Two years later, the Russians

Mystery in Space #56 ©1959 DC Comics, Inc.. Gil Kane, Joe Giella. "The Menace of the Super-Atom."

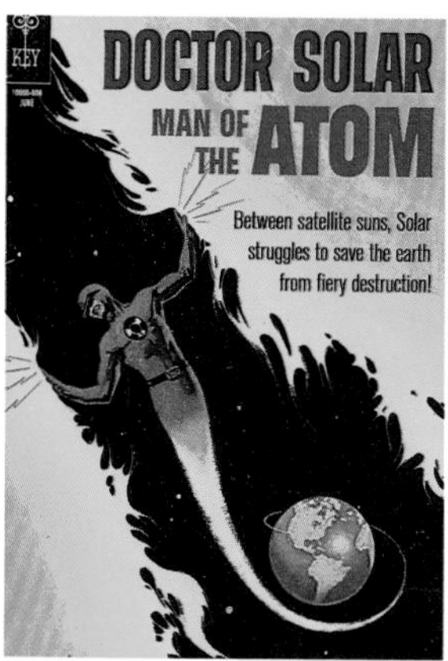

Doctor Solar #16 ©1966 Gold Key. Billed as "Man of the Atom."

crash-landed a rocket on the moon. America was terrified. We were two laps behind in the Space Race. Communist H-Bombs from outer space threatened our security.

To counter the Soviet space threat, the United States established the National Aeronautics and Space Administration (NASA) in 1958. That same year, President Eisenhower and Congress enacted the National Defense Education Act to accelerate the teaching of the sciences and technology to school children.

Science was the answer. Nuclear superiority tomorrow through science education today. Science fair exhibits by sixth grade students demonstrated the benefits of atom-splitting with colliding ping-pong balls. Kids joined Slide Rule Societies, formed model rocket clubs, and read about outer space.

The interest in science and space exploration was duly noted by one of the prime purveyors of literature for children at the time, DC Comics. A far-ranging editorial decision was made by the management in early 1958 to include more science and science fiction in all of their comic books. Batman would visit alien planets, comic book covers would feature more space ships, and there would be two new science fiction heroes, Space Ranger and Adam Strange.

Space Adventures #42 ©1961 Charlton Comics. Steve Ditko. Captain Atom, one of the earliest nuclear-created Silver Age superheroes.

Science, or perhaps more accurately science fiction, became the driving force behind old DC heroes like Superman and Batman and the catalyst for the resurrection of the Golden Age superheroes.

Green Lantern returned in 1959 after nearly sitting out the decade, modernized with a new costume and superpowers granted by a space alien. Hawkman and Hawkgirl, formerly down-to-earth 1940s crime fighters, began the 1960s as alien superheroes from the planet Thanagar.

The next nuclear age updating of a 1940s hero occurred in 1961. DC Comic's the Atom epitomized the scientific treatment given the new Silver Age superheroes:

Ray Palmer, a research scientist, is investigating ways to shrink matter to solve the world's food and transportation problems. Palmer tells the reader, "White dwarf stars are dense because they're formed of degenerate material—matter from which the electrons have been stripped, greatly compressing them! By studying the white dwarf fragment, I hope to learn how to compress matter without losing its physical and chemical properties!"

Later in the story, Palmer uses his knowledge of science to gain the super powers he needs to become the Atom:

"From the strange combination of white dwarf star and sunlight—product of the awesome forces of nature at her mightiest—steps a tiny titan into a world of giants—The Atom! Dedicated to overcoming evil—enlisting his services on the side of law and order against crime and injustice—he is to startle the world by the amazing inventiveness of his brilliant mind and the sheer physical power of his atomic body!"

Like the Atom, the other DC Silver Age superheroes also dedicated their superpowers (usually gained by science) against crime and injustice.

Barry Allen, a police chemist, gains his powers as the Flash in a science laboratory

World's Finest #105 ©1959 DC Comics, Inc. Curt Swan, Stan Kaye.

accident. The molecular-altered scientist muses: "There must be some way I can use this unique speed to help humanity!"

The combination of science, superpowers, and the desire to do good struck a responsive chord among young Cold War readers. The new DC superheroes were scientist-heroes with moral fibre. They possessed awesome powers, but they used those powers justly. We only hoped that our world leaders would wield their awesome nuclear powers so impeccably correct.

In the world of the DC superheroes of the Silver Age, rational thinking and scientific method could solve any problem, defeat any villain. There was a feeling of cheery optimism expressed through the heroes—a belief in ourselves and in our ability to actually make the Atomic Age a safe place to reach adulthood. As Green Lantern immediately realizes when he gains his superpowers, "Anything I *will* to happen, I *can* make happen!"

And so it seemed. For all our fears, we were entering a fabulous age of Science, Technology, and Space Exploration. The world of tomorrow promised to be a safer place than the world of today. We could learn to use those awesome powers justly. We could be scientific superheroes and bring order to a new world.

The DC superheroes were our solution to the pressures of an uncertain time. The conflicts of East and West, Communism and Democracy, nuclear destruction and technological progress, were all wrapped up into a single black and white confrontation. The Flash, Green Lantern, and all the other Justice League of America members fought and conquered outer space creatures, evil scientific geniuses, and megalomaniacs.

But never a single communist.

During the early years of the DC superhero renaissance, Nikita Khrushchev, then leader of the Soviet Union, was at a party in the United States hosted by author John Steinbeck. Among Steinbeck's guests was Mort Weisinger, editor of the *Superman* comic books.

Weisinger was introduced to Khrushchev as the editor of *Superman*. "You know," the translator prompted the Soviet leader, "the Man of Steel." Khrushchev then grinned and nodded to Weisinger. "The Man of Steel," said the feisty Kremlin leader, "will never pierce the Iron Curtain!"

Actually Khrushchev had it backwards. The Iron Curtain never pierced the world of the Man of Steel.

In the world of *Superman* comic books, communism did not exist. Superman rarely crossed national borders or involved himself in political disputes. Superman transcended all nationalities, all peoples, as did the other DC superheroes of the Silver Age.

The villains in Superman's world were apolitical. They, however, shared a common goal with the popularly conceived communists of the 1950s: they wanted to rule the world. Brainiac, a super-science android, shrinks and captures cities. Lex Luthor, a criminal mastermind, incessantly plots to conquer not only Metropolis but all countries of the world. Could political parallels be drawn?

In an April 1962 issue of *Action Comics*,

Nukla #1 ©1965 Dell Comics. Sal Trapani. Nuclear explosion hero.

Tales of Suspense #52 ©1964 Marvel Comics. Jack Kirby, George Roussos. Crimson Dynamo and Black Widow—Red agents!

a reader writes to editor Weisinger: "I am a great fan of Lex Luthor, and I've noticed something interesting about this character. Did you know that Luthor and Khrushchev resemble each other in many ways? Lex is bald, and so is Khrushchev. Lex is fat, K. is fat. And both of them want to rule the world. Therefore, I think it only logical for you to give us a story in which Luthor teams up with Khrushchev and the Man of Steel has to crash through the Iron Curtain."

"An interesting idea," Weisinger replies, "but we never go in for stories of a political nature."

Like sex, religion, constipation, and bad manners, politics did not exist in the fantasy world of the DC Comics superheroes. With these elements of realism removed, it was all the more important to make the superhero fantasy seem as real as possible within its constraints.

Superman's Girlfriend Lois Lane #51 ©1963 DC Comics, Inc. Kurt Schaffenberger.

Superman writers Edmond Hamilton and Jerry Siegel worked carefully with Weisinger to make sure that all their diverse stories never contradicted the basic ground rules for the character. The Superman legend must be respected and all the pieces of the ongoing mythos should fit together.

Fanciful stories, such as Superman's marriage to Lana Lang or his death by kryptonite, which could not fit into the developing Superman canon were printed as "Imaginary Stories." The other stories in the comic books, of course, were "real" and became a part of the well-ordered and internally consistent mythology for each DC superhero of the Silver Age.

Superman #166 ©1964 DC Comics, Inc. Curt Swan, George Klein.

By 1962, DC Comics had created a universe of superheroes that were comforting, positive, optimistic, reassuring, and rational. These new superheroes had awesome powers of destruction (like the new atomic missiles), but they used these powers responsibly and justly. It was Science married to Morality.

Still for a kid sitting in a fallout shelter in 1962, the world of DC Comics left a few nagging questions unanswered. For all its advancements, science was also what had made the world a dangerous place—at least in many people's minds. The hydrogen bomb and nuclear missiles were products of a science gone bad. We only had to look as far as movies like *The Day the World Ended* and *The Day The Earth Caught Fire* to see the dangers of science run amok.

Science, it seemed, was both our savior and our destroyer. With the Space Race and the New Frontier, we also got Geiger counters and the Iron Curtain. The perfect world of DC Comics and its science-superheroes was suddenly flawed for a kid who had just learned about the world threat of communism and the symptoms of radiation sickness.

Radiation—radioactive fallout from nuclear missiles—was the biggest fear. Science fiction movies fascinated us with horrors of mutated insects (*Them!*) and radioactive people (*The Amazing Colossal Man*).

Marvel Comics writer Stan Lee and artist Jack Kirby were also entertaining us with their stories of radiation-spawned monsters in comics like *Tales to Astonish* and *Strange Tales* of the late 1950s.

From their radioactive monsters, Lee and Kirby got the idea to create radioactive heroes, or "good" monsters like the Incredible Hulk and the Thing in the *Fantastic Four.*

In 1961, Lee and Kirby's Fantastic Four gain their superpowers when their experimental rocket ship is bombarded by cosmic radiation. The radiation accident turns them into horrible freaks, but also gives them superhuman abilities. Radiation—nuclear energy—seemed to have its light side as well as dark side.

"Together we have more power than any humans have ever possessed!" observes Mr. Fantastic. "We understand," rejoins a transformed Ben Grimm. "We've gotta use that power to help mankind, right?"

Radiation as a means of gaining superpowers became a Marvel Comics trademark. In 1962, Lee and Kirby tell the story of Bruce Banner, a nuclear physicist, who is blasted by the rays of an exploding "Gamma Bomb." He undergoes an involuntary transformation into a brutish green beast, the *Incredible Hulk.* He is all-powerful, but also less than human.

That same year, Peter Parker becomes the *Amazing Spider-Man* when he is bitten by a radioactive spider. But even that transformation has its drawbacks as it complicates the hero's personal life.

X-Men #4 © 1964 *Marvel Comics.* Jack Kirby, Paul Reinman.

Other radiation-created (or enhanced) Marvel superheroes of the Silver Age include *Daredevil* and the *X-Men,* the original teenage mutants.

The Marvel superhero, created by radiation, was a tempered yet ultimately optimistic reconciliation of the risks and benefits of the nuclear age. Sure, radiation was dangerous but there were also some awesome powers to be derived—powers which just might save the world instead of destroying it.

The Marvel superheroes inhabited a more

Fantastic Four #13 ©1963 Marvel Comics. Jack Kirby, George Roussos.

realistic, sobering, and dangerous world than did the DC superheroes. They lived in New York City, not the imaginary burgs of Metropolis or Central City. They wrestled openly with our fears of nuclear fallout, radiation, losing the space race, and that fear behind all fears, communism.

From 1962 to 1965, there were more communists in the stories of the *Fantastic Four*, *Ant-Man*, and *Iron Man* than on the subscription list of *Pravda*. Communist agents attack Ant-Man in his laboratory, red henchmen jump the Fantastic Four on the moon, and Viet Cong guerillas take potshots at Iron Man.

A typical issue of the *Fantastic Four* from 1963 (#13 April) introduces the evil space scientist Ivan Kragoff who lives "on the other side of the globe, behind the iron curtain." Kragoff is obsessed with "claiming the moon for the communist empire!"

Kragoff trains a group of apes to be his henchmen. "At last my crew of apes is ready! And now, we go to the *moon*—to claim it for the communist empire! Set the controls, Comrade Gorilla!"

Meanwhile on the "right" side of the Iron Curtain—in New York City—scientist Reed Richards, the leader of the Fantastic Four, makes a discovery:

"Now I've found a way to *harness* all that energy! All I have to do is expose this iron bar to the correct *radiation* . . . and it will furnish the power to send a huge rocket straight to the moon! This means *America* may win the space race!"

Radiation (read: nuclear power, science, etc.) correctly harnessed and used can help America beat her enemies. On the other hand, the awesome powers of science can also do great damage and harm in the wrong (read: communist) hands.

Indeed, radiation could create super-villains, such as the Puppet Master, Sandman, or Dr. Octopus as well as superheroes. Dr. Doom uses his scientific genius for evil, as does the Mandarin, Magneto, and others. Science was often the battleground in the morality plays of most superhero comics.

Kragoff, the Russian scientist who wants to claim the moon, deliberately exposes himself to heavy doses of space radiation in hopes of gaining superpowers like the Fantastic Four. The radiation turns the cosmonaut into the invisible and powerful Red Ghost.

The Fantastic Four pursue the radiation-charged Red Ghost and his mutant apes to the moon. He manages to imprison the Invisible Girl inside a force field with his apes. She frets:

"If I could only find a way to eliminate the force field to free his super-apes! I would rather take my chances with them, rather than the Red Ghost, for they are like the Communist masses, innocently enslaved by their evil leaders!"

There you have it. Super-apes and communist dupes on the moon. The comic book story sounded many themes running through the Silver Age comic books: good science, bad science, radiation, the space race, moral righteousness, self-sacrificing heroics, and communist world domination.

By the mid-1960s, however, Marvel Comics had pretty well replaced its communist villains with apolitical super-powered tyrants. Times were changing. The Cuban Missile Crisis faded and our attention turned to a southeastern Asian country called Vietnam.

Stan Lee, editor and writer of most of the Marvel comics at the time, recalled that the anti-communist rhetoric occurred well before the United States became heavily embroiled in the Vietnam War. Lee believed that the comic stories before then reflected "a time when most of us genuinely felt that the conflict in that tortured land really was a simple matter of good versus evil and that the American military action against the Viet Cong was tantamount to St. George's battle against the dragon. Since that time, of course, we've all grown up a bit. We've realized that life isn't quite so simple."

In many respects, the beginning of the Vietnam War era was also the ending of the Silver Age of Superheroes.

A gray moral relativism swept the country. Good and bad weren't black and white anymore. We were questioning ourselves, our country, and our values as a people. Riots on the streets of Chicago. Peace demonstrations. Robert Kennedy and Martin Luther King murdered.

The tensions of the Cold War, the perpetual anxiety about nuclear destruction, the race to embrace science as a solution to our problems—all the pressures of the late 1950s and early 1960s which had given birth to the superheroes—now seemed dwarfed by our domestic turmoil and our foreign entanglements. Equally important, our moral center was knocked off kilter. The end of the 1960s marked the end of a generation's naïvete. The Batman TV show, ending in 1968, was a smirking parody of our earlier innocent fascination and belief in all-powerful heroes who once had all the answers.

Spider-Man, Batman, Superman, and all the rest would prosper again in the 1970s, written by new writers and drawn by new artists. The 1980s and 1990s would see the return of still more 1960s superheroes, rediscovered, remembered, updated, and modernized for fourth and fifth generations of comic book readers.

Yet for all their familiarity, the superheroes of the 1970s, 1980s, and 1990s are still different—forever and far different—from their Silver Age counterparts and predecessors.

The Silver Age superheroes were born in the 1960s, in the middle of America's most frenzied myth-making. We had the Beatles, the Kennedys, the astronauts, and James Bond. We had heroes larger than life.

We had superheroes.

Journey Into Mystery #93
©1963 Marvel Comics.
Jack Kirby, Dick Ayers

The Heroes

Detective Comics #345 ©1966 DC Comics, Inc. Carmine Infantino, Joe Giella.

There were over three hundred comic book superheroes during the 1960s. Well over half of these were minor and fleeting characters, like Inferno, the Fab Four, and Polar Boy. Only the cognoscenti remember (or care) that the Terrific Three consisted of the Jaguar, Mr. Justice, and Steel Sterling.

Other Silver Age superheroes, however, like Superman, Batman, and Spider-Man, became American media icons, as widely recognized as any president. Several of the superheroes have inspired movies and television shows (Wonder Woman, Batman, Flash, Hulk, Superman, Supergirl, and Superboy).

The heroes profiled in this section are the most popular ones of the 1960s—the ones best remembered by readers and fans. Their origins, as well as their major and minor appearances in the Silver Age of comics, are noted, along with background information on their creation and history.

ANT-MAN (GIANT-MAN)

SECRET IDENTITY
Henry Pym, scientist

NICKNAMES
Ant-Size Avenger
High-Pockets (Giant-Man)

FIRST APPEARANCES
January 1962—*Tales to Astonish* #27 (Henry Pym)
September 1962—*Tales to Astonish* #35 (Ant-Man)
October 1963—*Tales to Astonish* #49 (Giant-Man)
May 1966—*Avengers* #28 (Goliath)
December 1968—*Avengers* #59 (Yellowjacket)

MAJOR SILVER AGE APPEARANCES
Tales to Astonish 27, 35–48 (Ant-Man) 49–69 (Giant-Man)

OTHER SILVER AGE APPEARANCES
Avengers 1–16, 28–60, 63–71
Fantastic Four 17 (Ant-Man)

Tales to Astonish #49 ©*1963 Marvel Entertainment Group, Inc.* Don Heck, Don Heck.

Henry Pym, a research scientist, invents "the most potent serum ever developed by man! A serum that can reduce a man to the size of an insect."

He splashes his new serum on his wrist to see if it works. It does. In fact, "the potion proved more powerful than Henry Pym had anticipated! It reduced him to the size of an insect—and led him to the most frightening encounter of his life—within a teeming ant-hill!"

After Pym escapes from the anthill and regains his normal size with his enlarging serum, he is a changed person. "After his experience in the anthill, Pym developed a growing interest in ants . . . secretly, continually, he made a thorough study of the ant world!"

Pym's obsession led to other inventions in his attempt to learn all about ants. "This helmet I devised will enable me to contact the ants—to tune in on their wave-length and actually communicate with them! And I designed a protective costume to wear which will shield me from an accidental ant-bite or sting."

Now Pym could safely shrink down again and enter the world of insects and ants, communicating with them via his cybernetic helmet.

His scientific curiosity, however, is put on hold when communist agents invade his lab in an effort to gain control of his reducing serum.

To escape from the communists, Pym puts on his special costume and helmet and uses his reducing serum to shrink down to ant-size. Squeezing through a crack in the laboratory door, he returns to the anthill to enlist their aid.

"I must communicate with the ants! I must make them understand what they are to do!"

Moments later, he succeeds in directing the ants to swarm over the legs of the spies, bite them, and plug their gun barrels with honey. The ants help Ant-Man win his first of many victories.

The Ant-Man grew out of the pages of Marvel's monster and science fiction comics. Jack Kirby had drawn the first appearance of Henry Pym as a straight adventure story of a shrinking scientist in a January 1962 issue of *Tales to Astonish* ("The Man in the Anthill!"). Writer and editor Stan Lee decided to bring the character back a few months later as a costumed superhero, the Ant-Man.

Lee had earlier expressed a desire for an insect-named superhero. The inspiration for a tiny, ant-sized hero may have came from the success of the Atom (The World's Smallest Hero) in DC Comics' *Showcase* the previous year. The first issue of the new *Atom* comic book was on sale the same month Lee discussed the idea of Ant-Man with artist Jack Kirby.

Kirby drew the first Ant-Man story based on Lee's plot, and Larry Lieber wrote the script. Early Ant-Man stories revolved around Pym enlisting the aid of his ant friends to help fight communism (Comrade X) and supervillains (Scarlet Beetle).

Within a year, Ant-Man was joined by yet another insect-sized superhero, the Wasp—also known as Janet Van Dyne. Janet had a crush on Pym and shamelessly pursued him. More often than not, however, the cool scientist seemed immune to her warm advances:

"Why couldn't I have fallen in love with a nice simple butcher or baker?" she asks him.

"Honey," he replies, "you're in love with the idea of being in love! Now button those ruby lips until we finish this job!"

"Even when you call me Honey," she pouts, "you make it sound . . . medicinal!"

Pym's scientific research eventually paid off, however. By late 1963, he discovered enlarging pills which turned him from an insect-sized hero into a Giant-Man! As Giant-Man, he can achieve a twelve-foot optimum fighting size (any larger and he becomes weaker).

Tales to Astonish #47 ©1963 Marvel Entertainment Group, Inc. Jack Kirby, Dick Ayers.

Evidently, becoming Giant-Man did wonders for Pym's self-image and his relationship with the Wasp. He no longer saw her as a lovesick youngster, but as a future marriage partner. Before wedding bells could ring, however, Henry Pym would undergo yet another, and still another, change of identity.

In 1966, Pym changes his name from Giant-Man to Goliath and dons a new costume. Two years later, he changes names and costumes again and calls himself the Yellowjacket.

Adventure Comics #267 ©1959 DC Comics, Inc. Ramona Fradon.

The Wasp, who has been with Pym as Ant-Man, Giant-Man, Goliath, and Yellowjacket, decided in 1969 that it was finally time for her to become Mrs. Pym. The two superheroes marry and take a leave of absence for a well-deserved honeymoon.

AQUAMAN

SECRET IDENTITY
Arthur Curry

NICKNAMES
King of the Seven Seas
Marine Marvel

FIRST APPEARANCE
November 1941—*More Fun* #73

FIRST SILVER AGE ORIGIN
May 1959—*Adventure Comics* #260

MAJOR SILVER AGE APPEARANCES
Adventure Comics 247–280, 282, 284
Aquaman 1–48
Brave and Bold 51, 73, 82
Detective Comics 293–300
Showcase 30–33
World's Finest 125–133, 135, 137, 139, 144, 147

OTHER SILVER AGE APPEARANCES
Action Comics 314, 366
Atom 8
Brave and the Bold 28–30, 54, 60
Doom Patrol 104
Flash 175
Green Lantern 29
Justice League of America 1–24, 26–29, 31, 33, 35, 36, 39–41, 44, 48, 50, 52, 53, 58–61, 63, 65, 67, 68, 76
Mystery in Space 75
Superman 138, 199
Superman's Girlfriend Lois Lane 12, 29
Superman's Pal Jimmy Olsen 115
Teen Titans 1

Brave and the Bold #54 ©1964 DC Comics, Inc. Bruno Premiani, Charles Paris.

"Tom Curry, an ex-sailor, lived a solitary existence as a light-house keeper. One evening while a hurricane raged over sea and land. . . . "

A beautiful woman is seen adrift alone in the stormy seas. Curry rescues her. They fall in love, marry, and have a son.

As their son Arthur grows older, he gradually learns more about his mother's mysterious past. One day she tells her son:

"I come from Atlantis, a continent that sank into the sea ages ago! Our people had to adapt to a watery existence. We gradually became like fish, capable of underwater feats!"

On her deathbed, Arthur's mother finally reveals the secret of his birth:

"You, my son, have inherited my ability to live underwater! You have the power to communicate with sea creatures . . . to perform great water feats . . . and to become Ruler of the Oceans!" He learns that he is truly a man of the water—Aquaman.

The boy discovers he can swim through the ocean at 100 miles per hour and telepathically control all the creatures of the sea. He can command squids, sea turtles, whales, and sharks to do his bidding. More than once, Aquaman's "finny friends" have come to his rescue, much like the jungle beasts of Tarzan. ("Look! He has commanded those octopi to catapult swordfish at us!")

Aquaman, however, has one serious weakness: He cannot survive more than one hour without some contact with water. Since even condensing spray from air conditioners and a well-aimed glass of water will usually do the trick, the King of the Seven Seas can maintain a fairly active schedule as a land-based crime fighter.

By the time writer Mort Weisinger and artist Paul Norris created Aquaman for DC Comics in 1941, there was already a school of underwater superheroes. Bill Everett alone created the Sub-Mariner in 1939, Hydroman in 1940, and the Fin in 1941.

Aquaman, however, was the most successful of all the watery superheroes. He had a continuing series in one DC comic or the other from 1941 to 1971. He was also a founding member of the Justice League of America.

Aquaman #3 ©1962 *DC Comics, Inc.* Nick Cardy.

Weisinger updated the character's origin in 1959 in *Adventure Comics*. In 1961, Aquaman appeared in several issues of *Showcase* and then received his own comic book in 1962.

In 1964, Aquaman married Mera, a princess from a watery dimension. She has the power of making water turn into any solid form she desires. The following year, they produced Arthur Curry, Jr., better known as Aquababy. Aquababy should not be confused with Aqualad, a boy who first teamed up with Aquaman as his teenage sidekick in 1960.

Aquaman first discovered Aqualad liv-

Aquaman #30 ©1966 *DC Comics, Inc.* Nick Cardy.

ing in an underwater capsule, frightened of all sea life, yet able to breathe naturally in the water. Aquaman became the boy's guardian and helped him adjust to a life in the ocean. He often affectionately referred to Aqualad as "Tadpole" and "Little Sardine." Aqualad gradually drifted away from his mentor, joined the Teen Titans, and got a steady girlfriend named (but of course) Aquagirl.

As the 1960s ended, Aquaman's personal life was in turmoil. His wife had been abducted, and he quit the Justice League of America in order to search for her. By the end of 1970, Aquaman returned as an active member, although his own comic book would be cancelled the following year.

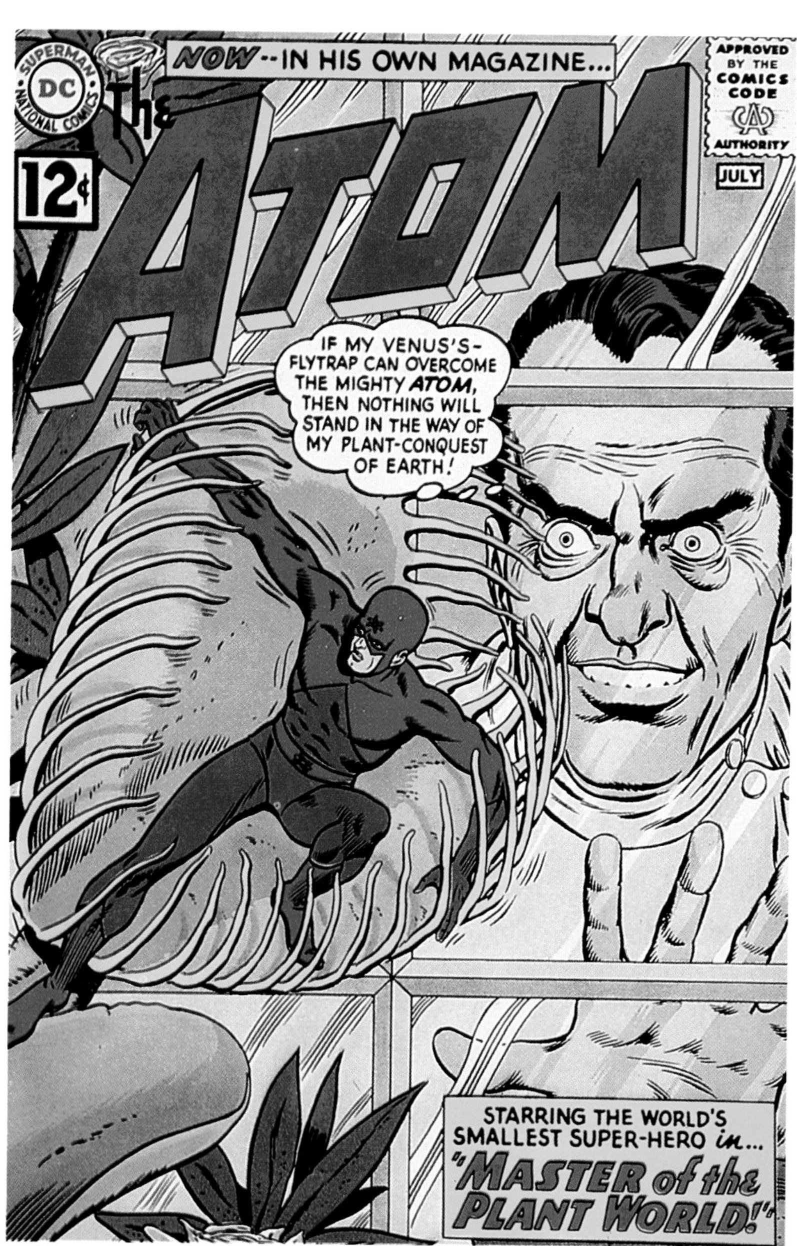

Atom #1 ©1962 *DC Comics, Inc.* Gil Kane, Murphy Anderson.

ATOM

SECRET IDENTITY
Ray Palmer, physics professor

NICKNAMES
Tiny Titan
World's Smallest Super-Hero

FIRST APPEARANCE
October 1940—*All American Comics* #19

FIRST SILVER AGE APPEARANCE
September 1961—*Showcase* #34

MAJOR SILVER AGE APPEARANCES
Atom 1–38
Atom and Hawkman 39–45
Brave and Bold 53, 55, 73, 77
Showcase 34–36

OTHER SILVER AGE APPEARANCES
Action Comics 314,
Aquaman 18
Detective 368
Flash 171
Hawkman 9

Like all idealistic scientists of the early 1960s comic books, Ray Palmer wanted to help humanity. His experiments with the compression of matter would enable farmers to grow more crops on less land, and the resulting compressed foods could be transported more easily.

His experiments in his lab at Ivy University, unfortunately, always ended in explosions. Palmer was frustrated:

"I was working hard on this experiment and getting nowhere, when three months ago—I saw a meteor falling from the night sky. Digging deep, I uncovered a fragment of what once must have been part of a dwarf star. . . . By studying the white dwarf fragment, I hoped to learn how to compress matter without losing its physical and chemical properties!"

Palmer discovers that when he passes

Atom #10 ©1963 DC Comics, Inc. Gil Kane, Murphy Anderson.

ultraviolet light through a lens made from the star fragment, matter does indeed compress and shrink. He takes the lens with him when he accompanies his fiancé Jean Loring on a field trip into a cave.

After a cave-in traps Palmer and his girlfriend, he uses the dwarf star lens upon himself in desperation. The lens shrinks him down to six inches, and he is able to reach a small opening. He is able to free them from the cave and return to his normal six-foot self, with no one the wiser.

As Palmer says later to his laboratory tape recorder, "Now that I am able to turn myself into a human atom—who knows what strange and wonderful things may happen?"

The first thing that happens is that Palmer devises a stretch-costume and refines his white dwarf lens so that he can shrink all the way down to subatomic size and return to full size at will. He discovers that his best fighting size is six inches. He also learns how to adjust his weight so that he can float through the air like a feather and then land with his full 180 pounds on a bad guy's jaw.

A favorite trick of writer Gardner Fox was to have Ray Palmer dial a phone number of his desired destination (like the Paris airport), then shrink down to the size of an a electron, hop into the phone receiver, travel along the electronic impulses of the phone lines, and then jump out of the receiver at the other end as a six-inch superhero. It was a great way to invade a crook's hideout or crash a friend's party.

The *Atom* comic book was crammed full of science fiction devices: subatomic universes, time pools, and supervillains armed with temporal displacers and light-ray machines.

Even the Atom's alter ego was inspired by science fiction. According to editor Julius Schwartz, he named the Atom after "Ray Palmer, the editor of *Amazing Stories* (the world's first s-f magazine). Raymond had an accident as a child and never grew too tall. So I figured that was a good name for the smallest hero of all time. Many of the names I created were based on my science fiction background."

The Atom, like the other 1960s DC superheroes who preceded him—the Flash, Green Lantern, and Hawkman—was originally a 1940s character. The Atom in the

Brave and the Bold #53 ©1964 DC Comics, Inc. Alex Toth.

Avengers #1 ©1963 Marvel Entertainment Group, Inc. Jack Kirby, Dick Ayers. Hulk *vs.* Iron Man.

1940s comic book got his name for his five-foot stature—not the ability to shrink down to the size of an atom.

Schwartz recalled that "I always felt that the Atom of the 1940s was misnamed. He was simply called the Atom because he was a short fellow. I got the idea of having him as a regular six-footer able to reduce himself to any size he wanted to."

The idea for a new Atom, according to Schwartz, came about during a 1961 brainstorming session when "It just struck us as we were groping around for a theme that wasn't being done by any superheroes."

Schwartz also felt that the time was right for a truly Atomic Hero. "In 1940, I'd venture to say not one person in ten knew what an atom was." By the time he was ready to introduce the new Atom, "everyone had heard about the atomic bomb, atomic reactors, atomic power."

The Atom was both a visual treat and nightmare for its artists, notably Gil Kane, who drew the character for the first seven years. The continual challenge was how to draw a six-inch hero so that he was dramatically visible but still in perspective to the normal-sized people around him.

The Atom first appeared in three issues of *Showcase* in 1961 and became a member of the Justice League of America in 1962. The "World's Smallest Super-Hero" starred in his own comic book series from 1962 until the end of 1969.

AVENGERS

NICKNAMES
Earth's Mightiest Heroes

MEMBERS
(Original Members—September 1963)
Thor
Iron Man
Ant-Man (aka: Giant-Man, Goliath, Yellowjacket)
Wasp
Hulk

(Subsequent Members)
Captain America (Joined March 1964)
Scarlet Witch (Joined May 1965)
Quicksilver (Joined May 1965)
Hawkeye (Joined May 1965)
Swordsman (Joined September 1965)
Hercules (Joined October 1967)
Black Panther (Joined May 1968)
Vision (Joined November 1968)
Black Knight (Joined December 1969)

FIRST SILVER AGE APPEARANCE
September 1963—*Avengers* #1

MAJOR SILVER AGE APPEARANCES
Avengers 1–71 Annual 1–3

OTHER SILVER AGE APPEARANCES:
Amazing Spider-Man 18 Annual 3
Captain America 100, 113, 114, 116
Captain Marvel 14, 17, 19
Dr. Strange 178
Fantastic Four 25, 26, 31, 36 Annual 3, 4
Incredible Hulk 115
Iron Man 18, 19
Journey Into Mystery 105, 108, 112, 116, 120
Nick Fury, Agent of SHIELD 15
Strange Tales 156
Sub-Mariner 14
Tales of Suspense 49, 56, 58, 59, 72, 91
Tales to Astonish 59, 78
X-Men 9, 43, 45

Ant-Man was the first to speak. "Each of us has a different power! If we combined forces, we could be almost unbeatable!"

"Work as a team?" responded Iron Man. "Why not? I'm for it!"

The Mighty Thor nodded his head. "There is much good we might do!"

"I'm sick of bein' hunted and hounded," snarled the Hulk as he looked at the other superheroes. "I'd rather be with you than against you! So, whether you like it or not, I'm joinin' the . . . the . . . hey! What are you callin' yourselves?"

The Wasp joined in. "That's right! We need a name! It should be something colorful and dramatic, like . . . The Avengers!"

"And thus is born," writer Stan Lee intones, "one of the greatest superhero teams of all time! Powerful! Unpredictable! Brought together by a strange quirk of fate, the Avengers are on the march, and a new dimension is added to the Marvel galaxy of stars!"

Composed of Marvel's most popular individual superheroes of the early 1960s (excepting Spider-Man), the Avengers were an immediate success. Like the other Marvel characters, the Avengers were a new breed. They were a team of superheroes that didn't always act like a team.

By the second issue, the temperamental Hulk had stamped off in a rampage. By the fourth issue, Captain America had joined the team. By the following year, all the original Avengers—Iron Man, Thor, Giant-Man, and the Wasp—had been written out of the series by Stan Lee. Lee's reason for dropping the popular characters was that it was becoming increasingly difficult to maintain the continuity between the stories in their own comics and their adventures in the *Avengers.*

The new Avengers consisted of Captain America and secondary characters like Quicksilver and the Scarlet Witch from *X-Men,* and Hawkeye from the Iron Man series in *Tales of Suspense.*

Quicksilver was Marvel's version of the "fastest man alive," while Hawkeye was an archer hero in the tradition of the Green Arrow. The Scarlet Witch added the requisite feminine touch. Captain America, by virtue

Avengers #3 ©*1963 Marvel Entertainment Group, Inc.* Jack Kirby, Dick Ayers.

Avengers #58 ©1968 Marvel Entertainment Group, Inc. John Buscema, George Klein.

of seniority, became the leader of the team—a position he maintained off and on all through the 1960s.

The appeal of the Avengers had a lot to do with the ever-changing group dynamics—the ways the characters played off each other and against each other:

"Only a fool fights on after the battle has been lost," the Scarlet Witch tells Captain America.

"Lady," he answers, "how did you ever get to be an Avenger?"

"I've heard enough," says Quicksilver, the Scarlet Witch's brother, "First, we are brought to defeat under your own leadership—then you have the gall to insult one who was your most loyal follower!"

"You hot tempered fool," Captain America yells as Quicksilver attacks him. "What do you think you're doing?"

"Hold it Speedy," says Hawkeye. "He'll make mincemeat out of you!"

"Let him go, Hawkeye," says Captain America, shaking his fist.

"Why? So you can build up your ego by battin' him around? Uh uh! If anyone fights you, it'll be *me*!"

One big happy family, and it got bigger.

Hercules became a member of the Avengers in 1967 and filled the god-gap left by Thor's departure two years earlier. "Taste thou the hammering fists of Hercules—and then say he is naught but the stuff of legend!"

The Black Panther, an African king turned superhero who first appeared in *Fantastic Four,* joined the Avengers in 1968: "Let the word go forth . . . that today you have gained a new ally . . . one who has given up a throne, that he may serve a greater kingdom . . . the whole of mankind itself! For now the Panther is truly an Avenger!"

The next new Avenger would be the stoic, humorless, and immensely powerful Vision—an evil android turned good. The artificially created Vision was accepted as a member of the team even though he wasn't a human. As Giant-Man observed: "Is a man any less human because he has an artificial leg or a transplanted heart? The five original Avengers included an Asgardian immortal and a green-skinned, tormented behemoth! We ask merely a man's worth—not the accident of his condition!"

Stan Lee remembered that back in 1963, "I was trying to come up with a new superhero feature. I remembered all the mail requesting team-ups of our main characters. So what could be more logical than for me to act upon that very idea and do a new feature consisting of a group of our most dazzling do-gooders, united together in a common bond? Once again, in a frantic flurry of excitement, I called Jack Kirby and told him to sharpen his pencil."

Kirby drew the *Avengers* for over a year before passing it on to Don Heck. John Buscema followed Heck as the other principal 1960s *Avengers* artist.

Heck recalled that while the Avengers were fun to draw, "the only problem is that when you have too many characters running around, you can only really devote one or two pages to each of them. If you put too many of them in there, then you'll never get a chance to see them do anything."

The Avengers continued to grow and evolve over the years. Captain America quit the Avengers. Giant-Man returned as Goliath. Thor and Iron Man came and went. The Vision married the Scarlet Witch. The Wasp married Yellowjacket (formerly Ant-Man). Hercules returned to Olympus.

Yet for all the changes in personnel, the Avengers always managed to rise above their decisive differences as individuals to fight—together—as a team.

It was, indeed, their battle cry:

"Avengers Assemble!"

BATMAN

SECRET IDENTITY
Bruce Wayne, socialite

NICKNAMES
The Caped Crusader
Masked Manhunter

FIRST APPEARANCE
May 1939—*Detective Comics* #27

MAJOR SILVER AGE APPEARANCES
Batman 113–217
Brave and Bold 59, 64 , 67–71, 74–87
Detective Comics 225–394
World's Finest 94–190

OTHER SILVER AGE APPEARANCES
Action 270, 313, 314, 344, 350, 365, 366
Adventure 275
Aquaman 18
Blackhawk 228
Brave and Bold 28–30
Justice League of America 1, 2, 4, 5, 7, 9–23, 40–47, 49–54, 60–63, 65, 66, 68–72, 74, 75, 77
Superman 132, 138, 142, 156, 173, 174
Superman's Girlfriend Lois Lane 29, 59, 70, 71, 89
Superman's Pal Jimmy Olsen 58, 92, 117
Teen Titans 1, 3

"One night some fifteen years ago, Thomas Wayne, his wife and son were walking home from a movie. . . . "

A robber leaps from the shadows and demands that Wayne's wife hand over her necklace. When Wayne defends her, he is murdered. When his wife calls for help, she, too, is gunned down. Only their son is left alive.

"The boy's eyes are wide in terror and shock as the horrible scene is spread before him. . . . "

After his mother and father are buried, the boy makes a solemn oath:

"And I swear by the spirits of my parents to avenge their deaths by spending the rest of my life warring on all criminals."

He devotes his life to training his body to physical perfection. He becomes a master scientist and criminologist. Finally . . .

"I am ready, but first I must have a disguise. Criminals are a superstitious cowardly lot, so my disguise must be able to strike terror into their hearts. I must be a creature of the night, black, terrible . . . a . . . a . . . a bat! That's it! I shall become a bat!"

Batman #156 ©1963 *DC Comics, Inc.* Shelly Moldoff, Charles Paris.

Batman #163 ©1964 DC Comics, Inc. Bob Kane, Shelly Moldoff.

"And thus is born this weird figure of the dark . . . this avenger of evil—*The Batman*."

The Batman was created in 1939 by artist Bob Kane and writer Bill Finger. With the success of Superman just the year before, DC Comics was looking for another costume hero. As a matter of fact, editor Vincent Sullivan needed one soon—like over the weekend. Kane recalled that he developed the basic concept for Batman in three days:

"I didn't want Batman to be a superhero with super-powers. He had to be original—I knew that DC wouldn't be interested if my new hero was too close to Superman. So I made Batman an ordinary human being; he's just an athlete with physical prowess."

Kane met with writer Bill Finger to help finalize the character. Finger suggested some costume changes and then developed the basic character and personality of Batman. He wrote many of the Batman stories over the next 30 years. Kane remembered that the two of them worked "together in simpatico relationship, as a team. Much of the Batman mythos evolved out of collaboration."

Much of that mythos had to do with the strip's characters (Robin, Alfred, Commissioner Gordon), its villains (Joker, Penguin), and its gadgets (Batmobile, Bat-Cave, Bat-Signal). All through the 1940s and into the early 1950s, Bill Finger, Bob Kane, and his growing stable of Batman artists (Jerry Robinson, George Roussos, Dick Sprang) turned out tales of mystery and detection. They featured the Caped Crusader and the Boy Wonder doing what they do best: solving crimes and foiling crooks with a little deductive reasoning, scientific methods, and some well-placed jabs to the jaw.

Although the stories were pure formula, the excitement and the mood always kept readers coming back for more. Batman and Robin, roaring across the darklands of Gotham City in their Batmobile, were among the most popular comic book characters of the 1940s.

By the mid-1950s, however, superheroes were being outsold by mystery, horror, and science fiction comics. With the growing interest in flying saucers, science fiction magazines, and the launching of Sputnik in 1957, DC Comics decided it was time to infuse their aging heroes with some extraterrestrial life.

The editor of the Batman titles at the time, Jack Schiff, remembered that word came down from management to put more science fiction elements into his books. He had already added a green-skinned Martian detective, J'Onn J'Onzz, to *Detective Comics* in 1955 as a backup series for the Batman stories.

Now, Batman and Robin themselves were to have adventures on other planets and fight alien invaders. By 1958, the Batman comic books were packed with Bug-Eyed Monsters from outer space. There was no room for mundane criminals or old villains like the Joker or the Riddler. Batman's scientific methods of deduction were pushed aside by pseudo-scientific mumbo-jumbo which tried to explain how yet another alien monster suddenly appeared in Gotham City.

Even Batman himself was regularly transformed into some alien-monster creature. He became a Zebra-Batman, a Giant Ape-Batman, a Rainbow Batman—even a Batbaby.

Editor Schiff did not like the changes he saw happening to his character. "I was having disagreements with the management about the 'monster craze' everybody was into. I fought against the introduction into Batman and Superman of this trend, but I was pressured into using them."

Every now and then, Schiff tried to restore Batman to his role as the Dark Detective. In the early 1960s, he reprinted the older Batman stories in annuals. He was vindicated by the fact that all the "letters from fans indicated their liking for the old stories I'd been editing all along." Still, Schiff sighed, "I didn't win out against that monster craze."

He did prove that readers preferred the old traditional Batman foes over the outer space aliens. "At one point, though, I managed to revive some of the old villains like the Joker and the Penguin. The sales went up with the villains featured."

In 1964, Schiff left as editor and the new Batman editor was Julius Schwartz—the editor of the *Flash, Green Lantern, Hawkman,* and *Atom*. Schwartz recalled that "before I took over, Batman was all robots and Martians."

Schwartz decided to give Batman what he called a "New Look." He added a yellow circle around the insignia on Batman's costume. He brought in new artists and writers. He emphasized plots and problem-solving over bizarre alien transformations.

"I did loads of changes with him," Schwartz remembered. "I couldn't believe they'd be going down into a Batcave on a long winding staircase, so I had an elevator installed. I changed the Batmobile, bringing it more up to date."

Following Schiff's earlier lead, Schwartz also "decided to go back to the villains they had neglected for awhile. I did a story about the Riddler (May 1965, *Batman* #171) . . . and there happened to be very shortly thereafter a story about the Joker (July 1965, *Detective Comics* #341)."

Both stories caught the attention of William Dozier, the future producer of the 1966 Batman television show. He liked the comics, and Schwartz recalled that those "two stories were pretty much the basis of the first Riddler and Joker stories that appeared on the *Batman* TV series. . . . If it hadn't been for the Riddler, Batman would never have appeared on television."

With the immense overnight popularity of the Batman TV show from 1966 to 1968, the Batman comic books skyrocketed in sales. But, with this new popularity came a price—the comic book turned into an offshoot of the TV show, subject to its needs.

Batman #113 ©1958 *DC Comics, Inc.* Bob Kane, Shelly Moldoff.

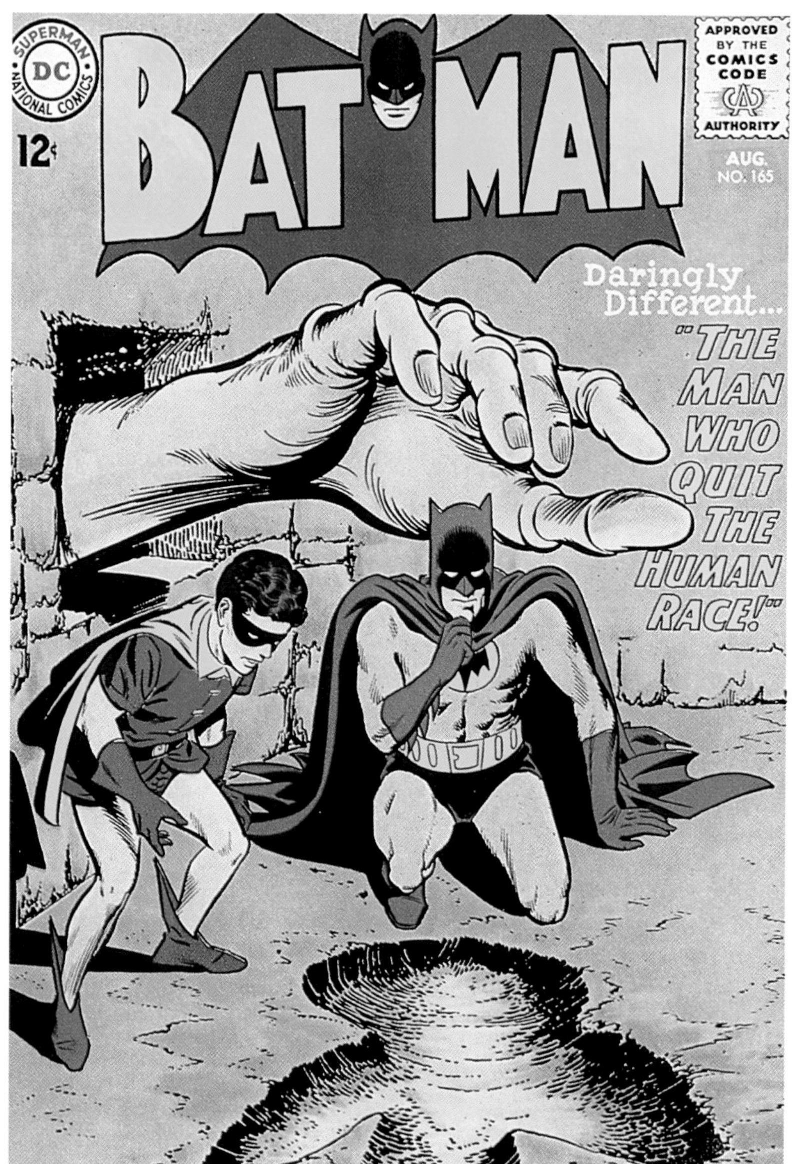

Batman #165 ©*1964 DC Comics, Inc.* Carmine Infantino, Joe Giella.

Schwartz recalled that "after the first year of Batman, Dozier said, 'We must do something to hype this program. Can we have a girl on the show?' . . . So I created Batgirl, and they wrote her into the show." Schwartz also had to bring Batman's butler, Alfred, back from the dead in order to satisfy the TV producers. As part of his new look for the Batman comic book in 1964, Schwartz had killed off Alfred in order to open up the series.

The television show had other effects on the comic book as well. The dialogue, plots, and villains in the Batman comic books of the later 1960s soon reflected the TV image of Batman as the "Camp Crusader."

Gardner Fox, one of DC's main writers at the time, admitted that "I myself personally preferred the more serious approach, but since the Batman show was such a craze, we felt it wouldn't hurt to take advantage of it. I knew the fad wouldn't last."

It didn't. By 1968, sales of Batman comics were falling fast. The pop culture craze was dying.

The following year, a new Batman slowly emerged from the ashes. Drawn by Neal Adams for *Brave and the Bold*, this Batman was hyper-realistic, deadly serious, and a creature of the night—a portent of the Batman that would emerge in the 1970s and 1980s.

Adams said that the changes he introduced into Batman in 1969 and in the early 1970s were what "fans have been aware of and wanting for years. The fact that Batman is a dark mysterious figure, a powerful athlete, a man who strikes terror into the hearts of criminals. Batman isn't the type of character to walk down the street in the daytime and have people say hello to him. They should kind of jump back. He's a creature of the night. A vengeful superhero. I found it a little hard to take credit for that, since I've known it since I was ten years old. That's the way he *should* be."

CAPTAIN AMERICA

SECRET IDENTITY
Steve Rogers, Army Private (World War II)

NICKNAMES
Cap
Star-Spangled Avenger
Winghead

FIRST APPEARANCE
March 1941—*Captain America* #1

FIRST SILVER AGE APPEARANCE
March 1964—*Avengers* #4

MAJOR SILVER AGE APPEARANCES
Captain America 100–120
Tales of Suspense 58–99

OTHER SILVER AGE APPEARANCES
Avengers 4–38, 42–47, 56, 58, 60, 69–71
Annual 1, 2

Daredevil 43, 51
Sgt. Fury 13
Strange Tales 159–162

The time is 1941. America prepares for war. Young men flock to enlist, but some are refused because they are physically unfit. One of these men is Steve Rogers.

Rejected by the army, Rogers volunteers for a secret government experiment. Timidly, he enters a laboratory where he meets a doctor holding a syringe.

"Don't be afraid son. . . . You are about to become one of America's saviors!"

He injects Rogers with a special serum which begins "rapidly building his body and brain tissues until his stature and intelligence increase to an amazing degree!"

Rogers becomes a superhuman. His muscles are huge. His strength is awesome. He is deemed to be "the first of a corps of super-agents whose mental and physical ability will make them a terror to spies and saboteurs."

The government researcher tells Rogers, "We shall call you Captain America, son! Because like you—America shall gain the strength and will to safeguard our shores."

Rogers puts on a red, white, and blue uniform and goes to work battling Nazi saboteurs and spies on the home front. After America enters the war, Captain America fights the Axis powers on both warfronts. He also gets a sidekick, Bucky Barnes, who "fights side by side with Captain America against the vicious elements who seek to overthrow the U.S. government."

Now, it is 1964. Captain America has been missing and presumed dead for fifteen years. Bucky, too, has vanished.

On an underwater mission to the Arctic Seas, the Avengers—Marvel's greatest team of superheroes—spot what appears to be a "frozen, petrified figure in a state of suspended animation" in an ice flow outside their submarine.

They rescue the ice-coated body and discover that it is Captain America! He is still alive and looks unchanged since the 1940s. As he thaws out, he tells the Avengers: "By some stroke of fantastic fate, I must have been frozen in an ice flow . . . all these years, being in a state of suspended frozen animation must have prevented me from aging!"

The last thing Captain America remembers was that he and his teenage partner Bucky were trying to stop an explosive-filled drone plane from taking off and killing American soldiers.

When the plane explodes, Bucky is killed and Captain America is hurled into the icy seas: "As for me, I didn't care if I lived or died! I struck the water off the coast of Newfoundland, and plummeted like a rock—with Bucky's face etched before me! And that's the last thing I remembered!"

The painful memory and guilt over his

Captain America #109 ©1969 Marvel Entertainment Group, Inc. Jack Kirby, Syd Shores.

Tales of Suspense #68 ©1965 Marvel Entertainment Group, Inc. Jack Kirby, Frank Giacoia.

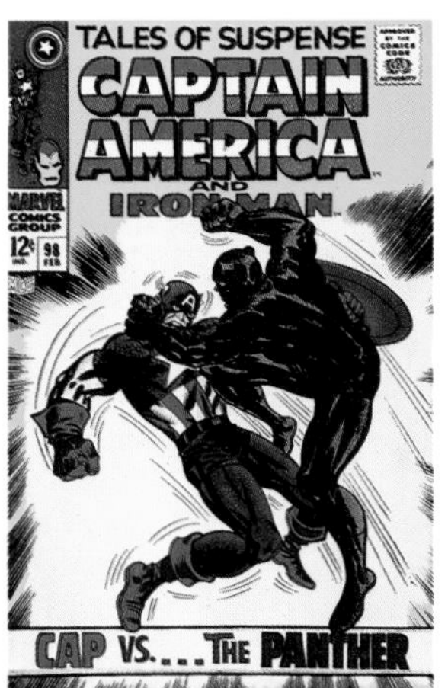

Tales of Suspense #98 ©1967 Marvel Entertainment Group, Inc. Jack Kirby, Syd Shores.

young partner's death were the necessary ingredients for transforming a gung-ho 1940s patriotic superhero into a 1960s Marvel character. Here was a man trapped outside of time—ageless but older, alive yet alone.

Jack Kirby, the cocreator (along with Joe Simon) of the original 1940s Captain America, also drew the first 1960s adventures of his character as well. He recalled that "I brought Captain America back from the dead and I made him human because Bucky was dead. He had to live with the fact that he no longer had Bucky." Bucky's death was done "as a gesture of reality," according to Kirby.

Captain America works through his grief by joining the Avengers as their newest member. Over the years, he became the official and unofficial leader of the team. He was the fulcrum of the Avengers, remaining the ultimate team player as other heroes left or joined the group.

Stan Lee and Jack Kirby began producing a series of Captain America adventures in late 1964 as a feature in *Tales of Suspense*. In 1968, Captain America was awarded his own comic book. In 1969, he got a new partner—the Falcon, a black crime-fighter from the ghetto.

Captain America's purpose and resolve, however, was fading in the Vietnam years of the late 1960s. He was having doubts about his superhero persona—perhaps he really was an anachronism, out of touch and out of time.

As the 1960s ended, Steve Rogers slipped into a major identity crisis which would cause him to temporarily abandon his Captain America role by the early 1970s.

The majority of the 1960s Captain America stories were written by Stan Lee and drawn by Jack Kirby. Kirby infused the same raw excitement and energy into his 1960s comics as he did in the 1940s stories.

"I see Captain America as you and me," Kirby revealed. "I see Captain America as a real person, as a guy under stress, as a guy in exuberant moods. . . . When Captain America was in a fight it was me doing a ballet. Fantasizing myself beating five or six guys, when in real life, of course, I'd get smeared!"

Captain America #110 ©1969 Marvel Entertainment Group, Inc. Jim Steranko, Jim Steranko.

DAREDEVIL

SECRET IDENTITY
Matt Murdock, attorney

NICKNAMES
The Man Without Fear

FIRST APPEARANCE
April 1964—*Daredevil* #1

MAJOR SILVER AGE APPEARANCES
Daredevil 1–59 Annual 1

OTHER SILVER AGE APPEARANCES
Amazing Spider-Man 16, 18, 43
Avengers 60
Fantastic Four 39, 40, 73 Annual 3
Journey Into Mystery 116
Strange Tales 156

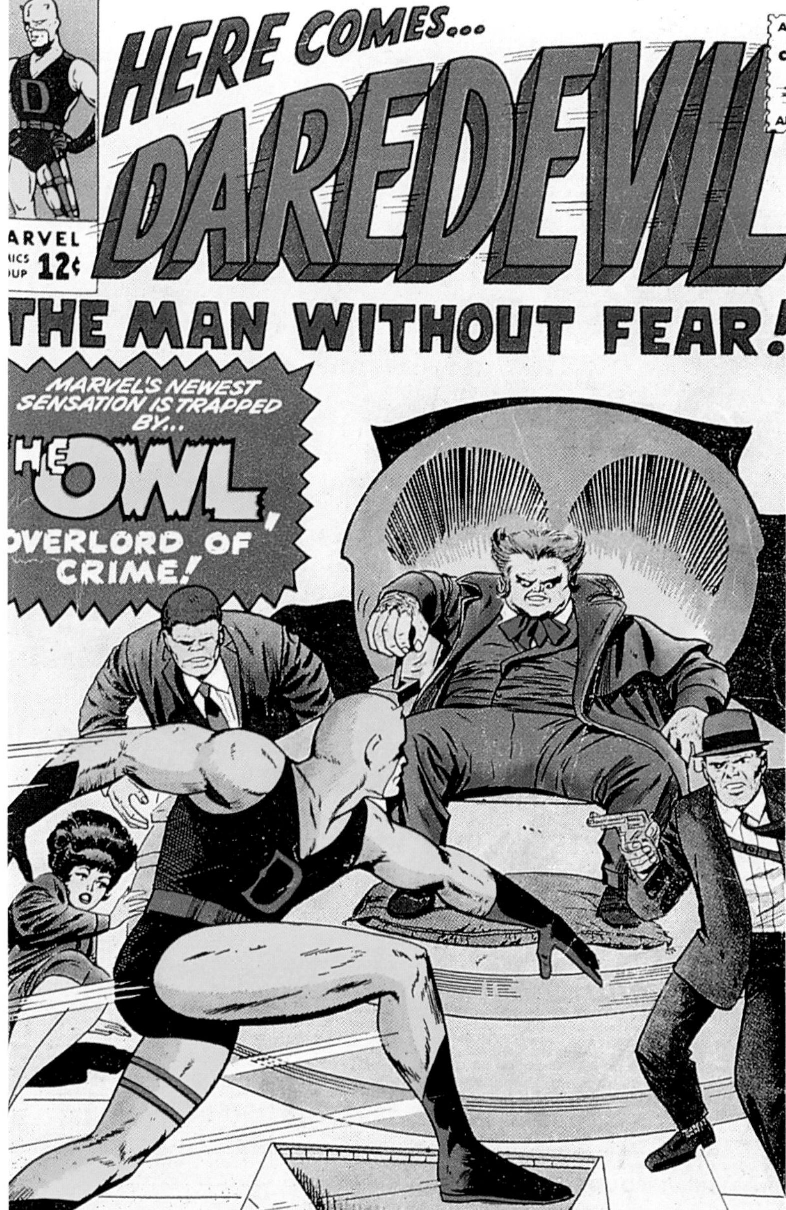

Daredevil #3 ©1964 Marvel Entertainment Group, Inc. Jack Kirby, Vince Colletta.

Matthew Murdock is returning from the library, taking what turns out to be the most important steps of his teenage life. He sees a blind man step into the path of a speeding truck. He reacts instantly.

"He hurtles toward the scene of impending disaster and hurls the unsuspecting blind man out of the truck's path. But he is not so fortunate. . . . "

A cylinder bounces from the truck—a radioactive cylinder—and it strikes Matt Murdock across the eyes, taking away his sight.

In the days after his accident, Matt rigorously trains his body to overcome his handicap. Slowly, he realizes that he is becoming an excellent acrobat, even though blind.

"I don't get it! Ever since my accident, I seem able to do everything lots better than before . . . even without my sight! It's as though nature made all my senses far more powerful to compensate for my blindness! I wonder . . . could the radioactive elements which stuck my eyes have anything to do with my increased powers? Stranger things have been known to happen."

Murdock discovers that he is also developing super-sensory powers.

"My hearing is so acute, that I can tell if someone is in a room with me by hearing the heartbeat! And I never forget an odor once I smell it! I could recognize any girl by her perfume or any man by his hair tonic. Even my fingers have become incredibly sensitive! I can tell how many bullets are in a gun just by the weight of the barrel."

He also develops a sixth sense—a built-in, biological radar. "It enables me to walk anywhere safely, without bumping into anything!"

When his father is murdered by the underworld, Murdock goes after the killers as a costumed figure called the Daredevil. Armed with a billy club which shoots out a grappling hook and a cable, Daredevil takes to the streets, swinging through the air, sightless above the city.

Daredevil #47 ©1968 Marvel Entertainment Group, Inc. Gene Colan, George Klein. Daredevil changed his yellow costume for a red one after the first year. An interesting decision for a blind superhero.

A large part of the appeal of Daredevil was the fact that nobody knew he was blind. He was able to fool everyone into thinking he had normal sight by the fantastic feats he performed. His secret identity, as a sightless attorney, seemed safe. Who would suspect a blind person could be a superhero?

Editor and writer Stan Lee described how he came to create Daredevil: "I was trying to think of a hero who would start out with a disability—a hero whose weakness would actually be more colorful, more unusual, than the power itself. And then it hit me. I remembered some mystery stories I had read years ago about a blind detective named Duncan Maclain. If a man without sight could be a successful detective, think what a triumph it would be to make a blind man a comic book superhero."

Lee delighted in showing readers how Daredevil triumphed over his blindness by developing and relying upon his other super senses. For example, Daredevil doesn't need to *see* people—his hearing is so acute that he can track and identify a person by picking out his or her distinctive heartbeat in a crowd.

"He doesn't realize that I can hear his pulse! It's like having a built-in lie detector! His pulse rate speeded up unnaturally! He has no intention of being here tomorrow."

Daredevil also used his super hearing in the affairs of the heart as well. Karen Page, his legal secretary and would-be girlfriend, has heart palpitations whenever he enters the office. He wonders, however, if it's love, embarrassment, or merely sympathy for his condition that sends her heartbeat racing.

"For a time I almost dared to hope" mused Daredevil, "that Karen might feel about me as I felt about her! Yet, the emotion I mistook for love was merely pity . . . pity for a man without sight! If only I didn't have to continue this pretense of helplessness! If only I could be myself—always!"

Meanwhile, Karen is seized with self-doubt about Matt's true feelings: "I'm sure it's his blindness that makes him so cold, so distant! If only I could convince him that it doesn't matter to me!"

Add to this a third part of the triangle: Foggy Nelson, Matt Murdock's law partner and also a want-to-be boyfriend of Karen Page.

All the thwarted love affairs, however, were just a small part of the Daredevil story.

Daredevil #7 ©1965 Marvel Entertainment Group, Inc. Wally Wood.

The real payoff was watching how a blind hero could excel over circumstances and defeat his foes, regardless of the odds.

At times, the reader's credibility was tested mightily by some of the feats Daredevil was able to pull off "blindfolded." For example, trapped on board a rocket ship, Daredevil is about to crash land in New York City. The blind hero thinks to himself:

"By *hearing* the slight movement of the astro-compass, I can gauge my direction perfectly. And by *feeling* the action of the radar-scope, I can pinpoint my landing. I'll bring the ship down in the middle of Central Park in New York, finding an open spot where I hear no human *heartbeats*!"

Believe it or not, he did it. In the age of Marvel angst and self-doubt, Daredevil was a refreshingly self-confident superhero.

DR. STRANGE

SECRET IDENTITY
Dr. Stephen Strange, ex-surgeon

NICKNAMES
Master of Black Magic
Master of the Mystic Arts

FIRST APPEARANCE
July 1963—*Strange Tales* #110

MAJOR SILVER AGE APPEARANCES
Strange Tales 110, 111, 114–168
Dr. Strange 169–183

OTHER SILVER AGE APPEARANCES
Amazing Spider-Man Annual 2
Avengers 60, 61
Fantastic Four 27 Annual 3

Dr. Stephen Strange is a world-famous surgeon. Arrogant and selfish, he cares more about money and his reputation than human suffering. ("When you are willing to pay me for my talent, I will listen. Not until then! Good day!")

One day, he has an auto accident and although he survives, the nerves in his hands are so damaged he can never perform surgery again. His life is ruined—his pride prevents him from becoming a surgeon's assistant or an ordinary doctor. "I must be the best . . . the greatest!!! Or else nothing!"

Strange becomes a homeless drifter. He searches for a fabled guru called "the Ancient One," who can perhaps use magic to heal his hands.

After finding the Ancient One in a remote cave in India, Strange is disappointed. He doesn't believe in the old man's sorcery and spells. The Ancient One tells Strange that "I heal none save those who deserve it! The power of magic must never be wasted on the undeserving! First, you must prove you are worthy!"

After a snowstorm forces Strange to spend several weeks with the Ancient One and his

Strange Tales #146 ©1963 Marvel Entertainment Group, Inc. Steve Ditko.

Strange Tales #127 ©1964 Marvel Entertainment Group, Inc. Steve Ditko.

disciple, Mordo, he sees that the magic is indeed real. He also discovers that Mordo is plotting to destroy the Ancient One and eventually take over the world with his powers of sorcery.

Determined to foil Mordo, Strange goes to the old man: "Ancient One, I crave a boon! I wish to study at your feet . . . to be taught your knowledge . . . to prove myself worthy of the mystic arts!"

So began the mystic career of Dr. Strange and his relationship with the Ancient One. Over the years, Dr. Strange would fight the powers of darkness, the nameless emissaries of evil, in cosmic, mind-blowing adventures that spanned dimensions, space, and time.

With his cloak of levitation and his eye of Agamotto (an amulet to peer into the souls of others), Dr. Strange fought otherworldly and other-dimensional villains like Eternity, Nightmare, The Mindless Ones, Mordo, Umar, and the "dreaded Dormammu."

Dr. Strange was created by Stan Lee and Steve Ditko as the second superhero feature for the comic *Strange Tales*. A magician-sorceror strip was a natural replacement for the supernatural stories that had filled up the back pages of *Strange Tales* for the last ten years. Lee remembered that his fondness for their new character came from a favorite childhood radio show, *Chandru, the Magician*. "I'll never forget the goosebumps that ran up and down my spine. . . . "

Ditko was the perfect artist to make the goosebumps roll again. He had drawn many of the weird mystery stories that had previously appeared in *Strange Tales* and other Marvel titles like *Tales of Suspense, Amazing Adult Fantasy*, and *Journey into Mystery*. In the 1950s, Ditko was also drawing atmospheric stories about other dimensions for Charlton Comics' *Tales of the Mysterious Traveler* and *This Magazine Is Haunted*. Although these stories, with their mystical hosts like Dr. Haunt and the Mysterious Traveler, could be considered forerunners of the Dr. Strange series, Ditko followed no precedents and threw away even his small rulebook when he drew Dr. Strange.

Ditko's Dr. Strange stories often had no anchor in reality, no familiar settings, and no normal perspectives. Strange would chase the Forces of Evil across astral dimensions—his etheric body plunging through pink fog, leaping across bridges of floating cubes, and falling into web-drapped sinkholes.

"Let there be silence absolute—" Strange would say as he tottered on an icicle precipice in the black hole of Eternity, "—as I send a vital thought throughout the endless void! By the Vapors of Voltorr wherein the nameless dwell, by the Roving Rings of Raggadorr, let my speed exceed her spell!"

Stan Lee, who wrote most of the 1960s Dr. Strange stories, admitted that he "didn't know a mystic chant from a Martian eggroll."

He knew, however, that the character

would have to somehow talk differently than the other Marvel characters. "When it came to Dr. Strange, I was in seventh heaven," Lee recalled. "At last I'd have a chance to be as alliterative and shmaltzy as I could wish. With Thor, I was influenced by Shakespeare and the Bible . . . 'Whither goest thou?' and similar phrases; but with Dr. Strange there were no landmarks, no points of reference. With Dr. Strange I had a chance to make up a whole language of incantations."

Lee did more than just make up chants. He gradually introduced a whole pantheon of spirits and mystical entities in his home-spun occult mythology.

There was the "Omnipotent Oshtar," "the eternal Vishanti," and the "All-Seeing eye of Agamotto." Dr. Strange was continually taking an oath—"By the Mystic Moons of Munnopor" or "By the shades of the shadowy Seraphim."

Lee's favorite oath for Dr. Strange was "by the hoary hosts of Hoggoth." As Lee said, "No matter what he did, no matter what he wanted, no matter what he said, it always seemed to sound more dramatic when preceded by 'By the hoary hosts of Hoggoth.' Even if he was just hungry, 'By the hoary hosts of Hoggoth, I feel like a pizza.'"

The Dr. Strange stories of the 1960s constructed a cohesive cosmology that would have thrilled any self-respecting theosophist. College students, minds freshly opened by psychedelic experiences and Eastern mysticism, read Ditko and Lee's Dr. Strange stories with the belief of a recent Hare Krishna convert. Meaning was everywhere, and readers analyzed the Dr. Strange stories for their relationship to Egyptian myths, Summarian gods, and Jungian archetypes.

"I'd get letters from kids who were doing term papers on the origins of Dr. Strange's incantations and they'd say, 'Well, it's obvious from my research that you're basing this on old Druid writings.' Which was nice to know," admitted Lee, "considering I wouldn't know any ancient Druid writings if they were tattooed on my dome."

After Ditko left the strip in 1966, Bill Everett took over Dr. Strange and tried, in his words, "to do Ditko-like work and that was next to impossible. Ditko is Doc Strange and vice versa. The artwork is very stylized. I tried to keep *my* drawing and Ditko's influence. It was very difficult, but fun. It was decorative design work."

Other artists, like Marie Severin, Dan Adkins, and Gene Colan, followed Everett and also expanded upon the supra-dimensional universe of Dr. Strange. In 1968, the magician doctor finally moved from the back pages of *Strange Tales* into his own comic book. He would spend the rest of the 1960s as the Marvel Master of the Mystic Arts.

By the hoary hosts of Hoggoth, let it be so.

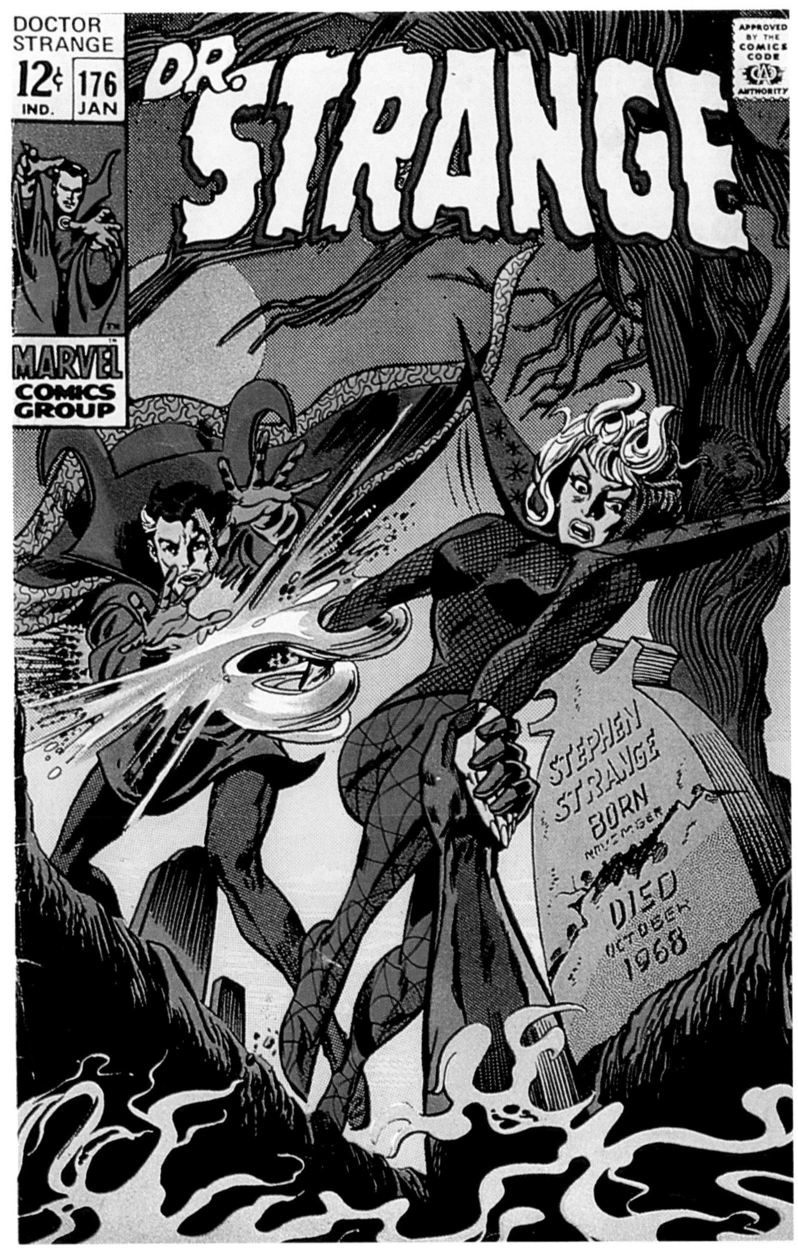

Doctor Strange #176 ©1969 Marvel Entertainment Group, Inc. Gene Colan, Tom Palmer.

FANTASTIC FOUR

MEMBERS:
Mr. Fantastic—Reed Richards
Invisible Girl—Sue Storm
Human Torch—Johnny Storm
The Thing—Benjamin Grimm

FIRST APPEARANCE
November 1961—*Fantastic Four* #1

MAJOR SILVER AGE APPEARANCES
Fantastic Four 1–93 Annuals 1–7

Fantastic Four #6 ©1962 *Marvel Entertainment Group, Inc.* Jack Kirby, Dick Ayers.

OTHER SILVER AGE APPEARANCES
Amazing Spider-Man 1, 5, 8, 18, 19, 21, 76, 77 (Human Torch only 19, 21, 76, 77) Annual 4
Avengers 60
Daredevil 2, 35 (Invisible Girl), 36–38
Incredible Hulk 122
Silver Surfer 5
Strange Tales 101–134 (Human Torch 101–134, Annual 2) (The Thing 101, 106, 116, 118, 123–134) (Invisible Girl 101, 105, 106, 118) (Mr. Fantastic 101, 106, 118, 127)
Submariner 8 (The Thing)

"If you want to fly to the stars," test pilot Ben Grimm tells scientist Reed Richards, "then you pilot the ship! Count me out! You know we haven't done enough research on the effect of cosmic rays! They might kill us all out in space!"

Sue Storm and her teenage brother Johnny watch the two men argue about testing Richard's new rocket ship. She tells the burly test pilot, "Ben, we've got to take that chance . . . unless we want the commies to beat us to it! I—I never thought you were a coward!"

"A coward!! Nobody calls me a coward! Get the ship! I'll fly her no matter what happens!"

And so, led by a determined Dr. Reed Richards, the group of four speeds toward the spaceport on the outskirts of town. Richards, Sue, her brother Johnny, and pilot Ben Grimm blast off in the experimental rocket. All goes well until they pass through a cosmic storm outside the atmosphere.

RAK-TAC-TAC-TAC-TAC!!

"Here that??" screams Ben Grimm. "It's the cosmic rays . . . they're penetrating the ship!! Our shielding isn't strong enough!"

The four lose control of the rocket and it returns to earth on automatic pilot "in a rough, but non-fatal landing."

Reed Richards pulls Susan from the wreckage. Ben and Johnny stumble out as well. "I'm grateful we're all alive," the scientist says, "but we're still not completely safe! We have to see whether the cosmic rays affected us in any way!"

Fantastic Four #55 ©*1966 Marvel Entertainment Group, Inc.* Jack Kirby, Joe Sinnott. The Thing.

Fantastic Four #5 ©*1962 Marvel Entertainment Group, Inc.* Jack Kirby, Joe Sinnott.

"Oh Reed," says Susan, holding her head, "I feel so strange!"

"Susan! You're—gasp—fading away! The cosmic rays have altered your atomic structure . . . making you grow invisible!"

Susan fades from sight and then grows visible again. Then the rays begin to affect Ben Grimm.

"Ben! Look what's happening to you!" Reed Richards says as his test pilot's face starts to become a lumpy, orange disfigured hunk of flesh. "You're changing!"

"Run, Reed darling!" Susan yells. "He's turned into a—a—some sort of a *thing*! He's as strong as an ox!"

Ben Grimm has become an orange-skinned behemoth—a monster. He uproots a tree and lashes out at Richards in anger and frustration. As the scientist tries to restrain the man-turned-monster, he discovers that his body has become elastic. He can wrap his arms around Ben Grimm like a rope. His entire body can stretch, bend, and mold itself like a piece of pliable plastic!

Sue's brother Johnny loses his cool. "You've turned into monsters . . . both of you!! It's those rays! Those terrible cosmic rays!" And then—the teenager bursts into flames!

"Now I know why I've been feeling so warm! Look at me!" His body has become a flaming human torch. "When I get excited,

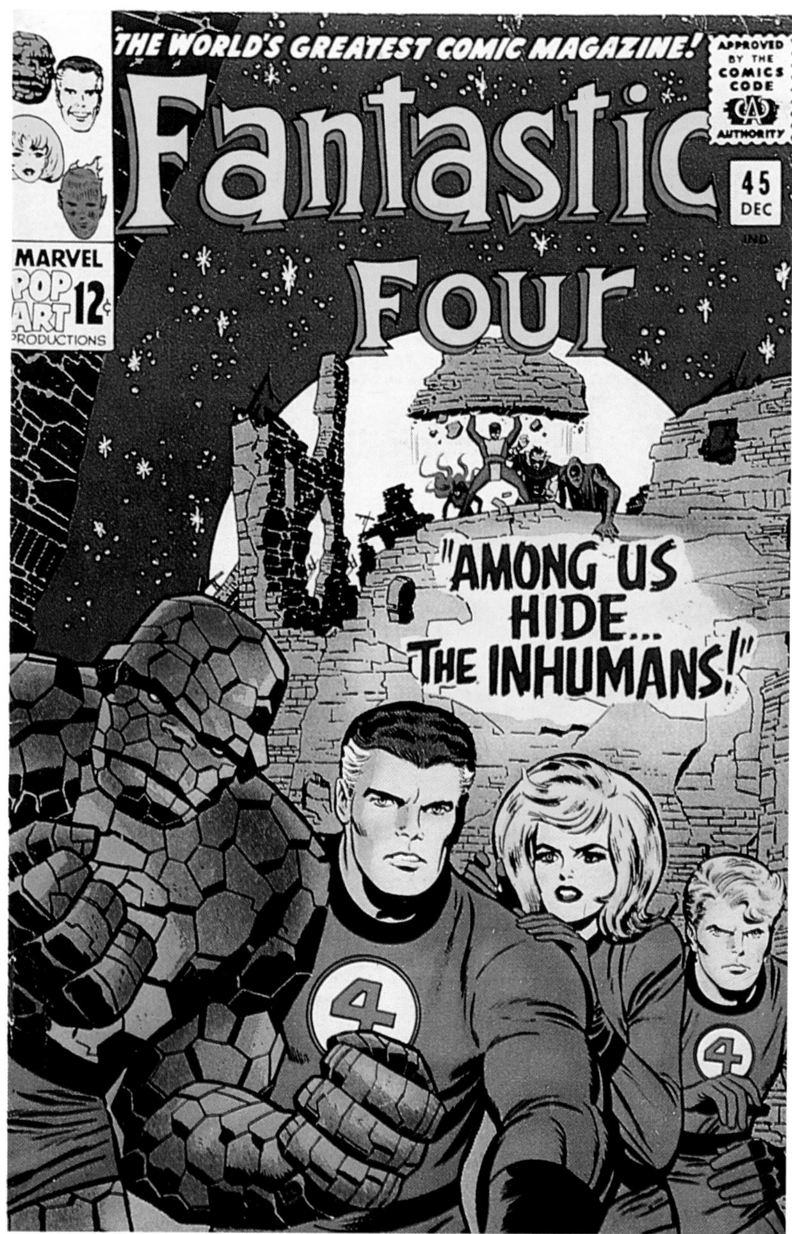

Fantastic Four #45 ©1965 *Marvel Entertainment Group, Inc.* Jack Kirby, Joe Sinnott.

I can feel my body begin to blaze! I'm lighter than air!! I can fly!! Look. . . . I can fly!"

As the teenager's body stops flaming, he returns to normal. The four suddenly realize: "We've changed! All of us! We're more than just humans!"

Reed Richards tells his three companions: "Listen to me, all of you! Together we have more power than any humans have ever possessed!"

"You don't need to make a speech, big shot!" Ben Grimm tells him. "We understand! We've gotta use that power to help mankind, right?"

Johnny replies, "I'm calling myself the Human Torch—and I'm with you all the way!"

"Same goes for me . . . the Invisible Girl" says his sister.

"I'll call myself Mr. Fantastic," says the elastic scientist. "There's only one missing . . . Ben??"

"I ain't Ben anymore—I'm what Susan called me—The Thing!"

The four grasp hands.

Stan Lee and Jack Kirby created the *Fantastic Four* in 1961 which launched the Marvel Age of Comics.

The Fantastic Four was in response to DC's *Justice League*. Lee discussed a synopsis with artist Jack Kirby and remembered that Kirby "contributed many, many ideas to it." Kirby drew the first *Fantastic Four* story and gave it back to Lee to write in the dialogue. Working together, the two men created a team of superheroes with distinct personalities—each one a well-realized and intriguing character.

"If anyone's gonna do any destroyin' around here, Aunt Petunia's blushin' blue-eyed nephew Benjamin is gonna git first crack at it . . . dig?"

With those words, Ben Grimm—the Thing—would then usually bellow, "It's clobberin' time!" and wade into a sea of super-villains.

While The Thing was the wise-cracking tough guy of the group, he had a heart as soft as a marshmallow. His true love, Alicia, was a blind sculptress, and he protected her ferociously. The irony of having a blind girlfriend was never lost on the incredibly ugly and misshapen Ben Grimm.

For artist Jack Kirby, The Thing was an incredibly tragic figure. "Can you imagine yourself as a mutation, never knowing when you were going to change, and what you'd look like to your folks or people that you love?"

Kirby was careful, however, to make the monstrous Ben Grimm believable and likeable. "No matter what he looked like, The Thing never changed his personality—he was always a human being despite his physical change. Ben Grimm always remained Ben

Grimm. I think that's why readers liked him—that touch of reality."

Another touch of reality was the budding relationship between Mr. Fantastic and Sue Storm, the Invisible Girl. Not only did the two eventually marry but they also had a son—a family, an early first in comic books. Married life among the superheroes, however, was never easy:

"For cryin' out loud, Sue—use your head for a change! How could we get any rest—how could we relax for a minute—so long as danger threatened! As leader of this temperamental team, I've got to do my job—no matter what!"

"That's it, Mr. Richards—yell at me! Act like a typical husband! You might as well put a huge billboard up on Times Square announcing that the honeymoon is over! You—never talked to me—like this—before we were married—!!"

It wasn't all soap opera and pathos, however. The Fantastic Four fought an amazing lineup of villains who were almost as colorful as they were: the Mole Man, the Sub-Mariner, the Red Ghost, the Frightful Four, and, the all-time Marvel archvillain, Dr. Doom!

Like each of the Fantastic Four, Dr. Doom had a distinct personality and character. Stan Lee thought that the villain was "far too complex to be neatly labeled a typical bad guy." Instead, he was a "man with his own drives, his own needs, his own pains and frustrations; a man to be feared, to be shunned, but also to be studied and—perhaps—even pitied."

Jack Kirby recalled that Dr. Doom was modeled after "the Man in the Iron Mask, which I felt was a classic character. I feel there are certain characters that will never die. We'll tell them in different versions for the rest of the centuries. Dracula will never die. Frankenstein. They live inside of us, and Dr. Doom will live inside of us."

All through the 1960s, Kirby and Lee introduced dozens of supporting characters, villains, and heroes through the pages of the *Fantastic Four* comic book. There was the Black Panther, who appeared in 1965. There were also the Silver Surfer and the Inhumans. Ant-Man, Daredevil, X-Men, Avengers, Hulk, Dr. Strange—almost every 1960s Marvel superhero made a guest appearance in the *Fantastic Four.*

Even Kirby and Lee themselves appear in an early *Fantastic Four* story ("Phone call for you, Reed! It's Lee and Kirby! They'd like you to go to their studio to work out a plot with 'em!").

It was only fitting for Stan Lee and Jack Kirby to appear as characters themselves in that 1963 issue. After all, they had already brought a little of themselves—the human

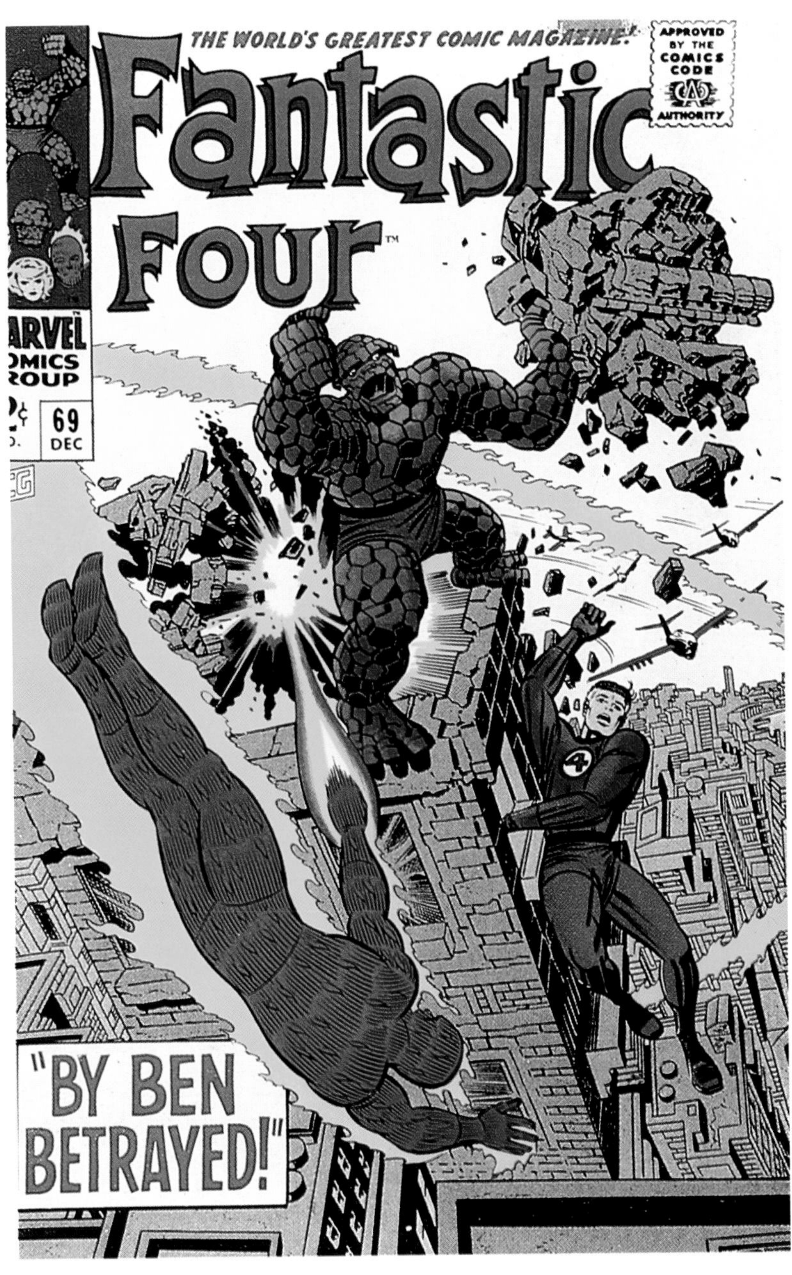

Fantastic Four #69 ©*1967 Marvel Entertainment Group, Inc.* Jack Kirby, Joe Sinnott.

element—to the *Fantastic Four*. It was like Kirby said: "It's not the heroics—it's the humanity that counts."

FLASH

SECRET IDENTITY
Barry Allen

NICKNAMES
The Fastest Man Alive
The Scarlet Speedster
Sultan of Speed

FIRST APPEARANCE
January 1940—*Flash Comics* #1

Flash #108 ©1959 DC *Comics, Inc.* Carmine Infantino, Joe Giella.

FIRST SILVER AGE APPEARANCE
September 1956—*Showcase* #4

MAJOR SILVER AGE APPEARANCES
Showcase 4, 8, 13, 14
Flash 105–193
Brave and Bold 53, 56, 65, 67, 72, 81

OTHER SILVER AGE APPEARANCES
Action Comics 314, 365, 366
Aquaman 18
Atom 8
Blackhawk 228
Brave and Bold 28–30, 54
Detective Comics 327, 336
Green Lantern 13, 20, 43
Justice League of America 1–33, 35, 36, 40–47, 49, 50, 53, 54, 56, 57, 59–63, 65, 69–71, 74, 77
Mystery in Space 75
Superman 199
Teen Titans 1

Over Central City, an electrical storm rages, casting lightning bolts in all directions. Inside the police laboratory, scientist Barry Allen is performing a chemical experiment. Suddenly, "the lab explodes with blinding light as a bolt of lightning streaks in . . . CRAAAAAK!"

Allen is covered in a bath of chemicals, supercharged by the storm's electricity. As he leaves his lab and sprints to catch a cab, he feels "a mysterious force rocket from him . . . until his feet vibrate with eye-blinding speed . . . and in that same split-second he flashes past the taxi as if it were standing still!"

Allen slowly realizes what happened. "A freak accident—caused by that lightning striking a strange combination of chemicals—I was drenched with a solution which must have changed my molecular structure! I am now . . . The Fastest Man on Earth!"

He ponders: "There must be some way I can use this unique speed to help humanity." As he picks up an old issue of a *Flash* comic book from the 1940s, he gets an idea.

He devises a costume and, in a case of art imitating art, assumes the identity of an old comic book superhero—the Flash.

"That was the thing I liked best about the Flash," remembered editor Julius Schwartz, who helped pioneer the character's revival in 1956, "is that he got his inspiration of naming himself for a comic book character he read as a kid after he got doused with that lightning bolt and realized he had super-speed himself."

Schwartz recalled that he "had worked on the Flash in the 1940s, and [then the Flash] died for several years. When the decision was made to put it out again, I didn't want to put out the same Flash. I just wanted to do something entirely different."

Schwartz knew that he could depend upon editor and writer Robert Kanigher to come up with something entirely different.

"One day, Mr. Schwartz asked me to write a new origin for the Flash," Kanigher explained. "Gardner Fox had originated the Flash (in 1939). He was, and in my mind, would always be the creator of the Flash. I merely reinvented the Flash."

Kanigher's script established the basic concept for the character—his secret identity, his new expandable costume, his personality, his girlfriend, and his capabilities as the Fastest Man Alive. "I wrote a completely finished script in every single detail," Kanigher recalled, "which he (Schwartz) gave to Carmine Infantino to draw."

Infantino, who had drawn the original Flash in 1947–1949, designed a sleeker and brighter costume for the new Scarlet Speedster. His lithe, lean Flash was perfectly suited for a character who could run ten times the speed of light.

Infantino remembered that he chose "a stark bland costume with lightning bolt accents. The bolts would help in creating speed

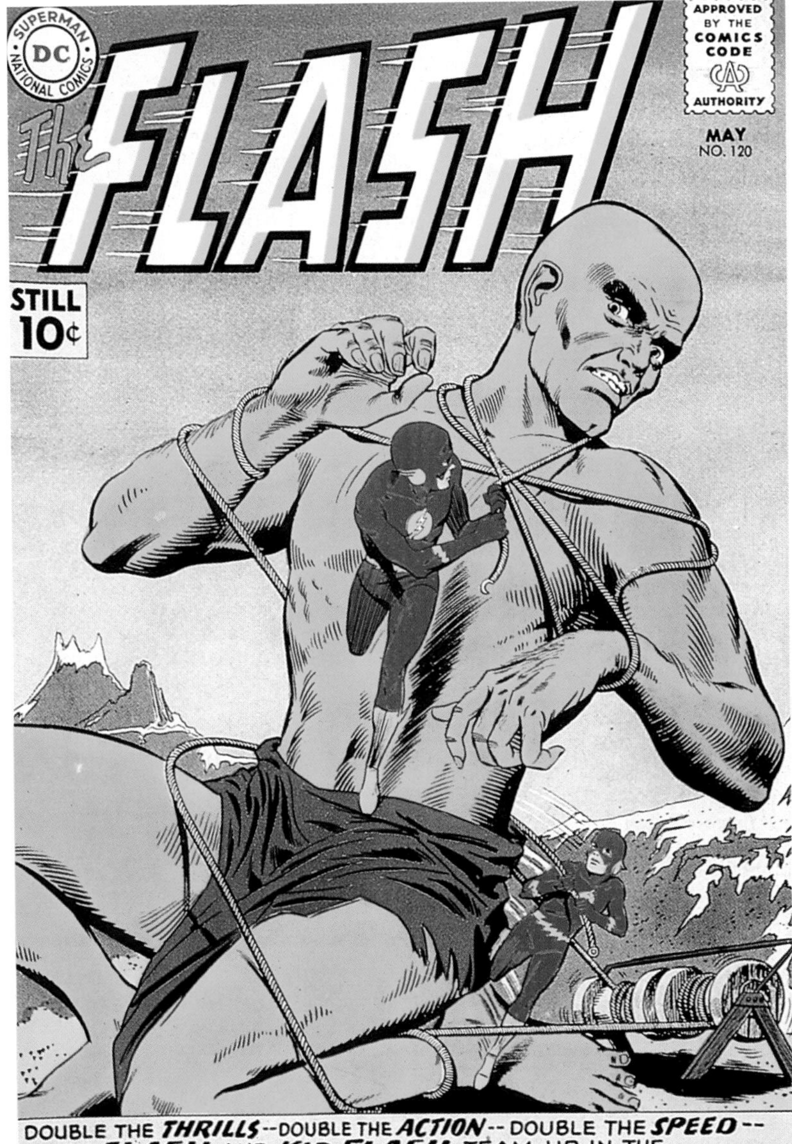

Flash #120 ©1961 DC Comics, Inc. Carmine Infantino, Joe Giella.

Flash #142 ©1964 DC Comics, Inc. Carmine Infantino, Murphy Anderson.

Mystery in Space #75
©1962 DC Comics, Inc.
Carmine Infantino, Murphy Anderson.

effects for the character. I always kept him slim, like a runner—wiry."

One of Infantino's trademarks was his "speed" effects which made it seem that the Flash was moving across the comic book page in super-blurred motion. "I start by lightly sketching in the final figure, the one with the most action," Infantino explained. "I then sketch in the first figure, the figure with the least action. Then the middle ones, a running figure is drawn with arms and legs going in opposite directions—then a few speed lines to give the drawing a flow."

And flow they did. Infantino would draw almost every Flash story from 1956 to 1967.

The other person responsible for most of the 1960s Flash adventures was writer John Broome. Broome's forte was super villains, and the Flash had perhaps the most imaginative rogue's gallery of any of the DC superheroes.

There was the Weather Wizard, who controlled the elements; Captain Boomerang, who used a giant boomerang to hurl his victims into outer space; the Pied Piper, whose supersonic flute caused tidal waves; the Trickster, whose crimes were a series of deadly practical jokes, and Super-Gorilla Grodd, a power-mad gorilla genius.

Broome introduced two other characters who also became superheroes in their own right. The Kid Flash, teenager Wally West, appeared in late 1959. He became a member of the Teen Titans in 1964, and would eventually take over the Flash's role in the 1980s.

Broome's other hero, the Elongated Man was a stretchable detective who appeared in 1960. He teamed up with the Flash several times before receiving his own series in *Detective Comics* in 1964.

But the real draw of the comic was the Flash. Part of the appeal was due to Barry Allen, Flash's likeable alter ego. As the Flash, he could run around the earth in a fraction of a second, but as Barry Allen, he could never show up on time for his dates with girlfriend Iris West.

"Honestly Barry! I thought you turned over a new leaf! You're late again! Why can't you be more like the Flash—the fastest man on earth? Instead, you're the slowest man alive!"

Barry Allen does manage to make it to his wedding *almost* on time. In 1966, he marries Iris West, yet continues leading a secret double life as the Flash. A year later, however, he tells her the truth: Her slowpoke husband really is, in fact, "the fastest man alive."

Boy, was she surprised.

GREEN ARROW

SECRET IDENTITY
Oliver Queen

POPULAR NICKNAME
The Emerald Archer

FIRST APPEARANCE
November 1941—*More Fun* #73

FIRST SILVER AGE APPEARANCE
January 1959—*Adventure Comics* #256

MAJOR SILVER AGE APPEARANCES
Adventure Comics 256–269
Brave and Bold 50, 71, 85
World's Finest 96–134, 136, 138, 140, 143, 145, 154, 159, 187

OTHER SILVER AGE APPEARANCES
Action Comics 350, 365
Justice League of America 4–8, 10–23, 26–28, 33, 36, 40, 44, 45, 50, 53, 56, 57, 60, 61, 63, 65, 66, 68, 69, 71, 72, 74, 75, 77
Superman's Girlfriend Lois Lane 29
World's Finest 178

Oliver Queen, wealthy playboy and world traveler, is on a South Seas voyage. As he recalled, "One night I accidentally fell off the ship and my shouts for rescue went unheard . . . by morning, I'd drifted far off course! Then I spotted it . . . an island!"

Alone on a deserted island, playboy Queen goes native. He fashions a crude bow and arrow to hunt for food. To catch fish, he makes a net from vines and attaches it to his arrow. The "net arrow" snares the fish, and Queen soon invents a "drill arrow" that can skewer coconuts off a tree. For hunting camouflage, he covers himself with green leaves and becomes an emerald archer.

When a ship anchors offshore, Queen swims out and discovers a mutiny in progress. Using his net and drill arrows, he foils the mutineers and saves the crew.

"I knew then, in that split-second, that my existence on the island could now serve a useful purpose! When I returned to civilization, I would fight crime with my trick arrows! From then on, I would become two people—Oliver Queen and . . . The Green Arrow!"

Being a wealthy playboy made Queen's career as a costumed crime fighter much easier. In his underground workshop beneath his sprawling estate, Queen developed a whole arsenal of trick arrows: the boomerang arrow, boxing glove arrow, exploding arrow, smokescreen arrow, handcuff arrow, and lasso arrow. He also used his money to build a special Arrowcar, with catapult seats, and even an Arrowplane.

When not fighting crime as Green Arrow, Queen continued his life as an idle socialite and adventurer. While hunting for a lost gold mine, he comes across a young

Brave and the Bold #85
©1969 DC Comics, Inc.
Neal Adams.

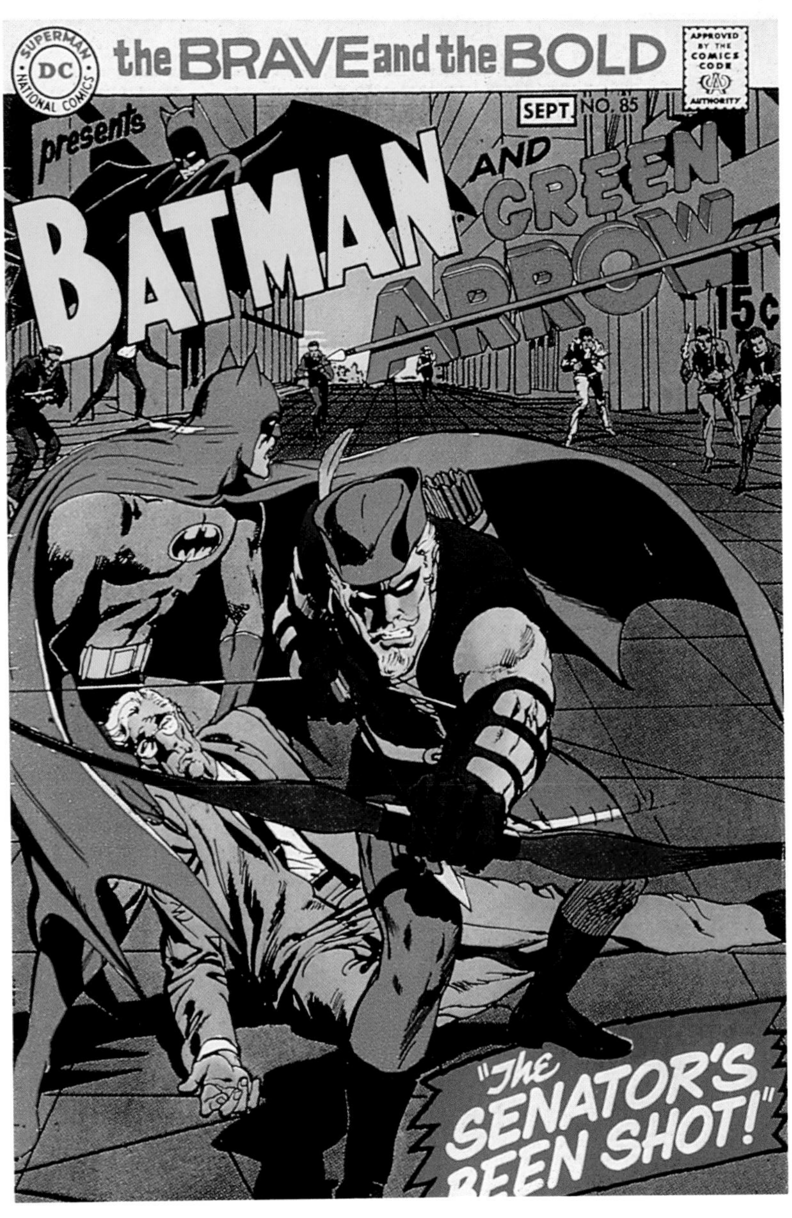

Adventure Comics #256 ©1958 DC Comics, Inc. Jack Kirby. Green Arrow.

boy, Roy Harper, who had been raised by an Indian. The boy's archery skills impress Queen and he adopts Harper as his young ward and sidekick, Speedy. Together they fight criminals with their collection of trick arrows.

Mort Weisinger created the original Green Arrow in 1941 (*More Fun Comics* #73), and rewrote the origin of the character again in 1959. "My Green Arrow was a streamlined Robin Hood—a law-abiding Robin Hood. Then I added props—the Arrowmobile, for one, and I got in the business of creating new kinds of arrows. He'd say, 'In this situation I'll use my drill arrow, or my gas arrow, or my net arrow. . . . '"

It was perhaps the suspense of not knowing what kind of arrow that Green Arrow and Speedy would pull out of their quivers that kept readers turning the pages. After all, in less than a dozen stories, Green Arrow made use of Acid Arrows, Balloon Arrows, Bolo Arrows, Cable Arrows, Clamp Arrows, Cocoon Arrows, Concussion Arrows, Electric Arrows, Flare Arrows, Grease Arrows, Grenade Arrows, Knockout Gas Arrows, Magnet Arrows, Parachute Arrows, Photo Arrows, Radar Arrows, Rope Arrows, Siren Arrows, Suction Cup Arrows, Torch Arrows, and Trip-Wire Arrows.

Weisinger remembered: "I was afraid a reader would say one day, 'How the hell can he carry that many arrows in his little bag?' He had everything from A to Z in there. In real life, he'd need fifty plastic garbage bags to haul them."

Although he never had his own comic book in the 1950s and 1960s, Green Arrow appeared in *Adventure* and *World's Finest Comics*. He was also a longtime member of the Justice League of America and appeared with the Martian Manhunter and Batman in several issues of *Brave and Bold*.

It was in the last *Brave and Bold* teamup with Batman (August 1969) that the Green Arrow of the 1950s and 1960s disappeared and the "new" Green Arrow emerged—a bearded, idealistic, and arrogant superhero who would become the definitive Green Arrow of the 1970s, 1980s, and 1990s.

Drawn by Neal Adams and written by Bob Haney, the comic book introduced readers to a new Green Arrow. In the words of

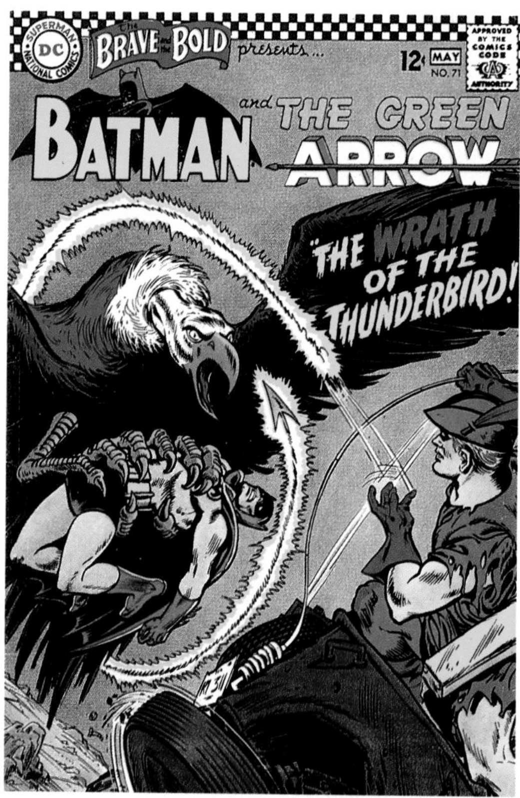

Brave and the Bold #71 ©1967 DC Comics, Inc. Carmine Infantino, Chuck Cuidera.

the editor, "Because of a climactic upheaval in his personal life, Green Arrow's costume, facial appearance and behavior pattern were affected."

This upheaval included the impending loss of his personal fortune and the replacement of his ward, Roy Harper, with a new Speedy. By the next year, Green Arrow is living in a ghetto apartment, has fallen in love with the Black Canary, and discovers that Speedy is addicted to drugs.

From a reliably one-dimensional character of the 1950s, the straight-shooting Green Arrow became a walking personal identity crisis, torn up and tortured by his own self-doubts and the failings and shortcomings of society around him.

GREEN LANTERN

SECRET IDENTITY
Hal Jordan, Test Pilot

NICKNAMES
Emerald Crusader
Green Gladiator

FIRST APPEARANCE
July 1940—*All American* #16

FIRST SILVER AGE APPEARANCE
September 1959—*Showcase* #22

MAJOR SILVER AGE APPEARANCES
Showcase 22–24
Green Lantern 1–73
Brave and Bold 59, 69

OTHER SILVER AGE APPEARANCES
Action Comics 350, 365, 366
Atom 8
Blackhawk 228
Detective Comics 350
Flash 131, 143, 168, 171, 191
Justice League of America 1–33, 35, 36, 40–42, 44, 46, 47, 49, 51, 52, 56, 60–63, 65, 66, 68, 70–72, 74, 77
Mystery in Space 75

At the Ferris Aircraft Company, Hal Jordan, test pilot, sits in a flightless trainer. Suddenly, a green glow surrounds the flyer and he is teleported through the air and to the crash site of an alien spaceship in the southwestern United States.

Jordan has been brought to the injured spacecraft by its pilot, a red-skinned alien: "I am Abin Sur . . . I am not of earth . . . but of a far distant planet—and I am dying!"

Jordan asks how he can help him. Abin Sur tells him that he must take possession of what appears to be a green lantern.

"Actually it is a battery of power," the alien tells the test pilot, "given only to selected space-patrolmen in the super-galactic system to be used as a weapon against forces

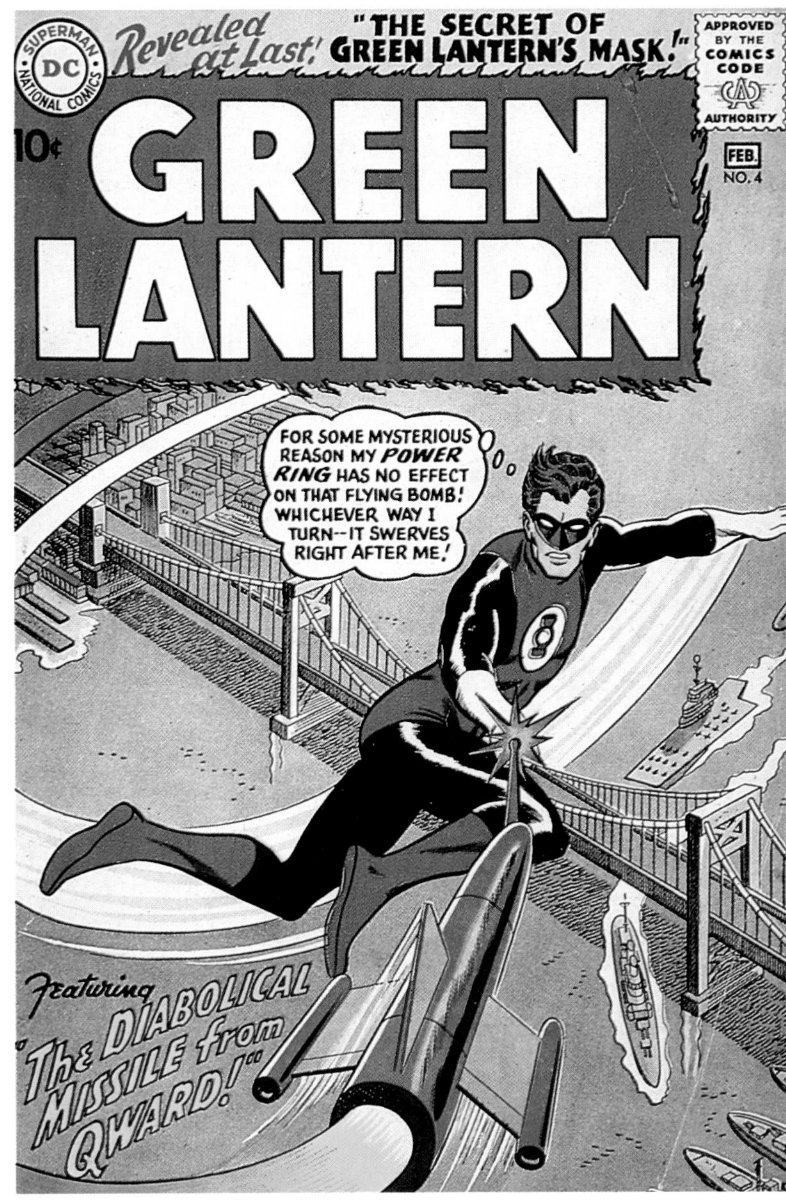

Green Lantern #4 ©1961 *DC Comics, Inc.*
Gil Kane, Joe Giella.

of evil and injustice. It is our duty, when disaster strikes, to pass on the battery of power to another who is fearless . . . and honest."

Abin Sur tells Jordan that he has been chosen to be the new guardian of the green lantern power battery. Before he dies, he gives the earthling his ring: "With this ring you will drain the power from the battery . . . effective for 24 hours."

Jordan puts on the ring and discovers that he can focus his willpower and make the ring do such things as "lifting a cliff into the air! I can do anything I want with this ring . . . anything I *will* to happen . . . I can make happen!"

He also realizes that "to be safe I must use it only in the greatest secrecy! I know! I'll adopt a secret identity—I'll call myself Green Lantern—after the power battery! And in time I hope to make Green Lantern a name feared by evildoers everywhere!"

"When the returns started coming in on the Flash," remembered DC editor Julius Schwartz, "we saw we had a hit. The natural instinct was to do something similar. That's how we decided to go ahead with Green Lantern."

Like the Flash, Green Lantern had been a popular character in the 1940s. When Schwartz revived the superhero for a 1960s readership, he wanted to give "him a new personality, a new costume, a new everything."

Gil Kane, one of Schwartz's science fiction artists, was given the job of designing the new Green Lantern. Kane quickly discarded the old 1940s costume with its theatrical cape.

"What I did with Green Lantern's uniform," Kane recalled, "was to make it an hourglass shape that started at the point of the shoulders and worked to a very narrow point at mid-chest and went out again at the waistline. I was trying for a balance between power and lyricism. A cape would have gotten in the way of the figure."

Kane drew all but a half dozen or so issues of the 1960s Green Lantern series. His Green Lantern flew effortlessly through the air, hair finely flying, injected with what Kane himself described as "some quality of grace."

It was writer John Broome who fashioned much of the modern Green Lantern mythos. There were the Guardians, a race of benign blue-skinned, godlike beings who supplied the power battery which made Green Lantern's ring work. There was also a whole universe full of Green Lanterns—alien Green Lanterns selected by the Guardians and equipped with a power battery and ring and assigned a sector of the universe to patrol.

Showcase #22 ©DC *Comics, Inc.* Gil Kane, Joe Giella.

Broome also created more mundane supporting characters. There was Pieface, Hal Jordan's friend, confidant, and airplane mechanic. Pieface knew that Hal was secretly Green Lantern, and he kept a casebook about the superhero's adventures.

And then there was Carol Ferris, Hal's "lovely boss," whose father owned the aircraft company where Hal worked as a test pilot. An interesting romantic triangle quickly sprang up between Carol, Hal, and Hal's alter ego, Green Lantern.

Even though Hal pursued her, Carol wouldn't give him a tumble. "Now, listen, Hal! You're a good friend, but that's all! It's Green Lantern that I love!"

Hal replies with a sly grin, "Now, let me tell you something! When you get married, it's going to be to me, Hal Jordan! I'll win out over that costume rival of mine yet!"

But it wasn't all romance and wisecracks. Most of the time, Hal Jordan was busy using his power ring in truly amazing ways:

"I can create such heat with my ring that it melts down the bullets coming at me in mid-air," and "The unbreakable net formed by my green beam has made the crooks helpless!"

Green Lantern used his power ring to erase people's memories, create objects out of nothingness, and even turn back atomic missiles. The more he focused his willpower through the ring, the stronger it became. The ring is so powerful, it almost makes Green Lantern an invincible—and hence boring—superhero.

Fortunately, there were two catches: First, the power ring could not work against anything yellow because of a "necessary impurity" in the power battery. This gave rise to all sorts of yellow-colored threats: "How can I battle these yellow creatures—when my ring is powerless against anything yellow?"

Second, the power ring could only be charged by the power battery for 24 hours. After that time, it became powerless. More than once, Green Lantern was caught with an expired meter.

When he recharged his ring each day, Green Lantern recited this following oath:

Green Lantern #16 ©1962 *DC Comics, Inc.* Gil Kane, Murphy Anderson.

"In brightest day, in blackest night,
No evil shall escape my sight.
Let those who worship evil's might
Beware my power—Green Lantern's
light!"

Green Lantern's light would indeed burn bright, all through the 1960s and then beyond. Like other heroes of the late 1960s, however, Hal Jordan (Green Lantern) would undergo an identity crisis. By the end of the 1960s, he left his job and girlfriend and took to the road for a journey of self-discovery. Even a power ring, it seemed, couldn't solve all the world's problems.

Hawkman #6 ©1965 DC Comics, Inc. Murphy Anderson.

HAWKMAN

SECRET IDENTITY
Carter Hall (Katar Hol), Museum Curator

NICKNAMES
The Winged Wonder
Flying Fury

FIRST APPEARANCE
January 1940—*Flash Comics* #1

FIRST SILVER AGE APPEARANCE
February 1961—*Brave and Bold* 34

MAJOR SILVER AGE APPEARANCES
Brave and Bold 34–36,42–44, 51, 70
Hawkman 1–27
Atom and Hawkman 39–45
Mystery in Space 87–90

OTHER SILVER AGE APPEARANCES
Action Comics 365
Atom 7, 31, 37
Brave and Bold 56 (Hawkgirl)
Aquaman 18
Justice League of America 31–34, 36, 40, 41, 43–47, 51–53, 57, 61–63, 65, 68, 71, 72, 74, 75
Mystery in Space 86, 91

A spacecraft hurtles through space with two police officers from the planet Thanagar, Katar Hol and his wife Shayera. They are in hot pursuit of an alien criminal who has escaped to earth.

The man and woman use their ship's electronic brain to quickly absorb encyclopedic knowledge about earth's customs and languages. Then, they don their Thanagarian "police uniforms," which turn them into giant hawks. Using their antigravity belts and their strapped-on wings, the couple fly down to earth to Midway City, where their quarry is hiding.

Like all good out-of-town cops, they first check in with the local police commissioner, who is at his home:

"Good gosh! A man and a woman dressed like hawks! If you're looking for a masquerade party, you've come to the wrong house!"

"We are police officers from . . . I know it'll be hard for you to believe, sir . . . from another world!"

"Fantastic as all that sounds, I'm convinced you're speaking the truth! Come in, please. . . . "

The police commissioner sets up a secret identity for the couple: He will be called Carter Hall, and his wife will be Shiera. They will take over the commissioner's brother's job as Midway museum curator, since he is retiring, and live in his apartment. As Hawkman and Hawkgirl, they can then pursue their criminal undetected on earth.

The Hawk couple use their advanced

Thanagarian science, as well as ancient earth weaponry from the Midway museum, to capture their alien foe.

After their mission is accomplished, Hawkman tells the commissioner that he and his wife want "to make an indefinite stay on your planet to study your police methods—secretly, of course, as Hawkman and Hawkgirl."

Hawkman was first created in 1939 by writer Gardner Fox, who had to fill up a new comic book with superheroes. The idea for Hawkman came to him when he saw a bird land outside his window and pick up some twigs. Hawkman appeared in *Flash Comics* throughout the 1940s and then disappeared.

By 1961, the new Flash and new Green Lantern were successful enough to bring back another 1940s hero. Editor Julius Schwartz remembered a discussion back then with writer Gardner Fox about reviving his old character, the Hawkman:

"We all recalled *Flash Comics*, and Flash featured Hawkman. In fact, the covers would be alternated; one issue devoted to the Flash, the following to Hawkman. Hawkman was almost as popular as the Flash. Somehow the readers always seemed to have a fascination with Hawkman."

Mystery in Space #90 ©1964 DC Comics, Inc. Murphy Anderson.

Schwartz asked Fox to bring his 1940s hero back for 1960s readers. They would retain Hawkman's original costume, but change his origin. Instead of Fox's original version of Hawkman as a reincarnation of an Egyptian prince, he would now be a policeman from the star-system Polaris.

The new Hawkman was drawn by Joe Kubert, who had also drawn the original version from 1945 until 1949. Kubert's version of the 1960s Hawkman and Hawkgirl appeared in a half dozen issues of *Brave and the Bold.*

Mystery in Space #87 ©1963 DC Comics, Inc. Murphy Anderson.

After another tryout as a cofeature in *Mystery in Space*, Hawkman and Hawkgirl landed their own comic book in 1964. Later that year, Hawkman joined the *Justice League of America*, the benchmark for a successful DC superhero.

Murphy Anderson penciled and inked all the stories in the first 21 issues of *Hawkman*. He enjoyed doing the comic book but felt that "Hawkman should have been like Flash Gordon, a high adventure kind of thing in a different kind of environment, not on present day earth."

Anderson recalled that both he and previous Hawkman artist Joe Kubert argued with editor Schwartz "that Hawkman shouldn't be just another kind of Batman. That was essentially what he was. On some of the stories, you could have just crossed out Hawkman and Hawkgirl and put in Batman and Robin. We weren't making use of what Hawkman could do. I remember in one story the only time he used his wings was when he did a somersault and knocked some crooks over with them. It just wasn't a Hawkman story."

Anderson did recall that for "a couple of times, I got Julie to let Hawkman off-planet. There were the flying gorilla stories, and the dinosaur-beasts, and the trips to Thanagar. . . . I felt those were good Hawkman stories."

Actually, there were many good Hawkman stories. After all, the stories did feature one of the most happily married couples in the superhero business. Carter

Hawkman #17 ©*1966 DC Comics, Inc.* Murphy Anderson.

and Shiera—Hawkman and Hawkgirl—shared more than just adventures. They had a relationship based on trust, mutual respect, and a strong common interest. The stress of saving the world day after day only seemed to strengthen the love the Hawks felt for each other:

"I kept telling myself over and over," Hawkman confesses to Hawkgirl, "I loved you and only you! I remembered our courtship and the wonderful times we had together! Ours was a love nothing could conquer!"

For adolescent readers outgrowing the buddy-buddy relationship of Batman and Robin, the coziness of Hawkman and Hawkgirl was certainly an attractive tradeoff.

THE HULK

SECRET IDENTITY
Dr. Bruce Banner, nuclear scientist

NICKNAMES
Green Goliath
Jolly Green Giant

FIRST APPEARANCE
May 1962—*Incredible Hulk* #1

MAJOR SILVER AGE APPEARANCES
Incredible Hulk 1–6, 102–122
Tales to Astonish 60–101

OTHER SILVER AGE APPEARANCES
Amazing Spider-Man 14
Avengers 1–3, 5, 17
Captain America 110
Fantastic Four 12, 25, 26
Journey Into Mystery 112
Silver Surfer 1
Tales to Astonish 59

In the blazing New Mexico desert, government scientists huddle behind bunkers for the Gamma-Bomb's first awesome testing. Dr. Bruce Banner, creator of the G-Bomb, begins the final countdown, but then . . . "Good Lord! It's a boy! A teenager! He's driving into the test area."

Banner dashes out and throws the teenager into a protective bomb trench. Then, the Gamma-Bomb explodes.

"Dr. Bruce Banner is bathed in the full force of the mysterious gamma rays! The world seems to stand still, trembling on the brink of infinity, as his ear-splitting scream fills the air. . . . "

Banner and the teenage boy, Rick Jones, are placed under observation. Jones turns out to be as normal as any 1960s comic book teenager can be, but Banner. . . .

"I—I'm beginning to feel strange! My head is throbbing! This must be . . . the end."

Instead of dying from the lethal radia-

Incredible Hulk #1 ©1962 Marvel Comics. Jack Kirby.

tion, however, Banner suddenly changes into a raging, brutish hulk. The Hulk is a green-skinned monster, but he is also gentle Bruce Banner. The gamma-rays cause him to change uncontrollably, back and forth. When he becomes Bruce Banner, he is tormented by his destructive rampages as the Hulk:

"When the sun sets, how do I know I won't change once more? How do I know I won't keep changing . . . into that brutal, bestial mockery of a human—that creature which fears nothing—which despises reason and worships power! Soon, the sun will set again! And here I sit helplessly, fearing I may again become . . . THE HULK!!"

Stan Lee, writer and cocreator of the Hulk, recalled that the idea of a monster as a superhero always appealed to him: "I always had a soft spot in my heart for the Frankenstein monster. He never wanted to hurt anybody; he merely groped his tortuous way through a second life trying to defend himself, trying to come to terms with those who sought to destroy him."

Lee took the monster-as-hero idea a step further: "We would use the concept of the Frankenstein monster, but update it. Our hero would be a scientist, transformed into a raging behemoth by a nuclear accident. And—since I was willing to borrow from *Frankenstein,* I decided I might as well borrow from *Dr. Jekyll and Mr. Hyde* as well—our protagonist would constantly change from his normal identity to his superhuman alter ego and back."

While the Hulk might be a 1960s nuclear retelling of Dr. Jekyll and Mr. Hyde, there was an important difference: The Hulk was a sympathetic monster. As the Hulk, he was

Incredible Hulk #105 ©1968 Marvel Entertainment Group, Inc. Marie Severin, Frank Giacoia.

misunderstood, persecuted, and hounded by fearful humans and the U.S. Army.

Moreover, as Bruce Banner, he was a prisoner of his brutish alter ego, unable to form friendships or to fall in love, always fearful that someone would discover his secret identity as the Hulk. As the Hulk, he hated his alter ego of weakling Bruce Banner. It was a perfectly closed circle of self-loathing.

Lee remembered that he "was envisioning a somewhat nice-looking monster, big and brutish enough to make him feared by all who met him and yet with a certain tragic appeal that would make our readers care about him and cheer him on."

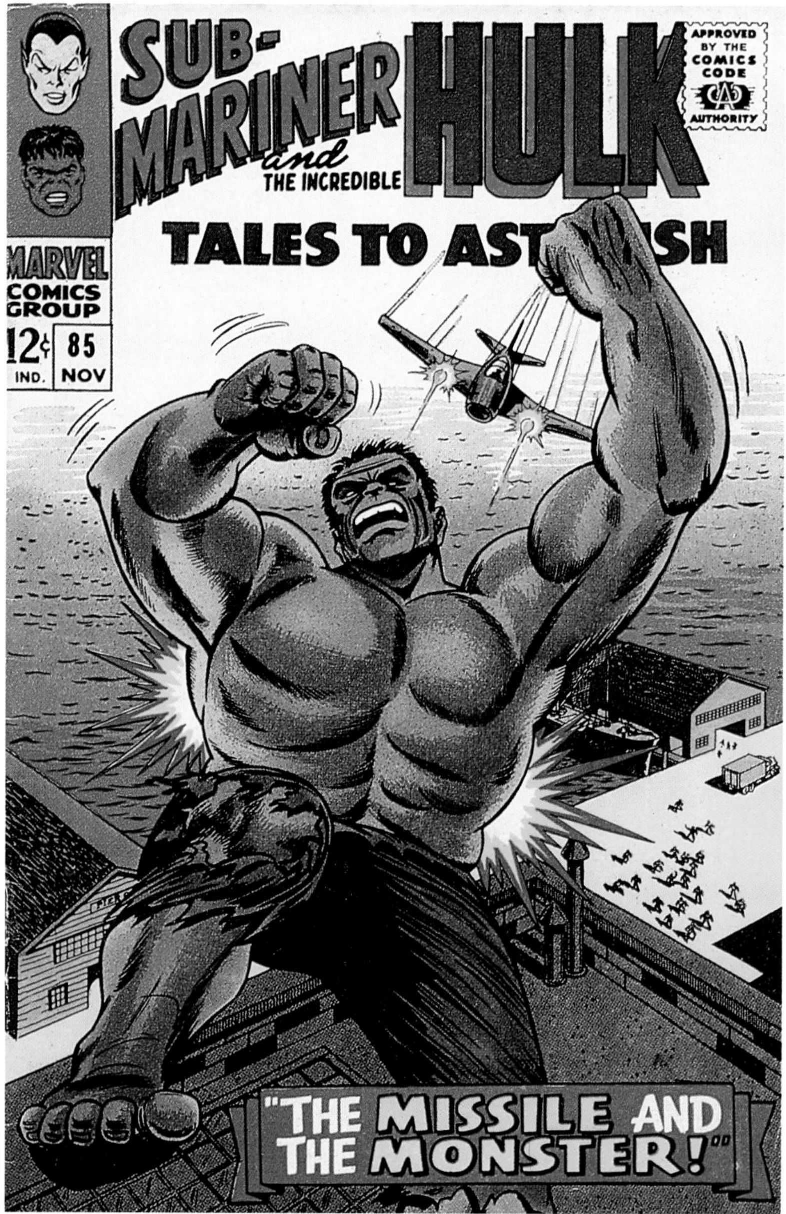

Tales to Astonish #85 ©*1966 Marvel Entertainment Group, Inc.* Jack Kirby, Bill Everett.

Jack Kirby, the artist and cocreator of the Hulk, recalled that his inspiration for the character came "from one of the monster stories I'd done (*Journey Into Mystery* #66). I took the Hulk name and made a superhero out of him because I felt it was realistic. There's a Hulk in all of us. It was a natural."

The Hulk in all of us that Kirby referred to was made obvious to him one day when he saw a mother perform a feat of superhuman strength: "I saw a woman lift a car. Her baby was caught under the running board of this car . . . this woman in desperation lifted the rear end of the car. It suddenly came to me that in desperation we can all do that—we can knock down walls, we can go berserk, which we do. You know what happens when we're in a rage—you can tear a house down. I created a character who did all of that and called him the Hulk."

The Hulk stories often centered on a quest for identity and a schizophrenic relationship. Banner's girlfriend Betty Ross loved him as Dr. Bruce Banner, but was terrified of him as the Hulk.

The green-skinned antihero appealed to many early 1960s college students. Kirby remembered that a "couple of guys from Columbia University came up with a list of 200 names saying that the Hulk was the mascot of their dormitory." Still, the first series of the Hulk comic books was cancelled because of poor sales with the sixth issue in March 1963, the same month that the *Amazing Spider-Man* began.

The Hulk made guest appearances in other Marvel comics, having a slugfest with the Thing in the *Fantastic Four* and going head-to-head with Thor the Thunder God in *Journey Into Mystery*.

By the fall of 1964, Marvel's "jolly green giant," as dubbed by Lee, rated his own series in *Tales to Astonish*. By 1968, he had his own comic book again, the *Incredible Hulk*, which would eventually launch a popular 1980s TV show.

It was the early 1960s comic book version by Kirby and Lee, however, that forever defined the appeal of the jade-skinned, man-monster superhero: "Puny humans! Hulk smash!"

IRON MAN

SECRET IDENTITY
Anthony Stark, scientist/weapons industrialist

NICKNAMES
Golden Avenger
Golden Gladiator
Shell Head
Bullet Head

FIRST APPEARANCE
March 1963—*Tales of Suspense* #39

MAJOR SILVER AGE APPEARANCES
Iron Man 1–20
Iron Man and Sub-Mariner 1
Tales of Suspense 39–99

OTHER SILVER AGE APPEARANCES
Avengers 1–16, 20, 22, 45, 47, 51, 58, 60, 63, 66–71 Annual 1, 2
Captain America 100
Captain Marvel 14
Daredevil 9–11
Journey Into Mystery 101
Strange Tales 156
Sub-Mariner 14
Tales to Astonish 82
X-Men 31

Tales of Suspense #42 ©1963 Marvel Entertainment Group, Inc. Jack Kirby, Don Heck.

"Anthony Stark is both a sophisticate and a scientist! A millionaire bachelor as much at home in a laboratory as in high society. . . ."

In his lab, Stark specializes in creating transistorized weapons, such as miniature mortars, for use in the early days of the Vietnam War.

Stark travels to South Vietnam to see his weapons in action and "to make sure they worked as planned! If not, I'll fix 'em on the spot!"

While in the jungle on observation, Stark trips over a Viet Cong booby-trap which explodes shrapnel up into his chest. The guerillas capture the injured Stark and discover "he is the famous Yankee inventor!"

The shrapnel is too close to his heart to operate. Within a week, he will die. Meanwhile, his communist captors try to force him to make new weapons for their army.

Stark cannily agrees, but instead uses their laboratory to invent a device which might keep his own heart beating. With his knowledge of transistors, circuitry, armory, and weaponry, Stark builds "a mighty electronic body" that will keep his heart beating after the shrapnel reaches it. When he puts on the life-support armor he has invented, he turns into an iron man.

As Iron Man, Stark breaks free of his communist captors with the aid of his built-in "transistor-powered air-pressure jets" and "electronically powered arms."

After returning to America, he leads a

Tales of Suspense #48 ©1963 Marvel Entertainment Group, Inc. Jack Kirby, Sol Brodsky.

double life as Iron Man and as Tony Stark, weapons manufacturer. As Stark, he must always wear the armor chest plate of Iron Man under his clothes in order to keep his weak heart beating:

"Inside my iron armor, I'm one of the strongest beings to walk the earth! My transistor-powered strength is capable of almost any task! The name of Iron Man makes strong men tremble! But, what good does it do me?? I can never relax . . . never be without my chest plate—never lead a normal life!!"

Stan Lee originally saw Iron Man, as "a Howard Hughes type with almost unlimited wealth—envied by other males and sought after by glamorous females from every walk of life. But, like virtually all the mixed-up Marvel heroes, he'd have to be flawed. There'd have to be some tragic element to his life to provide the necessary dimension of realism—some Achilles heel to make the reader feel pity even while envying him."

In this case, the Achilles heel was a heart—a weak heart that could only be maintained by wearing a chest plate which had to be recharged when its batteries ran down. Iron Man was in effect an invalid—connected to life by an electric cord.

Marvel artist Don Heck, who drew many of the early Iron Man stories, thought that was what made Iron Man so appealing. He wasn't an invincible, all-powerful being. "If a guy can't get hurt at all, it limits the interest as far as I'm concerned," Heck observed. "You know nothing's going to happen to him—that's why Iron Man in the beginning was good, because of the fact that his battery would drain down, and the guy could be in the middle of something, and have to get the hell out of there."

Of all the red-baiting Marvel superheroes, Iron Man was probably the most virulently anti-communist. His early enemies included the Red Barbarian, the Crimson Dynamo, and an evil Chinese mastermind called the Mandarin. In his alter ego as Tony Stark, he continued designing weapons to use on Vietnam battlefields.

A dozen years later, after the early Iron Man stories, Stan Lee observed that they were written "at a time when our government was telling us that we were the good guys, and that the communists were the bad guys. I had been conditioned. When the word came down from Washington that the commies are the bad guys, I just acted like one of Pavlov's dogs. Then came Vietnam, then came student protestors, then came a whole change in the country. I think you'll find at that point we got off the kick."

Lee did recall that he always "liked Iron Man because I liked the idea of taking a guy nobody's ever made a hero out of before—a guy who's a member of the military-industrial complex—and making a hero out of him."

Iron Man was first launched in 1963 in

Tales of Suspense #97 ©1967 Marvel Entertainment Group, Inc. Gene Colan, Frank Giacoia.

Tales of Suspense, one of the four Marvel monster comics that would soon be taken over by the new superheroes. The hero's name suggested "might and raw power" to Stan Lee. Jack Kirby designed the character's costume and drew the cover for the the first issue.

Lee turned the plot for the first Iron Man story over to Larry Lieber to script since he had to get the first issue of *Spider-Man* written. Kirby also had his hands full, so artist Don Heck, on a moment's notice, was assigned the story.

"I did the first issue of Iron Man," Heck recalled. "Jack Kirby created the costume but I did all the breakdowns and art. The second costume (the red-and-yellow one) was created by Steve Ditko. I found it easier than drawing that bulky old thing. The earlier design, the robot-looking one, was more Kirbyish."

Not only would Iron Man's armor costume change over the years, but so would the character himself. One of the original members of the Avengers, Iron Man left the group in 1965. By 1968, he had his own comic book, and in the 1970s, he would undergo a successful heart operation. As the 1970s ended, however, Tony Stark would face his greatest battle as he plunged into a six-year bout with alcoholism.

Justice League of America #31 ©1964 *DC Comics, Inc.* Mike Sekowsky, Murphy Anderson.

JUSTICE LEAGUE OF AMERICA

NICKNAME
World's Greatest Super-Heroes

MEMBERS
(Original Members—February 1960)
Aquaman
Batman
Flash
Green Lantern
Martian Manhunter
Superman
Wonder Woman

(Subsequent Members)
Green Arrow (Joined—April 1961)
Atom (Joined—September 1962)
Hawkman (Joined—November 1964)
Black Canary (Joined—September 1969)
Snapper Carr (Honorary Member)

FIRST APPEARANCE
February 1960—*Brave and the Bold* #28

MAJOR SILVER AGE APPEARANCES
Brave and the Bold 28–30
Justice League of America 1–77

OTHER SILVER AGE APPEARANCES
Action Comics 314, 365, 366
Aquaman 18, 30
Atom 8
Doom Patrol 104
Flash 171, 175, 199
Green Lantern 29

Justice League of America #2 ©1960 DC Comics, Inc. Murphy Anderson.

Mystery in Space 75
Superman 199
Superman's Girlfriend, Lois Lane 29

The World's Greatest Heroes, at least as far as comic books in 1960 were concerned, were finally together in one place. Superman, Batman, Wonder Woman, Aquaman, Martian Manhunter, Green Lantern, and the Flash had just defeated a band of meteorite-riding aliens.

The superheroes made a good showing. Together, as a team, they saved the earth from an extraterrestrial invasion. They felt pretty pleased with themselves.

Batman broke the silence and spoke the thoughts of his fellow superheroes: "We ought to form a club or society . . . "

"A league against evil!" the Flash responded. "Our purpose will be to uphold justice against whatever danger threatens it!"

And so was born the mightiest team of superheroes the world has ever known—The Justice League of America!

The JLA (as it was known) established its headquarters in a "modernistically outfitted cavern." They outfitted themselves with "signal devices" so any JLA member could summon the others for an emergency meeting. And they acquired an official and unlikely mascot—Snapper Carr, a jive-talking teenager from Happy Harbor.

Snapper Carr was adopted by the JLA when he inadvertently helped them defeat their first foe. He got his name from his constant habit of snapping his fingers:

Snap-Snap! "Like man, you might say it's endsville that ends well!" Snap-Snap!

His hipster lingo supposedly was for comic relief: "Man, like I'm primed for action! Maybe this time I won't be a stray cat where the JLA is concerned! I can't wait to get there and start cooking on the front burner!"

Julius Schwartz, after the success of the new Flash and Green Lantern, was ready to bring back DC's greatest superhero team of all time: the Justice Society of America. The Justice Society appeared in *All-Star Comics* from 1940 to 1951 and featured DC's most popular heroes fighting together as a team.

For the 1960s, Schwartz had to make some changes to attract a new generation of readers. He thought that the name Justice Society was too old-fashioned. "Society," said Schwartz, "was a dull word. In sports, everything is a League—the American League, the National League, the Football League, the Baseball League, so I said, 'We'll call ours the Justice League of America.'"

Schwartz premiered the new league of superheroes in *Brave and the Bold* at the beginning of 1960. After two more trial issues, the Justice League of America got its own comic book.

Gardner Fox, a writer of the 1940s Justice Society of America stories, was chosen

Justice League of America #21 ©1963 DC Comics, Inc. Mike Sekowsky, Bernard Sachs. JLA at headquarters.

by Schwartz to write the JLA adventures. Fox remembered that "there were so many characters to get into each story, it was a wonder that there was any room left for a plot. As for characterization, it was all but impossible."

As a result, many stories followed a formula of dividing the Justice League members into teams of two or three heroes, with each team fighting a simultaneous adversary or solving part of a puzzle. By the last page, all the members would regroup triumphantly, having beaten their foe through teamwork.

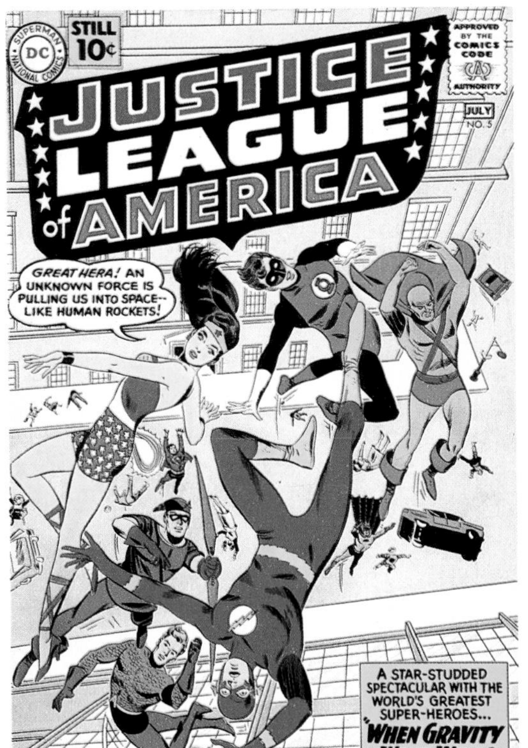

Justice League of America #5 ©1961 DC Comics, Inc. Mike Sekowsky, Bernard Sachs.

Schwartz knew well the problems of devising a challenging story with so many superheroes. "The Justice League is a very difficult book to write, maybe the hardest of all the DC books. One must not only come up with a menace worthy of the group's mettle, but also coordinate all of the team action."

Both Schwartz and Fox would work together on each JLA story. Fox remembered their regular working routine: "I'd bring in the plot around nine and then we'd kick it around and add to it, or subtract from it, until lunch."

After the script was completed, Schwartz turned it over to artist Mike Sekowsky. Sekowsky drew the adventures of the Justice League for its first eight years and Schwartz called it "the toughest assignment in comic-drawing, portraying a multitude of hero-creations of other artists."

Sekowsky did an admirable job of staging all the characters so that the stories unfolded gracefully. Long-time Justice League writer Gardner Fox explained that while "Sekowsky wasn't as polished as some others, he knew how to tell a story."

Dick Dillin became the book's artist in 1968 when Sekowsky became an editor at DC. Dillin also found the job of drawing so many characters a challenging task, but one he had prepared for by drawing *Blackhawk*, another team title, for almost 15 years.

Dillin recalled that of all the Justice League members, "I think I like the Green Lantern and the Green Arrow the best. They're both very well designed characters and it's very easy to draw an exciting picture if one or both of them are featured."

Over the years, the membership of the Justice League changed to reflect the addition of new DC superheroes (Atom, Hawkman, and Black Canary), as well as the departure of old ones (Wonder Woman and Martian Manhunter).

Regardless of its membership roll, however, the Justice League of America would always be, for some readers, "The World's Greatest Heroes."

Adventure Comics #337 *©1965 DC Comics, Inc.* Curt Swan, George Klein.

LEGION OF SUPER-HEROES

MEMBERS
(listed in order in which they joined):

Cosmic Boy (First appearance *Adventure Comics* #247)
Saturn Girl (First appearance *Adventure Comics* #247)
Lightning Lad (First appearance *Adventure Comics* #247)
Superboy (First appearance *More Fun Comics* #101)
Triplicate Girl (First appearance *Action Comics* #276)
Phantom Girl (First appearance *Action Comics* #276)
Chameleon Boy (First appearance *Action Comics* #267)
Invisible Kid (First appearance *Action Comics* #267)
Colossal Boy (First appearance *Action Comics* #267)
Star Boy (First appearance *Adventure Comics* #282)
Supergirl (First appearance *Action Comics* #252)
Braniac 5 (First appearance *Action Comics* #276)
Shrinking Violet (First appearance *Action Comics* #276)
Sun Boy (First appearance *Action Comics* #276)
Bouncing Boy (First appearance *Action Comics* #276)
Ultra Boy (First appearance *Superboy* #98)
Mon-El (First appearance *Superboy* #89)
Matter-Eater Lad (First appearance *Adventure Comics* #303)
Element Lad (First appearance *Adventure Comics* #307)
Light Lass (First appearance *Adventure Comics* #308)
Dream Girl (First appearance *Adventure Comics* #317)
Princess Projectra (First appearance *Adventure Comics* #346)
Ferro Lad (First appearance *Adventure Comics* #346)
Karate Kid (First appearance *Adventure Comics* #346)

Nemesis Kid (First appearance *Adventure Comics* #346)
Shadow Lass (First appearance *Adventure Comics* #365)
Chemical King (First appearance *Adventure Comics* #371)
Timber Wolf (First appearance, as Lone Wolf, *Adventure Comics* #327)

FIRST APPEARANCE
April 1958—*Adventure Comics* #247

MAJOR SILVER AGE APPEARANCES
Action Comics 377–383
Adventure Comics 247, 267, 282, 290, 293, 300–380
Superboy 147

OTHER SILVER AGE APPEARANCES
Action 267, 276, 284 (Mon-el), 285, 286, 287, 288 (Mon-el), 289, 290, 297 (Mon-el), 298, 306 (Braniac, Mon-el), 307 (Saturn Girl), 309, 319 (Shrinking Violet), 334 (reprint), 360 (reprint), 365, 373
Superboy 86, 89 (Mon-el), 93, 98, 100 (Ultra Boy, Chameleon Boy), 117, 125, 129 (Mon-el), 147, 148 (Polar Boy)
Superman 147, 149, 152, 155, 156, 162, 167 (Braniac 5), 172, 173, 213 (Braniac 5) Annual 4
Superman's Girlfriend Lois Lane 33 (Mon-el), 47, 50 (Triplicate Girl, Phantom Girl, Shrinking Violet), 56 (Saturn Girl)
Superman's Pal Jimmy Olsen 62 (Mon-el), 63, 70 (Element Lad), 72, 73 (Ultra Boy), 76, 85, 88 (Star Boy), 99, 100, 106, 117
World's Finest 142, 168 (adult Legion), 172 (adult Legion)

Three teenagers in the 30th century have special powers. Garth Ranzz can hurl lightning bolts from his fingertips. Rokk Krinn can magnetically attract and repel any object. Imra Ardeen can read others' minds. Together they accidentally save the life of the richest man in the universe.

In gratitude, he sets the teenagers up as an independent organization to combat crime and injustice, not only on earth but throughout the universe. He builds them a huge rocket ship-shaped clubhouse, and dubs the three teenagers Lightning Lad, Cosmic Boy, and Saturn Girl.

The three young superheroes draw up a constitution for their new club—the Legion of Super-Heroes. "According to our club's rules," Saturn Girl announces, "only persons under 18 years old who have super powers are eligible for membership!"

Evidently, there were plenty of qualified super-powered teens in the 30th century because membership in the Legion grew rapidly.

Adventure Comics #312 ©1963 DC Comics, Inc. Curt Swan, George Klein.

Adventure Comics #364
©1968 DC Comics, Inc.
Curt Swan, George Klein.

One of the first was Luornu Durgo from the planet Cargg. Cosmic Boy introduces her as a prospective member: "This gal wants to apply for membership! She's . . . huh?"

Suddenly Luornu Durgo has split into three identical people! "Popping planetoids!" says Lightning Lad. "The doll is triplets!"

She was called, naturally enough, Triplicate Girl. Her power to become a trio of clones earned her membership in the Legion.

At the next Legion meeting in their rocket ship clubhouse, Lightning Lad pronounces: "This is the safest place on earth! Nothing can get past our guard devices, and . . . ULP!"

A girl walks through the clubhouse walls. "I'm Tinya Wazzo of the four-dimensional planet, Bgztl! Everyone on my world can dematerialize and walk through walls."

To which Saturn Girl naturally concludes, "Let's make this . . . uh . . . Phantom Girl a member . . . if she'll help us make this place secure from ghostly intruders!"

Other teens with super-powers soon knocked at the doors of the Legion of Super-Heroes and they were accepted as well.

There was Bouncing Boy, who could swell up like a beach ball and bounce away from his enemies; Matter Eater Lad, who could eat his way out of any trap; Chameleon Boy, who could take the shape of any living creature, and many others.

Even Superboy and Supergirl, the two teens responsible for inspiring the original members to form the Legion, were invited to join the 30th-century group via time travel.

Besides the roster of regular members, there was also the Legion of Substitute Heroes—heroes whose powers were not quite "super" enough for the real Legion. This minor league contained players like Chlorophyll-Kid, Night Girl, Color Kid, and Stone Boy.

There was even a Legion Reserve—a backup group with members like Jimmy Olsen (as Elastic Lad), Lana Lang (as Insect Queen), and the uncontrollable Kid Psycho. Another group was the Legion of Super Pets, consisting of Superboy's dog Krypto, Supergirl's cat Streaky, a super-monkey named Beppo, and Comet the Flying Horse.

Jerry Siegel and Edmond Hamilton wrote many of the early 1960s stories, with E. Nelson Birdwell and Otto Binder contributing scripts as well. Jim Shooter became the youngest writer for the series at the age of fourteen when he "wrote and drew, as best I could, a story of the Legion of Super Heroes starring Superboy, for *Adventure Comics* and sent it off." Editor Mort Weisinger liked it and Shooter wrote most of the Legion stories from 1966 to 1969.

The Legion first appeared in a 1958 Superboy story in *Adventure Comics*. After popping up in a dozen stories, from *Action Comics* to *Superboy*, the Legion of Super-Heroes became a regular feature in *Adventure*

Comics in 1962. By the end of the 1960s, the Legion would be bounced to the back pages of *Action Comics.*

Wherever they appeared, however, the Legion of Super-Heroes attracted loyal fans. Readers often wrote Weisinger with their ideas for heroes who might be good future Legion members. Hopeful suggestions included Bacteria Boy (who could give anyone a deadly disease), Nasal Hazel (who has the power of super-smell and Gas Girl (who can turn into any gas).

All through the 1960s, other new superheroes would join the Legion, fight side by side, fall in love with each other, and even sometimes die. It was a 30th-century teenage science fiction space opera to beat all others.

MARTIAN MANHUNTER (J'ONN J'ONZZ)

SECRET IDENTITY
John Jones, police officer
Marco Xavier, playboy

NICKNAMES
Manhunter from Mars
Martian Marvel

FIRST APPEARANCE
November 1955—*Detective Comics* #225

MAJOR SILVER AGE APPEARANCES
Brave and Bold 50, 56
Detective Comics 225–326
House of Mystery 143–173

OTHER SILVER AGE APPEARANCES
Action Comics 365, 366
Brave and Bold 28–30
Flash 175
Justice League of America 1–23, 26–28, 33, 36, 40, 41, 44, 52, 54, 59, 61, 71

"In his observatory-lab, Professor Mark Erdel, world-famous scientist, works over a strange, humming contraption, dotted with twinkling lights . . . the robot brain of the century!"

When Dr. Erdel pushes a button that will allow the brain to "probe other dimensions . . . space . . . time," he accidentally teleports a man from Mars, J'Onn J'Onzz, into his laboratory. The professor timidly tells the giant green-skinned J'Onzz that he may not be able to get him back to Mars.

"You meant no harm, I realize that," said the magnanimous Martian, "But I must adapt myself to this planet until I can return to mine—so that my appearance won't frighten others. That is easily done."

And he suddenly metamorphosizes into a human being. The shock of seeing a green-skinned Martian changing into an Earthman in a blue serge suit causes Dr. Erdel to have a heart attack and die.

"The earth scientist is dead! I am a prisoner here on earth—unable to return to my own world . . . I am bound to stay here, disguised as an earthman."

House of Mystery #147
©1964 DC Comics, Inc.
Joe Certa.

Detective Comics #225 ©1955 DC Comics, Inc. Joe Certa.

The Martian molds his features into those of an earthman and adopts a secret identity as John Jones. As he explores his newly adopted planet, he notices newspaper headlines about a crime wave.

"Earth is far behind Mars in many ways—but that is natural, since it's a younger planet! But this evil they have—called crime . . . Mars once had crime—centuries ago! Until the great evolution we had wicked men who preyed on the good. But our enlightened science made all crime obsolete! There seems to be much crime here—so perhaps, while I am stranded on earth, I can help earthians by fighting this crime! Yes—I think I shall do that!"

John Jones gets a job as a police officer so that he will be better able to fight crime when he changes into his Martian identity as the Manhunter from Mars.

The Martian Manhunter series was initially written by Joe Samachson and edited by Jack Schiff in 1955, which makes the green-skinned detective one of the earliest new heroes of the 1950s. Schiff later assigned the writing chores to Jack Miller, who wrote many of the stories. Artist Joe Certa accompanied Miller as the series' mainstay. He drew the first J'Onn J'Onzz story and then went on to draw 132 more.

It was Mort Weisinger, however, the editor of Superman comics, who created J'Onn J'Onzz, the Manhunter from Mars. Like Superman, J'Onn J'Onzz is an alien from another planet who becomes super after arriving on earth. Like Superman, he has the power of super-vision, super-breath, and super-strength. Like Superman, he is almost invulnerable except for one weakness. Fire—even a lighted cigarette—can cause the Martian Manhunter to feel faint.

The Martian Manhunter gained a pet-friend called Zook in 1963. Zook was an orange imp from another dimension with cowlick antennae. He provided a comic balance to the cool and methodical Manhunter. His one drawback was his obfuscated pidgin-patter speech: "Manhunter, remember not to clobber him again or he split up into three again!" Zook was great at keeping the Manhunter's secret mountain hideout tidy and cozy.

Brave and the Bold #50 ©1963 DC Comics, Inc. George Roussos.

Justice League of America #22 ©1963 DC Comics, Inc. Mike Sekowsky, Bernard Sachs. Martian Manhunter and Black Canary.

In an interesting experiment, the Manhunter from Mars was given a new secret identity in 1966 as Marco Xavier, a jet-setting playboy. In this new guise, he was better able to battle a worldwide crime organization known as VULTURE.

By the end of the 1960s, J'Onn J'Onzz returned to his Martian roots. He resigned from the Justice League in 1969 and made his long-desired return to his home planet Mars. There he helped his people escape genocide from an insane ruler and became the new leader of his surviving race. The Martian Manhunter's 15-year sojourn as Earth's defender and benefactor was over.

SILVER SURFER

SECRET IDENTITY
Norrin Radd of the planet Zenn-La

NICKNAMES
Sentinel of the Spaceways
Sky-Rider of the Spaceways

FIRST APPEARANCE
March 1966—*Fantastic Four* #48

MAJOR SILVER AGE APPEARANCES
Silver Surfer 1–11

OTHER SILVER AGE APPEARANCES
Fantastic Four 48–50, 55–61, 72, 74–77
Annual 5
Tales to Astonish 92, 93
Incredible Hulk 102

"Somewhere in the deep vastness of outer space, an incredible figure hurtles through the cosmos! A being we shall call the Silver Surfer, for want of a better name! The Silver Surfer, zooming along the star ways like a living comet—with the freedom and wild abandon of the wind itself!

"On and on he soars, dodging meteors—skirting around asteroids—rocketing from planet to planet—with entire galaxies as his ports of call—with the known universe itself as his highway."

The Silver Surfer was previously known as Norrin Radd, a resident of the peaceful planet Zenn-La. When Galactus, a gigantic entity who roamed the universe and drained planets for their life-force, arrives at Zenn-La to drain it of its life-force in order to nourish himself, Norrin Radd offers him a deal: Spare my planet and I will become your scout. I will find other planets in the universe for you to feed upon.

Galactus accepts Radd's offer. He transforms him into his cosmic scout:

"Your body has been completely encased in a life-preserving silvery substance of my own creation! From this moment forth . . . neither the frigid, marrow-chilling emptiness of airless space, nor the all-consuming inferno of the hottest sun can cause you harm! And now . . . to transport you through the endless cosmos . . . an indestructible flying board . . . yours to control . . . but with a single thought! Now, and forevermore—you are my herald! Now, and forevermore

Silver Surfer #4 ©1969 *Marvel Comics*. John Buscema.

. . . you are truly . . . the Silver Surfer!"

The Silver Surfer. A cosmic being on a surfboard. He first appeared in the March 1966 issue of the *Fantastic Four*. Editor and writer Stan Lee recalled that he and artist Jack Kirby had plotted that particular issue over a quick bite in a little luncheonette, but he did not remember discussing any character called the Silver Surfer.

"When Jack brought the art to me so that I could add the dialogue and captions," Lee recalled, "I was surprised to find a brand new character floating around the artwork—a silver-skinned, smooth-domed, sky-riding surfer atop a speedy flying surfboard."

Kirby introduced the Silver Surfer to add an extra element of appeal for young readers. "He was drawn into the story," Kirby recalled, "when everybody, kids in California, were beginning to surf. I couldn't do an ordinary teenager surfing so I drew a surfboard with a man from outer space on it."

Stan Lee was quick to realize the potential for drama in Kirby's new cosmic hero. "Seeing the way Jack had drawn him," Lee remembered, "I found a certain nobility in his demeanor, am almost spiritual quality in his aspect and bearing. There seemed something biblically pure about our Silver Surfer, something totally selfless and magnificently innocent." As he scripted *Fantastic Four* stories which featured the Silver Surfer, Lee began turning the character into the voice of conscience for a 1960s generation:

"In all the galaxies . . . in all the endless reaches of space . . . I have found no planet more blessed than this . . . No world more lavishly endowed with natural beauty—with gentle climate—with every ingredient to cre-

Fantastic Four #50 ©1966 *Marvel Comics*. Jack Kirby, Joe Sinnott.

Fantastic Four #55 ©1966 Marvel Entertainment Group, Inc. Jack Kirby, Joe Sinnott.

ate a virtual living paradise! It is as though the human race has been divinely favored over all who live! And yet—in their uncontrollable insanity . . . in their unforgivable blindness . . . they seek to destroy this shining jewel—this softly-spinning gem—this tiny blessed sphere . . . which men call earth!"

Lee frankly admitted that he does his "most obvious moralizing" through the Silver Surfer.

As written by Lee and drawn by John Buscema in his late 1960s series, the Silver Surfer became one of Marvel's most tragic superheroes. He is exiled to spend the rest of his life on Earth, punished by Galactus for thwarting his plans to destroy the planet. Now the Silver Surfer is unable to return to his home planet and his lover, Shalla Bal.

"How much longer must I be an alien prisoner upon the savage planet earth? How much longer before the loneliness destroys me?? This cannot be my fate forever! Surely, in all the universe there can be no crueler mockery of fate! To think that I—possessed of power beyond the ken of mortal man . . . should be helplessly trapped—like the weakest of beasts! I am hated—and feared—by the very humans my heart longs to aid! My heart! Did I say—my heart? How can that be since I have no heart! For I have left it—countless galaxies away—with one whom I love—on the planet Zenn-La! It is there my world begins and ends . . . it is there that I left—Shalla Bal!"

Lee's pontificating and hand-wringing Silver Surfer struck a resonant chord with late 1960s college readers. In retrospect, some of it may seem a little heavy.

"I think Stan (Lee) wanted to make him a very compassionate character," observed Sal Buscema, who inked the *Silver Surfer* comic book. "There was a lot of emotion in the stories that he wrote. But I think it was overdone and got to the point where the Surfer

Amazing Fantasy #15 ©1962 Marvel Entertainment Group, Inc. Steve Ditko. Spider-Man realizes he could have prevented his uncle's death. Feelings of guilt and self-recrimination help launch the career of Marvel's teenage superhero.

was almost a weak sister, a wimpy kind of super-hero."

Perhaps others agreed. The *Silver Surfer* comic book was cancelled in 1970. The Surfer, however, lived on. He would eventually return, 17 years later, to star in his own series.

SPIDER-MAN

SECRET IDENTITY
Peter Parker, student

NICKNAMES
Spidey
Web-Head

FIRST APPEARANCE
August 1962—*Amazing Fantasy* #15

MAJOR SILVER AGE APPEARANCES
Amazing Fantasy 15
Amazing Spider-Man 1–79 Annuals 1–6
Marvel Super-Heroes 14
Spectacular Spider-Man 1, 2

OTHER SILVER AGE APPEARANCES
Avengers 3, 11, 32, 58–60, 69
Daredevil 16, 17, 27, 42, 54
Doctor Strange 179 (reprint)
Fantastic Four 35, 36, 73 Annual 1, 3
Strange Tales 115, 119, 156 Annual 2
Sub-Mariner 14
Tales to Astonish 57, 59
Thor 148
X-Men 27, 35

Peter Parker is a shy high school student, a "bookworm who wouldn't know a cha-cha from a waltz." One day he attends a public science exhibit which features—ahem—Experiments in Radioactivity.

As Parker stands next to a scientist who is blithely demonstrating a radioactive ray gun, a spider falls into its nuclear beam. Naturally enough, "the dying insect, in sudden shock, bites the *nearest* living thing, at that split second before life ebbs from its radioactive body!"

Peter Parker ("the nearest living thing") absorbs the full radioactive bite, and then: "What's happening to me? I feel—different! As though my entire body is charged with some sort of fantastic energy!"

The teenager soon discovers he can leap around on walls and ceilings and has the multiplied strength of a human spider. "It's the spider! It has to be! Somehow—in some miraculous way, his bite has transferred his own power—to me!"

He exploits his new powers by wrestling for money and then appearing on the Ed Sullivan television show as the costumed Spider-Man. His sudden fame and fortune go to his head. When a criminal runs past him at the TV studio, he refuses to help a policeman stop the fugitive.

"Sorry, pal! That's your job," Spider-Man tells the cop. "I'm tired of being pushed around by anyone! From now on, I just look out for number one—that means me!"

A few days later, Peter Parker returns home where he lives with his elderly aunt and uncle. He discovers the police waiting outside.

"Bad news, son—your uncle has been shot—murdered!"

"Uncle Ben—dead! No! No! It can't be!"

He quickly changes into his Spider-Man costume and catches up with his uncle's fleeing murderer. When he pulls the mask off the captured killer's face, he is horrified.

"That—that face! It's—oh no, it can't be! It's the fugitive who ran past me! The one I didn't stop when I had the chance!"

Parker is grief-stricken and guilt-ridden: "My fault—my fault! If only I had stopped him when I could have! But I didn't—and now—Uncle Ben—is dead!"

The first Spider-Man story ends as "a lean, silent figure slowly fades into the gathering darkness, aware at last that in this world, with great power there must also come—great responsibility!"

From the very beginning, Spider-Man was the Superhero-with-Problems. The guilt of his uncle's death and the resulting financial burden it placed upon him and his sweetly helpless Aunt May was only the beginning.

As Spider-Man, he is misunderstood and declared a menace by the media, particularly by newspaper publisher J. Jonah Jameson. It seems that public opinion often turns against him, and even his own aunt, who is unaware of his secret identity, declares that Spider-Man must be captured.

"Everything I do as Spider-Man seems to turn out wrong! What good is my fantastic power if I cannot use it?"

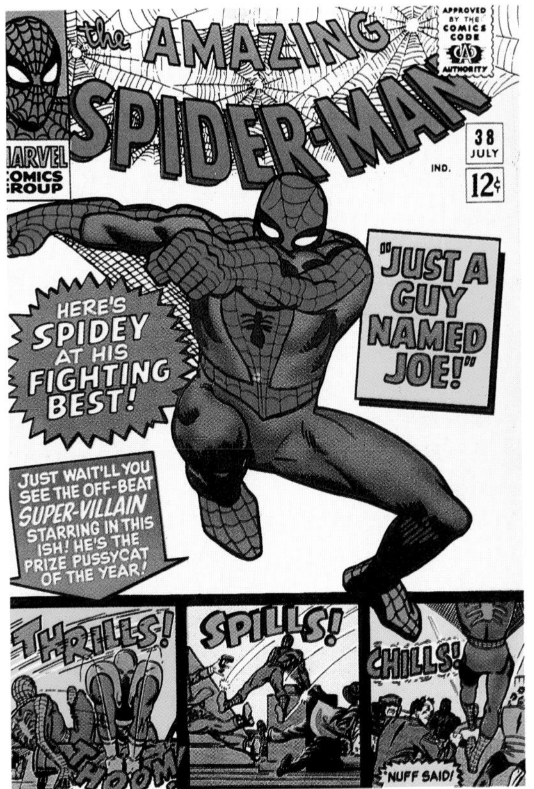

Amazing Spider-Man #38 ©1966 Marvel Entertainment Group, Inc. Steve Ditko.

Amazing Spider-Man #2 ©1963 Marvel Entertainment Group, Inc. Steve Ditko.

When Spider-Man finally establishes himself as a good guy, his alter ego Peter Parker has trouble paying the rent and avoiding misunderstandings with girlfriends. Furthermore, he is continually burdened by his frail aunt's health problems and her smothering protectiveness.

"Some superhero I am! I've got to find some way to get my aunt to let me out of the house!"

Parker's problems as Spider-Man go from love to money to self-image and even finally to wardrobe:

"If this doesn't take the cake!! I can't go

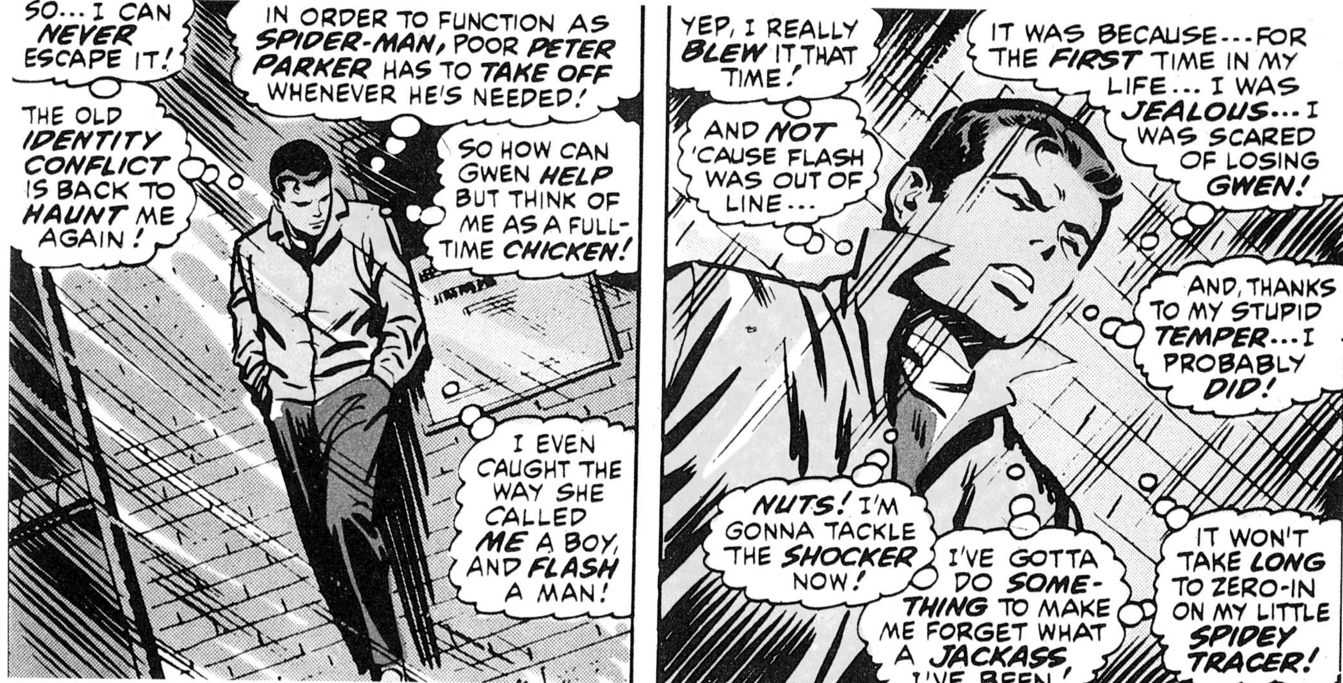

Amazing Spider-Man #72 ©1969 Marvel Entertainment Group, Inc. John Romita, Jim Mooney. By the end of the 1960s, Spider-Man was Marvel's best-selling comic. Stan Lee and John Romita hooked more and more readers with their blend of soap-opera romance and dashing heroics.

out in public as Spider-Man until my mask is sewn up, and when it comes to sewing, I'm all thumbs!"

That's what made Spider-Man so popular. Never before had a superhero sat in his bedroom and griped about patching his uniform. Never before had a teenager acted like a superhero, or a superhero like a teenager.

Spider-Man first appeared in the last issue of a failing science fiction comic book called *Amazing Fantasy*. The book previously had consisted of five-page stories drawn by Steve Ditko and written by Stan Lee.

Lee wanted to try out another superhero character in *Amazing Fantasy*. The Hulk and The Thing were Marvel's two most popular superheroes at the time. Lee decided that this new superhero should also be in the "monster" school—a slightly scary character. The idea for an insect-superhero appealed to Lee. He and artist Jack Kirby had just finished discussing the new Ant-Man character they would be introducing in *Tales to Astonish*.

Lee remembered, "I called Jack and told him: 'I want to do a character called Spider-Man who sticks to the walls, who does this and does that.' And I told him to draw it, how I wanted it done."

Kirby returned several days later with five pages of a preliminary story and a character design. The story featured a teenager living with his aunt and uncle, with a mad scientist lurking in the background.

Lee looked at the story and discussed it with artist Steve Ditko. Ditko recalled that "Stan said Spider-Man would be a teenager with a magic ring which could transform him into an adult hero—Spider-Man. I said it sounded like the *Fly* which Joe Simon had done for Archie Publications."

Kirby worked with Joe Simon a few years earlier on the Fly in 1959. In 1954, he and Simon had been involved in a superhero idea called the Silver Spider for Harvey Comics. It appeared that Kirby's preliminary Spider-Man story was indebted to these earlier characters and not in the style that Lee wanted.

Lee remembered that "Jack did a few pages. I saw them and said, 'No, it is all wrong. Let's forget it, Jack. It's just not your style.' . . . I didn't want him to look too heroic or too monsterlike. I wanted him to look like an average guy."

Lee recalled that he took Kirby's preliminary story and "gave it to Steve Ditko . . . . I don't know whether this is the case or not, but maybe when Ditko did the story, he used the costume Jack created. I don't remember."

It was not the case. Ditko designed a completely new costume for Spider-Man and, with Lee, created an 11-page origin story.

According to Ditko, "The first complete Spider-Man adventure, containing the legend and story, was published in *Amazing Fantasy* #15, from Stan's synopsis. With this story our working method was obviously more involved than with the 5-pagers because the ideas were greater. There were continuing characters (main and supporting), all with different personality types, on-going relationships, personal problems and conflicts. The heroes and villains had various motives and powers to be exploited. All needed consistency yet development and growth had to be considered."

Gradually, Ditko began taking over more control of the character, inventing subplots, supporting characters, and villains. According to Kirby, "Steve developed Spider-Man. He built Spider-Man. He's the one that refined the character." After awhile, Ditko both plotted and drew the stories and then turned them over to be dialogued by Lee.

Another Marvel artist, Gil Kane, recounted that "In the last two years Ditko never even spoke to Stan. They didn't speak at all. He would send in the stuff completely done and Stan put in the copy, and it's just that both had such a satisfying sense of narrative and drama that Stan could write for them. They were very good storytelling artists, and Stan was an adept lyricist."

The original Spider-Man team, however, broke up in 1966 when Ditko abruptly left Marvel Comics. John Romita stepped in the middle of a two-part story and became the major Spider-Man artist for the rest of the 1960s.

Romita recalled his early Spider-Man plotting sessions with writer and editor Stan Lee: "Whenever we used to do a story conference, it was hysterical to sit there and watch Stan go into gyrations. Because, whenever he was giving you a plot and he got excited about a certain point, he wanted to demonstrate it graphically, so he'd leap all over the furniture and shout, using the dialect and expression of the character. He'd change voices for women and villains, and he'd grab himself by the throat and throw himself around. It's true; it's exactly what he used to do, and I always loved to sit there and watch the reactions of strangers walking down the hall."

Romita's version of Spider-Man was handsome and dashing; his women vivacious and bouncy. His long years as a romance comic artist were paying off, and Spider-Man achieved even greater popularity as the 1960s ended.

Amazing Spider-Man #14 ©1964 Marvel Entertainment Group, Inc. Steve Ditko.

SUB-MARINER

SECRET IDENTITY
Namor

NICKNAMES
Prince of the Seas

FIRST NEWSSTAND APPEARANCE
November 1939—*Marvel Comics* #1

FIRST SILVER AGE APPEARANCE
May 1962—*Fantastic Four* #4

MAJOR SILVER AGE APPEARANCES
Sub-Mariner 1–20
Tales to Astonish 70–101
Iron Man and Sub-Mariner 1

OTHER SILVER AGE APPEARANCES
Avengers 3, 4, 16
Captain America 100
Captain Marvel 4
Daredevil 7
Fantastic Four 4, 6, 9, 14, 27, 33 Annual 1, 3
Incredible Hulk 118
Strange Tales 107, 125
X-Men 6

Incredible Hulk #118 ©1969 Marvel Comics. Herb Trimpe.

The man had lost his memory. Homeless and alone, he spent his days in a "flop house" in the company of bums and teenage runaways.

One of these teenagers is Johnny Storm, also known as the Human Torch, who had just run away from the Fantastic Four. He notices the man sitting on his bed, speechless and heavily bearded, lost in the world of the amnesiac.

He offers to help clean up the man, and uses his flame as a barber's razor to remove his beard. To the Human Torch's amazement, the shaved man looks almost exactly like a superhero from the 1940s, the Sub-Mariner.

To test his theory about the derelict's past, the Human Torch flies him over the ocean and drops him in, hoping that the sea will restore his memory.

"Once submerged in the mighty sea, a startling change comes over the strange derelict! In one sweeping motion, he hurls his outer garments from him . . . and stands revealed as the legendary prince of the sea . . . the invincible Namor, the Sub-Mariner!!"

His memory restored, the Sub-Mariner swims back to his underwater kingdom of Atlantis. When he reaches his almost forgotten land, he finds it has been . . .

"Destroyed!! It's all destroyed!! That glow in the water—it's radioactivity!! Now I know what happened!! The humans did it, unthinkingly, with their accursed atomic tests!"

From then on, Prince Namor, the Sub-Mariner, swears vengeance upon the human race for destroying his land. He also begins a quest to find the surviving members of his underwater people, and assume his rightful position as their monarch.

These two elements—a thirst for vengeance and a quest for identity—would dominate the Sub-Mariner stories of the 1960s. He was both a villain and a hero—striking out against the human race who destroyed his home, but also showing a great deal of noblesse oblige to individuals.

In particular, Sue Storm, the Invisible Girl of the Fantastic Four, was the original object of the Sub-Mariner's good intentions. Upon first meeting her, the Prince of the Seas remarks: "You're the loveliest human

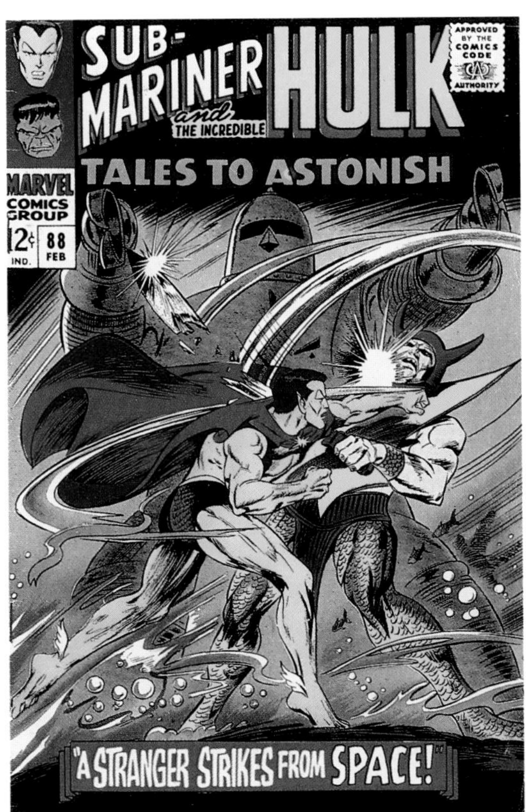

Tales to Astonish #88 ©1967 Marvel Entertainment Group, Inc. Gene Colan, Bill Everett.

I've ever seen! If you will be my bride, I might show mercy to the rest of your pitiful race!"

Sue, who is torn between her growing love for Reed Richards (Mr. Fantastic) and the noble charisma of Namor, replies: "How can I make such a choice?"

For the next three years, the Sub-Mariner would appear and reappear in battles with the Fantastic Four, the Hulk, the Avengers, the X-Men, and Daredevil—always as the villain with the heart of gold.

He began his regular series in 1965 in *Tales to Astonish*, and then received his own comic book three years later. He eventually found his long-lost people and reestablished his kingdom, although not without great suffering and difficulty. By the end of the 1960s, the Prince of the Seas found a steady girlfriend, the blue-skinned Lady Dorma, a fellow water breather.

The Sub-Mariner was one of the first Marvel superheroes, created in 1939 by Bill Everett. Everett named his character after the Mariner in Coleridge's poem, "The Rime of the Ancient Mariner."

Everett fashioned the Sub-Mariner as an anti-hero. "He was an angry character," Everett recalled. "He was probably expressing some of my own personality." The Sub-Mariner's anger at the human race came out in monumental battles of the 1940s with the original Human Torch. During the war years, however, the Sub-Mariner teamed up with Captain America and the Human Torch to fight the Nazis.

The idea of a 1940s superhero who was also a villain was shockingly original for comic books at that time. Everett recalled that he "was allowed full expression. There

Sub-Mariner #1 ©1968 Marvel Entertainment Group, Inc. John Buscema, Sol Brodsky.

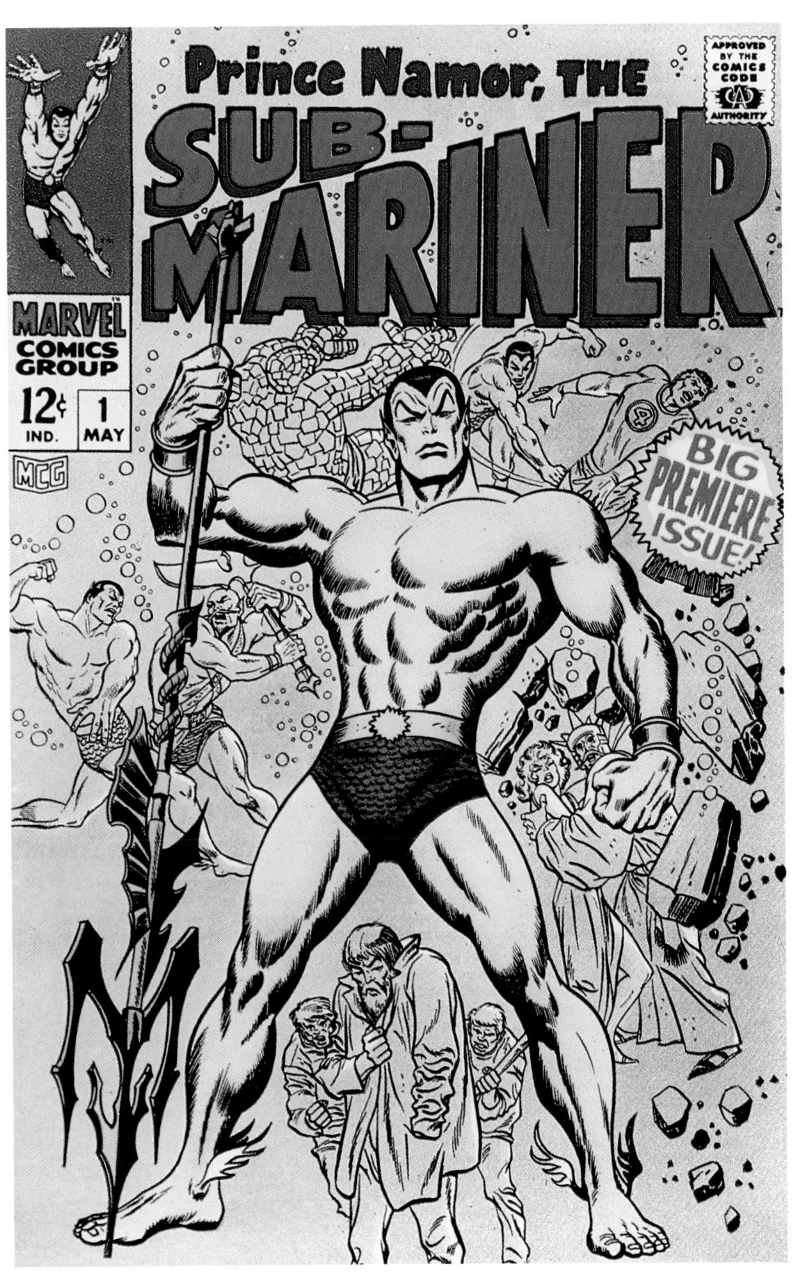

were no limitations by the editors or publishers or anyone. This was a case where the artist could freely express himself."

Along with many superheroes, the Sub-Mariner also disappeared by the end of the 1940s, although he did reappear briefly in the mid-1950s. With the successful revival of the Human Torch in 1961 for the *Fantastic Four*, Stan Lee and Jack Kirby felt the time was right to bring back another 1940s superhero.

As a superhero, the Sub-Mariner was perfect for the Marvel Age of angst-ridden protagonists. He was noble yet misunderstood, powerful yet thwarted, and ultimately, by the nature of his birth, completely schizophrenic. Yet for all of his contradictions, the Sub-Mariner was also portrayed as a regal monarch—a king without a country.

After appearing in a *Tales to Astonish* series, Sub-Mariner received his own comic in 1968. He would rule there for another six years.

"Imperious Rex!"

Superboy #100 ©1962 *DC Comics, Inc.* Curt Swan, John Forte.

SUPERBOY

SECRET IDENTITY
Clark Kent, student and grocery clerk

NICKNAMES
Boy of Steel

FIRST APPEARANCE
January 1945—*More Fun* #101

MAJOR SILVER AGE APPEARANCES
Adventure Comics 247–315 (317–345, 356 reprints)
Superboy 68–161

OTHER SILVER AGE APPEARANCES
Action Comics 358
Superman 131, 136, 144, 146
World's Finest 172

A baby hurtles through outer space in a rocket ship, launched by his parents from their dying planet Krypton. The ship enters the earth's atmosphere and crash lands in a farm field.

Driving by the field are Jonathan and Martha Kent, on the way to their farm from Smallville. When they see the rocket crash, they leap from their Model T Ford.

"Great Scott! That's a space rocket!" says Mr. Kent.

"Land sakes!" says Mrs. Kent as she pulls an infant boy from the rocket. "Then this child must be from another world! Oh, only if we had a baby of our own as sweet as he looks! Let's adopt him, Jonathan!"

Martha Kent tells her husband, "If we just adopt him, people will question it! We'll leave him on the orphanage doorstep and apply later for his adoption!"

Adventure Comics #253 ©1958 DC Comics, Inc. Al Plastino. Superboy meets Robin.

"We'll call him Clark," agreed the proud Mr. Kent, "after your maiden name."

The Kents raise their super son in secret on their farm. Ma Kent makes her child an indestructible costume from his swaddling clothes. Pa Kent moves the family to Smallville and opens a small grocery store. As Clark grows up, his parents help him preserve his secret identity as Superboy. He works in the family store and attends Smallville High School as Clark Kent.

As Superboy, he patrols Smallville (and the universe) by leaving through a secret underground tunnel from his home.

He has a best friend, Pete Ross, and a bothersome girlfriend, Lana Lang who (like her adult counterpart Lois Lane) continually tries to discover his secret identity. Superboy also has a super dog, Krypto, who also survived the explosion of Krypton.

In between his adventures in Smallville, Superboy is a time-traveling member of the 30th century Legion of Super-Heroes.

After graduating from Smallville High School, Clark attends Metropolis University as a journalism major in preparation for his career as a Daily Planet newspaper reporter.

Superboy was a natural way for DC Comics to introduce a juvenile version of their most popular hero.

The character was forst appeared in late 1944. DC Comics editor Jack Schiff remembered that it was "during the war and we had some extra paper which Jack Liebowitz (DC Comics business manager) had managed to acquire, so Whit (Ellsworth—the editor-in-chief) called Joe Shuster and told him we were going to put out a Superboy mag. Joe

Superboy #72 ©1959 DC Comics, Inc. Curt Swan, Stan Kaye.

Superboy #109 ©1963 DC Comics, Inc. Curt Swan, Shelly Moldoff.

spent a couple of days in the office, drawing different heads and figures of Superboy and other characters until we had it just right. I worked out a script with Don Cameron, who was writing Batman, Superman, and just about anything else we needed."

Superboy first appeared in *More Fun Comics* in 1945 before getting a permanent spot in *Adventure Comics* in 1946. He later received his own magazine three years later.

Superboy's adventures were always set in the past, before he became Superman, roughly between 1925 and 1950. As a result, the Superboy stories often had the nostalgic charm and values of small-town America, where people knew the grocer, police chief, and dog-catcher by first name.

Artist Curt Swan, who drew nearly a hundred Superboy stories in the 1950s and 1960s, recalled that "we always kept the same time period . . . the older cars, Ma and Pa Kent and the General Store." To help them keep the correct historical look in the Superboy stories, Swan remembered that "we all had picture files and subscribed to magazines. We'd clip out all the scrap and had a lot of reference material."

In the late 1950s, Mort Weisinger, the editor of the Superman line, began introducing new storylines and characters into Superboy.

There was the Bizzaro-Superboy, an imperfect replica of Superboy, and Beppo, the Super-Monkey from outer space. Lana Lang turns into a superheroine called Insect Queen. Clark Kent's friend Pete Ross accidentally discovers his identity but keeps it a secret. Superboy, through the twists of time travel, meets Supergirl, Lois Lane, Jimmy Olsen, Robin the Boy Wonder, and himself as an adult Superman. He even becomes a Superbaby ("Me not afraid of bad mans! Me spank you!").

The Superboy stories were written for a younger audience than the Superman stories. Stories about pets, friends, parents, and school dominated the Superboy plots. Otto Binder, Jerry Siegel, and Leo Dorfman wrote most of the late 1950s and 1960s adventures, with occasional stories by Bill Finger and Robert Bernstein. George Papp, Curt Swan, and Al Plastino drew the majority of the late 1950s and 1960s Superboy stories.

Superboy presented an attractive fantasy for young readers wrestling with the difficulties of growing up. Infinitely more powerful than his adopted parents, Superboy still basks in their love and protection in his secret identity. He can travel to other planets, romp through space with his super dog Krypto, and outwit his classmates and neighbors with his super powers and skills.

For kids who dreamed of being Superman, Superboy was an easy first step to take.

SUPERGIRL

SECRET IDENTITY
Linda Lee, orphan
Linda Lee Danvers, student

NICKNAMES
Girl of Steel
Maid of Steel

FIRST APPEARANCE
May 1959—*Action Comics* #252

MAJOR SILVER AGE APPEARANCES
Action Comics 252–376
Adventure Comics 381–387
Brave and Bold 63

OTHER SILVER AGE APPEARANCES
Adventure Comics 278, 334, 350, 351
Superboy 80
Superman 134, 140, 142, 144, 150, 154, 156, 157, 161, 176, 199
Superman's Girlfriend Lois Lane 14, 20, 35, 38, 39, 55
Superman's Pal Jimmy Olsen 40, 46, 57, 60, 63, 70, 75, 94, 101, 102, 117
Wonder Woman 177
World's Finest 167, 169, 176, 182

One day in Metropolis, where Clark Kent, who is secretly Superman, works as a reporter for the Daily Planet. . . .

"My super-hearing picked up a roaring sound far out of town! I'll check what it is with my telescopic vision!"

Superman sees that it is a guided missile, about to crash, and it has a human passenger on board!

As Superman races toward the missile, he notices that it's coming in "at greater speed than any rocket known on earth before! In fact, it reminds me of the rocket that brought me to earth the same way, when I was Superbaby years ago."

Too late to stop the missile from smashing into a field, Superman recalls that he was able to survive his crash landing on earth "because I came from Krypton, a world of a red sun! That gave me super-powers and invulnerability in earth's lesser gravitation! But," he sadly notices, "whoever was in this rocket won't come out alive!"

But then a voice from the wreckage: "Don't worry Superman! I'm alive without a scratch!"

Lo and behold, standing before the Man of Steel is a Girl of Steel—a supergirl, dressed in a costume like Superman!

"Great Scott! A young girl, unharmed! But . . . but that means you're invulnerable like me!"

Like Superman, the girl is also a survivor from the planet Krypton. She came from Argo City, one of Krypton's bubble cities which was safely hurled into space when her

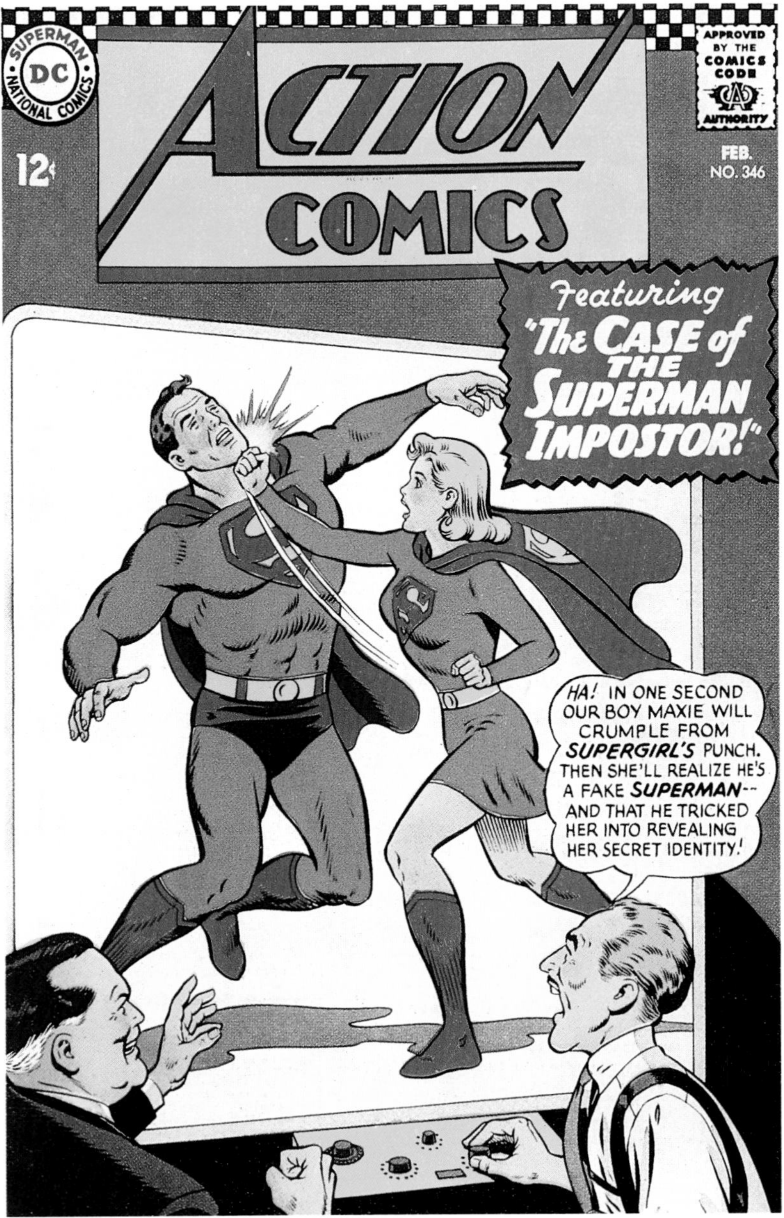

Action Comics #346
©1967 DC Comics, Inc.
Curt Swan, George Klein.

Action Comics #334 ©1966 DC Comics, Inc. Curt Swan, Shelly Moldoff.

planet exploded. Unfortunately, Argo City soon became contaminated by deadly Kryptonite. The girls' parents placed her in a rocket ship and launched her to earth—much in the same manner that Superman was.

Now there were two ex-Kryptonians on earth, male and female, Superman and Supergirl.

When Supergirl tells Superman that her father's name was Zor-El, he realizes that her father was the brother of his Kryptonian father, Jor-El.

"Great Scott! Then you're my . . . cousin!"

Superman and Supergirl embrace, the two surviving members of a family and a planet.

"We may be orphans, but we have each other! I'll take care of you like a big brother, cousin Kara!"

"Thanks cousin Superman! You mean I'll come and live with you?"

Cousin Superman quickly declines. He tells her that he can't be seen with her because "I've adopted a secret identity on earth which might be jeopardized!"

To solve the problem, Superman gets Supergirl a new identity as Linda Lee. Since she already is an orphan, they decide that she can maintain her secret identity in an orphanage.

Superman also tells Supergirl that she must keep her arrival on earth a secret—nobody must know there is a Supergirl yet. "At present you're my secret weapon! No one but me knows you exist! If Kryptonite ever destroys me, you can carry on!"

Supergirl's first year or so on earth was spent in an orphanage, where she tried her best *not* to be adopted. After all, having parents could put a crimp in her secret life as Supergirl. She had to remain hidden and alone.

Action Comics #276 ©1958 DC Comics, Inc. Curt Swan, Stan Kaye.

Supergirl's loneliness is helped when she discovers a super-cat which she names Streaky. Eventually, in spite of herself, she is adopted and leaves the orphanage. She now has an earth mom and dad, Mr. and Mrs. Danvers. Finally, Superman decides it's time to reveal Supergirl's presence on earth. She is greeted by the cheers of millions and becomes earth's newest hero.

For the rest of the 1960s, Supergirl would have a series of mild and romantic adventures, revolving around merman boyfriends, a superhorse, and bizarre encounters with everyone from Jimmy Olsen to the Legion of Super Heroes.

Supergirl first appeared in 1959 after the waters had been tested for a female version of Superman the year before in a story called "The Girl of Steel." Perhaps the biggest surprise is that it was over twenty years after Superman first appeared before there finally was a Superwoman.

Editor Mort Weisinger and writer Otto Binder came up with the idea for the Supergirl character. Binder was the perfect writer for the character. He had created Mary Marvel, the sister of Captain Marvel, so to speak, back in 1942. Like Mary Marvel, Binder also made Supergirl a relative to her male counterpart. Less messy that way.

In a series of stories written by Binder, Edmond Hamilton, and Leo Dorfman, Supergirl would eventually grow up, graduate from high school, fall in and out of love, and go off to college as the 1960s ended.

SUPERMAN

SECRET IDENTITY
Clark Kent, newspaper reporter

NICKNAMES
Man of Steel
Man of Tomorrow

FIRST APPEARANCE
June 1938—*Action Comics* #1

MAJOR SILVER AGE APPEARANCES
Action Comics 241–383
Superman's Girlfriend Lois Lane 1–97
Superman's Pal Jimmy Olsen 31–125
Superman 123–222
World's Finest 94–190

OTHER SILVER AGE APPEARANCES
Adventure 265, 266, 275
Batman 127
Blackhawk 228
Brave and Bold 28–30
Captain Action 1
Flash 175
Justice League of America 1, 2, 4, 5, 7, 9–13, 15–22, 25, 27–30, 32–34, 36, 40–44, 49, 52, 53, 56, 59–61, 63, 65, 66, 68–72, 74, 75, 77

"As a distant planet was destroyed by old age, a scientist placed his infant son within

Superman #156 ©1962 DC Comics, Inc. Curt Swan, George Klein.

Superman #180 ©1965 DC Comics, Inc. Curt Swan, George Klein.

a hastily devised spaceship, launching it to earth!

When the vehicle landed on earth, a passing motorist, discovering the sleeping babe within, turned the child over to an orphanage.

Attendants, unaware that the child's physical structure was millions of years advanced beyond their own, were astounded at his feats of strength.

When maturity was reached, he discovered he could easily:

Leap 1/8th of a mile; hurdle a twenty-story building . . . Raise tremendous weights . . . Run faster than an express train . . . And that nothing less than a bursting shell could penetrate his skin!

Early, Clark decided he must turn his titanic strength into channels that would benefit mankind.

And so was created . . . SUPERMAN! Champion of the oppressed, the physical marvel who had sworn to devote his existence to helping those in need!"

Superman started it all in 1938. Actually, Jerry Siegel and Joe Shuster, two teenagers from Cleveland, Ohio, started it all when they first came up with the idea for the character in 1933. They tried to sell Superman as a newspaper strip, but the syndicates rejected the character—a man from another planet—as too far-fetched for the family paper.

Superman finally caught the attention of Sheldon Mayer and M.C. Gaines at McClure Syndicate in the early spring of 1938. Gaines suggested to DC Comics that they use Superman in their *Action Comics*. They did.

Within three years, Superman was appearing on the radio, in a series of theatrical cartoons, as a newspaper strip, and in three different comic books. His success as the first comic book superhero inspired DC Comics and about three dozen other comic book publishers to come out with hundreds of superheroes in the 1940s.

Unlike many 1940s superheroes who disappeared by the end of the decade, Superman continued reaching a large audience in the 1950s, thanks in part to the Superman television show.

After ending his stint as story consultant on the TV show, DC Comics editor Mort Weisinger turned his full attention to the Superman line of comic books in 1957. Working with writer Otto Binder, Weisinger began creating a "Superman universe" that would last all through the 1960s.

Weisinger wanted to revitalize the nearly 20-year-old Superman with fresh concepts and new characters. In the late 1950s and early 1960s, the Superman legend grew to include a half dozen different types of Kryptonite (green, red, gold, white, silver, blue), a Fortress of Solitude, the Phantom Zone, the bottled Kryptonian city of Kandor, and another member of the Superman family, Supergirl.

Working with writers Binder, Edmond

Hamilton, Jerry Siegel, Leo Dorfman, and Jim Shooter, Weisinger kept reaching for new gimmicks, new twists, and new angles for the Superman mythology.

"I would bring out a new element every six months to keep the enraptured kids who were our audience involved," recalled Weisinger. "I enjoyed surprising the readers, giving them something new."

What if Superman became an old man ("The Oldest Man of Metropolis!")? What if he got married ("Mr. and Mrs. Clark—Superman—Kent!")? How about if he died ("The Last Days of Superman")? Or, how about if his parents from Krypton suddenly arrived on earth ("Superman's Lost Parents")? Or, maybe he visited his parents on Krypton by breaking through the time barrier ("Superman's Return to Krypton")? Or, how about if Superman fought Lex Luthor on a planet that had a red sun so that Superman is powerless, and Luthor was the hero and Superman is the bad guy ("The Showdown Between Luthor and Superman!")?

With a character as powerful as Superman, Weisinger realized that almost any fight was a foregone conclusion. To keep the stories interesting, he tried to bring the all-powerful Man of Steel down to the reader's level.

"One of the ways I was able to plot *Superman*," Weisinger recalled, "was to pretend that I was Superman. What would my problems be, and how would I solve them? How would I react if I was this magnificent character? It was like a schizoid personality . . . I often fantasized what I would do as the Man of Steel."

As a result, the Superman stories had a feeling of humanity—of family about them. There was Jimmy Olsen, Superman's pal, and Lois Lane, Superman's girlfriend. Superman looked after them, rescued them, occasionally tricked them, and obviously loved them. He built special rooms in his Fortress of Solitude where he kept lifelike statues of Jimmy, Lois, and his other friends, along with personal mementos and souvenirs of his times with them.

Without this human side, his friends, and his all-important identity as Clark Kent, Superman would be a god, and probably an uninteresting god at that. Under Weisinger's editorship, which lasted until 1970, the Superman character not only endured but increased in popularity. He was the most widely read superhero in the world, the best-selling superhero of the 1960s (briefly deposed by Batman in 1967), and the single character who first ensured the survival of the comic book industry in 1938.

Even for Superman, it was quite a job.

THOR

SECRET IDENTITY
Dr. Don Blake, physician

NICKNAMES
Son of Odin
God of Thunder
Goldilocks

FIRST APPEARANCE
August 1962—*Journey Into Mystery* #83

MAJOR SILVER AGE APPEARANCES
Journey into Mystery 83–125 Annual 1
Thor 126–171 Annual 2

OTHER SILVER AGE APPEARANCES
Avengers 1–16, 45, 51, 58, 66–71 Annual 1, 2
Daredevil 30
Fantastic Four 73
Silver Surfer 4
Strange Tales 123

Dr. Don Blake, a lame physician, is exploring a seaside cave when a flying saucer lands nearby. The Stone Men from Saturn are invading Earth and Dr. Blake is the only hu-

97, Journey Into Mystery #115 ©1965 Marvel Entertainment Group, Inc. Jack Kirby, Frank Giacoia. Thor and Loki.

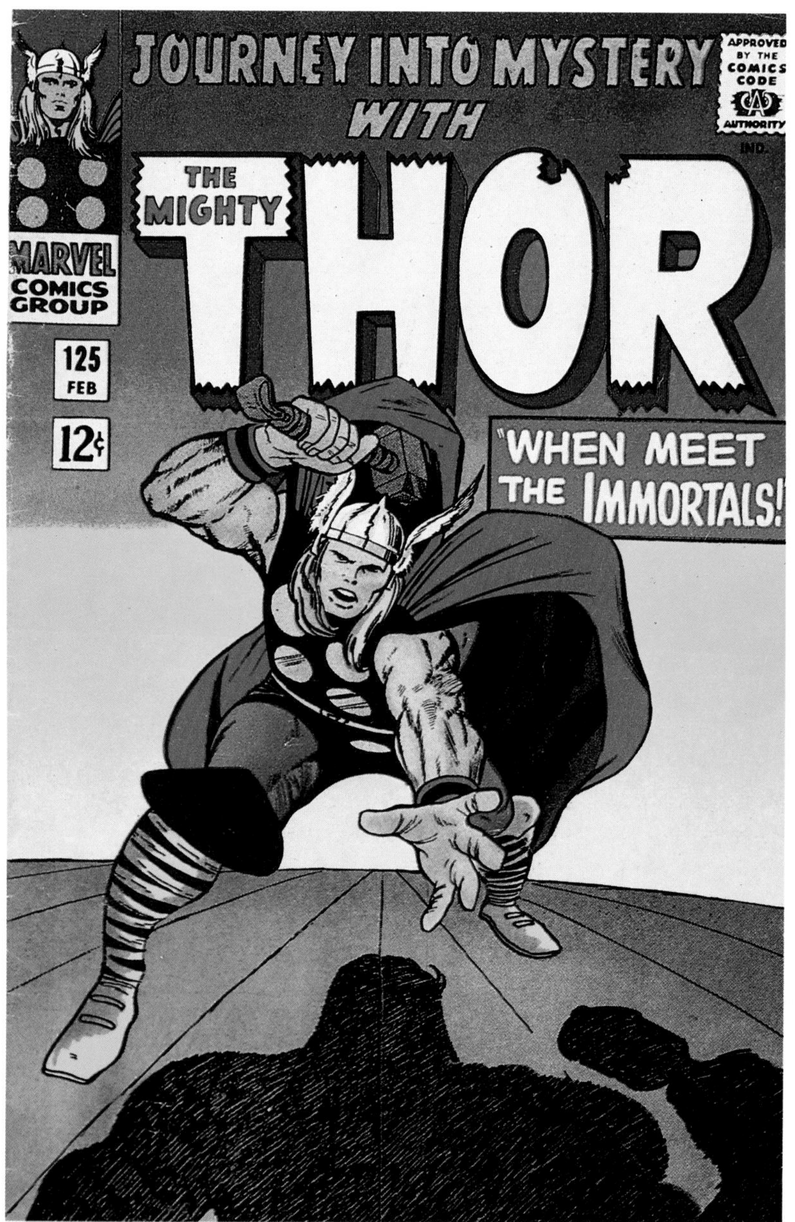

Journey Into Mystery #125 ©1966 Marvel Entertainment Group, Inc. Jack Kirby, Vince Colletta.

man witness. He slips inside the cave and discovers a secret chamber which holds an ancient wooden stick.

He grabs the stick and strikes it against the ground. Suddenly . . .

"The cave is bathed in blinding light! Like a fiery bolt of lightning! And the ancient cane—it—it's changing shape! And—I'm changing too!!"

The cane becomes the enchanted hammer of the ancient Norse god Thor when it is struck against the ground, and it also changes its owner into the legendary god of thunder. The frail Don Blake has now become one of the mightiest gods in mythology, and as Thor, he has the power to command the elements and fly through the air.

Returning to battle the Stone Men as Thor, he destroys their invasion weapons with his magical "Uru" hammer. "I've beaten them! I have proven that the power of the hammer and the might of the thunder-god are invincible! Nothing can conquer Thor! Nothing!"

Tapping his hammer on the ground, Thor changes back into Dr. Don Blake and the hammer becomes a walking cane.

Thor was the mightiest Marvel hero. More than merely a superman, he was, in writer Stan Lee's words, "a Super-God, the only one who could top the heroes we already had."

Lee saw Thor as a way he could have a godlike hero—a Norse mythological god—without offending any reader's religious beliefs. "I figured that Thor, God of Thunder, would be perfect for the job. I liked the sound of his name. It was short, simple, easy to remember, and if you lisped nobody would know."

Lee realized that the Norse legends would give him a ready-made framework for his adventure stories. "There was something about those mighty, horn-helmeted Vikings and their tales of Vahalla, of Ragnarok, of the Aesir, the Fire Demons, and immortal, eternal Asgard, home of the gods. If ever there was a rich lode of material into which Marvel might dip, it was there—and we would mine it."

"We" in this case meant artist Jack Kirby, who designed the character and drew the first story. He would draw more than one hundred Thor adventures over the next eight years.

Kirby recalled doing an earlier "version of Thor for DC in the 1950s (1957, *Tales of the Unexpected* #16) before I did him for Marvel. He had a red beard but he was a legendary figure, which I liked. I created Thor at Marvel because I was forever enamored of legends . . . which is why I knew about Balder and Heimdall and Odin."

Kirby's God of Thunder was a regal and proud figure with shoulder-length blond hair—over a year before the Beatles made long hair fashionable. Through the years,

Kirby created elaborate costumes and settings for many of the Norse gods—Odin, Heimdall, Balder, Lady Sif, and the evil and cunning Loki. His artistic vision of Asgard was complete—detailed down to the ornately designed handles of the Great Wooden Bathtub of Odin himself.

The super-fantastic, other-worldliness of Asgard and the colorful Norse gods was nicely balanced by Thor's alter ego, the lame Dr. Blake.

Lee recalled that he "realized it wouldn't be the easiest job in the world to make a reader in Hoboken develop an affinity for some long-haired nut in blue tights and helmet wings who also happens to be a Norse Thunder God."

Stan Lee used the ordinary Dr. Don Blake to give the Thunder God a necessary human side. As a doctor, he at least had a chance, as Lee put it, to "spend his spare time romping about with some ravishing registered nurse when the occasion demanded, or even when it didn't."

In this case, the ravishing nurse was Jane Foster, Dr. Blake's assistant and secret heartthrob. Jane and Don are in love, but there's a catch: As the immortal god Thor, he is forbidden by Odin to have a relationship with a mortal. He loves Jane Foster both as Don Blake and as Thor, but is unable to express that love.

Jane, unaware of Don's secret life as a Norse god, vacillates between loving the good doctor and becoming totally frustrated by his seemingly schizophrenic behavior ("I'm sure he loves me, but for some strange reason he never suggests marriage!").

Thor is an immortal trapped in a mortal's body—forbidden to engage in love with another human by the awesome responsibility of his godhood. "In truth, my soul is sad! But, neither man nor godling can do less than follow the urging of his heart . . . I must find Jane Foster and tell her everything! If she is to share my life, she must have the right to share my secrets! And never has a man carried such an awesome secret locked within his breast!"

Unlike the other Marvel heroes, Thor was not given to wisecracks or hip repartee. He was taciturn, noble, and aloof. Lee explained that when he began scripting the Thor stories, "I decided that I wanted the hammer holder to speak more like a god. And everyone knows that gods all speak with biblical and Shakespearean phraseology."

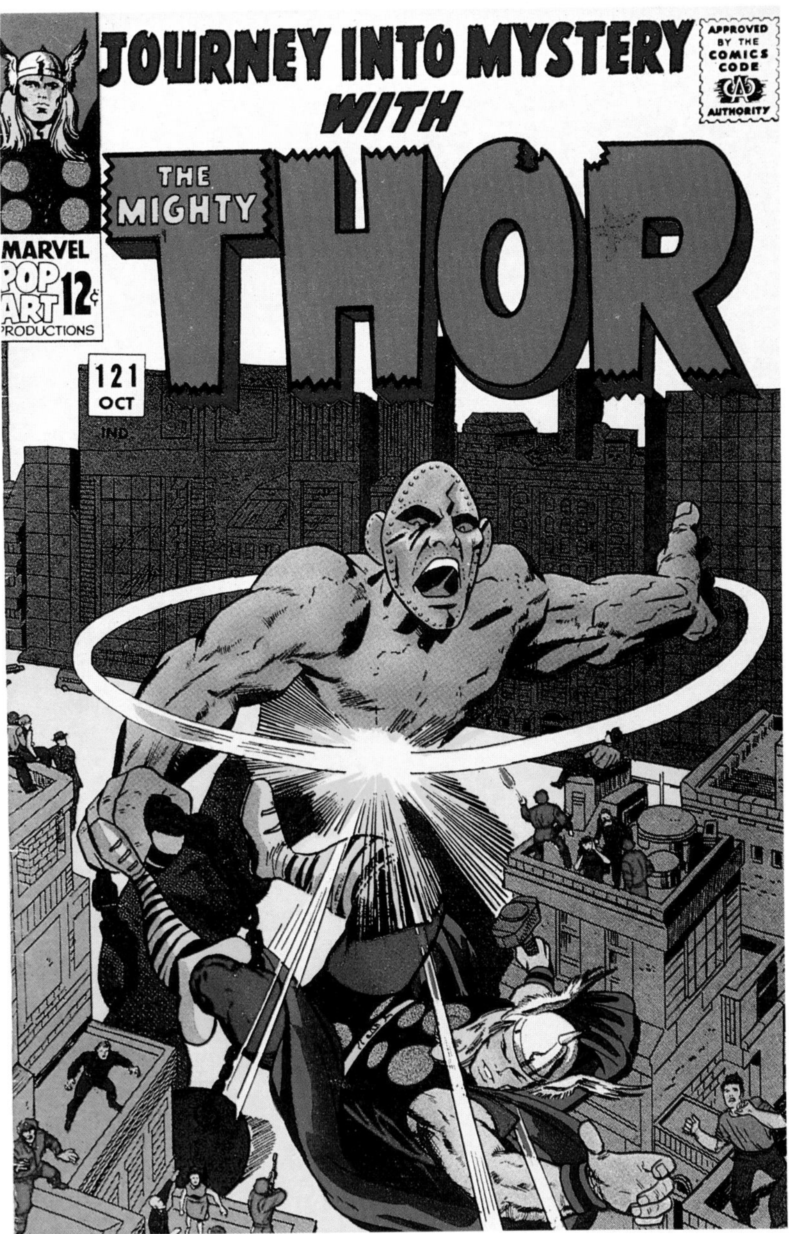

Journey Into Mystery #121 ©1965 Marvel Entertainment Group, Inc. Jack Kirby, Vince Colletta.

When the Thunder God did speak, it was as if Shakespeare had entered the body of Moses:

"Thou didst dare to threaten a female of Asgard! Thou didst profane her name by thine utterance! If ever thou had reason to expect victory over Thor, such reason is now forever vanished! I HAVE SPOKEN!"

So be it.

Thor #143, ©1967 Marvel Entertainment Group, Inc. Jack Kirby, Vince Colletta.

WONDER WOMAN

SECRET IDENTITY
Diana Prince, Army Major

NICKNAMES
Amazing Amazon

FIRST APPEARANCE
December 1941—*All-Star Comics* #8

MAJOR SILVER AGE APPEARANCES
Wonder Woman 98–185
Brave and Bold 63,78,87

OTHER SILVER AGE APPEARANCES
Action Comics 365
Justice League of America 1–31, 3–-36, 40, 41, 43–45, 50, 53, 54, 59, 61, 63, 65, 66, 69, 71
Superman's Girlfriend, Lois Lane 93
Teen Titans 1, 22

Wonder Woman #100
©1958 DC Comics, Inc.
Ross Andru, Mike Esposito.

Hippolyte is Queen of the Amazons, "a race of super women, stronger than men." To escape the mindless wars waged by men, the Amazons sail the far seas until they arrive at Paradise Island. There the women build a "splendid city which no man may enter—a paradise for women only!"

Queen Hippolyte, under the direction of Athena, goddess of wisdom, molds a statue of a baby girl. The goddess Aphrodite then imbues the statue with life, and the baby girl leaps into the queen's arms. "How marvelous—she is my little wonder child! I name thee Diana, after the moon goddess!"

At the age of three, Diana was pulling up trees by their roots ("Already our little princess has the strength of Hercules!"). By five, she was outracing the deer in the forest ("The Queen's child is swifter than Mercury!").

Indeed, Diana was more than just the Princess of the Amazons. She was "beautiful as Aphrodite, wise as Athena, stronger than Hercules, and swifter than Mercury." She was a creation of the goddesses, a Wonder Woman!

Her mother tells her that "beauty and happiness are your Amazon birthright so long as you remain on Paradise Island."

Diana, however, must leave Paradise Island in order to help America win World War II. She dresses in a red, white, and blue star-spangled costume and becomes known as Wonder Woman. Her secret identity is Diana Prince, an officer in the U.S. Army. With her invisible robot plane, magic lasso, and "feminium" bracelets (which can block bullets), Wonder Woman fights war villains and rescues her ineffectual boyfriend, Steve Trevor.

Wonder Woman was created in 1941 by Dr. William Moulton Marston, a psychologist, early feminist theorist, and inventor of the polygraph. Marston was serving as an educational consultant to comic book publisher M.C. Gaines when he suggested that Gaines feature a woman as his next new superhero.

"America's woman of tomorrow," Marston believed, "should be made the hero of a new type of comic strip—a character with all the allure of an attractive woman, but with the strength also of a powerful man."

Gaines said it couldn't be done. Marston responded: "Like hell it can't."

Marston set out to create a superheroine—a Wonder Woman—who would be a role model for girls growing up in the 1940s. He put his belief in the equality (if not the superiority) of women into action with his Wonder Woman stories.

Wonder Woman outwitted men instead of outfighting them, using brains instead of brawn. She was strong, self-reliant, and confident—never a frail hostage or unwilling captive as most of the other comic book women were.

Marston's wife remembered that for her husband, "Wonder Woman was an embodiment of his ideas, rather than mere entertainment. He was expressing a fundamental psychological doctrine. It wasn't just another action comic. Wonder Woman wouldn't battle people, but she would control them; she didn't pound them. Never."

After Marston's death in 1947, Robert Kanigher became sole editor and writer of the *Wonder Woman* comic book for the next 21 years. It was a fortunate choice because as Kanigher admitted: "I like women. I like my wife, I like my daughter, I like women in particular, and women in general."

Kanigher had no difficulty accepting Marston's original concept of Wonder Woman as a super woman, superior to men. As he explained, "There are matriarchies and patriarchies. There's room for both. Dominant people can either be male or female. Wonder Woman did come from a tribe of Amazons."

In 1958, Kanigher decided to give *Wonder Woman* a new look, a new art team, and a new origin. No more references to World War II origins and no more dowdy alter ego. Diana Prince became an attractive and fashionable woman, and Steve Trevor assumed a more active role as her boyfriend.

The new art team of Ross Andru and Mike Esposito gave the superheroine a modern look that was refreshing from the older, static style of the 1940s. Within a few months after Andru and Esposito began drawing Wonder Woman, the Amazon Princess got a new superpower—the ability to glide through the air. Andru remembered that he "enjoyed the sequences with her flying about. I like to do characters that are flying in mid-air, because I like that sense of vertigo, that sense of pull in your gut."

This new and superpowered Wonder Woman began to look and behave more like a female Superman or maybe even Lois Lane. The early 1960s stories were usually romantic melodramas revolving around her love

Wonder Woman #162
©1966 DC Comics, Inc.
Ross Andru, Mike Esposito.

for Steve Trevor and a merman boyfriend called Manno, who lived in the waters near Paradise Island.

Kanigher also tried to build interest among the young female readers by featuring stories about a teenage version of Wonder Woman—a Wonder Girl. There were even Wonder Tot adventures, palpable only to readers themselves a few years shy of puberty.

While the Wonder Woman stories of the early 1960s could certainly no longer be considered feminist fairy tales, they were popular with young female readers. The problem was that by 1965, there were fewer girls buying superhero-type comics—even those starring a Wonder Woman.

To reach the new and growing market of superhero fans in the mid-1960s, Kanigher decided to return to the original concept of Wonder Woman as a 1940s super woman. He instructed his artists to imitate the old Golden Age art style and he even set the stories back in the 1940s. This retro-look experiment failed to attract readers, and Kanigher ended his editorship on the title in 1968.

In the last two years of the 1960s, under a new editor, writer, and art team, Wonder Woman became ultra-hip. She divested herself of her gaudy star-spangled uniform and wore "mod" clothes. She bought a boutique shop, learned karate from an aged Oriental mentor, and became a plainclothes adventurer. And, in a nod to grim realism, her longtime boyfriend Steve Trevor was murdered.

By the end of the 1960s, Wonder Woman had come full-circle from William Marston's 1940s fantasy. She was liberated but also alone, freed of her past but also groping for her own identity. Painfully aware of both her weaknesses and strengths, Wonder Woman was entering the 1970s.

X-Men #1 ©1963 *Marvel Entertainment Group, Inc.* Jack Kirby, Paul Reinman.

X-MEN

NICKNAME
World's Strangest Superheroes

MEMBERS
(Original Members)
The Beast—Hank McCoy
Iceman—Bobby Drake
Cyclops—Scott Summers
The Angel—Warren Worthington III
Marvel Girl—Jean Grey

(Subsequent Member)
The Mimic—Calvin Rankin

FIRST APPEARANCE
September 1963—*X-Men* #1

MAJOR SILVER AGE APPEARANCES
X-Men 1–63

OTHER SILVER AGE APPEARANCES
Avengers 53, 60
Fantastic Four 28
Strange Tales 120
Tales of Suspense 49

Welcome to Professor Charles Xavier's School for Gifted Youngsters. It is not an ordinary

X-Men #1 ©1963 *Marvel Entertainment Group, Inc.* Jack Kirby, Paul Reinman.

school, nor is this professor an ordinary teacher. Professor X, as he is known to his "gifted" students, is a telepath—a mutant. His students, too, are mutants—teenagers who have powers which make them superior to normal homo sapiens.

Professor X, with his mutant powers, was able to locate and contact these gifted teenagers, and he offered to help prepare them for their place in the world.

"I realized the human race is not yet ready to accept those with extra powers," the Professor tells one of his new students, "So I decided to build a haven—a school for X-Men! Here we stay, unsuspected by normal humans, as we learn to use our powers for the benefit of mankind . . . to help those who would distrust us if they knew of our existence!"

The Professor introduces himself to his newest student, Jean Grey: "You, like the other four students at this most exclusive school are a mutant! You possess an extra power, one which humans do not!! That is why I call my students . . . X-Men, for *ex*-tra power!"

The members of the original X-Men are five teenagers:

Hank McCoy, the Beast, who has an agile, apelike body, super bestial strength, and a postgraduate vocabulary ("Why are we procrastinating? We've heard the clarion call to battle! Let us sally forth and slay some dragons!").

Bobby Drake, Iceman, a sixteen-year-old who has the power to freeze water right out of the air and hurl snow and ice bombs ("I'll just form a little ice shield out of my frozen breath . . . ").

Scott Summers, Cyclops, who must control his eyes with a visor because they emit powerful, destructive rays ("I worry about the awesome power in my eyes! If I should ever forget to shield them, *anything* might happen!").

Warren Worthington III, the Angel, a man with wings growing out of his back and a high-flying attitude to match ("Remember, I'm the Angel! Those earth-bound characters can't bother me! They're not in *my* class!).

And finally, Jean Grey, Marvel Girl, who can move objects at will by the power of thought ("I must admit it's a pleasure to practice teleportation openly, without fear of being discovered . . . ").

The X-Men (and X-Woman) practice using their mutant powers in the school's "Danger Room," a place where battles are simulated. Professor X tells the X-Men they must be ready to use their powers:

"There are many mutants walking the earth . . . and more are born each year! Not all of them want to help mankind! Some hate the human race, and wish to destroy it! Some feel that the mutants should be the real rulers of earth! It is our job to protect mankind from them . . . from the *evil mutants*!"

X-Men #49 ©1968 Marvel Entertainment Group, Inc. Jim Steranko, Jim Steranko.

Indeed, their first foe was an evil mutant— Magneto—who controlled the powers of magnetism. Magneto, and his Brotherhood of Evil Mutants, battled the X-Men time and again.

Other evil—and good—mutants came and went. Some, like the Mimic and Polaris, eventually joined the X-Men. Others, like Quicksilver and the Scarlet Witch, would turn up in other Marvel comics.

Stan Lee and Jack Kirby began the *X-Men* in 1963. Lee recalled that the concept of using mutants to create a new team of superheroes excited him. "It would allow Jack and me the fullest scope for our imaginations—whatever power we conceived of could be justified on the basis of its being a mutated trait." Lee even wanted to call the new comic book *The Mutants*, but his publisher vetoed the title out of fear that kids in 1963 might not understand the word.

The *X-Men* came out only a few years after the widespread public concern over atomic bomb testing in the 1950s. Artist Jack Kirby remembered that "this was only about 15 years after Hiroshima. That's no time at all. This was the period when we were first thinking about getting electricity from nuclear plants. We didn't know what radiation could do because we saw all the effects it had on the people of Hiroshima. How can we tell—radiation might help us as well as hurt us. We haven't explored it all yet."

With the X-Men, Kirby said he wanted to "give the beneficial side." While a comic book about mutants, even teenage superhero mutants, "could have been real scary," Kirby said that he used the X-Men to show that there is "a possible path through these dangerous courses that will steer us to permanent peace and make new people out of us."

In the early 1960s, the *X-Men* comic book made a statement that human will and spirit could win out over the dangers posed by mutations, radiation, and nuclear power. The X-Men may have been mutated freaks, but they were also teenagers. They were kids who fell in and out of love, had dreams, went to school, and regularly saved the world.

The Artists

Tales of Suspense #66 ©1965 Marvel Entertainment Group, Inc. Jack Kirby, Chic Stone.

Comic book artists are storytellers. They create a world, fill it with characters, and imbue it with life. They compose every scene and arrange each panel on the page so that the drawings themselves tell a story.

Using backgrounds and shadows, closeups and longshots, the artist is like a director, making our eyes race from image to image, now holding, now releasing, until suddenly all the words and all the pictures merge together and sweep us along until the last panel on the last page.

Comic book artwork is usually created in several steps: First, the artist lays out the panels or scenes for each story page. These "layouts" roughly indicate how the story will progress. The timing, pacing, and even the mood of the story can be set with the layouts.

Next, the artist uses the layouts as a guide to draw the artwork on the page with a pencil. This is called "penciling," and the artist who does this is the "penciler."

Penciled art can sometimes be very rough, showing only the major figures in a story, or it may be finely detailed, needing only darkening by a pen to complete the scene.

After the artwork is penciled, it is given to a letterer who draws the word balloons above the art and writes in the dialogue.

Next, the artwork is given to another artist to draw over the penciled drawings with an ink pen or brush. This artist is called the "inker." The inker darkens and shades the penciled drawings and embellishes the figures and the backgrounds.

In some cases, the penciler and inker may be the same artist. Some artists prefer to ink their own pencils, thereby giving them more control over what the final art looks like. For reasons of production and economics, however, comic book artwork is often the product of two artists, the penciler and the inker.

Since it is the pencilers who determine how a story is told and how the artwork looks, they are usually credited with drawing the comic book story.

The artists profiled in this section have drawn ("penciled") a superhero story in one of the over 100 comic book titles which make up the Silver Age of comics. Following each biographical sketch is a listing of all the superhero comic books which the artist had work in during the 1950s and 1960s. (In many cases, the superhero art credits may be only a fraction of an artist's total work in the comic book field.)

Please note: Only comic books with superhero or superhero-related *stories* from the Silver Age are listed. (Cover artwork is omitted.) Inking work done by artists is not noted. Work done outside of the superhero genre and the 1950s–1960s time period is also omitted from the artist lists.

Even so, there are still over 4,300 superhero stories indexed according to artist from this time period—a good indication of the vast richness and creativity to be found in the comic book art field as a whole.

For many years, comic book artists and writers labored in anonymity and obscurity, particularly during the 1940s and 1950s. Fortunately, artists began to be credited in some comics by the 1960s, but some information and art credits herein must depend upon detective guesswork.

NEAL ADAMS

Neal Adams had a background in modern advertising art as well as five years of experience on the Ben Casey newspaper comic strip when he started at DC Comics in 1968. He introduced a new "hip" Green Arrow in 1969, and also worked on the Spectre and Deadman that year as well.

"When I was twenty-five, I came to comics from the commercial art world, and to the editors at DC it was if I had arrived from outer space. I wasn't drawing in the conventional comic book style. I used illustration technique and reference. I knew how to draw things accurately, and I drew from some unusual angles."

Adams's slick comic book style would exert its influence throughout the 1970s on other artists. At the beginning of 1970, he turned the cartoony Batman into a more realistic and gritty Dark Detective. His best remembered superhero work was the 1971 Green Lantern–Green Arrow series with writer Denny O'Neil.

Brave and Bold 79–86 (Batman, Deadman, Creeper, Flash, Aquaman, Green Arrow)
Detective Comics 369 (Elongated Man)
Spectre 2–5
Strange Adventures 206–216 (Deadman)
Teen Titans 20–22
World's Finest 175, 176 (Superman and Batman)
X-Men 56–63

DAN ADKINS

Dan Adkins began his comic book career in 1964 as an assistant to Wally Wood. He worked with Wood on Tower Comics' *THUNDER Agents* as both writer and artist.

"The first important piece I did for Woody was an Iron Maiden job for *THUNDER Agents*. I ended up doing about 18 Tower jobs with him." As Wood's art assistant, Adkins remembered "practically living at Woody's apartment. All the work was done in one room. We were doing work for four of the top companies at once."

Later in the 1960s, Adkins left Wood and drew superhero stories for Marvel Comics, most notably the Dr. Strange series. His other 1960s work included horror, science fiction, and war stories for Warren's *Creepy*, *Eerie*, and *Blazing Combat*.

In the 1970s, Adkins worked primarlly as an inker for both Marvel Comics (*Conan*, *Master of Kung Fu*, etc.) and DC Comics (*Superman*, *Batman*, *House of Mystery*).

Doctor Strange 169, 170
Dynamo 2, 4
Strange Tales 161–165, 167, 168 (Dr. Strange)
Tales to Astonish 92, 93, 99 (Sub-Mariner)
THUNDER Agents 8, 9, 11, 13, 16, 19
X-Men 34

MURPHY ANDERSON

Murphy Anderson was the principal artist for DC's *Hawkman* in the 1960s. He is also remembered for his 1960s revivals of such Golden Age heroes as the Spectre, Dr. Fate, Starman, and the Black Canary. Anderson was often teamed as an inker with Gil Kane and Carmine Infantino to produce finely rendered heroic characters for titles edited by Julius Schwartz such as *Green Lantern*, *Atom*, *Flash*, and *Batman*.

Anderson began his comic book career at the age of 17 in 1944 with "Star Pirate," a science fiction series for Fiction House comics. In 1947, he drew the Buck Rogers daily newspaper strip for several years. Later in the 1950s, he penciled and inked many DC science fiction stories for *Strange Adventures* and *Mystery In Space*.

Strange Adventures #214
©1968 DC Comics, Inc.
Neal Adams.

After the 1960s, he continued working primarily as an inker for DC Comics through the 1970s and into the 1980s on such features as John Carter of Mars, Korak, and Superman.

"I think when an artist inks his own stuff, there's more art quality," Anderson observed. "No inker can think exactly like the penciler, he can only do it his own way and if he's a good inker, he'll carry the ball a little bit. But he'll miss some of the feeling, the mood that the penciler had intended."

Showcase #61 ©1966 DC Comics, Inc. Murphy Anderson.

Atom and Hawkman 39, 43, 44 (Hawkman)
Brave and Bold 61, 62 (Starman and Black Canary)
Detective Comics 357, 359, 360, 377 (Elongated Man)
Hawkman 1–21
Mystery In Space 87–90 (Hawkman)
Showcase 55, 56 (Dr. Fate & Hourman) 60, 61, 64 (Spectre)
Spectre 1

ROSS ANDRU

Ross Andru worked as an assistant to Brune Hogarth on the Tarzan newspaper strip in the late 1940s before taking a job at Hillman Comics. There he teamed up with Mike Esposito, who would be his longtime inker and business partner.

The Andru-Esposito art team eventually landed a job at DC Comics in the early 1950s drawing war stories. Much of their work at DC comics in the 1950s and 1960s were for titles edited by Robert Kanigher. Their best remembered 1960s superhero series were *Wonder Woman* and *Metal Men.*

Andru and Esposito moved on to Marvel Comics in the early 1970s, where they worked on Spider-Man among other characters. Andru was later selected as the penciler for the 1976 Marvel-DC team up comic book featuring both Superman and Spider-Man.

"I try to make my mind and eye think like a camera," he explained. "Any optical effect that creates shock and surprise, I'm impressed by, and I try to incorporate it to the best of my ability if I can."

Showcase #37 ©1962 DC Comics, Inc. Ross Andru, Mike Esposito.

Batman 213
Brave and Bold 74, 75, 77 (Metal Men, Batman, Spectre, Atom)
Detective Comics 386 (Robin)
Flash 175–177, 179–186, 188–193
Marvel Super-Heroes 14 (Spider-Man)
Metal Men 1–29
Rip Hunter, Timemaster 1–3
Sea Devils 13
Showcase 28 (Sea Devils), 37–40 (Metal Men)
Superman 204, 211, 216
Wonder Woman 98–171
World's Finest 180–183, 185–187, 189, 190 (Superman and Batman)
X-Men 36, 37

JIM APARO

Jim Aparo's first comic book work was a 1966 feature for Charlton's *Go-Go* comics called "Miss Bikini Luv." After drawing other features for Charlton like the *Phantom* and a science fiction western strip for *Cheyenne Kid,* Aparo followed editor Dick Giordano over to DC Comics. His first job there was drawing *Aquaman.*

Aparo is perhaps best known for his 1970s

work on DC Comics' *Brave and the Bold*, drawing over a hundred issues featuring Batman.

"When I read a script," Aparo said, "I start seeing pictures right away."

Aquaman 40–48
Captain Atom 87–89 (Nightshade)
Thunderbolt 60 (The Prankster)

DICK AYERS

Dick Ayers remembered his beginnings as a comic book artist in 1947: "I got my first break and helped pencil a book called *Funnyman*. And after that, the assignments began to roll in. Over the next few years, I drew *Jimmy Durante* comics, a Calico Kid strip which was featured in *Tim Holt* Comics, and *Bobby Benson and the Bar-B-Riders*. Then in 1951, I entered the House of Marvel for the first time—and they've kept me 'hawgtied' ever since."

After inking the *Human Torch* (1954), the *Rawhide Kid*, and *Wyatt Earp* for Marvel, Ayers remembered that "in 1962, things really started to swing. As Stan and Jack came up with characters by the dozen, I found myself busily inking a number of superhero books as well as penciling several fantasy stories." During his twenty-year association with Marvel alone, Ayers drew (by his own count) 10,330 comic book pages.

Ayers worked on many of the 1960s Marvel heroes, often as an inker, and was usually paired with Jack Kirby. His most memorable 1960s work as a penciler was for Marvel's *Sgt. Fury* war comic. After leaving Sgt. Fury in the 1970s, Ayers worked for DC Comics.

Adventures of the Fly 2
Avengers 11, 12
Double-Dare Adventures 2 (Bee-Man)
Dynamo 2
Spyman 2
Strange Tales 106, 107, 110–113, 115–119, 121, 122, 124–129 (Human Torch, Thing and Human Torch)
Tales of Suspense 75 (Captain America)
Tales to Astonish 52, 53, 55–60 (Giant-Man)
THUNDER Agents 2 (NoMan)

Strange Tales #124 ©1964 Marvel Entertainment Group, Inc. Dick Ayers, Steve Ditko.

C.C. BECK

"Shazam!"

In 1939, Charles Clarence Beck helped create the most popular superhero of the 1940s—Captain Marvel. Beck was the principal artist and guiding light behind almost all of the Captain Marvel adventures until 1953, when the character ceased publication. Twenty years later, Beck helped resurrect Captain Marvel for DC Comics, but with unimpressive results.

Before his second bout with Captain Mar-

Superman's Girlfriend Lois Lane #63 ©1966 DC Comics, Inc. Wayne Boring, Kurt Schaffenberger.

vel, however, Beck had returned to comics in the 1960s. Along with veteran Captain Marvel writer Otto Binder, Beck created *Fatman, the Human Flying Saucer*. Similar to the good-natured and wholesome Captain Marvel tales of the 1940s, the comic book was lost in the flood of new superhero comics of the time.

"Nobody ever found out if the public would have bought *Fatman* or not," Beck explained, "because they had no distributorship. Old-time fans were looking for it, but they couldn't find it. It never got out on the stands."

Fatman, The Human Flying Saucer 1–3

FRANK BOLLE

Frank Bolle was still a teenager when he went to work for the Lloyd Jacquet art studio in 1943. He remembered that even as a young child, he "started drawing on any scrap of paper I could find."

In the late 1940s and throughout the 1950s, Bolle drew crime, western, war, and humor comics for over a dozen comic book companies.

His best known 1960s superhero work was *Dr. Solar* for Gold Key comics. He also drew many movie and TV movie comic adaptations for Dell and Gold Key comics. His other 1960s work included stories for DC's romance comics *Girls' Love Stories* and *Heart Throbs*.

In the 1970s, he drew romance and war stories for Charlton Comics and inked a number of Marvel titles in 1973 (*Avengers, Defenders, Sub-Mariner*, etc.).

Doctor Solar 6–19

WAYNE BORING

Wayne Boring began drawing Superman stories in 1938 in response to a "help wanted" ad placed by Superman creators Jerry Siegel and Joe Shuster. Boring recalled his job interview with Shuster: "Joe was living over on Third Avenue in a real rat-hole on the elevated (subway). He had a room with a cot that you had to walk over to get to the other side. Joe was a very timid little guy who wore elevator shoes. He got up and we shook hands over the bed!"

He worked with Siegel and Shuster at their studio in Cleveland, and took over the Superman daily newspaper strip in 1940. In 1942, he began a 25-year stint as one of the principal artists for *Action* and *Superman* comics, with a five-year break from 1961 to 1966. Throughout the early to mid 1950s, Boring's Superman was the definitive version.

After leaving DC Comics, Boring returned to Marvel Comics in 1972 to draw *Captain Marvel*.

Action Comics 241, 243, 245, 246, 248, 250, 257, 258, 261–264, 266–268, 275, 276,

342–344, 346, 348–353, 355–357 (Superman)
Adventure Comics 285 (Bizarro World)
Showcase 10 (Lois Lane)
Superman 124–130, 132–-136, 138–143, 155, 183, 187, 189, 190, 195–197, 200, 202, 207, 208, 215, 217
Superman's Girlfriend Lois Lane 2, 4, 6–8, 10, 13, 77, 78

PAT BOYETTE

Pat Boyette completed his first comic book assignment, a mystery story for Charlton Comics, and then was assigned by editor Dick Giordano to draw a new 1960s superhero series, *Peacemaker*.

After leaving Charlton, Boyette drew two issues of *Blackhawk* for DC Comics. He also worked briefly for Marvel Comics and has drawn stories and covers for Warren Publishing (*Creepy, Eerie*).

"I'm strictly a guy who loves to draw pictures," Boyette said in regard to his desire to experiment with his artwork. "I get terribly bored with the fact that you have to draw everybody with five fingers. On occasion, a guy should have two . . . or one."

Blackhawk 242, 243
Charlton Premiere 1 (Spookman)
Fightin' Five 40, 41 (Peacemaker)
Peacemaker 1–5
Thunderbolt 57, 59, 60

SOL BRODSKY

Sol Brodsky was Marvel Comics' production manager from 1954 to 1971. He also had a career as a comic book editor, writer, publisher, and artist. He broke into the business in 1941 by writing and drawing for Victor Fox's *Blue Beetle* comic. He drew stories for a half dozen comic book companies in the 1940s and also served as art director for Holyoke Publishing.

At Marvel in the 1950s, he wrote and drew science fiction, western, war, horror, and satire comics. In the 1960s, he inked many of the early Marvel heroes, including Fantastic Four, Ant-Man, and Iron Man. He is also known as the creator of the 1960s title logos for *Fantastic Four, Tales of Suspense, Tales to Astonish*, and *Strange Tales*.

Adventures of the Fly 4 (Fly, Shield)

BOB BROWN

Bob Brown began his comic book career at the end of World War II. After two years of art school, he joined Stan Lee at Marvel Comics where he served as an assistant editor in the late 1940s. He later joined Jack Kirby and Joe Simon and worked on their *Black Magic* comic book in the early 1950s.

Brown began drawing stories and covers for DC in the early 1950s, including the last

Doom Patrol #93 ©1965 DC Comics, Inc. Bob Brown.

X-Men #43 ©1968 Marvel Entertainment Group, Inc. John Buscema, George Tuska.

Vigilante story for *Action Comics* in 1954. Along with writer Gardner Fox, he helped create Space Ranger for *Showcase* in 1958 and then drew almost all the subsequent Space Ranger adventures in *Tales of the Unexpected*. In 1959, he took over the *Challengers of the Unknown* with Kirby's departure from the title. For the next nine years, he penciled and inked almost every Challenger story, including covers.

After leaving the Challengers in 1968, Brown worked on *Superboy*, drawing most of the issues until 1973. He drew Supergirl and Wonder Woman in the mid-1970s and also began working for Marvel Comics where he penciled *Daredevil* as well. He worked for both companies until 1977.

Brave and Bold 78 (Batman, Wonder Woman)
Challengers of the Unknown 9–63
Doom Patrol 94, 98, 99
Showcase 15, 16 (Space Ranger)
Superboy 150–155, 157–161
Tales of the Unexpected 47, 48, 50–82 (Space Ranger)

CARL BURGOS

Carl Burgos joined Harry "A" Chesler's comic book studio in 1938. He later worked for Centaur Comics and for Lloyd Jacquet's Funnies Inc., before entering the service in 1942. Burgos's most famous creation during those years was the Human Torch, which he scripted and drew in 1939 for *Marvel Comics*.

Burgos recalled the early days of comics when he created the Human Torch: "We just called them characters. The word superhero didn't even exist until much later. When we created them, we never knew what characters would catch on. We just did the best we could."

In the middle 1950s, Burgos drew a few horror stories for Marvel as well as a cover for the newly revived Human Torch in 1954.

In the 1960s, he returned to Marvel after a nine-year absence and again drew the Human Torch as well as Giant-Man. In 1966 Burgos helped create a short-lived version of a Captain Marvel character for M.F. Enterprises.

Captain Marvel 1–5
Strange Tales 123 (Thing and Human Torch)
Tales to Astonish 62–64 (Giant-Man)

JOHN BUSCEMA

John Buscema spent much of the late 1940s and early 1950s drawing cowboy-and-Indian comics for Dell Comics and romance and adventure comics for Marvel.

After drawing for nearly a half dozen other comic companies, he returned to Marvel in 1966 and was soon drawing the Incredible Hulk and the Avengers. His most popular 1960s Marvel work was the *Silver Surfer*.

In 1971, Buscema was one of the first to succeed Jack Kirby as the artist for the *Fantastic Four*. He remembered his feelings at the time: "When you follow Jack Kirby, it's not very easy to work on a book. You're always thinking of him. What would Jack Kirby do in this situation? Jack could be very intimidating. The guy's a genius! I draw 180 degrees different from Kirby. Jack's very stylized. My style is, I think, very realistic. Jack depends more upon the tremendous impact of the panel. I try to create personalities. How does a woman stand and a man stand? How would a villain sit as opposed to how a superhero would sit. These are the things I'm interested in."

In 1973, he became the artist on *Conan the Barbarian* for many of its next 160 issues. During the 1970s, he drew almost every major Marvel character and helped develop a "house style" that was expounded in his book with Stan Lee called *How to Draw Comics the Marvel Way*.

Avengers 41–47, 49–62 Annual 2
Captain America 115
Silver Surfer 1–11
Strange Tales 150 (Nick Fury)
Sub-Mariner 1–8, 20
Tales to Astonish 85–87 (Incredible Hulk)

SAL BUSCEMA

Sal Buscema was a teenager in the 1950s when he helped his older brother John with some of his art chores on various Dell comics, like *Roy Rogers*.

After working for 13 years in commercial art, Buscema entered the comic book field by joining his brother John at Marvel Comics in 1968. Besides penciling the *Avengers*, he also inked the *Silver Surfer* and other titles in the late 1960s.

In the 1970s and 1980s, Sal Buscema drew several features for Marvel including the *Defenders*, the *Incredible Hulk*, and *ROM*.

"If you can illustrate your story and get it across to the reader without any dialogue, captions, or balloons—just with pictures—then you have told a beautiful pictorial story. If you can tell your story with just your pictures, and make it dynamic and dramatic and moving—and grab your reader—then that's storytelling and you're doing your job."

Avengers 68–71

NICK CARDY

Nicholas Viscardi (Cardy) began his comic book career as a teenager in 1939 in Will Eisner's comic shop. His first regular work appeared in 1940 for Quality Comics (Wonder Boy) and Fiction House (Kaanga). In the

Avengers #71 ©1969 Marvel Entertainment Group, Inc. Sal Buscema, Sam Grainger.

Aquaman #9 ©1963 DC Comics, Inc. Nick Cardy.

late 1940s and early 1950s, he drew crime, horror, war, and a fairly good amount of romance stories for several publishers, including DC Comics.

Cardy would spend most of his career at DC Comics, from 1948 to 1975, drawing such characters as Tomahawk, Daniel Boone, Congo Bill, and Gang Busters. His most memorable 1960s superhero work was on *Aquaman,* which he drew for eight years.

In the early 1970s, Cardy drew romance stories (*Heart Throbs*) and mystery stories (*Witching Hour*) for DC Comics.

Aquaman 1–39
Detective Comics 293–296, 298–300 (Aquaman)
Rip Hunter, Timemaster 4, 5
Showcase 31–33 (Aquaman) 59 (Teen Titans)
Teen Titans 1–7, 13, 14, 16, 17
World's Finest 125, 126 (Aquaman)

JOE CERTA

Joe Certa cut his cartooning teeth by assisting Ham Fisher on the Joe Palooka newspaper strip for six years. "In 1946, I started freelancing for comic magazines," Certa recalled. "In 1950, I did the Straight Arrow newspaper strip and worked again on the Palooka strip from 1956 to 1959."

His late 1940s and early 1950s comic book work for DC Comics included the Robotman series for *Detective Comics* and Captain Compass for *Star Spangled Comics.*

Certa is usually remembered as the original and principal artist of the Martian Manhunter. He drew every one of the more than 130 J'Onn J'Onzz—Manhunter from Mars stories that appeared from 1955 to 1968 in *Detective Comics* and *House of Mystery.* Some of his later work included the *Dark Shadows* TV comic book for Gold Key.

Detective Comics 225–326 (Martian Manhunter)
House of Mystery 143–173 (Martian Manhunter)

ERNIE COLAN

Ernie Colan began as a pasteup production worker for Harvey Comics and soon became an artist. For 25 years, he drew stories featuring all the Harvey Comics characters: *Richie Rich, Casper, Little Dot,* and *Little Lotta* ("A despicable character—ate everything in sight, including the furniture!").

His only 1960s superhero work was *Doctor Solar* for Gold Key Comics. In the 1970s, Colan worked for Atlas Comics (*The Grim Ghost*), Marvel Comics (*Conan*), and served as both artist (*Arak, Amethyst*) and editor at DC Comics as well.

"I'm a real admirer of a craftsman. A good carpenter, a good pottery maker—not people who are on the assembly line, but people who craft things with their hands and minds. As far as I'm concerned, all I've ever aspired to is to be as good as an honest pottery maker. To me, that's a big thing."

Doctor Solar 24–26 (Dr. Solar)

GENE COLAN

Gene Colan loved airplanes and comic strips as a young man. In 1944, he drew aviation adventure strips for Fiction House's *Wing Comics*. Colan worked for at least nine other comic book companies in the 1940s and 1950s, including EC Comics, Dell Comics (*Ben Casey*), and DC Comics (*Hopalong Cassidy*).

Beginning in 1948, he drew war, horror, and romance comics for Marvel Comics all through the 1950s.

In the 1960s, Colan worked on almost every major Marvel superhero. From 1965 to 1972, he drew the majority of the *Daredevil* and *Sub-Mariner* stories (sometimes under the pen name of Adam Austin). His majestic and noble heroes were perfectly suited for the Marvel style.

During the 1970s, Colan drew all 70 issues of *Tomb of Dracula*.

House of Mystery #148 ©1965 DC Comics, Inc. Joe Certa.

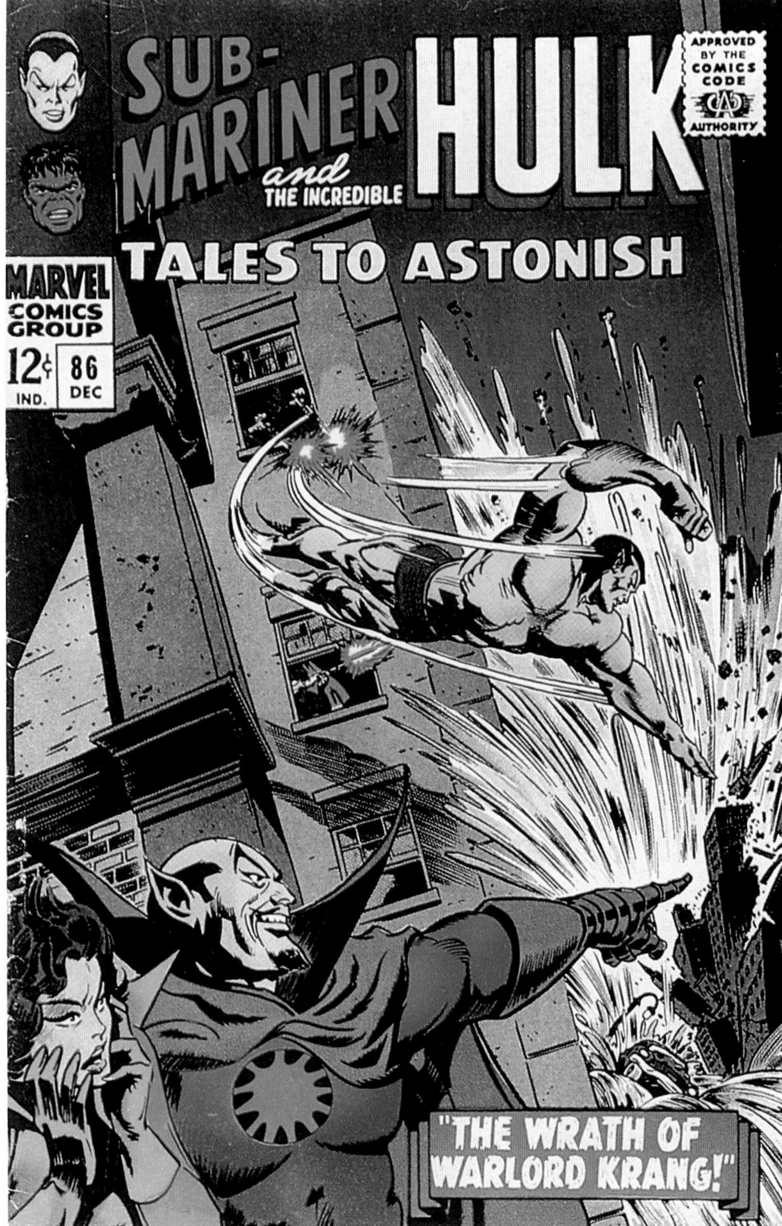

Tales to Astonish #86 ©1966Marvel Entertainment Group, Inc. Gene Colan, Bill Everett.

Avengers 63–65
Blackhawk 211
Captain America 116–120
Captain Marvel 1–4
Daredevil 20–49, 53–59 Annual 1
Doctor Strange 172–178, 180–183
Iron Man 1
Iron Man and Sub-Mariner 1
Marvel Super-Heroes 12, 13, 15, 18 (Captain Marvel, Medusa, Guardians of Galaxy)

Sea Devils 13
Silver Surfer 1–3 (The Watcher)
Sub-Mariner 10, 11
Tales of Suspense 73–99 (Ironman)
Tales to Astonish 70–82, 84, 85, 101 (Sub-Mariner)

PETE COSTANZA

Pete Costanza illustrated pulp magazines in the early 1930s. He began his comic book career in 1940 by drawing Golden Arrow for the second issue of Fawcett's *Whiz Comics.*

While working at Fawcett, he formed an art studio with C.C. Beck in 1945 to meet the huge demand for new Captain Marvel stories. By 1947, Costanza recalled that "the tempo of the business had changed, leaving Beck and myself as the sole artists of Captain Marvel until the Superman lawsuit closed us down in 1953."

Costanza later worked for Classics Illustrated, and then began drawing science fiction stories for the American Comics Group in the 1960s, where he also worked on its superhero, Magicman. His other superhero work during this period was primarily on DC Comics' *Jimmy Olsen.*

Forbidden Worlds #132 ©1965 American Comics Group/ACG. Pete Costanza.

Adventure Comics 362–364 (Legion)
Adventures into the Unknown 154–156 (Nemesis)
Forbidden Worlds 125–141 (Magicman)
Superboy 147 (Legion)
Superman 185, 203
Superman's Pal Jimmy Olsen 91–94, 96–103, 105–107, 109, 111, 112, 114–121, 123–125
World's Finest 174 (Superman and Batman)

JOHNNY CRAIG

Johnny Craig was twelve years old when he became an art assistant in 1938 to DC Comics' artist Harry Lampert. After World War II, Craig became a full-time comic book artist for such publishers as Fox, ME, and Lev Gleason. In 1948, he joined EC Comics, where he worked on its crime comics. He helped introduce the EC horror line with his art and stories, and was editor of the *Vault of Horror.*

After the EC crime and horror comics went out of business, Craig became a commercial artist. He worked occasionally in the 1960s on ghost stories for ACG's suspense comics (*Adventures into the Unknown, Unknown Worlds*) and for Warren's *Creepy* and *Eerie* magazines.

Craig's superhero 1960s artwork was limited to four issues of *Ironman* for Marvel and an issue of *Brave and Bold* for DC Comics. In the 1970s, he continued his lifelong association with the suspense genre by working on several ghost and mystery stories for DC.

Brave and Bold 70 (Batman, Hawkman)
Iron Man 2–4, 14

REED CRANDALL

Reed Crandall became the main artist of Quality Comics' *Blackhawk* in 1942 just two years after entering the comic book field. From 1942 to 1953 (with a two-year break for the Army Air Force in 1944–46), Crandall drew most of the Blackhawk stories in *Blackhawk*, *Military*, and *Modern Comics*.

After working on other Quality titles (like *Dollman*, *Feature Comics*, and *T-Man*), Crandall moved over to EC Comics, where he drew both crime and horror stories. He later worked on *Treasure Chest* and *Buster Brown* comics in the 1950s, and in the 1960s contributed to comics like the *Twilight Zone*, *Flash Gordon*, and *Creepy* magazine.

Crandall's only brush with superheroes in the 1960s was his work for Tower Comics.

Dynamo 1
THUNDER Agents 1, 4, 5, 18, 20 (NoMan, Dynamo)

World's Finest #126
©1962 DC Comics, Inc.
Dick Dillin, Shelly Moldoff.

JACK DAVIS

Jack Davis began his comic career in 1950 by assisting artist Mike Roy on the *Saint* newspaper strip. He got a job in 1951 working for EC Comics, and quickly became its most prolific horror artist. He drew a lead story for almost every issue of *Tales from the Crypt*, worked on the EC war titles and the early *Mad*.

From 1956 to 1963, he worked for Marvel on a half dozen western titles, as well as a few science fiction stories. He was persuaded to do the cover for the first issue of *Creepy* magazine in 1964 and helped design its horror host, Uncle Creepy.

Davis became a well-known advertising and magazine cover artist (*Time*, *TV Guide*) in the 1970s. His only venture into superhero comics was a story he did in 1959 for editor Joe Simon for *Adventures of the Fly*.

Adventures of the Fly 3

JOSÉ DELBO

José Delbo, an Argentinean artist, broke into American comic books by drawing western stories for Charlton Comics in 1965 (*Billy the Kid*, *Outlaws of the West*). He also drew several movie and TV comic book adaptations for Dell Comics in the 1960s, including the *Monkees* and the *Brady Bunch*.

He began working at DC Comics in 1969, primarily on mystery stories. During the 1970s and 1980s, Delbo drew many DC titles and characters, including Batgirl, Green Arrow, Jimmy Olsen, Superboy, Teen Titans, and Wonder Woman.

Doctor Solar 27
Spectre 10

DICK DILLIN

Dick Dillin drew the *Blackhawk* comic book for nearly 15 years, first at Quality Comics and then for DC, when it took over the title in 1956. After ending his run on *Blackhawk* in 1968, he moved over to another team title, the *Justice League of America*. He then drew almost every issue of that title until late 1980. Dillin's work throughout the years was often inked by Chuck Cuidera.

"I always wanted to do comics," remembered Dillin. "My favorites when I was a kid

Amazing Spider-Man #17 ©*1964 Marvel Entertainment Group, Inc.* Steve Ditko.

were all the standards: Prince Valiant, Flash Gordon, you know. I studied at Syracuse University and, after graduation I started pounding the streets looking for work. I hit all the publishers, picking up a job here and a job there. My first assignment was for Fiction House Comics. I did a Korean War hero named Buzz Bennett for *Wings Comics*. That was 1951."

Atom and Hawkman 40–45 (Atom, Hawkman)
Blackhawk 108–241
Hawkman 22–27
Justice League of America 64–66, 68–75, 77
Spectre 7 (Hourman)

STEVE DITKO

Steve Ditko got his start in 1953 by drawing horror stories for several small comic book publishers (Ajax-Farrell, Charlton, and Prize). Most of his later 1950s work appeared in science fiction comics from Charlton (*Out of This World, Unusual Tales*, etc.) and Marvel Comics (*Strange Tales of the Unusual, Journey into Mystery*, etc.).

Ditko's first superhero character was Captain Atom who appeared in a 1960 issue of *Space Adventures*. Two years later, he drew the first appearance of Spider-Man in *Amazing Fantasy*. Ditko's Spider-Man, and later his Dr. Strange, provided the counterpoint to a Marvel universe otherwise dominated by Jack Kirby. Ditko did much of his own plotting for both Marvel heroes until 1966.

From 1966 to 1968, Ditko returned to Charlton and drew new Captain Atom stories as well as a new *Blue Beetle* comic book. The following year, he created *Beware the Creeper* and *Hawk and Dove* for DC Comics.

A man of strong principles, Ditko's objectivistic philosophy found a voice in his later 1970s creations, *Mr. A* and *Avenging World*.

"I never talk about myself. My work is me. I do my best, and if I like it, I hope somebody else likes it, too."

Amazing Fantasy 15 (Spider-Man)
Amazing Spider-Man 1–38 Annuals 1–3, 6
Beware the Creeper 1–6
Blue Beetle 1–5 (Blue Beetle, The Question)
Captain Atom 78–89 (Captain Atom, Blue Beetle, Nightshade)
Dynamo 1 (Dynamo)
Hawk and Dove 1, 2
Mysterious Suspense 1 (The Question)
Nukla 4
Showcase 73 (The Creeper), 75 (Hawk and Dove)
Space Adventures 33–40, 42 (Captain Atom)
Strange Suspense Stories 75–77 (Captain Atom reprints)
Strange Tales 110, 111, 114–147 (Dr. Strange)
Tales of Suspense 47–49 (Iron Man)
Tales to Astonish 61 (Giant-Man), 60–67 (Incredible Hulk)
THUNDER Agents 6, 7, 12, 14, 16, 18 (NoMan, Menthor, Dynamo)

BILL DRAUT

Bill Draut worked for Joe Simon and Jack Kirby in the late 1940s and early 1950s on such comics as *Black Magic, Justice Traps the Guilty, Young Romance,* and other crime, horror, and romance titles. Draut later drew romance stories for Harvey and Marvel in the 1950s, and then for DC in the 1960s.

When editor Joe Simon launched the 1960s Harvey superhero line, he asked Draut to work on some of the new titles (*Jigsaw, Spyman,* etc.).

In the 1970s, Draut inked several DC characters, including Green Lantern, the Creeper, and the Legion of Super Heroes. He also penciled a wide range of stories in the 1970s for DC, including *Jonah Hex* and *Lois Lane*.

Double-Dare Adventures 1 (Bee-Man)
Jigsaw 2
Spyman 3
Teen Titans 18
Unearthly Spectaculars 3 (Jack Frost)

LEE ELIAS

Lee Elias began his comic book career in 1943 drawing Captain Wings, Suicide Smith, Firehair, Space Rangers, and other features for Fiction House comics. In the late 1940s, he worked for Harvey (*Black Cat, Green Hornet*), DC Comics (*Green Lantern, Black Canary*), Hillman, Dell, and Marvel Comics.

After working on several newspaper comic strips in the 1950s, notably *Beyond Mars*, Elias returned to DC Comics in 1959. His best remembered 1960s superhero work was Green Arrow in *Adventure* and *World's Finest*. Elias also drew Cave Carson (*Showcase*), Tommy Tomorrow (*Showcase*), Eclipso (*House of Secrets*), and Adam Strange (*Mystery in Space*) for DC in the 1960s as well.

After a short break, Elias returned to DC Comics in 1972 to draw ghost and horror stories.

Adventure Comics 258–269 (Green Arrow)
Black Cat 63–65 (reprints)
Flash 160
Mystery In Space 92–100, 102 (Adam Strange)
Tales of the Unexpected 91 (Automan)
Teen Titans 15
World's Finest 100–134, 136, 138, 140, 143, 145, 154, 159 (Green Arrow)

BILL ELY

Bill Ely worked at DC Comics on such features as "Larry Steele" and "Johnny Law" for *Detective Comics* in the days before there even was a Superman. He was quickly typecast as a crime and detective comic book artist. For DC Comics, Ely worked on *Gang Busters* and *Mr. District Attorney*. He drew an Ellery Queen strip for Dell Comics in the early 1940s, and contributed stories to Hillman's crime comics in the early 1950s.

Ely did most of his 1950s and 1960s work for DC Comics science fiction and mystery comics like *House of Mystery, House of Secrets, My Greatest Adventure,* and *Tales of the Unexpected*. Although rarely associated with a character or continuing series, Ely did draw the majority of the *Rip Hunter, Timemaster* adventures.

Rip Hunter, Timemaster 8–29
Tales of the Unexpected 94 (Automan)

BILL EVERETT

Bill Everett is best known as the creator of the Sub-Mariner. His underwater "anti-hero" appeared in 1939 in *Marvel Comics* #1—the first Marvel comic book. The idea of a water hero was so appealing that Everett created Hydroman for *Heroic Comics* in 1940 and The Fin in 1941 for Marvel's *Daring Mystery Comics*.

He continued working for Marvel Comics all through the 1940s (with a break for duty in the armed forces) and into the 1950s. From 1950 to 1955, Everett drew dozens of science fiction, horror, and romance stories for Marvel Comics.

After an eight-year sojourn in commercial art, Everett returned to comics in 1964 as the first artist for the new Marvel superhero, *Daredevil*. From 1966–67, he drew Sub-Mariner in *Tales to Astonish* and then later in his own book in 1972.

"I was sort of led into cartooning by my father's wish," Everett remembered in 1970.

Strange Tales #150
©1966 Marvel Entertainment Group, Inc.
Bill Everett.

"My formal art training was never complete. I have to say I was born with the talent . . . and the desire to put something down on paper. I've had a pencil in my hand almost all my life."

Daredevil 1
Strange Tales 148–152 (Dr. Strange)
Tales to Astonish 78–84 (Incredible Hulk)
87–91, 94–96 (Sub-Mariner)

CREIG FLESSEL

Creig Flessel was one of DC Comics' first artists, working there in 1936 when the company was run by Major Malcolm Wheeler-Nicholson and known as "Nicholson Pub. Co."

He drew stories and covers for many of the early issues of *More Fun*, *New Adventure*, and *Detective Comics* ("Some good, some rotten. All done in hurry, with a smoking pen," according to Flessel). His best known comic book works were the 1940s Sandman and Shining Knight stories in *Adventure Comics*.

Throughout the 1940s, he did numerous advertising comic strips for Sunday comic sections as well as other commercial work. "To keep my sanity," Flessel recalled, "I occasionally did a comic book cover or feature." Those other occasional features included several Superboy stories in the 1950s.

As an early DC staff artist, Flessel saw a lot of history made in the offices. "I got to see everybody who came in," he recalled, like "Siegel and Shuster, a couple of kids from Cleveland with this idea of theirs. And everybody said, 'That's for the birds. Who believes in a guy who wears a cape and goes into a phone booth to change his pants?'"

Adventure Comics 248 (Superboy)
Superboy 72, 149

JOHN FORTE

John Forte began drawing comic books in 1942. One of his first assignments was drawing the Destroyer, a Captain America-type superhero written by teenager Stan Lee for Marvel Comics.

In the early to mid-1950s, Forte drew dozens of mystery, romance, and horror stories for Ajax-Farrell, Avon, ACG, Marvel, Orbit, St. John, Trojan, and Superior.

He broke in at DC Comics by drawing romance stories for *Girls' Love Stories* and *Girls' Romances*. By 1961, he moved over to the Superman family of magazines and drew *Jimmy Olsen*, *Lois Lane*, and the totally demented "Tales of the Bizarro World" series in *Adventure Comics*.

In 1962 Forte became the major artist for the new "Legion of Super-Heroes" series in *Adventure Comics*, a job he held until his death in 1965.

Action Comics 279 (Superman), 377 (Legion reprint)
Adventure Comics 286–299 (Bizarro World), 300–312, 314–327, 332–339 (Legion)
Superman 143, 153, 202
Superman's Girlfriend Lois Lane 9, 24, 25, 28, 29, 31, 50, 57
Superman's Pal Jimmy Olsen 56, 58, 59, 61–77, 80, 81, 83–85, 87, 88

BILL FRACCIO

Bill Fraccio spent the better part of his comic book career drawing romance, western, and war comics for Charlton Comics from 1955 to 1967. In 1956, he drew *Mr. Muscles*, one of Charlton's early efforts at a superhero character. In 1964, he helped revive the *Blue Beetle* for a new audience. Two years later, he worked with Tony Tallarico on a short-lived line of monster/superhero comics for Dell (*Wolfman, Frankenstein, Dracula*).

Fraccio began drawing comics in 1943 for Fawcett Publishing (Commando Yank) and Hillman Publications (Iron Ace). He worked for at least ten other comic book publishers in the 1940s and early 1950s, including a four-year stint at Youthful Publications (1949–53) and some romance work for EC Comics in its salad days (1949–50).

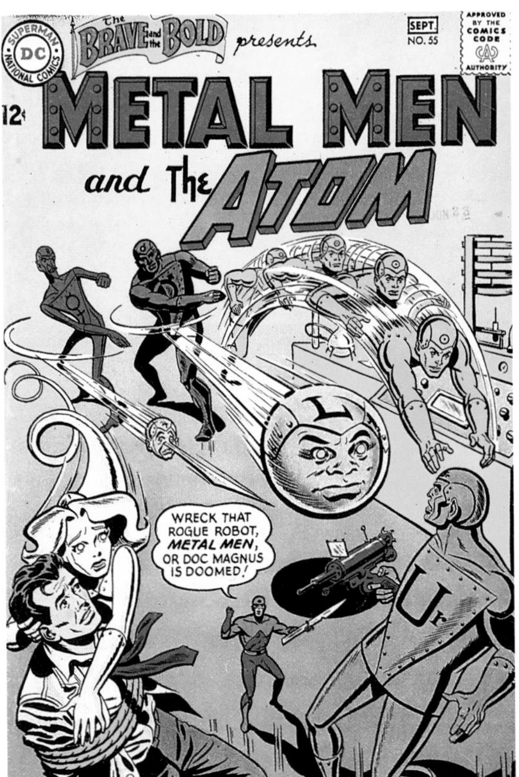

Brave and the Bold #55 ©1964 DC Comics, Inc. Ramona Fradon, Charles Paris.

Adventure Comics #295 ©1962 DC Comics, Inc. John Forte.

Blue Beetle 1–5, 50–54
Mysteries of Unexplored Worlds 46–48 (Son of Vulcan)
Son of Vulcan 49, 50

RAMONA FRADON

Ramona Fradon was one of the few woman artists in the comic book field during the 1960s. She began working for DC Comics in the early 1950s, where she drew Aquaman in *Adventure Comics* for nearly ten years. In 1965, she help create Metamorpho the Element Man.

She left comics for seven years and returned in the 1970s to work on such titles as *Plastic Man, Superman,* and *Super Friends*. In the 1980s, Fradon drew the Brenda Starr newspaper strip.

"I really like drawing characters and characters interacting, but there's none of that

Adventures of the Fly #9, ©1960 Archie Comics. John Giunta, John Giunta.

when you're drawing super heroes. It's all action, which I found to be strenuous." Fradon also observed that "most women artists tend to have a more open style [than men], use less shadow, and work in bigger, open patterns. I think that's probably true—at least I always did."

Adventure Comics 247–280, 282 (Aquaman)
Aquaman 47, 48 (reprints)
Brave and Bold 55 (Metal Men, Atom) 57, 58 (Metamorpho) 59 (Batman, Green Lantern)
Metamorpho 1–4
Showcase 30 (Aquaman)
World's Finest 127–133, 135, 137, 139, 144, 147 (Aquaman)

BOB FUJITANI

Bob Fujitani assembled an impressive line of early 1940s superhero credits: the Black Hood, the Hangman, Shock Gibson, Lash Lightning, Mr. Scarlet, and Catman.

In the late 1950s and early 1960s, he worked for Dell Comics on adaptations of *Prince Valiant, Jungle Jim, Lassie, Sherlock Holmes,* and *King of the Royal Mounted.*

Fujitani drew the first adventures of *Doctor Solar,* Gold Key's premier superhero in 1962. He left comic books in 1963 to work on the daily Flash Gordon newspaper strip.

Doctor Solar 1–5

TOM GILL

Tom Gill began drawing comic book stories in 1943. After World War II, Gill worked at Dell Comics for over 20 years on several western titles. He is best remembered for his longtime work on the *Lone Ranger* comic book in the 1950s and 1960s.

In the mid- and late 1960s, his work appeared in several Gold Key comics, including *The Twilight Zone, Bonanza, Ripley's Believe It or Not,* and *The Owl*—his only superhero work.

The Owl 1, 2

DICK GIORDANO

Dick Giordano worked as an artist for a number of comic book companies, starting with Fiction House in 1951 (*Sheena*). In 1952, he began a 17-year association with Charlton Comics as artist, assistant editor, and editor.

While editor at Charlton, he launched a series of highly regarded superhero titles, including the *Blue Beetle, Judomaster,* and *Peacemaker.* His best remembered 1960s work as an artist for Charlton was the adventure/spy strip, *Sarge Steel.*

Giordano also worked for Dell Comics (1964–66), Archie Comics (1974), and Marvel Comics (1970–75), usually as an inker. In the 1980s, he became managing editor at DC Comics.

Brave and Bold 65 (Flash and Doom Patrol)
Judomaster 91–98 (Sarge Steel)
Nukla 2, 3

JOHN GIUNTA

John Giunta worked as a letterer and colorist for Harry Chesler's comic book studio in 1938. He was later an artist for a number of comic book companies in the 1940s, and also illustrated science fiction magazines during a 33-year period.

Although he worked briefly for Marvel Comics in 1965 (as the inker of a Giant Man story in *Tales to Astonish*), Giunta's major superhero work was for Tower Comics (*THUNDER Agents*) and Archie Comics (*Fly* and *Jaguar*).

Adventures of the Fly 6–10, 27–30
Adventures of the Jaguar 14, 15
Dynamo 1 (Weed)
Laugh Comics 127–136, 138–143 (Jaguar, Fly)
NoMan 1
Pep Comics 150–156, 158, 159 (Jaguar, Fly, Fly Girl)
THUNDER Agents 3–9, 11, 12, 14, 20 (NoMan, Menthor)

JERRY GRANDENETTI

Jerry Grandenetti began his comic book career in 1949. He drew adventure, war, and science fiction stories for Fiction House, Gleason, and DC Comics in the early 1950s. One of his better known features during this time was the "Secret Files of Dr. Drew," an atmospheric horror series which appeared in *Rangers Comics*.

In the 1960s, he was chosen to illustrate another supernatural series, the *Spectre*. Grandenetti's other 1960s work included war stories for Charlton and Tower comics.

Showcase 82 (Nightmaster)
Spectre 6–10
Tales to Astonish 86 (Sub-Mariner)

SID GREENE

Sid Greene began his comic book career in 1941 as an artist in the Lloyd Jacquet comic studio, where he drew features for *Target* comics. After working at Marvel Comics, Holyoke, and Ace Comics, Greene came to DC Comics in 1955.

He drew many science fiction and mystery stories for DC from 1955 to 1964, including the Star Rover series for *Mystery in Space* and *Strange Adventures*. In the 1960s, Greene spent much of his time as one of the principal inkers for the superhero titles edited by Julius Schwartz, such as *Green Lantern* and *Atom*.

Although an acclaimed inker, Greene often expressed a desire to do more penciling. "I feel that, where inking is concerned," Greene stated in 1964, "my job is to complement the pencils with my inking according to the penciler's technique. If you'll notice, my inking of Elongated Man or Batman is, in my opinion, different from the Atom inks."

Detective Comics 358, 361, 365, 378–383 (Elongated Man)
Green Lantern 67

AL HARTLEY

Al Hartley's involvement with the Marvel superheroes began in 1963 when he drew an early Thor story for *Journey Into Mystery*. Hartley also wrote early Iron Man and Giant-Man stories for *Tales of Suspense* and *Tales to Astonish*.

He became an artist at Archie Comics in 1966. Eight years later, he drew a series of Christian comic books featuring the Archie characters which were sold in religious bookstores. In his words, Hartley hoped that the comics would reach young people who "are realizing a lot of values they've been holding onto aren't as lasting as they thought."

Journey into Mystery 90 (Thor)

RUSS HEATH

Russ Heath began working in comic books in 1942 at the age of 17. He was later an assistant on the "Terry and the Pirates" and "Flash Gordon" newspaper strips.

From 1946 to 1957, he drew western, war, and horror comics for Marvel Comics, including *Two-Gun Kid* and *Kid Colt Outlaw*. In the 1960s, Heath is often remembered for his stories in *Our Army at War* and *G.I. Combat*.

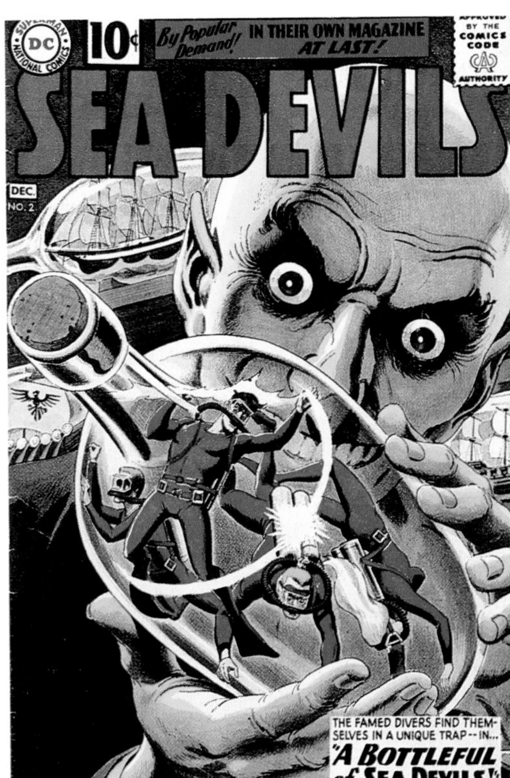

Sea Devils #2 ©1961 DC Comics, Inc. Russ Heath, Jerry Serpe.

X-Men #44 ©1968 Marvel Entertainment Group, Inc. Don Heck, John Tartaglione.

Although he rarely worked in the superhero genre, Heath was the original artist on DC's *Sea Devils*, a costumed team of underwater adventurers.

"A lot of people in the industry knock the work out with the dollar as their only goal," Heath observed. "You know, 'It's only comics.' I thought, 'If I become a hack, will I still be able to do anything good?' So I always try to improve my technique. It cost me a lot of money because that attitude slowed me down, but that's my temperament."

Sea Devils 1–10
Showcase 27–29 (Sea Devils)

DON HECK

Don Heck drew almost every Marvel superhero at one time or another during the 1960s. Along with Jack Kirby and Steve Ditko, Heck was one of the three major Marvel Comics artists of the early 1960s, best remembered for his work on *Iron Man* and the *Avengers*.

Heck began his career in 1952 by drawing horror and mystery stories for Comic Media, Ajax-Farrell, and ME Publishing. From 1961 to 1965, he worked for Gold Key on comic book adaptations of *The Man from UNCLE* and *Voyage to the Bottom of the Sea*. Most of his comic book career, however, was spent at Marvel.

After working at Marvel for over 17 years, Heck went to DC Comics in 1971, where he drew Batgirl and the Flash.

"I left Marvel for a change of pace," Heck recalled. "I kept getting all the new inkers. Everyone who walked in, I got them. A bad inker can kill artwork. I once got some pages back from inking, and I just tore them up, that's how bad they were . . . I would much

Flash #129 ©1962 DC Comics, Inc. Carmine Infantino, Joe Giella.

rather finish my own work. I like to get into the characters. I like to work with the whole feel of the story . . . do the whole drawing."

Avengers 9–15, 17–40 Annuals 1, 2
Captain Marvel 5–10, 16
Journey into Mystery 98–100 (Thor)
Strange Tales 140, 145–148 (Nick Fury)
Tales of Suspense 39, 42, 44–46, 50–72 (Iron Man)
Tales to Astonish 41–43, 45–48 (Ant-Man) 54 (Giant-Man)
X-Men 38–42 (X-Men, Cyclops)

CARMINE INFANTINO

Born in 1925, Infantino's first published comic book work was Jack Frost in a 1942 Marvel comic. By 1946, he was working at DC Comics, where he drew such features as the Green Lantern, Black Canary, and the Flash. After these 1940s heroes were retired, Infantino drew western and science fiction stories for DC Comics in the 1950s. In 1956, he was assigned to draw the Flash in a new version for *Showcase* comics.

Carmine Infantino's artwork on the Flash from 1956 to 1967 helped define the classic look of the Silver Age superhero. His other fondly remembered 1960s feature was Adam Strange, a science fiction romance-adventure series in *Mystery in Space*.

Recalling his working habits, Infantino described his usual approach to a comic book story: "I'd read the script, as a rule, and then I'd rough out the page—lay it out. I'd look at it as a whole and if I didn't like it, I'd change panels—the angles, in and out. Then I'd finish the page. In the beginning, I was fast, but as the years went on, I got slower and slower. A page and a half was the most I could do in a day. Of course, when I say a day, I'm talking about ten or eleven hours. I used to have a reputation as a speed demon, but I really wasn't. I just put more hours into it!"

Brave and Bold 67 (Batman, Flash) 72 (Flash, Spectre)
Detective Comics 327–357, 362, 363, 366, 367, 369 (Batman, Elongated Man)
Flash 105–174, 178, 187 (Flash, Kid Flash)
Green Lantern 53

Atom #18 ©1965 DC Comics, Inc. Gil Kane, Murphy Anderson.

Mystery in Space 53–91 (Adam Strange)
Showcase 4, 8, 13, 14 (Flash)
Strange Adventures 180, 190, 205 (Animal Man, Deadman)

GIL KANE

Gil Kane began his comic book career as a teenager in 1942. He worked for almost all of the major publishers in the 1940s, and spent much of the 1950s drawing science fiction, mystery, and western strips for Marvel and DC comics.

Kane was perhaps DC Comics' quintessential 1960s superhero artist. He drew al-

199, Thor #140, ©1967 Marvel Entertainment Group, Inc. Jack Kirby, Vince Colletta.

most every issue of the new *Green Lantern* and *Atom* and was responsible, along with Carmine Infantino and Murphy Anderson, for developing the 1960s DC superhero "look."

During the 1960s, his superhero work for other companies included Marvel Comics (*Hulk, Captain Marvel*), Tower Comics (*THUNDER Agents*), and Dell Comics (*Brain Boy*).

Kane recalled when he first realized he wanted to be a comic book artist: "I had a feeling for this material [comics], but I had to inform it, I had to learn it. I had to understand anatomy and design and so forth, and once I began to gain a certain amount of control, I found my personality beginning to express itself, and then it became easier. I found a direction for myself, and I knew what I wanted to do. I knew what I had to learn in order to achieve . . . a kind of grace and power. Gymnastics sort of suggest everything I ever wanted to do in my work. A lyricism and strength."

Atom 1–37
Batman 208
Brain Boy 1330
Captain Action 2–5
Captain Marvel 17–19
Detective Comics 368, 370, 372–374, 384, 385, 388–394 (Elongated Man, Batgirl, Batman, Robin)
Green Lantern 1–61, 68–73
Hawk and Dove 3–6
Metal Men 30, 31
NoMan 1
Plastic Man 1
Showcase 22–24 (Green Lantern) 34–36 (Atom)
Strange Adventures 184 (Animal Man)
Tales of Suspense 88–91 (Captain America)
Tales to Astonish 76, 88–91 (Incredible Hulk)
Teen Titans 19, 22–24
THUNDER Agents 1, 5, 14, 16 (Menthor, NoMan, Raven)
Unearthly Spectaculars 2 (Tiger Boy)

JACK KIRBY

Jack Kirby created a universe full of superheroes—Captain America, Incredible Hulk, the Mighty Thor, Iron Man, Giant-Man, the Fantastic Four, the Silver Surfer, and dozens more. He was the most influential superhero comic book artist of the 1960s. He combined a prodigious imagination with peerless technical skill and a huge drive for production. For Marvel Comics alone in the 1960s, he drew over 300 issues of superhero comics—still only a small measure of his lifelong output.

Kirby began drawing comic books in 1939. Two years later, he formed his partnership with Joe Simon, and they created Captain America in 1941. Throughout the 1940s, Kirby worked with Simon on various projects, from drawing superheroes for DC Comics (Boy Commandos, Sandman) to creating the first romance comic book (*Young Romance*).

In the 1950s, Kirby helped launch the Fly and the Shield for Archie Comics and Challengers of the Unknown for DC Comics. He then went over to Marvel and began a successful run of monster and science fiction comics (*Tales to Astonish, Amazing Adventures*, etc.).

From 1961 to 1970, he would turn out thousands of pages of superhero stories for Marvel Comics. Kirby left Marvel to work at DC Comics in 1970. There, he was writer/

editor/artist of nearly a dozen titles, from *Kamandi* to the *New Gods*.

"I write from a people's point of view," Kirby explained. "I write what I know about the next guy and what I know about myself. My characters are always myself. I suppose I must be a lot like Ben Grimm (the Thing from the Fantastic Four). I never duck out of a fight. I don't care what the hell the odds are, and I'm rough at times, but I try to be a decent guy all the time. That's the way I've lived."

Adventure Comics 250–257 (Green Arrow)
Adventures of the Fly 1, 2
Amazing Spider-Man 8 (Human Torch and Spider-Man)
Avengers 1–8 Annual 3
Captain America 100–109, 112
Challengers of the Unknown 1–8
Double Life of Private Strong 1, 2
Fantastic Four 1–93 Annuals 1–7
Fighting American 1
Incredible Hulk 1–5 Annual 2
Journey into Mystery 83–89, 93, 97, 101–125 Annual 1 (Thor, Tales of Asgard)
Showcase 6, 7, 11, 12 (Challengers)
Strange Tales 101–105, 108, 109, 114, 120, 135, 141, 142 Annual 2 (Human Torch, Nick Fury)
Tales of Suspense 40, 41, 43 (Ironman) 59–70, 72–74, 78–86, 92–99 (Captain America)
Tales to Astonish 27, 35–40, 44 (Ant-Man) 49–51 (Giant-Man) 68–70 (Incredible Hulk) 83 (Sub-Mariner)
Thor 126–171 Annual 2 (Thor, Tales of Asgard, The Inhumans)
World's Finest 96–99, 187 (Green Arrow)
X-Men 1–11

JOE KUBERT

Joe Kubert is perhaps best remembered by 1960s comic readers for his work in DC's war comics, like Sgt. Rock in *Our Army At War* and Enemy Ace in *Star Spangled War Stories*. He also drew the first new version of Hawkman for *Brave and the Bold* in 1961. After drawing six issues of the revived Hawkman, Kubert reluctantly relinquished the character in order to concentrate on other projects.

"I started drawing comics when I was about 12 1/2 years old (in 1939), at a time when there were about twenty or thirty comic book publishers. At a time when a kid like myself could go the full rounds of places in an afternoon, hopping from one place to the other trying to get them to purchase some of my art."

Kubert worked for a half dozen publishers before settling down at DC Comics in 1943. For the next seven years, he worked for DC, drawing Hawkman, among other characters. In the early 1950s, he worked on a variety of comics for St. John Publishing, including the Three Stooges, horror stories, and 3-D comic books.

Kubert also drew the Viking Prince in addition to his war stories for DC in the 1950s. In the late 1960s, he left comics to draw the "Tales of the Green Berets" newspaper comic strip. He returned to DC as an editor and artist when the strip ended.

Atom and Hawkman 40, 41 (Hawkman)
Brave and Bold 34–36, 42–44 (Hawkman)
Sea Devils 13
Showcase 25, 26 (Rip Hunter)

Brave and the Bold #34
©1961 DC Comics, Inc.
Joe Kubert.

LARRY LIEBER

Larry Lieber began writing and drawing for Marvel Comics in 1951. In addition to the usual mystery, love, and crime stories, he drew science fiction stories and worked on almost every Marvel western, most notably the *Rawhide Kid*.

He scripted some of the first Thor, Iron Man, Ant-Man, and Human Torch stories in 1962 and 1963. He rarely drew features, but often illustrated science fiction stories for the back pages of *Tales of Suspense*, *Tales to Astonish*, *Journey into Mystery*, etc.

Lieber continued working for Marvel into the 1970s on features like the Living Colossus and the Living Mummy. In the 1980s and 1990s, he was the artist for the *Spider-Man* newspaper strip.

Amazing Spider-Man Annual 4, 5
Marvel Super-Heroes 20 (Dr. Doom)
Tales of Suspense 49–57 (Watcher)
Tales to Astonish 51–58 (The Wasp)
Spectacular Spider-Man 1

FRANK MCLAUGHLIN

Frank McLaughlin began his career at Charlton Comics in 1959 by drawing stories for most of its western comics. From 1966 to 1967, he wrote and drew the adventures of *Judomaster*, one of Charlton's new superheroes.

In the late 1960s and early 1970s, McLaughlin worked as an inker for DC Comics (Flash, Aquaman, Green Arrow, Atom) and Marvel Comics (Captain America, Captain Marvel).

Judomaster 89–98
Thunderbolt 52, 53

AL MCWILLIAMS

Al McWilliams began illustrating pulp magazines and comic books in 1935 at the age of 19. His realistic style was well suited for the many crime and war stories he drew from 1940 to 1952.

McWilliams recalled his first years as a comic book artist for Dell Comics: "I was in the business before the war. Oscar Lebeck was a comic book editor, and it so happened that five or six of his artists lived in Scarsdale. So he'd hand out the work and we'd do it, and we'd then all arrange to meet one day on the turnpike under a big maple tree, and we'd sit there for an hour with the cars parked under the maple tree, exchanging work while he gave us checks. It was a haphazard way of doing business."

Most of McWilliams's comic book work was for Dell and Gold Key comics. His art appeared in such titles as *Tom Corbet, Space Cadet*, *Flash Gordon*, *I Spy*, and *The Man from UNCLE*. McWilliams was also a noted comic strip artist, and worked on *Rip Kirby*, *On Stage*, *Dan Flagg*, *Davy Jones*, *Twin Earths*, *Dateline: Danger!*, and *Star Wars*.

Doctor Solar 20–23 (Dr. Solar)

SHELDON MOLDOFF

Sheldon "Shelly" Moldoff began drawing covers and adventure stories for DC Comics in 1938. Among his more memorable 1940s features was Hawkman for DC's *Flash Comics*.

In the 1950s and 1960s, he drew *Mr. District Attorney* and a few other titles for DC, but most of his career was spent penciling several hundred Batman stories.

"I was there at the very beginning. I worked with Bob Kane when he just started Batman, lettering and backgrounds. I was just out of high school. In 1953, I began working for Kane again, ghosting Batman. Nobody knows Bob better than I."

The most prolific Batman artist of the 1950s and 1960s, Moldoff worked in virtual anonymity from 1953 to 1968 as Bob Kane's ghost artist in both *Batman* and *Detective Comics*. His Batman stories were usually inked by Charles Paris.

Adventure Comics 346 (Legion)
Batman 113–196, 198, 199
Detective Comics 225, 227, 228, 230, 231, 233–239, 241, 242, 244–247, 249–295, 297, 298, 300–307, 309, 310, 312–317, 319–326, 328, 330, 332, 334, 336, 338, 340, 342, 344, 346, 348, 350, 352, 354, 356, 358, 360, 362, 364, 365, 368, 370, 372 (Batman, Aquaman)

JIM MOONEY

Jim Mooney's first comic book work was drawing superheroes like Lash Lightning, Magno, Vulcan, and Captain Courageous for Ace Publishing in 1940.

Mooney spent most of his career at DC Comics from 1947 to 1968. He drew such features as Tommy Tomorrow, Blackhawk, Space Ranger, as well as mystery and science fiction stories.

Mooney's best remembered 1960s superhero work was the Supergirl series in *Action Comics*, a feature he drew for nine years. He also drew dozens of new superheroes for the "Dial H for Hero" series in *House of Mystery*.

During the 1970s, Mooney drew *Spider-Man*, *Ghost Rider*, and *Son of Satan* for Marvel Comics, and also served as an inker on *Sub-Mariner*, *Thor*, *Daredevil*, *Avengers*, and others.

Action Comics 253–342, 344–350, 353–358, 360, 373 (Supergirl, Superman)
Adventure Comics 284 (Aquaman), 328–331, 361 (Legion)
Batman 148, 150, 203 (Batman), 199, 213 (Robin)
Detective Comics 296, 299, 311, 318 (Batman)
House of Mystery 156–170 (Dial "H" for Hero)
Superman 185
Superman's Pal, Jimmy Olsen 92
World's Finest 120–122, 125–130, 132–134, 136–140, 188 (Superman and Batman)
Tales of the Unexpected 40–46, 49 (Space Ranger)

PETE MORISI

Pete Morisi (known as "PAM" to 1960s comic readers) wrote and drew *Thunderbolt*, a Charlton superhero in 1966.

His previous work consisted mostly of crime and western comics for nine different publishers from 1948 to 1955. One of his better known series from that time was his hard-boiled detective stories featuring Johnny Dynamite. Beginning in 1957, Morisi drew western stories for Charlton's *Kid Montana* (which he also wrote), *Billy the Kid*, *Lash Larue*, and *Wyatt Earp*.

World's Finest #79
©1955 DC Comics, Inc.
Win Mortimer.

According to Morisi, *Thunderbolt* was the result of "tortured thinking, late-night artwork, and a burning desire to present a realistic costumed hero to the public."

Judomaster 90 (Thunderbolt)
Thunderbolt 1, 51–56, 58

WIN MORTIMER

From 1945 to 1958, Win Mortimer drew Superman, Superboy, Batman, and a variety of mystery and crime stories for DC Comics. For *Star Spangled Comics* in the late 1940s, he worked on several features, including Robin the Boy Wonder, the Star Spangled Kid, and Merry, the Girl of 1000 Gimmicks.

In the mid-1960s, Mortimer contributed mystery stories to Gold Key titles like *Boris Karloff* and the *Twilight Zone*. He returned to DC Comics in 1967, where he worked on the newly revived *Plastic Man* comic book. In 1969, he drew the Legion of Super-Heroes and Supergirl. Mortimer worked for Marvel Comics in the early 1970s, drawing horror stories and *Night Nurse*.

Action Comics 378–383 (Legion)

Detective Comics #374
©1968 DC Comics, Inc.
Irv Novick.

Adventure Comics 373–381, 383–387 (Legion, Supergirl)
Brave and Bold 64 (Batman)
Doctor Solar 15–27 (Professor Harbringer)
Plastic Man 2–7
Wonder Woman 177

IRV NOVICK

Irving Novick was in on the superhero business from the very beginning. In late 1939, he helped create the Shield, the first patriotic superhero, for MLJ (Archie) Comics. Novick drew other MLJ heroes in the early 1940s, including the Black Hood, the Hangman, and Steel Sterling. From 1940 to 1941, he worked on the first *Green Hornet* comic book.

Novick came to work for DC Comics in the late 1960s, where he drew war stories, including some Sgt. Rock appearances, as well as some superhero stories. In the early 1970s, Novick was one of the principal artists for both Batman and the Flash.

Batman 204–207, 209–212, 214–217
Detective Comics 364 (Elongated Man)
Superman's Girlfriend Lois Lane 82–85, 87, 88, 90, 93, 96, 97
Teen Titans 8–12
Wonder Woman 172–175

JOE ORLANDO

Joe Orlando and Wally Wood formed a comic book art studio in 1950 and sold science fiction stories to publishers like Avon, Youthful, and Ziff-Davis. Orlando later joined Wood at EC Comics, where he continued to draw science fiction and horror stories.

When EC went out of business, Orlando drew science fiction and mystery stories for Marvel Comics in the 1950s, as well as doing some work for *Mad* magazine.

After a period of painting and advertising art, Orlando returned to comics in 1964. He drew horror stories for James Warren's *Creepy* and *Eerie* magazines, and also worked briefly on Marvel's *Daredevil*. In 1966, he became an artist-editor at DC Comics, and helped launch the *Swamp Thing* comic book in 1972.

"My first job in 1949 was on a strip called Chuck White, which was done for a Catholic-oriented series for *Treasure Chest* comics. I was getting something like nine dollars a page for pencils and inks, and the joy of getting that first art check is absolutely unbelievable. I was standing outside the studio with my check, but I also was on cloud nine—I just kept looking at that first real money for artwork. I just got on the first bus that came along, rode up and down 5th Avenue staring at my check and I didn't even care where the bus was going."

Daredevil 2–4
Metamorpho 5–9
Showcase 62, 63 (Inferior Five)
Unearthly Spectaculars 3 (Miracles, Inc.)

TOM PALMER

Tom Palmer learned the basics of the comic book business while working as an assistant to Wally Wood in 1967 on *Jungle Jim*.

He penciled a few Marvel stories in 1968, but the majority of his work has been as an inker. Beginning in 1969 on the *X-Men*, Palmer began an 18-year stretch as an inker for Marvel Comics, where he worked on over 25 titles.

Doctor Strange 171
Marvel Super-Heroes 23 (The Watcher)

GEORGE PAPP

George Papp began working at DC Comics in 1938 by drawing one- and two-page "filler" comic strips. He continued working at DC for the next 28 years (with a 4-year interim for World War II). He drew crime, mystery, and war strips for DC in the 1950s, and worked on *Jimmy Olsen* and the Legion of Superheroes in the 1960s.

Papp is best known for his longtime work on two characters: Green Arrow, which he drew for over 17 years, beginning with the character's first appearance in 1941, and Superboy, which he drew from 1958 to 1968.

Adventure Comics 247–249, 251, 254, 255, 258, 259, 261, 262, 264–267, 269, 270, 272–275, 277, 282, 283, 287–290, 295, 299, 300, 303–310, 312–315, 322, 323, 325, 326, 342, 343, 348, 356, 358 (Green Arrow, Superboy, Legion)
Brave and Bold 71 (Batman, Green Arrow)
Superboy 68–73, 75–79, 81, 83–97, 99–102, 104–146, 148, 156 (Superboy)
Superman 152, 173, 177, 212
Superman's Pal Jimmy Olsen 79, 80, 82, 84, 86, 88, 90, 94
World's Finest 94, 95 (Green Arrow)

AL PLASTINO

Al Plastino, like many young cartoonists of the late 1930s, passed through a series of comic book studio shops. Beginning in 1938 with Harry "A" Chesler, Plastino went on to studios run by Jack Binder, Jerry Iger, and finally Lloyd Jacquet. He worked at Jacquet's shop until 1946 where he drew superhero characters like the Patriot, the Vision, and Captain America.

Plastino landed a job at DC Comics in 1948 by drawing a Superman story. Editor Mort Weisinger liked Plastino's smooth style so much that he made him one of his main Superman artists. For the next 20 years, Plastino worked almost exclusively on all of the Superman titles. He was also the ghost artist on the Batman newspaper strip from 1966 to 1972.

Action Comics 242, 247, 249, 251, 252, 254, 255, 259, 260, 271, 273, 281, 282, 289, 291–294, 296, 299–302, 306, 308, 313, 314, 317, 322-324, 328, 329, 331–335, 337, 340, 341, 345, 354, 361 (Superman, Supergirl)
Superboy 79, 81, 83, 86, 88, 90, 93, 96, 98, 102, 105, 107, 108, 110, 114, 116, 125, 128, 133, 137, 140, 143, 149
Superman 124, 125, 129–131, 133, 135, 136, 138, 139, 144–147, 150–153, 157, 160, 161, 163–165, 169–174, 178–180, 183, 184, 186, 188, 191, 193, 194, 196, 198, 201, 203–207, 212–214, 217, 218, 222
Superman's Girlfriend Lois Lane 5, 12, 18, 20
Superman's Pal Jimmy Olsen 50, 55, 56, 60, 64, 73, 76, 78, 87
World's Finest 165 (Superman and Batman)

BOB POWELL

Bob Powell entered the comic book field in 1938 as an artist and writer in the Will Eisner studio. There, he illustrated Sheena, Queen of the Jungle, and Blackhawk. After World War II, Powell returned to comics and opened his own art studio. He drew stories for Harvey Comics (The Man in Black, Green Hornet, etc.) and Street and Smith (The Shadow, Doc Savage). A versatile artist, Powell turned out an enormous quantity of quality work in the 1950s in almost every genre: horror, romance, war, western, jungle, and superheroes.

Besides his superhero work for Marvel and Harvey Comics in the 1960s, he also worked on a teenage humor title (*Henry Brewster*) and served as art director for *Sick*, a satire magazine in the *Mad* tradition.

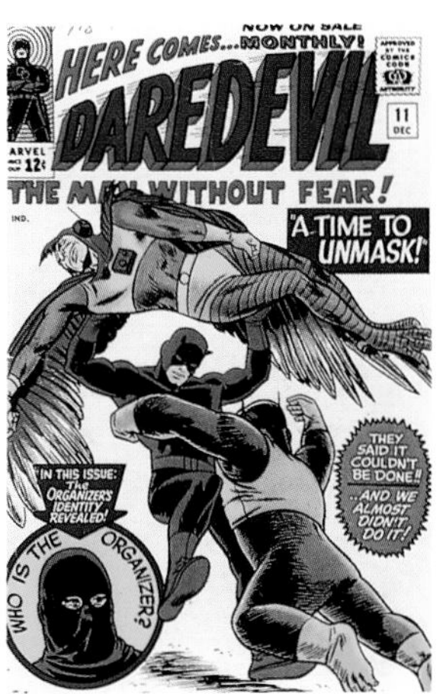

Daredevil #11 ©1965 *Marvel Entertainment Group, Inc.* Bob Powell, Wally Wood.

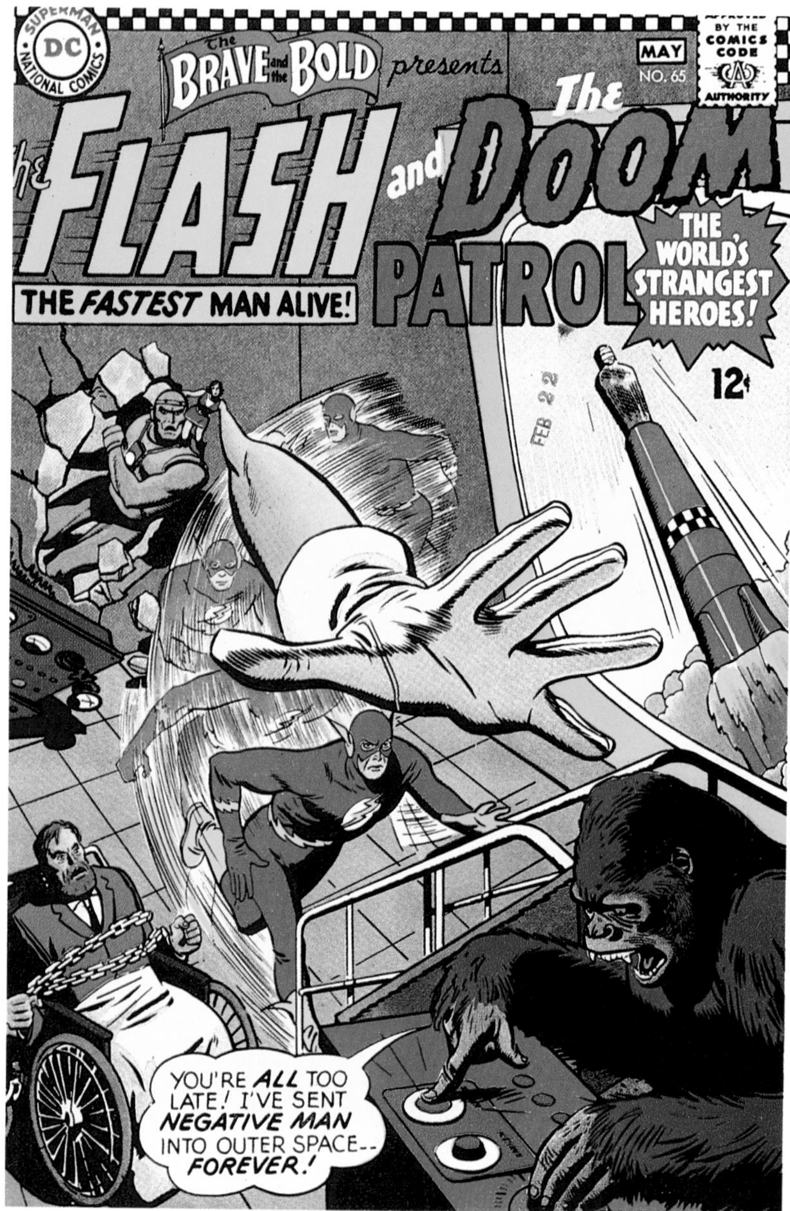

Brave and the Bold #65
©*1966 DC Comics, Inc.*
Bruno Premiani.

Daredevil 9–11
Double-Dare Adventures 1 (Glowing Gladiator)
Strange Tales 130-134 (Thing and Human Torch)
Tales to Astonish 65, 68, 69 (Giant-Man) 73, 74 (Hulk)
Thrill-O-Rama 1 (Man in Black)

BRUNO PREMIANI

Bruno Premiani was an Italian editorial cartoonist before moving to Argentina. For 15 years, he was a cartoonist for that country's leading newspaper and illustrated a series of biographical comics of famous South Americans. His book *El Caballo* ("The Horse") is recognized as the leading reference source for animal anatomy by artists.

Premiani drew crime and western stories for various American comic book publishers in the 1950s before working for DC Comics.

At DC, he drew stories in the early 1960s for *Tomahawk*, *Brave and the Bold* (Cave Carson, Teen Titans), and *My Greatest Adventure*. His most famous comic book work was his five-year stint on the *Doom Patrol*.

A prolific artist outside the comic book field, Premiani listed his leisure time pursuits as "working, studying, and working some more."

Brave and Bold 54, 60 (Teen Titans)
Doom Patrol 86–98, 100–121
My Greatest Adventure 80–85 (Doom Patrol)
Sea Devils 16

HOWARD PURCELL

Howard Purcell worked as a studio animator in the late 1930s and became interested in cartooning for comic books. He worked for DC Comics in the early 1940s on such characters as Green Lantern and Sargon the Sorcerer.

He was a longtime artist on DC's crime comics *Mr. District Attorney* (1948–57) and *Gang Busters* (1950–57). He also drew for several DC science fiction titles in the 1950s.

In addition to his work on a half dozen superhero titles in the 1960s, Purcell also drew stories for DC's romance comics.

Brave and Bold 51 (Hawkman, Aquaman)
Marvel Super-Heroes 17 (Black Knight)
Mystery in Space 96–99, 103 (Space Ranger)
Sea Devils 16–33, 35
Silver Surfer 4, 5, 7 (The Watcher)
Strange Adventures 187, 200 (Enchantress)
Strange Tales 143, 144 (Nick Fury)

PAUL REINMAN

Paul Reinman is remembered by most 1960s comic book readers as the principal artist of Archie Comics' *Mighty Crusaders*, *Shadow*, and *Fly Man*. Reinman drew almost all of the superhero stories for Archie from 1964 to 1967.

Reinman had actually drawn many of the original Archie superheroes as early as 1941 when he worked on the Shield, Wizard, and Steel Sterling. He also drew superheroes for DC Comics (Green Lantern, Atom, Wildcat) and Marvel Comics (Whizzer) in the 1940s.

During the 1950s and 1960s, Reinman drew mystery, western, war, and crime comics for nearly a dozen publishers, including ACG, Charlton, Harvey, Hillman, and Marvel. Some of his last comic book work was as an inker for Marvel Comics in the mid-1970s.

Shadow 2–8
Dynamo 3
Fly Man 31–39 (Fly Man, The Shield, Black Hood, The Web, Steel Sterling)
Mighty Comics 40–50 (Web, Shield, Black Hood, Steel Sterling, Hangman, Mr. Justice, Fox)
Mighty Crusaders 1–7
THUNDER Agents 19 (Dynamo, NoMan)

Brave and the Bold #51 ©1963 DC Comics, Inc. Howard Purcell.

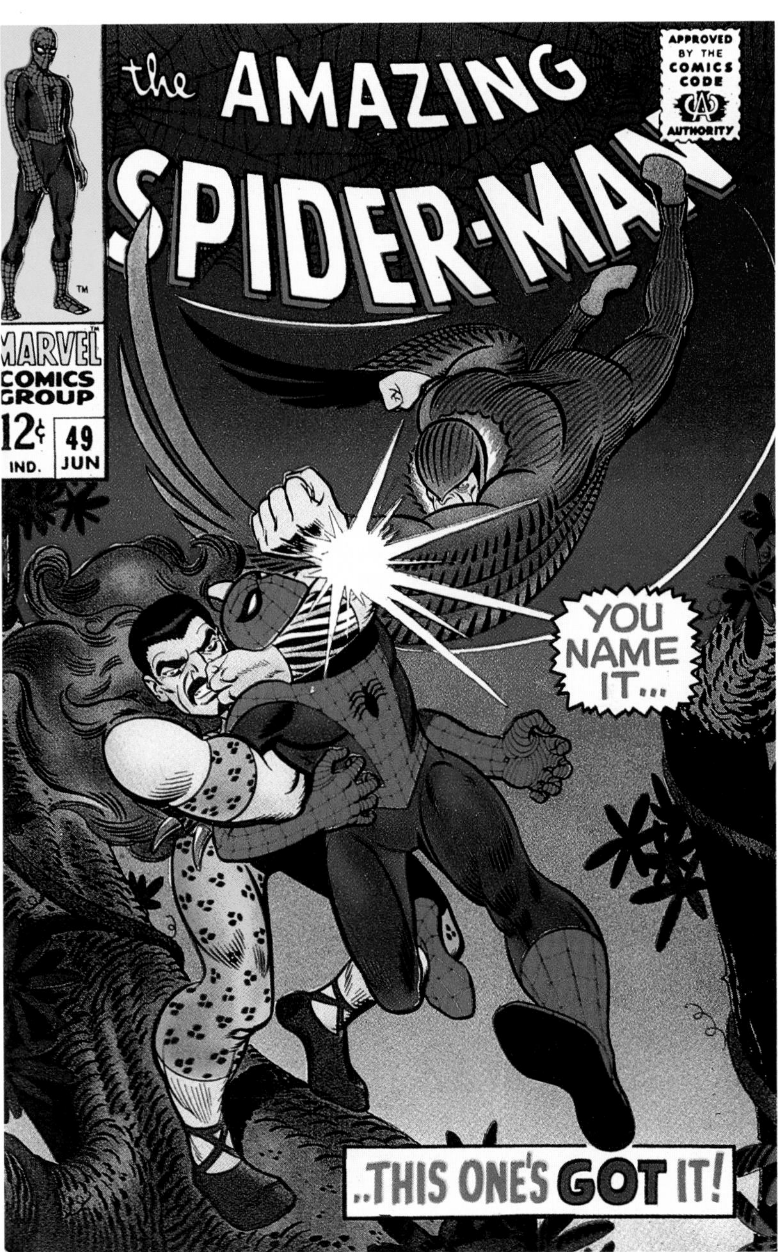

Amazing Spider-Man #49 ©1967 Marvel Entertainment Group, Inc. John Romita.

JOHN ROMITA

John Romita was 19 years old when he began drawing stories for Marvel Comics. "From 1951 to the middle of 1957 I worked for Stan [Lee] and during that time I did everything: mysteries, romance, science fiction, war, westerns—I even did some *Captain America*."

From 1957 to 1965, Romita worked at DC Comics as one of its major romance artists (*Heart Throbs*, *Girls' Romances*, etc.).

He returned to Marvel Comics in 1965 and worked as an inker on the *Avengers* before

Adventures of the Jaguar #10 ©*1962 Archie Comics*. John Rosenberger.

being assigned as the penciler for *Daredevil*. Romita recalled that Jack Kirby helped him lay out his first few stories because "my approach was still a lot like romance books, somewhat sedate. It was a way to teach me storytelling . . . a way of breaking in an unfamiliar artist to their way of thinking."

When Romita's *Daredevil* began picking up in sales, the artist remembered that Stan Lee "asked me to take home a stack of *Spider-Man* books, and to get used to the character, in case I ever had to back it up. I spent the weekend looking them over . . . then, three months later, Steve Ditko is leaving Marvel. Suddenly, I was doing Spider-Man!"

Under Romita, *Spider-Man* became Marvel's bestselling title. He drew most of the stories until 1971, cutting back to become art director for Marvel in 1972.

Amazing Spider-Man 39–79 Annual 3
Captain America 114
Daredevil 12–19
Tales of Suspense 76, 77 (Captain America)
Tales to Astonish 66, 67 (Giant-Man) 77 (Incredible Hulk)
Spectacular Spider-Man 1, 2

JOHN ROSENBERGER

John Rosenberger first worked for Dell Comics in 1940. In the late 1940s and through the 1950s, he drew crime, western, and romance comics for 13 different publishers.

For Archie Comics in the 1960s, Rosenberger drew the majority of the Fly, Fly Girl, and Jaguar stories. Besides superheroes, he also drew stories for *Archie*, *Jughead*, and *Betty and Me*.

Rosenberger's clean and attractive style was also welcomed at DC Comics, where he drew 1960s and 1970s romance comics, as well as the *Lois Lane* series from 1970 to 1972.

Adventures of the Fly 11–28 (Fly, Fly Girl)
Adventures of the Jaguar 1–15
Brave and Bold 63 (Supergirl, Wonder Woman) 69 (Batman, Green Lantern)
Pep Comics 157, 160 (Jaguar, Fly)
Laugh Comics 137, 144 (Fly Girl, Jaguar)
The Shadow 1, 2

WERNER ROTH

Werner Roth's first comic book job was at Marvel Comics in 1950 on its crime and western books. Roth drew stories for Marvel until the company laid off most of its artists in 1957.

He started up his comic book career again in 1961 by drawing romance stories for DC Comics. His first superhero job was penciling Jack Kirby's layouts for the *X-Men*. He eventually took over the X-Men in 1966 and drew it off and on for the next three years. His other 1960s work included Marvel's *Kid Colt Outlaw* and a brief stint on *The Man from UNCLE* comic book. Some of his last work was on the *Lois Lane* comic in 1972.

Tales to Astonish 97, 98 (Sub-Mariner)
X-Men 13–29, 31–33, 35, 42–57

KURT SCHAFFENBERGER

Kurt Schaffenberger drew almost every issue of the *Lois Lane* comic book in the 1960s. His clean, attractive style was so perfectly suited

Superman's Girlfriend Lois Lane #50 ©*1964 DC Comics, Inc*. Kurt Schaffenberger.

for "Superman's Girlfriend" that editor Mort Weisinger soon assigned him the job of drawing Lois's face whenever she appeared in stories drawn by other artists.

Schaffenberger polished his wholesome storytelling approach by working on the Captain Marvel family of comic books all through the 1940s and 1950s. When *Captain Marvel* ceased publication, he produced several educational comic books in the 1950s and later worked for ACG Comics in the 1960s under the name of Lou Wahl. He also drew the Supergirl series for DC in the late 1960s, but his more than two hundred Lois Lane stories is his best remembered work from that time period.

"Otto Binder was the writer of most of the stories I had drawn for Fawcett, and when they folded [in 1953], he moved right over to DC immediately. He was friends with Mort Weisinger (then Superman editor) and he was directly responsible for me coming over in 1957. At the time, they were doing a Lois Lane book as a spin-off of Superman and during the conversation with Mort, Otto brought up my name. At the time, I was on vacation with my family in Maine, and I got a call from Otto telling me he'd recommended me to Mort for this new Lois Lane book. Well, immediately I called Mort from Maine, and he told me to work up some samples and show them to him right away!"

Action Comics 359, 361–372, 374–376 (Supergirl)
Adventure Comics 382–387 (Supergirl)
Superman 124–126, 128, 131, 142, 150
Superman's Girlfriend Lois Lane 1–28, 30–81, 84–88, 94, 95, 97
Superman's Pal Jimmy Olsen 56, 66, 81, 89, 117

MIKE SEKOWSKY

Mike Sekowsky is known to 1960s comic book readers as the *Justice League of America* artist, drawing all of their adventures from 1960 to 1968.

Sekowsky cut his teeth at Marvel Comics in the early 1940s, going back and forth between superhero strips (*Human Torch*, *Captain America*) and humor titles (*Silly Seal and Ziggy Pig*, *Super Rabbit*).

Justice League of America #22 ©1963 DC Comics, Inc. Mike Sekowsky, Murphy Anderson.

In the early 1950s, he drew crime, western, horror, and romance stories for a dozen comic book companies. In 1953, he drew the adventures of *Captain Flash*, one of the first new 1950s superheroes.

Sekowsky spent much of his career at DC Comics, from 1954 to 1972, first as an artist (romance, war, and science fiction), then as a writer and editor.

Atom 38
Brave and Bold 28–30, 66, 68, 76, 87 (Justice League of America, Metamorpho, Metal Men, Batman, Plastic Man, Wonder Woman)

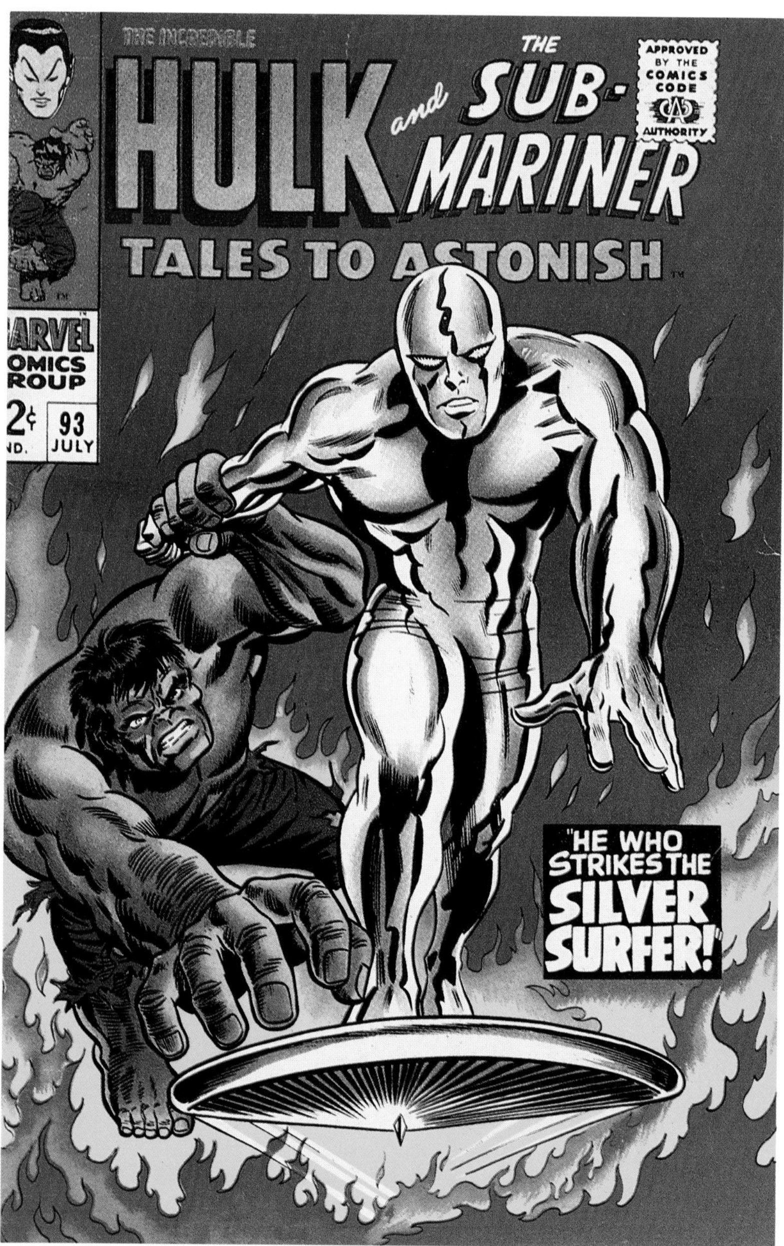

Tales to Astonish #93 ©1967 Marvel Entertainment Group, Inc. Marie Severin, Frank Giacoia.

Detective Comics 371, 374–376 (Elongated Man)
Dynamo 1, 2
Fly Man 34 (The Shield)
Green Lantern 64–66
Justice League of America 1–63, 67, 76
Metal Men 32–41
Mighty Crusaders 2, 7 (Mighty Crusaders, Steel Sterling)
Showcase 17–19 (Adam Strange) 21 (Rip Hunter) 65 (Inferior Five)
THUNDER Agents 1–12, 19 (THUNDER Agents, Menthor, NoMan, Lightning)
Wonder Woman 178–185

JOHN SEVERIN

John Severin entered the comic book field in 1947 and soon became an editor, writer, and artist for *Prize Western Comics*. His most memorable character for Prize was American Eagle, one of the first serious and sympathetic portrayals of the American Indian in a comic book.

Severin joined EC Comics in 1953 and worked on war and adventure books with Harvey Kurtzman, where he further refined his illustrative approach to storytelling.

Throughout the 1950s, he drew mostly western stories for Charlton and Marvel and he also began a long-term association with *Cracked* magazine, a *Mad* magazine imitation.

Severin's realistic penciling more often appeared in straight adventure rather than superhero strips. He worked on Marvel's *Agent of SHIELD* comic book in the 1960s (a nod to the James Bond superspy genre), and also inked several titles, including *Sgt. Fury* and the *Incredible Hulk*. In 1973, he collaborated with his sister Marie on Marvel's *King Kull* comic book.

Strange Tales 136–138 (Nick Fury)

MARIE SEVERIN

Marie Severin, one of two women artists who drew superhero comics in the 1960s, began her career as a colorist in 1953, when she joined her brother, artist John Severin, at EC Comics. After EC went out of business in the mid-1950s, Severin worked for a year and a half in the production department at Marvel Comics before being laid off with almost all the rest of the staff in 1957.

She returned to Marvel in 1964 again as a production worker. Two years later, she was asked to draw illustrations of some Marvel characters for an article in *Esquire* magazine. Shortly afterward, Severin was assigned the Incredible Hulk for *Tales to Astonish* in 1967 and soon started on Dr. Strange for *Strange Tales*.

She also drew several satire stories for Marvel's *Not Brand Echh* and worked on *The Cat* and *King Kull* in the 1970s.

Severin recalled that her artistic influences were "all the old stuff, by Howard Pyle, N.C. Wyeth, the fairy tale artists—I loved that stuff. Growing up, we didn't have TV, and I was discerning enough, probably because of the books available to me, to pick out the good stuff and retain it. I gobbled up everything I could. . . . I think the best kind of artist absorbs everything. The thing is to constantly feed your imagination. If you don't, you're going to fall back, because the style is always evolving. We reflect the period of the day because we are a mirror."

Amazing Spider-Man Annual 5
Incredible Hulk 102–105 Annual 1
Strange Tales 153–160 (Dr. Strange)
Sub-Mariner 9, 12–19
Tales to Astonish 92–101 (Incredible Hulk)

JOHNNY SIKELA

Johnny Sikela began as an art assistant for Superman cocreator Joe Shuster in 1940. He drew Superman stories from 1942 to 1948 for *Action* and *Superman Comics*.

When Superboy received his own comic book in 1949, Sikela was assigned the task of drawing the "Boy of Steel" adventures. For the next eleven years, Sikela drew Superboy in his own comic book and for his series in *Adventure Comics* as well.

Adventure Comics 250, 252, 263, 317–319, 321, 329, 331, 332, 337, 338, 340, 345 (Superboy)
Superboy 69–72, 74–80, 82, 129, 138, 142, 146

JOE SIMON

Joe Simon began his career as a comic book writer, artist, and editor in 1940. He formed a partnership with artist Jack Kirby in 1941, and created *Captain America* for Marvel Comics. In 1942, the Simon-Kirby team created heroes like the Boy Commandos and Newsboy Legion for DC Comics. In the late 1940s and early 1950s, Simon worked with Kirby on such comics as *Young Romance* (the first romance comic book), *Black Magic* (horror), *Headline* (crime), and *Fighting American* (a patriotic superhero). Simon formed his own comic book company in 1954 (Mainline Publications) and published comics for almost two years.

In 1957, Simon joined Harvey Publications to turn out a new line of adventure comics (*Race for the Moon*, *Alarming Tales*, etc). Two years later, he would be at Archie Comics as artist, editor, and writer on a new line of superhero comics consisting of the *Adventures of the Fly* and the *Double Life of Private Strong*. In the mid-1960s, he worked at Harvey Comics again as an artist, editor, and writer on a new line of superhero comics (*Spyman*, *Thrill-O-Rama*, etc.).

Simon returned to DC Comics in 1968 to create a hippie-mannequin-hero called *Brother Power, The Geek*. In 1973, he created other new (and offbeat) hero titles for DC, including *Prez* and the *Green Team*.

Simon recalled his early beginnings in 1940 as a superhero artist: "The pattern was to first invent a hero. And after that, to write the story. Complicated plotting wasn't necessary. Few publishers read the copy. They were

Thrill-O-Rama #1 ©1965 *Harvey Comics*. Joe Simon.

Captain Marvel #11 ©1969 Marvel Entertainment Group, Inc. Barry Smith, Herb Trimpe.

interested in exciting graphics and action. The drawings evolved into a stock format. . . . It wasn't even necessary to draw an open mouth when the character was speaking. Almost always, our comic people spoke through clenched lips."

Adventures of the Fly 2–4
Fighting American 1

JOE SINNOTT

Joe Sinnott began working for Marvel Comics in 1951 when it was a two-room office in New York on 60 Park Avenue. "You'd show up every Friday for a new script," Sinnott recalled, "and it might be a Western, science fiction, detective—you never knew what to expect."

When superheroes became popular in the 1960s, Sinnott drew Thor for *Journey into Mystery* in early 1963. He soon devoted all of his time to inking and worked on almost every Marvel feature in the mid-1960s. In 1965, he began a 15-year run as the principal inker for the *Fantastic Four.*

Sinnott recalled that his favorite Marvel artist to ink in the 1960s was Jack Kirby: "All those years we spent working together were never boring because he made it interesting and fun. Every month I looked forward to receiving that package of art from him and seeing those fantastic pages."

Journey into Mystery 91, 92, 94–96 (Thor)
Strange Tales 139 (Nick Fury)

BARRY SMITH

Barry Smith (later known as Barry Windsor-Smith) was 19 years old and fresh out of art school in England when he came to the United States and landed a job at Marvel Comics in 1968. He worked on several titles with editor and writer Roy Thomas in 1969 before drawing *Conan the Barbarian* (1970–72).

Smith remembered his early work on *Daredevil* at the end of 1968 and the beginning of 1969: "It was just at the time when Stan [Lee] had quit the book and Roy [Thomas] had taken over, and Roy didn't know what the heck to do with Daredevil. It seemed like right from the outset Roy had a trust in me for some reason, so he just left me alone. He just said, 'All right what are you going to do now?' I said, 'I really don't know. I'll do it and show it to you tomorrow.' Which is just what I did. I just made up the story as I went along."

Avengers 66, 67
Daredevil 50–52
Nick Fury, Agent of SHIELD 12
X-Men 53

JACK SPARLING

Jack Sparling was never closely associated with any one character or comic book series, but he certainly got around. "I was born several centuries ago at a drawing board, foresaking the slab only to wed two wives and father three children."

Besides drawing over a half dozen different DC superheroes in the 1960s, Sparling also contributed fantasy and science fiction stories to *House of Mystery*, *Mystery in Space*, and *Strange Adventures*. He also drew *Bomba the Jungle Boy* and Eclipso for *House of Secrets* in the 1960s.

Sparling drew for Harvey, Dell, and Gold Key Comics in the 1960s, including a 1966 *Doc Savage* comic book. In the 1970s, he drew mystery and romance stories for DC Comics.

Beware the Creeper 6
Blackhawk 196
Challengers of the Unknown 64–71
Double-Dare Adventures 1, 2 (Magicmaster, Glowing Gladiator)
Green Lantern 62, 63
Metamorpho 17
Neutro 1
Plastic Man 8–10
Secret Six 3–7
Spectre 9, 10
Strange Adventures 177, 185, 190, 195, 198, 201, 203 (Immortal Man, Animal Man, Split Man)
Tales of Suspense 87 (Captain America)
Thrill-O-Rama 2, 3 (Piranha, Man in Black)
Tiger Girl 1
Unearthly Spectaculars 2 (Jack Frost)
X-Men 30

DICK SPRANG

Dick Sprang drew for pulp magazines and advertising accounts from 1936 to 1940 before beginning his 25-year career at DC Comics. Sprang worked almost exclusively on Batman, and his stories were often inked by Charles Paris.

Sprang's cartoony, yet dynamic, style was perfect for the Batman and Superman stories he did for *World's Finest*—his best work, by his own admission.

"With comics, we have to tell the story in a few pages with a few frames on each page. To do this I found that my best illustrations moved around the characters the way a good director moves the camera around the main actors," Dick Sprang observed in 1989.

"When Batman would be in a fight with some crook and he would strike the crook on the jaw, I didn't stop Batman's fist right at the jaw. I found it was more effective to have Batman's fist strike the jaw, have the arm follow through with appropriate speed lines and then go beyond the jaw. This is the way to activate the frozen frame and simulate a great deal of motion in a static medium."

Batman 113, 114, 123, 125, 127, 129–131, 133, 193, 203 (Batman)
Detective Comics 226, 229, 232, 240, 243, 248, 308 (Batman)
Superman 123
World's Finest 94–108, 110–115, 118, 119, 123, 131, 135, 161, 170, 179, 188 (Superman and Batman)

FRANK SPRINGER

Frank Springer remembered he "started freelancing in 1954 and did everything from straight illustration to big-foot drawing."

Some of his earlier comic book work was done in 1962 when editor L.B. Cole hired him to work on Dell Comics' new line of adventure titles. One of Springer's first comic book assignments was *Brain Boy*, an early 1960s mutant-superhero. Springer's other work for Dell in the 1960s included *Toka, Jungle King* and *Naza*.

He worked at DC Comics from 1967 to 1969 on several titles, including *Batman* and *House of Mystery*, and also drew a few features for Marvel in 1968. In the 1970s, he inked over 30 different characters and titles for both DC and Marvel Comics.

In the 1980s, Springer worked primarily as an inker for Marvel, although he did pencil several issues of *Captain America* and *Spider-Woman*. "If I had to do it over, I'd be a steely-eyed, leather-jacketed, bi-plane pilot."

Batman 203
Brain Boy 2–6

Strange Tales #167 ©*1968 Marvel Entertainment Group, Inc.* Jim Steranko.

Captain Marvel 13, 14
Detective Comics 377 (Batman)
House of Mystery 171, 172 (Dial "H" for Hero)
Nick Fury, Agent of SHIELD 4, 6–11
Secret Six 1, 2

MANNY STALLMAN

Manny Stallman began his 40-plus-year comic book career in the mid-1940s by selling his stories to some of the smallest and most obscure publishers of the time: Bailey, Rural Home, Spotlight, Catholic, Holyoke, and Star.

In the 1950s, Stallman drew crime, horror, romance, and western comics for publishers like DC Comics (*Big Town*, *Mystery In Space*), Marvel (*Strange Tales*), and Harvey Comics (*Teen Age Brides*, *Tomb of Terror*).

His 1960s work was mostly for DC's romance comics (*Heart Throbs*, *Girls' Love Stories*), but he did turn in some superhero work for Tower Comics' *THUNDER Agents*. After leaving DC Comics in 1969, Stallman did commercial artwork, including a 1980s promotional comic book series for a restaurant chain called *Adventures of the Big Boy*.

THUNDER Agents 9–12 (Raven)

JIM STERANKO

Jim Steranko came to the comic book field from an advertising and movie art background. He created three superheroes (Spyman, Golden Gladiator, and Magicmaster) for Harvey Comics in 1966. Later that year, he began inking the Nick Fury SHIELD stories in *Strange Tales*, and then became the series' primary artist until 1968. His other stories for Marvel during this period, *Captain America* and the *X-Men*, were almost cinematic in execution, with their innovative and dynamic layouts. Steranko left the comic book field in 1969 to become a publisher.

When discussing the new look he and other artists brought to comics in the late 1960s, Steranko observed: "From my own point of view, an influence by illustrators from the paperback field on through magazine illustrations, movie posters, and book covers was dominant."

Captain America 110, 111, 113
Nick Fury, Agent of SHIELD 1–3, 5
Strange Tales 151–167 (Nick Fury)
X-Men 50, 51

CHIC STONE

Chic Stone's first comic book story was "Booby Sox," drawn at the age of sixteen in 1939 for Lloyd Jacquet's comic art studio. He drew other humor strips in the 1940s and worked on Fawcett's *Captain Marvel* from 1941–43.

In the 1950s, Stone drew crime, horror,

and romance stories for the American Comics Group, Ace Publications, and Charlton Comics.

From 1964 to 1965, he was Jack Kirby's inker on the *Fantastic Four* and Thor in *Journey into Mystery*. Although Stone penciled a number of superhero stories for Tower Comics in the 1960s, he is often remembered as the artist of Nemesis, a supernatural superhero who appeared in *Adventures into the Unknown* from 1965 to 1967.

In the 1970s and 1980s, most of Stone's work was for Archie Comics, with occasional inking for DC (*Jimmy Olsen*) and Marvel (*Conan*).

Adventures into the Unknown 157–170 (Nemesis)
Batman 163, 197, 200–202 (Batman)
Detective Comics 373, 375, 376 (Batman)
Dynamo 3, 4
NoMan 1, 2 (Lightning)
Sea Devils 34
THUNDER Agents 11, 13–18, 20 (THUNDER Agents, Lightning, Dynamo)

CURT SWAN

Curt Swan was the principal Superman artist for almost 30 years (1955–85). He drew the majority of *all* the covers, as well as nearly 500 stories, for the Superman family of comic books (*Action, Superman, Superboy, Adventure, Jimmy Olsen*, etc.) from the mid-1950s through the 1960s.

Swan began work at DC Comics in 1945 drawing *Boy Commandos*. After working on features like Tommy Tomorrow and Gangbusters, Swan began his Man Of Steel tenure with the 1953 3-D *Superman* comic book. He drew many of the early *Jimmy Olsen* stories and also worked on *Superboy* before becoming the primary artist for *Superman* in 1955.

"I didn't have any conscious models for Superman," Swan remembered. "I wanted to show strength, of course, and ruggedness. And character. He had to be the kind of person you'd want to have on your side. When I drew Clark Kent, on the other hand, I deliberately softened his features, made them less angular than Superman's. I wanted him to appear more meek. Just sort of a good Joe."

Action Comics 244, 256, 265, 269, 270, 272, 277, 278, 280, 283, 284, 286–288, 290, 295, 297, 298, 303–305, 307, 309–312, 318–321, 325–327, 330, 336, 338, 339, 351, 352, 358, 359, 367, 369–372, 374–383 (Superman, Supergirl)
Adventure Comics 249, 257, 279, 280, 284, 285, 293, 301, 302, 313, 320, 327, 328, 330, 334, 336, 340–345, 347, 349–357, 359, 360, 365–372 (Superboy, Legion)
Superboy 73, 80, 89, 91, 98, 100, 103–107, 112, 117, 118, 121, 123, 126, 132, 136, 147, 148, 156

Superman #130 ©1959 DC Comics, Inc. Curt Swan, Stan Kaye.

Superman 127, 130, 137, 139, 147–182, 186, 187, 192–195, 197–199, 201, 207–215, 218–222
Superman's Girlfriend Lois Lane 17, 27, 29, 32, 33, 35–39, 41, 45, 54, 59, 68, 72, 86, 89, 91, 92, 94, 96
Superman's Pal Jimmy Olsen 31–55, 57–72, 74–79, 81–91, 95, 104, 106–114, 116, 119, 121–123, 125
World's Finest 109, 116, 117, 124, 141–160, 162–164, 166–169, 171–173, 177, 178, 184 (Superman and Batman)

TONY TALLARICO

Tony Tallarico was born in 1933. He was both an artist and a writer for Charlton and Dell Comics during the 1960s.

In 1964, Tallarico inked the *Blue Beetle* for Charlton Comics. In the 1960s, he drew *Dracula, Frankenstein,* and the *Wolfman* as superhero characters for Dell Comics.

Dracula 2–4
Frankenstein 2–4
Werewolf 1–3

Marvel Super-Heroes #16 ©*1968 Marvel Entertainment Group, Inc.* Herb Trimpe.

ALEX TOTH

Alex Toth was a high school student when he started freelancing in 1944 for Eastern Color Printing Company, the very first comic book publisher. In 1947, he started working at DC Comics, where he drew the Atom, Dr. Midnight, and the Green Lantern. In the 1950s, Toth drew crime, war, horror, western, and romance comics for a half dozen companies. Rarely associated with any one character or comic book, he did draw several memorable issues of *Zorro* in the late 1950s.

Toth rarely drew superheroes in the 1960s, and his style and storytelling approach was perhaps better suited for the mystery stories he drew for DC Comics, Archie Comics, and Warren Publishing in the 1970s. Toth's keen sense of panel composition, coupled with his economy of line, earned him the title of "the artist's artist."

"Formula is just a way to keep doing the same thing, repeating the same mistakes, and keeps you from growing. If you can throw aside formula, you'll keep developing toward better quality—storytelling—economy. It's hard work. Even if you don't make it, you've tried. I see so many artists accept one way of working, thinking it's as far as they have to go, and stay with it. That's a killer. A real killer."

Brave and Bold 53 (Atom, Flash)
Rip Hunter, Timemaster 6, 7
X-Men 12

SAL TRAPANI

Sal Trapani recalled that he was "hired as a staff artist for the S.M. (Jerry) Iger comic book studio in 1950 and worked there for two years. Quit to go freelance for three years. I went on staff again for Charlton Press in Derby, Connecticut."

For Charlton Comics, he drew mystery, science fiction and adventure stories for nearly seven years. "I quit in 1961 to work with Alex Toth on the Space Angel animation in Hollywood."

In 1964, Trapani returned to comic books and worked for several companies, including American Comics Group, Gold Key, and Dell. For Dell Comics, Trapani drew the first issue of *Nukla*, an atomic-powered superhero, and all four issues of a superhero group known as "The Fab Four" for *Super Heroes*.

Trapani's other noteworthy 1960s superhero work included a seven-issue run of *Metamorpho* for DC Comics.

Brave and Bold 73 (Aquaman, Atom)
House of Mystery 173 (Dial "H" for Hero)
Metamorpho 10–16
Nukla 1
Super Heroes 1–4

HERB TRIMPE

Herb Trimpe started out in 1960 as an assistant to Tom Gill, the artist of the Lone Ranger comic book. Trimpe inked several issues of the *Lone Ranger*, *Lone Ranger's Horse Silver*, and *Bonanza* in the early 1960s.

His experience as a cowboy artist landed him a job at Marvel Comics in 1967 working on *Kid Colt Outlaw*, *Ghost Rider*, and the *Rawhide Kid*. Trimpe became the chief artist on the *Incredible Hulk* in 1968 and drew most of the title's stories for the next seven years.

During the 1970s and the 1980s, Trimpe worked on many comics for Marvel, including the *Avengers*, *Captain America*, *Defenders*, *Godzilla*, *Iron Man*, *Spider-Man*, *Thor*, and *X-Men*.

Incredible Hulk 106–122
Marvel Super-Heroes 16 (Phantom Eagle)
Nick Fury, Agent of SHIELD 13–15

Avengers #48 ©1968 Marvel Entertainment Group, Inc. George Tuska.

GEORGE TUSKA

George Tuska has drawn everything—Buck Rogers, Captain Marvel, Bee-Man, The Fly, Man from UNCLE, Captain America, Godzilla, Two-Gun Kid, Dynamo, G.I. Joe, and dozens and dozens of others. He has worked for at least 28 comic book publishers in his 50-year career.

He became one of the most prolific and capable crime comic artists during the late 1940s and early 1950s, making regular appearances in Lev Gleason's *Crime Does Not Pay* and *Crime and Punishment*.

During the 1960s, Tuska pinch-hit on a half dozen superhero titles, and turned in a two-year run of artwork on Marvel's *Iron Man*. In the 1970s and 1980s, he worked on superhero titles for both Marvel and DC Comics, including *Superman*, *Green Lantern*, *Teen Titans*, and *Luke Cage, Powerman*.

Avengers 48
Double Life of Private Strong 2 (The Shield)
Dynamo 2, 3 (Weed)
Iron Man 5–13, 15–20
Marvel Super-Heroes 19 (Ka-Zar)
Spyman 1
Strange Tales 166 (Dr. Strange)
Tales of Suspense 58 (Watcher) 71 (Captain America)

Herbie #14 ©1965 American Comics Group/ACG. Ogden Whitney.

THUNDER Agents 7, 8, 10, 13–17, 19
(THUNDER Agents, Raven, Dynamo)
X-Men 43–47 (The X-Men, Ice Man)

OGDEN WHITNEY

Ogden Whitney has long been associated with two unlikely characters. He drew the adventures of an aviator superhero called Skyman from 1940 to 1943, and again from 1946–49. Skyman was dashing; his women were beautiful. Then from 1963 to 1967, for the American Comics Group (ACG), Whitney drew the misadventures of "a little fat nothing" called Herbie, a rotund preadolescent who gained supernatural powers by sucking on magical lollipops. For several issues of his comic, Herbie became the Fat Fury, a parody on the popular 1960s superheroes.

Whitney began his comic book career in 1939 at DC Comics, where he drew the Sandman for a short time. From the 1940s to 1960s, he supplied hundreds of romance, western, fantasy, and mystery stories to over a half dozen comic book companies, most notably ACG.

His 1960s superhero work was primarily for Tower Comics' *THUNDER Agents*.

Herbie 14 (Magicman, Nemesis, Fat Fury)
NoMan 1, 2
Strange Tales 149 (Nick Fury)
THUNDER Agents 9, 10, 13, 15, 17, 18
(THUNDER Agents, NoMan)

AL WILLIAMSON

Al Williamson worked as an assistant to Burne Hogarth on the Sunday *Tarzan* newspaper comic in the late 1940s. By the early 1950s, he was drawing western and science fiction stories for comic books like *Forbidden Worlds*, *John Wayne Adventure Comics*, and *Jet Powers*.

During the 1950s, Williamson drew science fiction stories for EC Comics (*Weird Science*, *Weird Fantasy*) as well as western stories for Marvel Comics (*Wyatt Earp*, etc.) and Charlton Comics (*Texas Rangers in Action*, etc.).

In the 1960s, Williamson was able to work on one of his favorite projects, *Flash Gordon*, for King Comics. He also drew fantasy stories for *Creepy* and *Eerie* magazines in the 1960s. He was not tempted to venture into the superhero boom of the time, but he did work with longtime friend Wally Wood on covers for *THUNDER Agents* #10 and *NoMan* #1.

Williamson recalled one of his rare experiences in the superhero genre when he drew the Shield for Archie Comics' *Double Life of Private Strong* in 1959: "Joe Simon called me about it and I penciled it. I did the best I could. Ordinarily I never did that kind of work [superheroes], so I brought it in and he didn't like it. He was very unhappy with first couple of pages. . . . I think he only paid me $30 for those five pages."

Williamson later worked at DC Comics in the 1970s and 1980s, primarily as an inker on many superhero titles, including *Superman*.

Adventures of the Fly 2 (Fly)
Double Life of Private Strong 2 (Shield; partial art only)
Thrill-O-Rama 2 (Clawfang)

WALLY WOOD

Wally Wood has been called the dean of the science fiction comic book artists. He first drew romance and crime comics in the late 1940s before hitting his stride in 1950 and 1951 with stories for comics like *Flying Saucers*, *Strange Worlds*, and *Space Detective*. His reputation was established with EC Comics in the early 1950s on such titles as *Weird Science* and *Weird Fantasy*. After EC folded, Wood drew stories for Marvel, Charlton, Harvey, and DC Comics, where he worked with Jack Kirby on *Challengers of the Unknown*.

Wood inked several issues of 1960s Marvel superheroes and drew (as well as wrote) *Daredevil* for a brief time in 1965. His most fondly remembered 1960s superhero work was for Tower Comics' *THUNDER Agents*.

Wood gradually penciled less and inked more for Marvel and DC Comics throughout the 1960s and 1970s. Toward the end of his life in 1981, he became increasingly bitter and disenchanted with the field he had devoted his life to:

"One day, a few years ago, as I was watching a small boy busily defacing a subway poster, the thought occurred to me, 'That kid's going to grow up to be an art director!' It was only much later that it occurred to me that what I said was based on a glimpse of truth. The world is composed of two kinds of people: those who create things and those who deface them. The latter category includes all editors, art directors, critics, and not a few publishers."

Captain Action 1
Daredevil 5–8
Dynamo 1, 3 (Dynamo) 4 (Weed)
THUNDER Agents 1–8, 10, 15, 17, 20 (THUNDER Agents, Dynamo)
Unearthly Spectaculars 2 (Miracles, Inc.)

BERNI WRIGHTSON

Berni Wrightson is primarily known as the consummate 1970s horror comic artist (*Swamp Thing*, *House of Mystery*). He rarely worked in the superhero genre, although he drew the *Spectre* and the Nightmaster in *Showcase* comics during his first few months at DC Comics in 1969.

After leaving the comic book field in the mid 1970s, Wrightson returned to work on a 1985 X-Men comic (*Heroes for Hope*) whose profits were used to fight world famine.

"No work of art is ever finished," Wrightson once observed, "it is only abandoned."

Showcase 83, 84 (Nightmaster)
Spectre 9

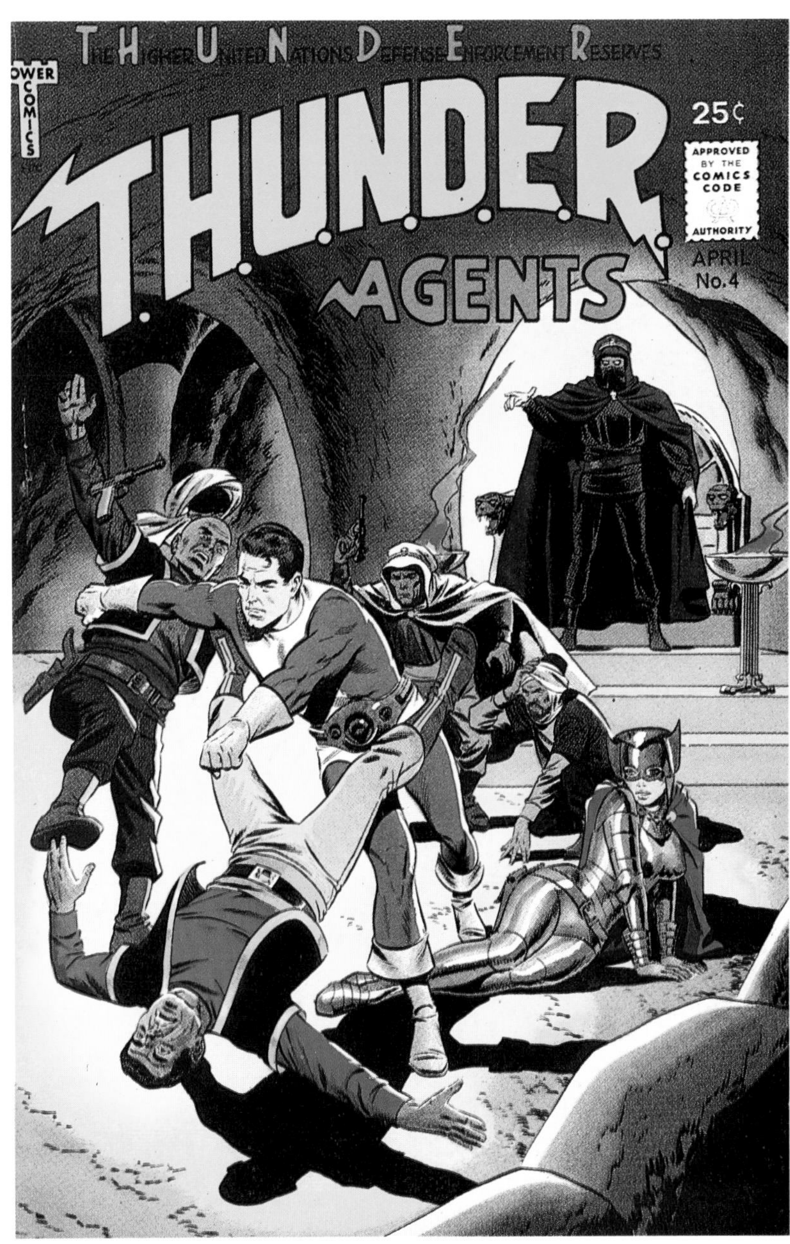

THUNDER Agents #4
©1966 Tower Comics.
Wally Wood.

The Comics

Tales of Suspense #39 ©1963 *Marvel Entertainment Group, Inc.* Don Heck. First appearance of Iron Man.

Nearly 3,500 comic books make up the Silver Age of Superheroes (late 1950s through 1969). What follow are descriptions and a collector's checklist of the 100-plus comic book titles that fall into the Silver Age era.

For each title, two dates are given. The "Publication Date" lists the date and number for both the first and last issues published.

The "Silver Age Date" lists the date and number of what is considered to be the first Silver Age issue for each title. For some long-running titles like *Superman, Batman, Wonder Woman*, etc., the first "Silver Age" issue is determined (and sometimes quite arbitrarily) by a significant change or event in the title which reflected a new editorial approach.

The last Silver Age issue is also listed for each title. Throughout this book, the Silver Age is taken to mean superhero comics published until the end of the 1960s. If a title was published beyond the cutoff date of December 1969, only those issues up to that date are listed as Silver Age issues.

The "Artists" section lists the artists who worked on the title, along with the issue numbers that their art appeared in. If it is not obvious from the title of the book which character the artist drew, then the character's name is listed after the appropriate issue numbers.

The "Significant Issues" listed for each title indicate first appearances of major characters, origin stories, guest appearances by other characters, and important story changes. In short, anything that would make an issue significant to a collector.

Finally, there is a brief description of the title and its contents. When known, writers and creators are listed for the book in this section, along with the other highlights.

Collecting the original Silver Age superhero comic books can be challenging and sometimes expensive. Fortunately, many of the DC and Marvel Silver Age superhero comics have been reprinted in other comic books and in hardback collections. Collectors may wish to obtain these relatively inexpensive reprints before investing in the original issues.

Action Comics #242
©1958 DC Comics, Inc.
Curt Swan, Stan Kaye.

ACTION COMICS

DC Comics

		Issue #s
Published	6/38–	1–
Silver Age	6/58–12/69	241–383

Major Characters
Superman 241–383
Supergirl 252–376
Legion of Super-Heroes 377–383

Significant Issues
241—First appearance of Superman's Fortress of Solitude.
242—First appearance of Braniac, Superman's enemy.
249, 254, 257, 259, 267, 271, 277, 286, 291, 292, 294, 296–298, 309, 317–319, 332, 333, 335, 363–365—Lex Luthor appears.
252—Origin, first appearance of Supergirl. Supergirl series begins; ends #376.
254—First appearance of Bizarro-Superman.
255, 263, 264, 336—Bizarro appears.
255—Supergirl meets Tommy Tomorrow.
261—Origin, first appearance of Streaky the Super Cat.
262—Supergirl's origin retold.
266, 271, 277–292—Streaky appears.
267, 276, 285, 287, 289, 290, 298, 309, 365—Legion of Super-Heroes appear.
276—Supergirl joins Legion of Super-Heroes.
270—Batman and Robin appear at Supergirl's 16th birthday party.
285—Supergirl's presence on earth revealed.
292--First appearance of Comet.
293—Origin, Comet the Superhorse.
294, 300, 301–302, 311, 318, 336, 356—Superhorse appears.
309—Supergirl's parents from Krypton reappear.
310—Jewel Kryptonite.
313, 314, 344—Batman appears.
314—Origin Supergirl reprinted.
314, 364, 366—Justice League of America appears.
334, 347, 360, 373—80-Page Giants; contain reprints.
334, 360—Origin Supergirl reprinted.
344—Batman appears.
350—Batman, Green Lantern, and Green Arrow appear.
377—Legion of Super-Heroes series begins.

Artists
Al Plastino 242, 247, 249, 251, 252, 254, 255, 259, 260, 271, 273, 281, 282, 289, 291–294, 296, 299–302, 306, 308, 313, 314, 317, 322–324, 328, 329, 331–335, 337, 340, 341, 345, 354, 361 (Superman, Supergirl)
Wayne Boring 241, 243, 245, 246, 248, 250, 257, 258, 261–264, 266–268, 275, 276, 342–344, 346, 348–353, 355–357 (Superman)
Curt Swan 244, 256, 265, 269, 270, 272, 277, 278, 280, 283, 284, 286–288, 290, 295, 297, 298, 303–305, 307, 309–312, 318–321, 325–327, 330, 336, 338, 339, 351, 352, 358, 359, 367, 369–372, 374–383 (Superman, Supergirl)
Jim Mooney 253–342, 344–350, 353–358, 360, 373 (Supergirl, Superman)
John Forte 279 (Superman), 377 (Legion reprint)
Kurt Schaffenberger 359, 361–372, 374–376 (Supergirl)
Win Mortimer 378–383 (Legion of Super-Heroes)

The birthplace of Superman in 1938, *Action Comics* has chronicled the Man of Steel's adventures through several generations. Over the years, Superman has changed as editors, writers, and artists came and went. The Superman of the 1950s and 1960s was shaped to a great degree by editor Mort Weisinger, who edited all the *Superman* comic books from 1941 to 1970.

Weisinger and writer Otto Binder introduced many new concepts and characters into the Superman mythos in *Action Comics* beginning in 1958. The first such change occurred when readers first got a glimpse of Superman's Fortress of Solitude. The following issue introduced Braniac, a supervillain who had shrunk the Kryptonian city Kandor into a bottle.

The following year, Weisinger and Binder presented the origin of Supergirl, Superman's super-cousin from Krypton. For the next ten years, Supergirl appeared in every issue of *Action*.

A number of writers worked on the Superman stories (Otto Binder, Jerry Siegel, Bill Finger, Robert Bernstein, Leo Dorfman) and the Supergirl stories (Binder, Siegel, Dorfman), but the guiding hand of Weisinger was evident throughout all of the 1950s and 1960s issues.

ADVENTURE COMICS

DC Comics

	Issue #s
Published 11/38–9/83	32–503
Silver Age 4/58–12/69	247–387

Major Characters

Superboy 247–315 (317–345, 356 reprints)
Green Arrow 247–269
Aquaman 247–280, 282, 284
Tales of Bizarro World 285–299
Legion of Super-Heroes 300–380
Supergirl 381–387

Significant Issues

247—First appearance of Legion of Super-Heroes.
253—Superboy and Robin meet for first time.
256—Origin of Green Arrow retold.
258—Superboy meets young Oliver Queen (Green Arrow).
260—Origin of Aquaman retold.
261—Superboy meets Lois Lane.
262—Origin of Speedy (Green Arrow's sidekick) retold.
265, 266—Superman appears.
267, 282, 290, 293—Legion of Super-Heroes appears.
269—First appearance of Aqualad.
270–283—Congorilla stories appear.
271—Origin of Lex Luthor, as teenager.
275—Origin of Superman–Batman team retold.
276—First appearance of Sun Boy.
278—Supergirl appears.
280—Superboy meets Lori Lemaris.
282—First appearance of Star Boy.
283—First appearance of Phantom Zone.
286—Bizarro World series begins; ends #299.
292, 293, 300, 301, 325, 387—Lex Luthor appears.
293—First appearance of Legion of Super-Pets.
299—First Gold Kryptonite.
300—Legion of Super-Heroes series begins; ends #380.
301—Origin of Bouncing Boy.
303—First appearance of Matter Eater Lad.
304—Lightning Lad dies.
306—First appearance of Legion of Substitute Heroes.
307—Element Lad joins Legion of Super-Heroes.
308—Lightning Lass joins Legion of Super-Heroes.
311, 351—Legion of Substitute Heroes.
312—Lightning Lad returns. Proty dies.
317—Dream Girl joins Legion of Super-Heroes.
327—First appearance of Timber Wolf.
329—Bizarro-Legion of Super-Heroes appear.
346—Karate Kid joins Legion of Super-Heroes.
348—Origin of Sunboy.
351—First appearance of White Witch.
353—Ferro Lad dies.
365—Shadow Lass joins Legion of Super-Heroes.
372—First appearance of Chemical King.
375—First appearance of Quantum Queen.
381—Batgirl appears.
381—Supergirl series begins.

Artists

Al Plastino 247, 253, 256, 268, 271, 276, 278, 281, 286, 292, 294, 296, 298, 324, 333, 335, 341, 344 (Superboy)
George Papp 247–249, 251, 254, 255, 258, 259, 261, 262, 264–267, 269, 270, 272–275, 277, 282, 283, 287–290, 295, 299, 300, 303–310, 312–315, 322, 323, 325, 326, 342, 343, 348, 356, 358 (Green Arrow, Superboy, Legion)
Ramon Fradon 247–280, 282 (Aquaman)
Creig Flessel 248 (Superboy)
Curt Swan 249, 257, 279, 280, 284, 285, 293, 301, 302, 313, 320, 327, 328, 330, 334, 336, 340–345, 347, 349–357, 359, 360, 365–372 (Superboy, Legion)

Adventure Comics #326
©1964 DC Comics, Inc.
Curt Swan, George Klein.

Adventures into the Unknown #154, ©*1964 American Comics Group/ACG.* Pete Costanza.

Johnny Sikela 250, 252, 263, 317–319, 321, 329, 331, 332, 337, 338, 340, 345 (Superboy)
Jack Kirby 250–257 (Green Arrow)
Lee Elias 258–269 (Green Arrow)
Jim Mooney 284 (Aquaman), 328–331, 361 (Legion)
Wayne Boring 285 (Bizarro World)
John Forte 286–299 (Bizarro World), 300–312, 314–327, 332–339(Legion)
Shelly Moldoff 346 (Legion)
Pete Costanza 362–364 (Legion)
Win Mortimer 373–381, 383–387 (Legion, Supergirl)
Kurt Schaffenberger 382–387 (Supergirl)

Adventure Comics has been the home for many superheroes, starting with the Sandman, Hourman, and Starman in the early 1940s. By the 1950s, Superboy had taken over the comics' starring role, and was joined by Aquaman and Green Arrow.

In the late 1950s, editor Mort Weisinger and writer Otto Binder were busy creating a whole new mythology for the Superman family, including *Adventure Comics*. One such creation was the Legion of Super-Heroes, a team of futuristic, super-powered teenagers who first appeared in 1958.

Within a year after introducing the Legion, Weisinger also gave readers new origins for Green Arrow and Aquaman. Aquaman and Green Arrow were later shuttled off to other books to make room for one of Weisinger's more demented series, "Tales of the Bizarro World." On the Bizarro World, everything is opposite than what occurs on earth. Using such reverse logic, Bizarro World has clocks that run backwards, firemen who set fires, and people who are fired when they do a good job at work. Adult readers no doubt saw disturbing similarities between Bizarro World and real life.

The Legion of Super-Heroes replaced the Bizarro World series in issue #300, and eventually pushed Superboy to the back pages. After a successful seven-year run, the Legion moved over to *Action Comics*, and Supergirl became the star of *Adventure Comics* in 1969.

ADVENTURES INTO THE UNKNOWN

American Comics Group/ACG

	Issue #s
Published Fall/48–8/67	1–174
Silver Age 2/65–2/67	154–170

Major Characters
Nemesis 154–170

Significant Issues
154—Origin and first appearance of Nemesis.
Note: Nemesis also appears in *Herbie* #14 (January 1966) and *Forbidden Worlds* #136.

Artists
Pete Costanza 154–156 (Nemesis)
Chic Stone 157–170 (Nemesis)

Adventures into the Unknown was the first regularly published horror comic book. After the 1954 Comics Code prohibited graphic horror scenes in comic books, the title switched over to mild science fiction and supernatural tales for the next ten years. When sales declined in 1965, editor Richard Hughes decided to exploit the growing interest in superheroes.

Writing under one of his many pen names (Shane O'Shea), Hughes and artist Kurt Schaffenberger created Nemesis, a spectral avenger from beyond the grave. The reborn superhero was in the tradition of other "dead" comic book heroes like the Spirit, the Spectre, and Deadman. Ex-detective Steve Flint is killed while pursuing the "Mafia Chief of the United States." He is granted a reprieve from the Unknown by the Grim Reaper and given special powers and a costume so he can fight crime as Nemesis. He can fly, travel through time, grow to giant size, and disappear at will. Although dead, Nemesis still maintains an active relationship with his mortal girlfriend, Lita Revelli Craig.

ADVENTURES OF THE FLY

Archie Comics

	Issue #s
Published 8/59–10/64	1–30
Silver Age 8/59–10/64	1–30

Major Characters
The Fly 1–30
The Shield 2, 4
Fly Girl 19–21, 24, 27, 30

Significant Issues
1—Origin of the Fly.
2, 4, 8, 9—The Shield appears.
3—Origin retold.
7, 10, 29—The Black Hood appears.
9—First appearance of Cat Girl (also see *Adventures of the Jaguar*).
13—First appearance of Kim Brand (later Fly Girl).
14—Origin and first appearance of Fly Girl.
16-25, 27, 29, 30—Fly Girl appears.

23—Jaguar appears.
30—Comet (first 1960s appearance) meets Fly Girl.

Artists
Jack Kirby 1, 2 (Fly)
Dick Ayers 2 (Fly)
Al Williamson 2 (Fly)
Joe Simon 2, 3, 4 (Shield, Fly)
Jack Davis 4 (Fly)
Ted Galindo 4 (Fly)
Sol Brodsky 4 (Fly, Shield)
Bob White 5 (Fly)
John Giunta 6–10, 27–30 (Fly, Fly Girl)
John Rosenberger 11–28 (Fly, Fly Girl)

Adventures of the Fly #19, ©1962 Archie Comics. John Rosenberger.

Tommy Troy is hired by an elderly couple to clean out their attic. The young boy discovers a fly-shaped ring and rubs it. The ring opens a door to another dimension—the World of the Fly People. Turan, an emissary of the Fly People, appears and tells Tommy that because he is "pure of heart," he now has the power to become the Fly by rubbing the ring and saying, "I wish I were the Fly."

As the Fly, Troy's muscles are 100 times stronger than an ordinary human's. He has the power to fly, see in all directions, and crawl up walls. He later acquires a Buzz-Gun and the ability to telepathically communicate with insects.

After the first four issues, Tommy Troy changes from a young boy into an adult attorney. As the Fly, he fights supervillains like the Spider and the Metal Monster. Later, he is joined by Fly Girl who has the same insectlike powers. Both the Fly and Fly Girl can be harmed by the insecticide chlordane. Both also exclaim, "Great Grasshoppers!" when surprised.

Joe Simon created the Fly in 1959 for the new Archie Adventure Series. Artist Jack Kirby originally drew the hero and Simon's studio packaged the first four issues. The rest of the 1960s stories were drawn by John Giunta and John Rosenberg and written by Robert Bernstein (1960–64) and Jerry Siegel (1964).

The series was continued in 1965 as *Fly Man.*

ADVENTURES OF THE JAGUAR

Archie Comics

	Issue #s
Published 9/61–11/63	1–15
Silver Age 9/61–11/63	1–15

Major Characters
Jaguar 1–15

Significant Issues
1—Origin and first appearance.
3—First appearance of Kree-Nal, the Sea Circe from Space.
4, 5, 6, 13, 14—Cat Girl appears.
6, 7—Kree-Nal appears.
13—Origin retold.

Note: Jaguar also appeared in *Pep Comics, Laugh Comics, Adventures of the Fly,* and the *Mighty Crusaders.*

Artists
John Rosenberger 1–15
John Giunta 14, 15

While fleeing from a dinosaur awakened by a jungle earthquake, zoologist Ralph Hardy stumbles into an Incan temple. He discovers a jaguar-skin belt filled with "nucleon-energy." The belt can transform its wearer into a "human jaguar with supreme power over animals everywhere in the universe." Hardy becomes the Jaguar when he wears the belt and says, "The Jaguar!" As the Jaguar, he has the strength of a "million elephants" and can fly through space.

An early 1960s superhero who predated Marvel's *Fantastic Four* by two months, the Jaguar was created and written by Robert Bernstein for the same young readers who were reading the Archie teen comics.

"I am the Jaguar, Master of the Animal Kingdom! My magic powers, given to me by the animal world, are as great as yours. . . perhaps greater!"

Adventures of the Jaguar #6, ©1962 Archie Comics. John Rosenberger.

AMAZING FANTASY

Marvel Comics

	Issue #s
Published 8/62	15
Silver Age 8/62	15

Major Characters
Spider-Man 15

Significant Issue
15—First appearance and origin of Spider-Man.

Artist
Steve Ditko 15

The birthplace of the Amazing Spider-Man, *Amazing Fantasy* was originally called *Amazing Adventures* (June 1961) and featured supernatural and science fiction stories by Jack Kirby and Steve Ditko. Renamed *Amazing Adult Fantasy* with issue #7, the title became an exclusive showcase

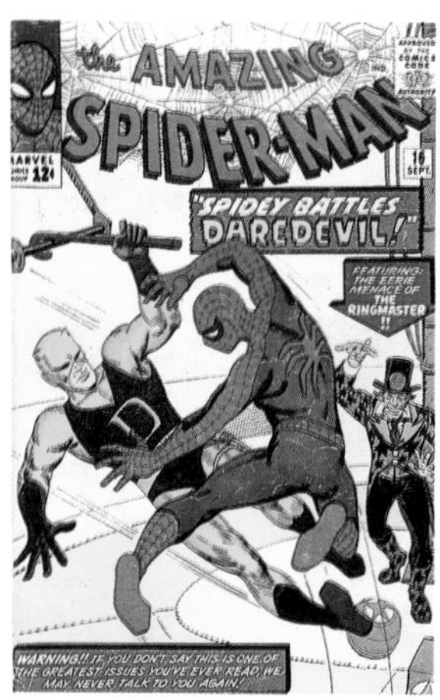

Amazing Spider-Man #16 ©1964 Marvel Entertainment Group, Inc. Steve Ditko.

Aquaman #2 ©1962 DC Comics, Inc. Nick Cardy.

for Stan Lee and Steve Ditko short stories with twist endings. Unfortunately, the word "adult" in the title caused some distribution problems and the title was to be canceled with the 15th issue. The Spider-Man story, according to Stan Lee, was stuck in because they figured it couldn't hurt the book anyway. It turned out that he was absolutely right.

AMAZING SPIDER-MAN

Marvel Comics

		Issue #s
Published	3/63–	1–
Silver Age	3/63–12/69	1–79
		Annuals 1–6

Major Characters

Spider-Man 1–79 Annuals 1–6

Significant Issues

Note: Spider-Man first appears in *Amazing Fantasy* #15 (August 1962).

1—Origin retold. Fantastic Four appears.
3—First appearance and origin of Doctor Octopus. Human Torch appears.
4—First appearance and origin of the Sandman.
5—Dr. Doom appears.
6—First appearance and origin of the Lizard.
8, 17, 19, 21, 77—Human Torch appears.
11, 12, 31, 32, 33, 53–56—Doctor Octopus appears.
14—First appearance of the Green Goblin. Hulk appears.
16, 18, 43—Daredevil appears.
17, 23, 26, 27, 39, 40, 66—Green Goblin appears.
18—Avengers and Fantastic Four appear.
28—Peter Parker graduates from high school.
40—Origin of the Green Goblin.
42—First appearance of Mary Jane Watson, Spider-Man's future wife.
50—First appearance of the Kingpin.
51, 59–61, 68–71—Kingpin appears.
Note: The following issues contain continued stories— #s 17–19, 26, 27, 31–33, 39, 40, 41–43, 44, 45, 48, 49, 50–52, 53–57, 59–61, 63–65, 66, 67, 68–77, 78, 79.

Artists

Steve Ditko 1–38 Annuals 1–3, 6
John Romita 39–79 Annual 3
Larry Lieber Annual 4, 5
Marie Severin Annual 5
Jack Kirby 8 (Human Torch and Spider-Man)

It was a half year before Spider-Man got his own comic book after first appearing in *Amazing Fantasy*. The first four issues were bimonthly, and then the comic became a monthly. Within a few years, Spider-Man was Marvel's most popular superhero.

Stan Lee, who made Spider-Man "the first superhero to wear his neuroses on his sleeve," wrote or scripted all of the 1960s issues. Steve Ditko, who penciled and inked the first 38 issues, also helped plot many of the stories and was cowriter on issues #26–38.

Ditko and Lee developed a full cast of supporting characters: J. Jonah Jameson, Aunt May, Betty Brant, Gwen Stacy, Harry Osborne, as well as a worthy assortment of spider-hating villains: Doctor Octopus, the Vulture, The Lizard, The Sandman, and—most villainous of all—the Green Goblin.

The story and character continually evolved all through the 1960s and into the years beyond. Spider-Man graduates from high school, gains and loses girlfriends, goes off to college, and ends the decade torn between his love for a woman and his destiny as a superhero.

AQUAMAN

DC Comics

		Issue #s
Published	1/62–8/78	1–63
Silver Age	1/62–12/69	1–48

Major Characters

Aquaman 1–48

Significant Issues

11—First appearance of Mera, Aquaman's girlfriend.
18—Justice League of America appears.
18—Marriage of Aquaman and Mera.
23—Birth of Aquababy.
29—First appearance of Ocean Master.
33—First appearance of Aquagirl.
36, 40, 41, 43, 46–48—Aquagirl appears.
48—Origin of Aquaman reprinted.

Artists

Nick Cardy 1–39 (Aquaman)
Jim Aparo 40–48 (Aquaman)
Ramona Fradon 47, 48 (Aquaman—reprints)

After years as a second-string character in the back pages of *World's Finest* and *Adventure Comics*, Aquaman was given his own comic book after a successful four-issue tryout in *Showcase* comics.

The full-length comic book allowed Aquaman to develop more fully as a character, and he finally got an active social life. Within three years, he was married and the proud father of—what else—Aquababy.

ATOM

DC Comics

	Issue #s
Published 6/62–8/68	1–38
Silver Age 6/62–8/68	1–38

Major Characters
Atom 1–38

Significant Issues
7, 31, 37—Hawkman appears.
8—Justice League of America appears.
29, 36—Atom of Earth-Two (1940s) appears.

Artists
Gil Kane 1–37
Mike Sekowsky 38

The Atom became the third new DC superhero in the 1960s to receive his own book, after the Flash and Green Lantern.

Gardner Fox wrote all the stories. Gil Kane, assisted by inkers Murphy Anderson and Sid Greene, drew the first 37 issues.

The comic was retitled *Atom and Hawkman* after issue #38, and the World's Mightiest Mite shared his book with Hawkman and Hawkgirl.

ATOM AND HAWKMAN

DC Comics

	Issue #s
Published 11/69–11/69	39–45
Silver Age 11/68–11/69	39–45

Major Characters
Atom 39–45
Hawkman 39–45

Significant Issues
39—Atom and Hawkman team-up.

Artists
Murphy Anderson 39 (Atom and Hawkman), 43, 44 (Hawkman)
Joe Kubert 40, 41 (Hawkman)
Dick Dillin 40–45 (Atom, Hawkman)

As superhero comics plunged in popularity by the late 1960s, titles were being dropped. When *Hawkman* was canceled, DC moved the character over to the *Atom* comic book and made it a double feature called *Atom and Hawkman*.

After the first issue (#39), each hero had his own half of the book. Gardner Fox and Robert Kanigher wrote most of the stories.

AVENGERS

Marvel Comics

	Issue #s
Published 9/63–	1–
Silver Age 9/63–12/69	1–71
	Annuals 1–3

Major Characters
Avengers 1–71 Annuals 1–3

Significant Issues
1—Origin and first appearance of the Avengers (Thor, Iron Man, Giant-Man, Wasp, and the Hulk).
2—Hulk leaves the Avengers. Ant-Man becomes Giant-Man.
3—Avengers versus the Hulk and Sub-Mariner.
4—First appearance of 1960s Captain America, who joins Avengers.
5, 17—Hulk appears.
11—Spider-Man appears.
16—New Avenger lineup: Captain America, Quicksilver, Scarlet Witch, and Hawkeye.
19—Origin of Hawkeye and the Swordsman.
20—Swordsman becomes a member of the Avengers.
28—Giant-Man becomes Goliath and rejoins Avengers, along with Wasp.
30—Quicksilver and Scarlet Witch leave.
36—Quicksilver and Scarlet Witch return.
39—Captain America leaves.
39–42—Hercules appears.
40—Sub-Mariner appears.
42—Captain America returns.
45—Hercules joins the Avengers.
45, 51—Thor and Ironman appear.
47—Captain America leaves.
48—First appearance of Black Knight (Dane Whitman).
49—Quicksilver and Scarlet Witch leave.
52—Black Panther joins the Avengers.
53—X-Men appear.
56—Captain America appears.
58—Thor, Iron Man, and Captain America appear. Vision joins Avengers.
59—Goliath becomes Yellowjacket.
60—Yellowjacket marries the Wasp.
63—Yellowjacket and Wasp return.

Atom #8 ©1963 DC Comics, Inc. Gil Kane, Murphy Anderson.

Avengers #11 © 1964 Marvel Entertainment Group, Inc. Jack Kirby, Chic Stone.

Batman #139 ©1961 DC Comics, Inc. Bob Kane, Shelly Moldoff.

65—Origin of Hawkeye retold.
71—First appearance of the Invaders. Black Knight joins Avengers.

Artists
Jack Kirby 1–8 Annual 3
Don Heck 9–15, 17–40 Annuals 1, 2
Dick Ayers 16
John Buscema 41–47, 49–62 Annual 2
George Tuska 48
Gene Colan 63–65
Barry Smith 66, 67
Sal Buscema 68–71

The *Avengers* were Marvel's best and brightest superheroes of 1963: Iron Man, Giant-Man, Wasp, Thor, and (for a couple of issues) the Hulk. Soon, the team would be joined by Captain America.

The membership of the Avengers often changed throughout the 1960s. Captain America anchored the title as original members were replaced by secondary heroes from other Marvel comics, such as Quicksilver, Scarlet Witch, and Hawkeye.

Stan Lee and Jack Kirby created the *Avengers*. Lee wrote the comic for its first three years. Roy Thomas succeeded Lee with a run of Avengers adventures that lasted into the early 1970s.

Beware the Creeper #1 ©1968 DC Comics, Inc. Steve Ditko.

BATMAN

DC Comics

	Issue #s
Published Spring/1940–	1–
Silver Age 2/58–12/69	113–217

Major Characters
Batman 113–217

Significant Issues
113—Introduction of science fiction themes in Batman stories.
116, 119, 122, 125, 126, 128, 129, 131, 133, 139, 141, 144, 151, 153, 157, 159, 162,
163—Batwoman appears.
129—Origin of Robin retold.
123, 127, 136, 140, 144, 145, 148, 152, 159, 163, 176, 182, 186, 187, 198, 200, 201, 213—Joker appears.
127—Superman appears.
130—Lex Luthor appears.
131, 145, 154, 159—Batman II and Robin II stories.
139—First appearance of early 1960s Batgirl.
141, 144, 153, 159, 163—Batgirl appears.
155—First 1960s appearance of the Penguin.
164—New Batmobile and updating of Batman with new editor and artists.
169, 200—Penguin appears.
171—First 1960s appearance of the Riddler.
176, 182, 185, 187, 193, 198, 203, 208, 213—Contain reprints; 80-page giant-sized issues.
179—Riddler appears.
197—New Batgirl appears.
198—Origin of Batman reprinted.
200—Origin of Batman and Robin retold.
208—New origin of Batman.
213—New origin of Robin.
217—Batman goes solo as the Dark Detective.

Artists
Shelly Moldoff 113–196, 198, 199
Dick Sprang 113, 114, 123, 125, 127, 129–131, 133, 193, 203
Jim Mooney 148, 150, 203, 199, 213
Chic Stone 163, 197, 200–202
Frank Springer 203
Irv Novick 204–207, 209–212, 214–217
Gil Kane 208
Ross Andru 213

The original Batman of the 1940s was a fist-fighting detective—a down-to-earth, analytical crime fighter. By 1958, however, elements of science fiction—aliens, spaceships, and giant monsters—were creeping into many DC comics. The new science fiction look for the Caped Crusader was introduced in *Batman* #113 in a story called "Batman—Superman of Planet X!"

For the next six years, Batman and Robin battled alien creatures and outer-space crime bosses. Even stranger, Batman himself was often transmogrified, by aliens or failed scientific experiments, into such bizarre creatures as a Giant Bat-Ape, a Zebra Batman, an Invisible Batman, and a Rainbow Batman.

In 1964, editor Julius Schwartz took over the title and restored the Batman character to his original role as a self-assured crime detective—the thinking man's superhero.

Two years later, however, the Batman TV show undid Schwartz's efforts. The comic fell victim to Robin's hip lingo ("Holy Deception! That was a robot Penguin!") and a pop art mentality that dogged it to nearly the end of the 1960s.

BEWARE THE CREEPER

DC Comics

	Issue #s
Published 5/68–3/69	1–6
Silver Age 5/68–3/69	1–6

Major Characters
The Creeper 1–6

Significant Issues
Note: The Creeper first appeared in *Showcase* #73. Other 1960s appearances include *Brave and the Bold* #80 and *Justice League of America* #70.

Artists
Steve Ditko 1–5
Jack Sparling 6

Jack Ryder is a security investigator for TV station WHAM. A Russian scientist who possesses a super-serum has been kidnapped. Ryder tracks the scientist to a costume party, but is discovered by the kidnappers. Ryder uses the scientist's serum to give himself super strength and agility so he can defeat the kidnappers. He decides to continue using his new powers to battle evil. Since he is already wearing a creepy costume he donned for the party, Ryder calls himself the Creeper.

As the Creeper, he can rearrange his molecules to become weightless and invisible like a ghost. Ryder also takes advantage of his unearthly appearance and shrieks in deranged laughter (HA-HA-HA-HA-HA-HA!!!) to terrify his enemies.

Steve Ditko created the Creeper in early 1968 for DC's *Showcase* comics. Proclaimed the "World's Weirdest Hero," the Creeper was somewhat like a darker version of Spider-Man. Hanging off skyscraper ledges like a gargoyle, the Creeper didn't possess the boyish charm of Ditko's Peter Parker—but then again, he didn't need to.

BLACK CAT

Harvey Comics

	Issue #s
Published 10/62–4/63	63–65
Silver Age 10/62–4/63	63–65

Major Characters
Black Cat 63–65

Significant Issues
63—Origin of Black Kitten, the Black Cat's sidekick.

Artist
Lee Elias 63–65 (reprints)

Linda Turner, an actress and movie stunt girl, fights criminals and supervillains as the Black Cat. Her natural athletic abilities and knowledge of judo are her only powers.

Originally appearing in the April 1942 issue of *Speed Comics* and later in her own comic, the Black Cat was one of only a handful of 1940s superheroines. The stories in these 1960s issues were recycled from the original 1940s *Black Cat* comic book and featured new covers by Joe Simon.

Black Cat #63 ©1962 Harvey Features Syndicate. Joe Simon.

BLACKHAWK

DC Comics

	Issue #s
Published Winter 1944–11/84	9–273
Silver Age 1/57–10/68	108–243

Major Characters
Blackhawk 108–243

Significant Issues
108—First issue published by DC Comics.
133—First appearance of Lady Blackhawk.
164, 189, 198—Origin retold.
166, 186—Lady Blackhawk appears.
197—Blackhawks get new uniforms.
203—Origin of Chop Chop.
228—Appearances by Batman, Green Lantern, Flash, and Superman.
230–241—Blackhawks become superheroes with new names and costumes.
242—Return to old Blackhawk uniforms.

Artists
Dick Dillin 108–241
Jack Sparling 196
Gene Colan 211
Pat Boyette 242, 243

The Blackhawks were a team of freedom-fighting aviators who first appeared in *Military Comics* #1 at the beginning of World War II. The multiethnic team of heroes (French, German, Polish, American, Swedish, and Chinese) fought around the world for democracy. Their militaristic uniforms and adventures fit in well during the war and postwar years of the 1940s and in the Korean War years of the early 1950s.

Originally published by Quality Comics, DC Comics acquired the rights to the characters in late 1956 when Quality went out of business. With DC's takeover of the comic, new elements were slowly introduced into the series by writers Arnold Drake, Bob Haney, Ed Herron, and others. Notably, there was now a Lady Blackhawk, although she was more a guest than a regular member. The Blackhawks also got a mascot, "Blackie," a rather ingenious black bird that pulled their fat out of the fire a couple of times.

Blackhawk #117 ©1957 DC Comics, Inc. Dick Dillin, Chuck Cuidera.

Blue Beetle #3 ©1967 Charlton Comics. Steve Ditko.

Brain Boy #3 ©1963 Dell Comics.

The biggest change DC made in the Blackhawks was to introduce science fiction elements into nearly every story. Like just about all the DC heroes in the late 1950s and early 1960s, the Blackhawks fought a plethora of alien monsters and outer space-spawned geeks.

When the science fiction stories faltered, the Blackhawks were transformed into a team of super-powered heroes in 1967 with new identities, costumes, and powers.

BLUE BEETLE

Charlton Comics

	Issue #s
Published 6/64–11/68	1–5, 50–54, 1–5
Silver Age 6/64–11/68	1–5, 50–54, 1–5

Major Characters

Blue Beetle 1–5 (1964–65), 50–54 (1965), 1–5 (1967–68)
The Question 1–5

Significant Issues

1 (1964)—Origin of Dan Garrett as the Blue Beetle.
1 (1967)—First appearance of new Blue Beetle (Ted Kord) by Ditko.
1 (1967)—First appearance of the Question. (Also see Mysterious Suspense.)
2 (1967)—Origin of new Blue Beetle.
5 (1967)—Blue Beetle and The Question team-up.

Artists

Bill Fraccio 1–5, 50–54 (Blue Beetle)
Steve Ditko 1–5 (Blue Beetle, The Question)

The Blue Beetle was one of the first comic book superheroes, appearing in 1939. After a brief revival of the character in the mid-1950s, Charlton Comics brought the Blue Beetle back again in the 1960s.

Archaeologist Dan Garrett discovers a magic blue scarab in an Egyptian tomb. Whenever he holds the scarab and speaks the incantation, "Kaji Dha," he becomes the Blue Beetle and gains super strength and super vision.

The comic was discontinued in 1965, and then revived in 1967 by artist Steve Ditko as a new character. Ted Kord discovers that the previous Blue Beetle (Dan Garrett) has been attacked by Kord's evil uncle. As Garrett dies, Kord promises him that he will carry on the fight for justice as the new Blue Beetle. Kord uses his scientific knowledge to develop a fireproof costume, a Beetle-Gun, and a large beetle-shaped vessel called The Bug, which can fly and travel under water.

Issues 1–5 of the first series (1964–65) and issues 50–53 were written by Joe Gill. Roy Thomas made his second scripting appearance in issue #54. The Blue Beetle stories in the second series (1967–68) were plotted by artist Steve Ditko.

BRAIN BOY

Dell Comics

	Issue #s
Published 4/62–9/63	1330, 2–6
Silver Age 4/62–9/63	1330, 2–6

Major Characters

Brain Boy 1330, 2–6
Mr. Ozimandias 2–6

Significant Issues

1330 (#1)—Origin and first appearance of Brain Boy.

Artists

Gil Kane 1330 (Brain Boy)
Frank Springer 2–6 (Brain Boy, Mr. Ozimandias)

A woman's car crashes into a high-voltage tower. She receives a massive dose of electricity, but survives. Two months later, she gives birth to a son, Matt Price.

As Matt grows up, he discovers he has fantastic mental powers. He can use his mind to lift objects, fly through the air, read the thoughts of others, and even control them with his increased brain power.

"You are frozen solid," Brain Boy tells a crazed dictator. "I take your mind and make it mine! You will keep smiling, keep acting normal, but you will not move!"

Brain Boy uses his powers as a U.S. Secret Service agent. He wears no special costume and needs no weapon, other than his advanced, mutated brain. He is often seen nonchalantly flying through the air in his street clothes.

Brain Boy was the first of the many "mutant" superheroes who appeared in the 1960s, appearing a year before Marvel's X-Men.

BRAVE AND THE BOLD

DC Comics

	Issue #s
Published 8/55–7/83	1–200
Silver Age 2/60–12/69	28–87

Major Characters

Justice League 28–30 Hawkman 34–36,42–44,51,70 Green Arrow 50,71,85 Martian Manhunter 50,56 Aquaman 51,73,82 Atom 53,55,73,77 Flash 53,56,65,67,72,81 Teen Titans 54,60,83 Metal Men 55,66,74 Metamorpho 57,58,66,68 Green Lantern 59,69 Batman 59,64 67–71,74–87 Starman & Black Canary 61,62 Supergirl 63 Wonder Woman 63,78,87 Doom Patrol 65 Spectre 72,75 Plastic Man 76 Deadman 79,86 Creeper 80

Significant Issues

28—First appearance of Justice League of America.
34—First appearance of 1960s Hawkman.
43—Origin of Hawkman.
50—Beginning of team-ups in *Brave and the Bold.*
54—First appearance and origin of Teen Titans.
57—First appearance and origin of Metamorpho.
60—First appearance of new Wonder Girl.
61—Origin of Starman and Black Canary.
74—Batman appears in all remaining issues until end of title.
85—First new costume and update of Green Arrow.

Artists

Mike Sekowsky 28–30, 66, 68, 76, 87 (Justice League of America, Metamorpho, Metal Men, Batman, Plastic Man, Wonder Woman)
Joe Kubert 34–36, 42–44 (Hawkman)
George Roussos 50 (Green Arrow, Martian Manhunter)
Howard Purcell 51 (Hawkman, Aquaman)
Alex Toth 53 (Atom, Flash)
Bruno Premiani 54, 60 (Teen Titans)
Ramona Fradon 55 (Metal Men, Atom) 57, 58 (Metamorpho) 59 (Batman, Green Lantern)
Bernard Bailey 56 (Flash, Martian Manhunter)
Murphy Anderson 61, 62 (Starman and Black Canary)
John Rosenberger 63 (Supergirl, Wonder Woman) 69 (Batman, Green Lantern)
Win Mortimer 64 (Batman, Eclipso)
Dick Giordano 65 (Flash, Doom Patrol)
Carmine Infantino 67 (Batman, Flash) 72 (Flash, Spectre)
Johnny Craig 70 (Batman, Hawkman)
George Papp 71 (Batman, Green Arrow)
Sal Trapani 73 (Aquaman, Atom)
Bob Brown 78 (Batman, Wonder Woman)
Ross Andru 74,75,77 (Metal Men, Batman, Spectre, Atom)
Neal Adams 79–86 (Batman, Deadman, Creeper, Flash, Aquaman, Green Arrow, Teen Titans)

The *Brave and the Bold* was originally an anthology of adventure stories. The early issues featured heroes like Robin Hood, the Silent Knight, and Joe Kubert's dashing and lusty hero, the Viking Prince.

In 1960, DC Comics turned the title into a proving ground for new superheroes, much like *Showcase* had already become. Issue #28 featured the first appearance of the Justice League of America. Other new heroes like Hawkman, Metamorpho, and the Teen Titans also first appeared in *Brave and the Bold.*

By the 50th issue, the comic book became a team-up title for popular DC superheroes. Characters like Atom and Flash or Supergirl and Wonder Woman joined together to battle supervillains and sometimes each other. With the success of the Batman TV show in 1966, the comic became a Batman team-up title. Nearly every imaginable DC comic character (including Sgt. Rock) appeared in a joint appearance with Gotham's Caped Crusader.

Bob Haney wrote almost all of the team-up stories in the 1960s as well as many of the first 24 pre-superhero issues.

Brave and the Bold #59 ©1965 DC Comics, Inc. Gil Kane.

Captain Action #3 ©1969 DC Comics, Inc. Gil Kane, Dick Giordano.

CAPTAIN ACTION

DC Comics

	Issue #s
Published 11/69–6/69	1–5
Silver Age 11/69–6/69	1–5

Major Characters

Captain Action 1–5

Significant Issues

1—Origin of Captain Action. Superman appears.
3—Origin of Dr. Evil
Note: Captain Action first appeared in a 1967 Ideal Toy giveaway comic that came with the action-figure doll. Art was by Kurt Schaffenberger.

Artists

Wally Wood 1
Gil Kane 2–5

Archaeologist Clive Arno discovers ancient coins in Spain bearing the faces of Greek, Norse, Hindu,

Captain America #100 ©1968 Marvel Entertainment Group, Inc. Jack Kirby, Syd Shores.

Captain Atom #87 ©1967 Charlton Comics. Steve Ditko, Rocke Mastroserio.

Captain Marvel #1, ©1966 M.F. Enterprises. Carl Burgos, Leon Francho.

and Aztec gods. When he holds a coin, he gains the power of the god pictured on it. He devises a costume, returns to America to fight crime, and makes his son, Carl, his sidekick, Action Boy.

Captain Action's archenemy, Dr. Evil, is also his father-in-law who is now a radioactive, blue-skinned supervillain. "Hear me, all of mankind. I am Dr. Evil. I have no hatred for you. Indeed, I have no feeling at all toward you, save you are an outmoded evolutionary step. I am the first of my kind, and it is my destiny to usher in the new higher level of existence where mind reigns supreme. Humanity is a blemish upon nature and I shall remove it!"

Based on a 1966 action-figure doll from Ideal Toys, *Captain Action* was originally written by Jim Shooter under the editorship of Mort Weisinger. After Shooter's two-issue origin tale, Gil Kane wrote issues 3–5 and penciled issues 2–5 (with inking by Wally Wood). Julius Schwartz began his editorship of the title with the third issue.

CAPTAIN AMERICA

Marvel Comics

		Issue #s
Published	4/68–	100–
Silver Age	4/68–12/69	100–120

Major Characters
Captain America 100–120

Significant Issues
100—Avengers, Sub-Mariner appear in a flashback.
101–104, 114–119—Red Skull appears.
109—Origin of Captain America.
110—Hulk appears.
112—Origin retold.
113, 114, 116—Avengers appear.
117—First appearance of the Falcon.
118–120—Falcon appears.

Artists
Jack Kirby 100–109, 112
Jim Steranko 110, 111, 113
John Romita 114
John Buscema 115
Gene Colan 116–120

Captain America joined Iron Man as a cofeature in *Tales of Suspense* #59 in 1964. Four years and 41 issues later, he took over the title when Iron Man was given his own comic book. Jack Kirby, cocreator of the original 1940s Captain America and principal artist for the *Tales of Suspense* series, continued drawing the character for the first ten issues of his new book. Stan Lee scripted all the 1960s issues. In 1969, Lee introduced another black superhero, the Falcon, who later became Captain America's partner.

CAPTAIN ATOM

Charlton Comics

		Issue #s
Published	12/65–12/67	78–89
Silver Age	12/65–12/67	78–89

Major Characters
Captain Atom 78–89
Blue Beetle 83–86
Nightshade 87–89

Significant Issues
82—First appearance of Nightshade.
83–84—Two-part story. Captain Atom's powers are reduced.
87–88—Origin of Nightshade.

Artists
Steve Ditko 78–89 (Captain Atom, Blue Beetle)
Jim Aparo 87–89 (Nightshade)

Steve Ditko first drew Captain Atom in 1960 for *Space Adventures*, two years before first working on Spider-Man. In 1966, Ditko returned to Charlton and gave readers a new version of the space-age superhero. The longer stories took a turn for the better under the editorship of Dick Giordano with issue #82. Issue #s 78–81 were written by Joe Gill and issue #s 82–89 were written by Dave Kaler with Steve Ditko.

The comic also featured Blue Beetle stories by Steve Ditko and Gary Friedrich. Nightshade, a martial-arts-trained superheroine, was introduced as first a foe and later a sidekick of Captain Atom. Written by Dave Kaler, Nightshade was one of the first liberated 1960s superheroines.

CAPTAIN MARVEL

Marvel Comics

		Issue #s
Published	5/68–5/79	1–62
Silver Age	5/68–12/69	1–19

Major Characters
Captain Marvel 1–19

Significant Issues
4—Sub-Mariner appears.

14—Iron Man appears.
17—New costume.
Note: Captain Marvel first appears in *Marvel Super-Heroes* #12 (December 1967).

Artists
Gene Colan 1–4
Don Heck 5–10, 16
Dick Ayers 11, 12
Frank Springer 13, 14
Tom Sutton 15
Gil Kane 17–19

Mar-Vell is a member of a super-scientific alien race called the Kree. He is sent to earth as the commander of a space crew which will decide if earth is a potential threat to the Kree Empire. While on earth, he grows to like the human race. His sympathy incurs him the wrath of a Kree political faction. He disavows his Kree heritage and decides to use his super strength to become earth's defender.

Rick Jones, the teenager who used to be the Hulk's buddy and Captain America's would-be sidekick, now becomes mixed up—literally—with Captain Marvel. For a period of time, Rick Jones and Captain Marvel switch bodies whenever the teenager claps his "nega-band" bracelets together.

Captain Marvel first appeared in 1967, the last 1960s superhero created by Stan Lee. Roy Thomas, Arnold Drake, Gary Friedrich, and Archie Goodwin all wrote stories for the 1960s series. The title went through a half dozen art teams in 18 months, a couple of refinements on the character's origin, as well as a change in costume. Small wonder that readers were often confused as to who the "real" Captain Marvel was.

The title suspended publication with the December 1969 issue, was published briefly in 1970, and then went through another major revision and incarnation in 1972.

CAPTAIN MARVEL

M.F. Enterprises

	Issue #s
Published 4/66–9/67	1–5
Silver Age 4/66–9/67	1–5

Major Characters
Captain Marvel 1–5

Significant Issues
1—Origin and first appearance of Captain Marvel (1966).
5—Retitled as *Captain Marvel Presents the Terrible 5.*
Note: This version of Captain Marvel also appears in *Captain Marvel Presents the Terrible 5* #1 (August 1966).

Artists
Carl Burgos 1–5 (Captain Marvel)

"I'll fight you all at once!" Captain Marvel yells at the four villains. He says the magic word, "Split!" and suddenly his arms, legs, and head all fly off from his body and chase after the different villains. Now he says the magic word, "Xam!" and his body parts reattach themselves.

Captain Marvel was a little weird for a superhero, but perhaps that's because he was originally an android invented by scientists on another world to preserve the peace. The alien scientists are too late, however, to save their own world. As Captain Marvel heads to earth, his planet explodes. "From 1,000 miles up, I watched the planet I was born on disintegrate into a million pieces!"

He arrives on earth and adopts the secret identity of Roger Winkle, archaeology professor. Besides being able to split off any part of his body down to his fingertips, he also has laser-beam vision and jet-propelled booties.

Created by Carl Burgos, the original artist and writer of the 1940s Human Torch, this Captain Marvel was primarily an attempt to capitalize on the 1960s superhero fad by exploiting the name of the original 1940s Captain Marvel.

CHALLENGERS OF THE UNKNOWN

DC Comics

	Issue #s
Published 4/58/–6/78	1–87
Silver Age 4/58–12/69	1–71

Major Characters
Challengers of the Unknown 1–71

Significant Issues
Note: Origin and first apppearance of Challengers in *Showcase* #6 (January 1957).
14—Origin and first appearance of the Challengers' archenemy, Multi-Man.
15, 20, 24, 30, 34, 40, 42, 45, 48, 55, 61—Multi-Man appears.
18, 21, 25, 32—Cosmo, the Challengers' space pet appears.
27, 32—Volcano Man appears.
31—Origin retold and expanded.

Captain Marvel #14 ©1969 Marvel Entertainment Group, Inc. Frank Springer, Vince Colleta.

Challengers of the Unknown #34 ©1963 DC Comics, Inc. Bob Brown.

Daredevil #44 ©1968 Marvel Entertainment Group, Inc. Gene Colan, Jim Steranko.

34—Origin and first appearance of Multi-Woman.
43—Challengers get new yellow uniforms.
48—Doom Patrol appears.
51—Sea Devils appear.
64, 65—Reprints Challenger origin in two parts.

Artists
Jack Kirby 1–8, 64, 65
Bob Brown 9–63
Jack Sparling 64–71

Four men are flying to appear on a radio program called "Heroes." They are Rocky Davis (Olympic wrestling champion), Professor Haley (master skin diver), Red Ryan (circus daredevil), and Ace Morgan (war hero and fearless jet pilot). A storm, however, causes their plane to violently crash-land.

"When the echoes of the crash have faded into the cool night air, there is no sign of life in the gloomy silence surrounding the wreckage! Then, amid the torn and twisted metal of the smashed plane, come faint stirrings. One by one, the men crawl from the shadows of the wreck—miraculously alive!"

"We should be dead but we're not," says Red.

"Borrowed time—we're living on borrowed time," observes Ace.

"Somehow I feel that too!" added the professor. "And I'm not scared—in fact, I might enjoy taking a few more risks!"

"Well," offered Ace, "there's no reason why we can't do it together—challenge the unknown!"

"Win or lose," Rocky nodded, "it sounds great to me! Count me in!"

The Challengers of the Unknown were a team of born-again, heroic daredevils who readily risked their lives for science and justice. Arnold Drake and Ed Herron wrote most of the stories through the mid-1960s. Other writers included Bill Finger, Robert Kanigher, Bob Haney, and Dennis O'Neil.

CHARLTON PREMIERE

Charlton Comics

	Issue #s
Published 9/67–5/68	Vol 2 #1–4
Silver Age 9/67–5/68	Vol 2 #1–4

Major Characters
The Shape 1
Tyro Team 1
Spookman 1
Sinestro 3

Significant Issues
1—Origin and first apperance of the Shape, Tyro Team, and Spookman.
3—Blue Beetle and Peacemaker appear.

Artists
Pat Boyette 1 (Spookman)
Bill Montes 1 (Tyro Team)
Grass Green 1 (The Shape)
Henry Scarpelli 3 (Sinestro)

Charlton Comics introduced three new superheroes in the first issue of this "tryout" title. The Shape was a plastic-pliable hero created in the laboratory of Professor Scuba S. Duba. The Shape can take on any form—a basketball, a sword, a horse—even a sportscar convertible.

The Tyro Team was a group of three college students who communicated with each other by mental telepathy. They become costumed crime-busters who must juggle thug-bashing with their collegiate lives of cram-studying and homecoming dates.

Spookman, the last hero, was originally archaeologist Aaron Piper, who discovers a moonstone amulet which gives him superstrong powers. He travels back in time to Nero's Rome with his sidekick Crispin X. Crispin.

The third issue featured Sinestro, Boy Fiend, a supervillain type of character, who meets up with two other Charlton heroes, the Blue Beetle and the Peacemaker.

Issue #s 2 and 4 do not contain superhero stories.

DAREDEVIL

Marvel Comics

	Issue #s
Published 4/64–	1–
Silver Age 4/64–12/69	1–59
	Annual 1

Major Characters
Daredevil 1–59 Annual 1

Significant Issues
1—Origin and first appearance of Daredevil.
2, 36–38—Fantastic Four appear.
7—Daredevil gets new costume.
7—Sub-Mariner appears.
12–14, 24—Ka-Zar appears.
16, 17, 27, 54—Spider-Man appears.
30—Thor appears.

35—Invisible Girl appears.
36–38—Dr. Doom appears.
43—Daredevil versus Captain America.
43, 53—Origin retold.
51—Captain America appears.
52—Black Panther appears.
57—Daredevil reveals secret identity to girlfriend Karen Page.

Artists
Bill Everett 1
Joe Orlando 2–4
Wally Wood 5–8
Bob Powell 9–11
John Romita 12–19
Gene Colan 20–49, 53–59 Annual 1
Barry Smith 50–52

Daredevil was the last major new Marvel superhero of the early 1960s. Stan Lee created the blind superhero and wrote almost all of the first fifty issues. Roy Thomas wrote the remainder of the 1960s issues.

After a series of costume changes and art teams, the title settled into a long run of stories by Gene Colan, who remained the Daredevil artist until 1973.

DETECTIVE COMICS

DC Comics

	Issue #s
Published 3/37–	1–
Silver Age 11/55–12/69	225–394

Major Characters
Batman 225–394
Martian Manhunter 225–326
Aquaman 293–300
Elongated Man 327–383
Batgirl 385, 388, 389, 392, 393
Robin 384, 386, 390, 391, 394

Significant Issues
225—First appearance of the Martian Manhunter.
226—Origin of Martian Manhunter continued.
231, 287—Origin of Martian Manhunter retold.
233—Origin and first appearance of Batwoman.
235, 265—Origin of Batman retold.
246—First appearance of Diane Meade, girlfriend of Martian Manhunter.
250—Science fiction themes begin in Batman.
249, 276, 285, 286, 292, 302, 307, 309, 311, 318, 321, 325—Batwoman appears.
267—Origin and first appearance of Bat-Mite.
311— First appearance of Martian Manhunter's sidekick, Zook.
322—Batgirl appears.
326—"Death" of John Jones, Martian Manhunter's alter ego.
327—New Batman begins with change of editors and artists.
327—Elongated Man strip begins; ends #383.
328—Death of Alfred, Batman's butler and confidant.
331, 343—Batman and Elongated Man team up.
351—Elongated Man gets new uniform.
356—Alfred resurrected.
332, 341, 365, 388—Joker appears.
350—Green Lantern appears.
359—First appearance and origin of new Batgirl.
362, 373—Riddler appears.
363, 369, 371—New Batgirl appears.
368—Atom appears.
387—Reprints first Batman story from 1939.
384, 386, 390, 391, 394—Robin stories.
385, 388, 389, 392, 393—Batgirl stories.

Artists
Joe Certa 225–326 (Martian Manhunter)
Shelly Moldoff 225, 227, 228, 230, 231, 233–239, 241, 242, 244–247, 249–295, 297, 298, 300–307, 309, 310, 312–317, 319–326, 328, 330, 332, 334, 336, 338, 340, 342, 344, 346, 348, 350, 352, 354, 356, 358, 360, 362, 364, 365, 368, 370, 372 (Batman, Aquaman)
Nick Cardy 293–296, 298–300 (Aquaman)
Jim Mooney 296, 299, 311, 318 (Batman)
Dick Sprang 226, 229, 232, 240, 243, 248, 308 (Batman)
Carmine Infantino 327–357, 362, 363, 366, 367, 369 (Batman, Elongated Man)
Murphy Anderson 357, 359, 360, 377 (Elongated Man)
Sid Greene 358, 361, 365, 378–383 (Elongated Man)
Irv Novick 364 (Elongated Man)
Gil Kane 368, 370, 372–374, 384, 385, 388–394 (Elongated Man, Batgirl, Batman, Robin)
Neal Adams 369 (Elongated Man)
Mike Sekowsky 371, 374–376 (Elongated Man)
Chic Stone 373, 375, 376 (Batman)
Frank Springer 377 (Batman)
Bob Bown 378–394 (Batman)
Ross Andru 386 (Robin)

Detective Comics #303
©1962 DC Comics, Inc.
Bob Kane, Shelly Moldoff.

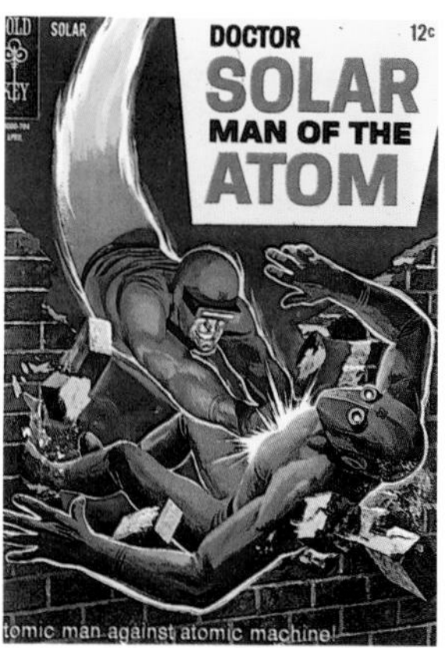

Doctor Solar #5 ©1963 *Western Publishing Co.*

Doctor Strange #171 ©1969 *Marvel Entertainment Group, Inc.* Dan Adkins.

Detective Comics was one of the first DC comics, and its initials (DC) eventually became part of the company's name. The first 26 issues featured ordinary crime-fighting detectives like Larry Steele and Flat Foot Flanigan. Batman first appeared in May 1939 and was joined by Robin a year later.

By late 1957, science fiction elements were being introduced into all the comics edited by Jack Schiff, including *Batman* and *Detective Comics*. With issue #250, the new science fiction look was established when Batman and Robin battled outer-space aliens on the planet Skar. The next issue featured "The Alien Batman," and for the next six years, *Detective Comics* relied heavily upon bug-eyed monsters and science fiction plots.

With issue #327, Julius Schwartz began editing the title and introduced a "new look" for Batman which featured new art, a new costume, and the old detective approach to stories and villains. This new look lasted until the end of the 1960s, although later issues reflected the influence of the Batman TV show.

Other costumed detectives shared the title with Batman. J'onn J'onzz, the Martian Manhunter, first appeared in 1955, and his series lasted until 1964. He was replaced by the Elongated Man, the "world's first stretchable sleuth," whose stories appeared in *Detective*'s back pages from 1964 to 1969.

DOCTOR SOLAR

Gold Key

	Issue #s
Published 10/62–3/82	1–31
Silver Age 10/62–4/69	1–27

Major Characters
Dr. Solar 1–27
Professor Harbringer 2–27

Significant Issues
1—Origin and first appearance of Dr. Solar.
2—Professor Harbringer series begins.
5—Dr. Solar dons a superhero costume.
15—Origin retold.
20–23—Continued storyline.

Artists
Bob Fujitani 1–5
Frank Bolle 6–19
Al McWilliams 20–23
Ernie Colan 24–26
José Delbo 27
Mel Crawford 2–14 (Professor Harbringer)
Win. Mortimer 15–27 (Professor Harbringer)

"The fiery impact of a premature atomic explosion engulfs Dr. Solar during a secret energy-to-matter experiment at Atom Valley. He is converted into atomic energy and hurtled into space. But though Dr. Solar has been converted to pure energy, his conscious mind has not been stilled. . . ."

The nuclear scientist discovers he can convert his body back and forth between matter and energy. He is a glowing, radioactive being—"a walking atomic power plant!"

With such power must come isolation: "Because of my radioactivity, I must remain isolated from the world and avoid all human contact for more than a few minutes!"

To boost his atomic powers, Dr. Solar gulps down cobalt pills and swallows liquified radioactive isotopes. Later, he develops a red-cowled, cadmium-lined bodysuit with a transluscent visor to contain his deadly radioactive rays.

Like many other Gold Key comics, the covers of Dr. Solar were painted—not drawn. Science fiction illustrator Richard Powers painted the first two covers, while J.P. Sternberg and George Wilson painted later covers.

Writers included Paul Newman (responsible for many of the stories after #5), Dick Wood, Marshall McClintock, and Otto Binder.

DOCTOR STRANGE

Marvel Comics

	Issue #s
Published 6/68–2/87	169–183, 1–81
Silver Age 6/68–11/69	169–183

Major Characters
Dr. Strange 169–183

Significant Issues
169—Origin of Dr. Strange retold.
177—New costume.
178—Black Knight appears.
179—Spider-Man appears. (Reprint from Amazing Spider-Man Annual 2).

Artists
Dan Adkins 169, 170
Tom Palmer 171
Gene Colan 172–178, 180–183
Steve Ditko 179 (Spiderman reprint)

After years as a secondary feature in *Strange Tales*, Dr. Strange took over the title in 1968. The comic was renamed *Doctor Strange* with issue #169.

Roy Thomas, who had written Dr. Strange

almost a year ago for *Strange Tales*, wrote the stories for the series until its end in 1969.

DOOM PATROL

DC Comics

	Issue #s
Published 3/64–6/73	86–124
Silver Age 3/64–9/68	86–121

Major Characters
Doom Patrol 86–121
Robotman 100, 101, 103, 105
Negative Man 106, 107, 109, 111
Beast Boy 112–114

Significant Issues
86—Origin of Doom Patrol retold. First appearance of the Brotherhood of Evil.
88—Origin of the Chief.
91—First appearance of Mento.
93—Origin retold.
92, 97, 102, 104, 106–113, 116, 119, 120—Appearances by Mento.
99—First appearance of Beast Boy.
100—Origin of Beast Boy.
101, 102—Appearances by Challengers of the Unknown.
102–113, 116, 118–120—Appearances by Beast Boy.
104—Elasti-Girl marries Mento. Justice League of America appears.
121—The Doom Patrol is destroyed. Elasti-Girl, Negative Man, and the Chief die.

Artists
Bruno Premiani 86–98, 100–121
Bob Brown 94, 98, 99

The Doom Patrol premiered in *My Greatest Adventure*. The writing by Arnold Drake and the artwork by Bruno Premiani was so well received that the Doom Patrol took over the title with issue #86.

The Doom Patrol began when Niles Caulder, a wheelchair-bound scientific genius (also known as "the Chief"), summoned "three victims of a cruel and fantastic fate" to join him in turning their handicaps into assets. The three victims were: Larry Trainor, an experimental rocket plane pilot, who was blasted by cosmic rays so that now his body splits into a "radio wave figure" of negative energy (Negative Man); Cliff Steele, a daredevil racer whose brain is transferred to a robot body after a near-fatal crash (Robotman); and Rita Farr, an actress who is exposed to dangerous chemical vapors which allow her to shrink or grow at will (Elasti-Girl).

Later characters included Mento (who became Elasti-Girl's husband) and Beast Boy (later known as the Changling). Writer Drake remembered that Beast Boy was added because "we wanted a character who could assume many different animal forms, and also wanted a kid in the strip, someone the kids could relate to."

As sales dropped in 1968, Drake ended the series with a dramatic flourish: He killed the characters in the last issue.

Doom Patrol #112 ©*1967 DC Comics, Inc.* Bruno Premiani.

DOUBLE LIFE OF PRIVATE STRONG

Archie Comics

	Issue #s
Published 6/59–8/59	1, 2
Silver Age 6/59–8/59	1, 2

Major Characters
The Shield 1, 2

Significant Issues
1—Origin and first appearance of the Shield.
1, 2—Tommy Troy (alter ego of the Fly) appears.

Artists
Jack Kirby 1, 2
George Tuska 2
Al Williamson/Larry Ivie 2

Lancelot Strong grew up as a child in a plastic germ-free bubble. His father, a research scientist, stimulated his son with "microelectricity" in order to make him a superbeing. When his father is destroyed by communists who want his scientific secrets, Lancelot is adopted by a kindly farm couple.

As he grows up, Lancelot discovers his father's experiments with microelectricity have given him unusual powers. He can see in the dark, hurl bolts of lightning, leap as "far as a cannonball," and move fast enough to dodge bullets. Drafted by the army, Private Strong assumes a secret identity as the Shield to battle super bad guys like Doctor Diablo.

According to Joe Simon, Archie publisher John Goldwater asked him to "Give me a cross between the Shield (of the 1940s) and Captain America." Working with his old partner Jack Kirby, the two came up with the *Double Life of Private Strong*.

Double Life of Private Strong #2 ©*1959 Archie Comics*. Jack Kirby, Joe Simon.

Double-Dare Adventures #1, ©1966 Harvey Publications. Joe Simon, Jack Sparling.

Dracula #2 ©1966 Dell Comics, Inc. Tony Tallarico.

DOUBLE-DARE ADVENTURES

Harvey Publications

	Issue #s
Published 12/66–3/67	1, 2
Silver Age 12/66–3/67	1, 2

Major Characters
B-Man 1, 2
Glowing Gladiator 1, 2
Magicmaster 1, 2

Significant Issues
1—Origin and first appearance of B-Man, Glowing Gladiator, and Magicmaster.

Artists
Bob Powell 1 (Glowing Gladiator)
Jack Sparling 1, 2 (Magicmaster, Glowing Gladiator)
Bill Draut 1 (Bee-Man)
Dick Ayers 2 (Bee-Man)

This giant-sized comic book contained reprints of science fiction stories by Jack Kirby and Al Williamson, as well as three original 1960s superheroes. Jim Steranko created the first two: Magicmaster and the Glowing Gladiator.

Magicmaster possesses a mystic dagger which allows him to fly and conjure up objects. The magician superhero was reminiscent of a 1940s Fawcett hero, Ibis the Invincible, who wielded a mystic Ibis Stick.

The Glowing Gladiator gains his powers from the magic Amulet of Hannibal. The Glowing Gladiator possesses the Sword of Hercules, "the ultimate weapon, for by mere mental command, it has the power to change into any armament!"

B-Man, the third hero, was written by longtime author Otto Binder. Astronaut Barry E. Eames is attacked by a swarm of Martian bees from a synthetic meteorite sent by would-be alien invaders. The alien venom turns Eames into an insect-powered superhero, B-Man but it also makes him dependent upon Martian honey to stay alive. The Martian invaders use B-Man to terrorize the Earth in exchange for his honey dose. "The day is not far away when insects will indeed rule the humans of Earth. You will fulfill the duties of our worker bees. You will become our slaves. Any questions?" Fortunately, B-Man is rescued from the Martians by the "F.Bee.I." in the second issue.

DRACULA

Dell Comics

	Issue #s
Published 11/66–3/67	2–4
Silver Age 11/66–3/67	2–4

Major Characters
Dracula 2–4

Significant Issues
2—Origin and first appearance of Dracula.
4—Origin and first appearance of Fleeta.

Artists
Tony Tallarico 2–4

Count Dracula, a descendant of the original Dracula, is a millionaire scientist who hopes to clear his family's name by discovering a cure for brain damage. He concocts a serum from bat brains, but when he tests the potion by drinking it (yum!), it gives him the power to turn into a bat at will.

The scientist decides to use his new talent for the good of mankind: "I pledge by the strange powers which have become mine to fight against injustice, corruption, evil and greed which fills this earth in the hopes that somehow my example will be an example to all men."

By the last issue, Dracula got some help in fighting evil, greed, corruption, and injustice in America. He was joined by another superbat creature, a female assistant (B.B. Beebe) known as Fleeta.

DYNAMO

Tower Comics

	Issue #s
Published 8/66–6/67	1–4
Silver Age 8/66–6/67	1–4

Major Characters
Dynamo 1–4
Weed 1–4

Significant Issues
1—NoMan and Lightning appear.

Artists
Wally Wood 1, 3, 4 (Dynamo)
Reed Crandall 1 (Dynamo)
Mike Sekowsky 1, 2 (Dynamo)
Steve Ditko 1 (Dynamo) 4 (Weed)
Dan Adkins 2, 4 (Dynamo)

Dick Ayers 2 (Dynamo)
Paul Reinman 3 (Dynamo)
Chic Stone 3, 4 (Dynamo)
John Giunta 1 (Weed)
George Tuska 2, 3 (Weed)

Leonard Brown is a paper pusher in the administration department at THUNDER headquarters, a United Nations defense agency. He is suddenly summoned to THUNDER's secret inner council and asked to become a special agent.

"Because of your physical stamina, you've been selected to use the *Thunderbelt* . . . It will change your body's atomic structure . . . Put it on!"

Brown puts on the belt and a special uniform. When he turns the dial on his Thunderbelt, he becomes Dynamo—"the strongest man alive!" As a THUNDER Agent, Dynamo must fight all sorts of international terrorists. One of the first, and most persistent, is the Iron Maiden, a beautiful woman seemingly poured into a suit of armor. She is first a foe and later a secret friend—half of a real love-hate relationship: "My patience is limited!" she snarls at the captured Dynamo. "I command you to tell me why you wore that belt!" "I thought you would have guessed by now sister . . . to hold up my pants!"

Dynamo was the most popular member of Tower's *THUNDER Agents*, appearing in its first issue in 1965. He received his own comic book a year later. Wally Wood created Dynamo and drew many of his adventures. Stories were written by Leonard Brown (the character's namesake) and Larry Ivie.

FANTASTIC FOUR

Marvel Comics

	Issue #s
Published 11/61–	1–
Silver Age 11/61–12/69	1–93
	Annuals 1–7

Major Characters
Fantastic Four 1–93 Annuals 1–7

Significant Issues
1—Origin and first appearance of Fantastic Four.
3—Fantastic Four get costumes and a headquarters.
4—First appearance of 1960s Sub-Mariner.
5—First appearance of Dr. Doom.
6—Fantastic Four versus Dr. Doom and Sub-Mariner.
9, 14, 27, 33, Annual #1—Sub-Mariner appears.
10, 16, 17, 23, 56–60, 84–87, Annual #s 2, 3—Dr. Doom appears.
11—Origin retold.
12, 25, 26—Hulk appears.
13—First appearance of the Watcher.
17—Ant-Man appears.
22—Invisible Girl gains new powers.
25, 26—Avengers appear.
27—Dr. Strange appears.
28—X-Men appear.
39–40—Daredevil appears.
44–47, 54, 56, 57, 59–64, 82, 83, Annual #5—Inhumans appear.
48—First appearance of Silver Surfer.
49, 50, 55–61, 72, 74–77, Annual #5—Silver Surfer appears.
52—First appearance of Black Panther.
53—Origin of Black Panther.
54, Annual #5—Black Panther appears.
73—Daredevil, Thor, and Spider-Man appear.
80—Sue (Invisible Girl) becomes inactive member.
81–95—Crystal joins Fantastic Four.
95—Sue (Invisible Girl) becomes an active member again.
Annual 1—Origin of Sub-Mariner.
Annual 2—Origin of Dr. Doom.
Annual 3—Reed Richards (Mr. Fantastic) and Sue Storm (Invisible Girl) are married. Avengers, Spider-Man, Daredevil, X-Men, and Nick Fury appear.
Annual 6—Birth of Franklin Richards.

Artists
Jack Kirby 1–93 Annuals 1–7

Mr. Fantastic, Invisible Girl, Human Torch, and The Thing made up the group known as the Fantastic Four. Created by writer Stan Lee and artist Jack Kirby, they were the first superheroes, in Lee's words, that were made of "flesh and blood."

The *Fantastic Four* was Marvel's best-selling comic book in the early and mid-1960s, and every Marvel superhero made an obligatory guest appearance in its pages at one time or another. Characters which first appeared in the *Fantastic Four* and then received their own comic books included the Sub-Mariner, Silver Surfer, Black Panther, and the Inhumans.

Lee and Kirby worked on every 1960s issue of the *Fantastic Four*. Kirby's artwork was inked by a variety of people during the title's first three years, from letterer Artie Simek to production manager Sol Harrison, as well as artists Larry

Dynamo #4, ©1967 Tower Comics. Wally Wood.

Fantastic Four #25 ©1964 Marvel Entertainment Group, Inc. Jack Kirby, George Roussos.

Fatman,The Human Flying Saucer ©1967 Milson Publishing Company. C.C. Beck.

Fighting American #1, ©1966 Harvey Features Syndicate. Jack Kirby, Joe Simon.

Lieber, Steve Ditko, Dick Ayers, and George Roussos. After Chic Stone and Vince Colletta inked the *Fantastic Four* in 1964 and 1965, Joe Sinnott took over for the rest of the 1960s, and beyond, as the title's most distinctive inker.

FATMAN, THE HUMAN FLYING SAUCER

Milson Publishing Company

	Issue #s
Published 4/67–8/67	1–3
Silver Age 4/67–8/67	1–3

Major Characters
Fatman 1–3

Significant Issues
1—Origin and first appearance of Fatman and Tinman.

Artists
C.C. Beck 1–3

Van Crawford is a likeable young millionaire who enjoys 15-course meals and birdwatching on his parents' vast estate. His large bulk comes in handy when he is able to save a flying saucer from crashing by pulling down a tree to cushion its impact. The grateful occupant of the saucer gives Crawford a special chocolate-flavored drink which gives him superpowers and turns him into—Fatman!

As Fatman, he can move his huge body quickly and easily. He can also communicate telepathically and hear radio messages. Most impressive, he can turn into a human flying saucer and zip through the air at 5,000 miles per hour. His only weakness was, of course, food: "First I think I'll raid the refrigerator . . . ah, yes! A baloney, ham, egg salad, sardine, liverwurst, tongue sandwich!"

Fatman was the creation of C.C. Beck and Otto Binder, the renowned artist and writer, respectively, of the 1940s Captain Marvel series. The publishers were two former Captain Marvel editors, Wendall Crowley and Will Liberson. Not surprisingly, Fatman followed in the footsteps of the good-natured, cheerful captain, albeit with tongue planted even more firmly in cheek.

Even for the camp days of the Batman TV show, however, the hero may have been too much of a parody ("Holy strawberry shortcake!"). After three issues, Fatman bit the dust.

FIGHTING AMERICAN

Harvey Publications

	Issue #s
Published 10/66	1
Silver Age 10/66	1

Significant Issues
1—Reprints origin.

Artists
Joe Simon 1
Jack Kirby 1

Joe Simon and Jack Kirby created this 1950s version of Captain America in 1954, when anti-communist feelings were running strong. Crippled war veteran Johnny Flag is murdered by communist agents after he exposes one of their plots on his show at radio station USA. Flag's brother takes his corpse to a government laboratory where they revitalize and strengthen the body and turn it into a superpowered shell. Flag's life force is transferred into the body of this new "fighting American" and he becomes an ardent anti-communist avenger.

As the Fighting American, he recruits a teenage sidekick, Speedboy, to help him fight such villains as Hotsky Trotsky, Poison Ivan, and Two-Ton Tessie, a communist man-killer who uses a blowtorch to light her cigars.

The first 1950s issue was very patriotic, but Simon said he and Kirby "found out we were being very stupid, or very naïve. We changed it to a lot of jokes. It turned out to be one of the book's great strengths. We had a lot of fun with it." Kirby agreed: "*Fighting American* is a kind of burlesque on the patriotic thing."

This 1966 issue was packaged by Joe Simon for Harvey Comics, and contained 1950s reprints as well as two stories from that era which had not been previously published.

FLASH

DC Comics

	Issue #s
Published 2/59–10/85	105–350
Silver Age 2/59–12/69	105–193

Major Characters
The Flash 105–193
Kid Flash 111, 112, 114, 116, 118, 122, 130, 133, 138, 144, 164, 167

Significant Issues
105—Origin of Flash retold.

110—First appearance and origin of Kid Flash.
111, 112, 114, 116, 118, 122, 130, 133, 138, 144, 156, 164, 167—Kid Flash appears.
112—First appearance and origin of Elongated Man.
115, 124, 130, 134, 138—Elongated Man appears.
119—Elongated Man gets married.
123—First appearance of 1940s Flash, Earth-One and Earth-Two.
129, 137, 151, 170, 173—Team-up of 1960s Flash and 1940s Flash.
130—Kid Flash meets the Elongated Man.
131, 143, 168, 191—Green Lantern appears.
137—First 1960s appearance of Justice Society of America.
158—Flash appears as Green Lantern, Hawkman, Aquaman, and the Atom.
160, 169, 178, 187—80-page, giant-sized issues; contain reprints.
165—Flash marries longtime girlfriend, Iris West.
167—Flash's origin retold.
170—Dr. Midnite and Dr. Fate appear.
171, 175—Justice League of America appears.
174—Flash reveals secret identity to wife.
175—Flash and Superman race.
179—Flash visits the offices of DC Comics.

Artists
Carmine Infantino 105–174, 178, 187
Lee Elias 160
Ross Andru 175–177, 179–186, 188–193

The *Flash* comic book is perhaps the most significant DC superhero title of the 1960s. Not only was it the first comic book starring a newly revived DC character, it also featured a story ("Flash of Two Worlds") which introduced the parallel universes of Earth-One and Earth-Two in which superheroes of the 1940s met their 1960s counterparts. The "Earth-One/Earth-Two Universe" allowed DC Comics to introduce other 1940s superheroes, including the Justice Society of America, into its 1960s comics.

The *Flash* comic book also featured stories of Kid Flash and the Elongated Man, two characters who grew in importance over the next twenty years.

John Broome wrote the majority of the Flash stories until 1969. Writer Gardner Fox was responsible for the team-up stories, which featured the Flash of Earth-One and the Flash of Earth-Two.

Carmine Infantino drew the comic from its beginning until 1967, when he assumed an editorial position. His hyperkinetic visuals and long, lean panels were perfectly suited for the "fastest man alive."

FLY MAN

Archie Comics

		Issue #s
Published	5/65–9/66	31–39
Silver Age	5/65–9/66	31–39

Major Characters
Fly Man 31–39
Mighty Crusaders 32, 33
The Shield 34, 36, 37
Black Hood 35
The Web 36, 38
Steel Sterling 39

Significant Issues
31—Shield, Black Hood, and Comet appear. First mention of the Mighty Crusaders.
32—First appearance of Mighty Crusaders as a team (Fly Man, Fly Girl, Black Hood, Shield, and Comet)
33—Fly Man versus the Mighty Crusaders.
34—Fly Man and Black Hood team up. Shield and Comet team up.
35, 39—Fly Man and Fly Girl team up.
35, 36, 37—Shield appears.
35—Black Hood origin retold.
36—Web origin retold.
38—Web appears.
39—Steel Sterling appears.

Artists
Paul Reinman 31–39 (Fly Man, Mighty Crusaders, Shield, Black Hood, Web, Steel Sterling)
Mike Sekowsky 34 (Shield, Comet)

The Fly first appeared in the *Adventures of the Fly* from 1959 to 1964. The comic book ceased publication for six months and then returned under a new title and a new name for its main character: *Fly Man.*

Along with his new name, Fly Man got a new art and writing team (Paul Reinman and Jerry Siegel). When the superhero boom began in the mid-1960s, other Archie heroes appeared in the comic. The comic book underwent another name change in 1966 when it became *Mighty Comics* with its 40th issue.

Flash #131 ©1962 DC Comics, Inc. Carmine Infantino, Joe Giella.

Fly Man #34, ©1965 Archie Comics. Paul Reinman.

Forbidden Worlds #136 ©1966 American Comics Group/ACG. Kurt Schaffenberger.

Frankenstein #4 ©1967 Dell Comics, Inc. Tony Tallarico.

Green Lantern #40 ©1965 DC Comics, Inc. Gil Kane, Murphy Anderson.

FORBIDDEN WORLDS

American Comics Group/ACG

	Issue #s
Published 7/51–8/67	1–145
Silver Age 1/66–1/67	125–141

Major Characters
Magicman 125–141

Significant Issues
125—Origin and first appearance of Magicman.
136—Nemesis teams up with Magicman.
Note: Magicman also appears in *Herbie* #14 (January 1966).

Artist
Pete Costanza 125–141

Forbidden Worlds was the companion comic for *Adventures into the Unknown.* Editor Richard Hughes, who wrote nearly all the stories for both comics and artist Kurt Schaffenberger created Magicman as a superhero who would fit in with the comic's supernatural lineup.

Writing under the pen name of Zev Zimmer, Hughes and artist Pete Costanza told the story of the 200-year-old son of the master magician Cagliostro, who kept himself forever young through magic.

After bumming around the world for a couple of centuries, the magician's son (now known as Tom Cargill) decides to enlist in the U.S. Army just in time for the Vietnam war. When his buddy Al is killed by the Viet Cong, Tom decides to become Magicman and use his magic powers to melt tanks and blow up enemy camps. "It's more than just getting even for Al. A war's half won when you can strike fear into your opponent—and I've got to strike that fear as Magicman!"

FRANKENSTEIN

Dell Comics

	Issue #s
Published 9/66–3/67	2–4
Silver Age 9/66–3/67	2–4

Major Characters
Frankenstein

Significant Issues
2—Origin and first appearance of Frankenstein as superhero.

Artists
Tony Tallarico 2–4

After publishing a comic book adaptation of the 1933 Frankenstein movie in 1963, Dell Comics decided to capitalize on the monster's eternal popularity by publishing a superhero comic of the same name three years later.

This Frankenstein is an artificial monster from the 19th century who is awakened in the 20th century by a bolt of lightning. Adapting the name of Frank Stone, the monster decides to devote his life to doing good. "None will learn my secret identity, for as Frank Stone, millionaire playboy, I can go about unquestioned . . . while as Frankenstein I can use my extraordinary strength and super brain to fight crime and injustice wherever it appears on the face of the earth."

GREEN LANTERN

DC Comics

	Issue #s
Published 7/60–10/86	1–205
Silver Age 7/60–12/69	1–73

Major Characters
Green Lantern 1–73

Significant Issues
1—Origin retold. First appearance of the Guardians.
2—First appearance of Pieface, Green Lantern's friend and confidant.
7—First appearance of Sinestro, arch enemy of Green Lantern.
9, 11, 15, 18—Sinestro appears.
9—Green Lantern Corps first appearance.
13, 20, 43—Flash appears.
16—Origin and first appearance of Star Sapphire (Green Lantern's girlfriend, Carol Ferris, turned villianess).
17, 41—Star Sapphire appears.
29—Justice League of America appears.
40—Origin of the Guardians. Green Lantern (1940s) of Earth-Two appears.
45, 52, 61—Earth-Two Green Lantern appears.
59—First appearance of other Green Lantern, Guy Gardner.

Artists
Gil Kane 1–61, 68–73
Carmine Infantino 53
Jack Sparling 62, 63
Mike Sekowsky 64–66
Dick Dillan 67, 71
Sid Greene 67

Six months after a three-issue tryout in *Showcase* and three more appearances in *Brave and Bold* as a member of the Justice League of America, Green Lantern finally received his own comic book in 1960.

There were several recurring themes and characters in the *Green Lantern* series. Villains like Sinestro, the renegade Green Lantern, and Star Sapphire, Green Lantern's mind-controlled girlfriend, made several appearances. His team-ups with fellow Justice League member Flash became an almost annual event; likewise, the appearances of the Earth-Two Green Lantern of the 1940s.

Artist Gil Kane and writer John Broome were the chief creative team on the title throughout the 1960s. Gardner Fox also contributed scripts beginning in 1963.

HAWK AND DOVE

DC Comics

	Issue #s
Published 8/68–6/69	1–6
Silver Age 8/68–6/69	1–6

Major Characters
Hawk and Dove 1–6

Note: Hawk and Dove first appear in *Showcase* #75.

Artists
Steve Ditko 1, 2
Gil Kane 3–6

Hank and Don Hall are brothers—students at the time of the Vietnam war demonstrations. Hank belives you should never walk away from a fight, or a war: "Force is the only way to make them quit!" Don replies, "Hey now, wait a minute! If we give in, everybody will be happy and we'll have peace."

Their father is a judge who has made many enemies. After gangsters try to kill him with a bomb, his sons track them to a warehouse hideout. While hiding there, the boys wish they had the power to "stop those creeps who are after dad!"

A disembodied voice suddenly tells them: "I have heard your wish . . . you both should have powers, if that is what you seek!"

The unknown entity changes Hank into the Hawk and Don into the Dove. In their costumes, they have "extensions of the abilities they already possess . . . whatever you could do moments ago, you can do infinitely better, with greater ease and consummate skill." Hank, the Hawk, has the athletic ability to kick, smash, and beat up the gangsters. Don, the Dove, relies on finesse to capture the crooks without fisticuffs ("Got past them easy enough—didn't have to result to violence."). Together the two brothers would become a well-balanced crime-fighting team, relying upon brute force and quiet skill.

Steve Ditko created the characters in the war protest years of 1968–69. Steve Skeates scripted Ditko's stories.

HAWKMAN

DC Comics

	Issue #s
Published 4/64–8/68	1–27
Silver Age 4/64–8/68	1–27

Major Characters
Hawkman 1–27

Significant Issues
4—First appearance of Zatanna the Magician.
9—Atom appears.
18, 19—Adam Strange appears.
25—Reprints Hawkman story from *Flash Comics* #12 (December 1940).

Artists
Murphy Anderson 1–21
Dick Dillin 22–27

Hawkman received his own comic book in 1964 after a six-issue tryout in *Brave and Bold* and a series in *Mystery in Space.*

As sales dropped in the late 1960s with the departure of artist Murphy Anderson, the comic was canceled. Hawkman moved over to share the Atom's comic and it was renamed *Atom and Hawkman.*

Gardner Fox wrote the majority of the Hawkman stories. Bob Haney also contributed some 1967–68 stories.

HOUSE OF MYSTERY

DC Comics

	Issue #s
Published 12/51–10/83	1–321
Silver Age 6/64–3/68	143–173

Major Characters
Martian Manhunter 143–173
Dial "H" for Hero 156–173

Significant Issues
143—Martian Manhunter series begins.
56—"Dial 'H' for Hero" series begins.

Hawk and Dove #2 ©1968 DC Comics, Inc. Steve Ditko.

Hawkman #3 ©1964 DC Comics, Inc., Murphy Anderson.

House of Mystery #166 ©1967 DC Comics, Inc. Jim Mooney.

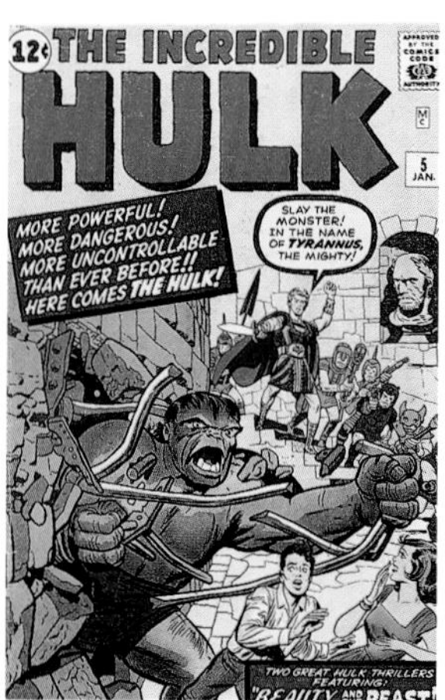

Incredible Hulk #5 ©1963 Marvel Entertainment Group, Inc. Jack Kirby, Dick Ayer.

Journey Into Mystery #98 ©1963 Marvel Entertainment Group, Inc. Jack Kirby, George Roussos.

160—First appearance of DC's Plastic Man.
160—Martian Manhunter gets new secret identity.
173—Last issue to feature superheroes; changes back to mystery format with the next issue.

Artists
Joe Certa 143–173 (Martian Manhunter)
Jim Mooney 156–170 (Dial "H" for Hero)
Frank Springer 171, 172 (Dial "H" for Hero)
Sal Trapani 173 (Dial "H" for Hero)

Originally one of DC Comics' first (and few) early 1950s horror comics, *House of Mystery* soon settled into stories like "I Was Tried by an Insect Jury!" and "Captives of the Alien Fishermen" by the 1960s.

When the Elongated Man dislodged the Martian Manhunter from his original niche in *Detective Comics*, the alien sleuth moved over to *House of Mystery* in 1964. The artwork remained the same, but the stories began establishing a continuity that culminated in a 14-issue series centered on the Manhunter's battle with the Vulture Crime Organization.

With issue #156, the Martian Manhunter was again pushed into a secondary spot by a new series, "Dial 'H' for Hero." Robby Reed, boy genius, discovers an extraterrestrial "telephone dial" that changes him into one of a 1,000 different superheroes whenever he dials "O-R-E-H." When danger threatens, Reed dials the letters and turns into such heroes as Balloon Boy, Giant Boy, Sphinx-Man, Super Nova, the Human Bullet, etc.

In each story, Reed changes into two or three heroes, with all the ease of dialing a phone. The "Dial 'H' for Hero" stories, written by Bill Finger, provided plenty of goofy and forgettable superheroes.

INCREDIBLE HULK

Marvel Comics

		Issue #s
Published	5/62–6/63, 4/68–	1–6, 102–
Silver Age	5/62–12/69	1–6, 102–122
		Annual 1, 2

Major Characters
Incredible Hulk 1–6, 102–122 Annual 1, 2

Significant Issues
1—Origin and first appearance of the Hulk (colored grey instead of green).
3, 4—Origin retold.
6—First appearance of Teen Brigade.
102—New series begins (1968). Origin retold.
109–111—Ka-Zar appears.
118—Sub-Mariner appears.
122—Fantastic Four appear.
Annual 1—Inhumans appear.

Artists
Jack Kirby 1–5 Annual 2
Steve Ditko 2, 6
Marie Severin 102–105 Annual 1
Herb Trimpe 106–122

The Hulk was the second 1960s Marvel superhero title, appearing in 1962 (almost a year before Spider-Man received his own book). After six issues, the first Hulk comic book was cancelled, and the "jolly green giant" bounced around as a guest-villain/hero in the *Avengers*, the *Fantastic Four*, and other Marvel titles.

After a successful 43-issue run as a cofeature in *Tales to Astonish*, the Hulk took over the magazine in 1968 and it was retitled the *Incredible Hulk*. This second Hulk series was one of Marvel's best-selling titles, and was helped along by the success of the Incredible Hulk TV show in the 1980s.

All six issues of the early 1960s series were written by Stan Lee, who also continued to write most of the later 1960s Hulk stories as well. Roy Thomas took over the scripting of the title in 1969.

IRON MAN

Marvel Comics

		Issue #s
Published	5/68–	1–
Silver Age	5/68–12/69	1–20

Major Characters
Iron Man 1–20

Significant Issues
1—Origin of Iron Man retold.
17—First appearance of Madame Masque.
18, 19—Avengers appear.
Note: Iron Man first appears in *Tales of Suspense* (#s 39–99).

Artists
Gene Colan 1
Johnny Craig 2–4, 14
George Tuska 5–13, 15–20

After a five-year sojourn as a feature in *Tales of Suspense*, Iron Man moved into his own magazine in 1968. Archie Goodwin wrote the *Iron Man* comic through the 1960s and took advantage of the book-length stories to develop the character and introduce new villains.

IRON MAN AND SUB-MARINER

Marvel Comics

	Issue #s
Published 4/68	1
Silver Age 4/68	1

Major Characters
Iron Man 1
Sub-Mariner 1

Artists
Gene Colan 1

One month before Iron Man and Sub-Mariner each got his own comic book, they appeared in this one-issue title.

JIGSAW

Harvey Comics

	Issue #s
Published 9/66–12/66	1, 2
Silver Age 9/66–12/66	1, 2

Major Characters
Jigsaw 1, 2

Significant Issues
1—Origin and first appearance of Jigsaw.

Artists
Bill Fracchio 1
Bill Draut 2

Jigsaw, "Man of a Thousand Parts," was originally Colonel Gary Jason, a U.S. Space Force astronaut. While on a space photography mission, he is sucked up by a magnetic vortex and taken to an alien base on the moon. His injuries are treated by an advanced alien race, the Krellites, who reconstruct his body so that he can stretch like "some gigantic-jointed doll."

When he returns to earth, his newly reassembled body horrifies his fiancé. After she leaves him, he decides to use his new stretching abilities as Jigsaw to do good deeds around the Milky Way. Otto Binder wrote both issues.

JOURNEY INTO MYSTERY

Marvel Comics

	Issue #s
Published 6/52–2/66	1–125
Silver Age 8/62–2/66	83–125
	Annual 1

Major Characters
Thor 83–125 Annual 1
Tales of Asgard 97–125

Significant Issues
83—Origin and first appearance of Thor.
84—First appearance of Loki, Thor's evil half-brother and rival.
86—First appearance of Odin.
89—Origin retold.
97—Tales of Asgard series begins.
102—First appearance of Lady Sif, Thor's future girlfriend.
112—Thor versus the Hulk.
116—Daredevil appears.
124—Thor reveals his secret identity to Jane Foster.
124, 125—Hercules appears.
Annual 1—First appearance of Hercules.

Artists
Jack Kirby 83–89, 93, 97, 101–125 Annual 1 (Thor, Tales of Asgard)
Al Hartley 90 (Thor)
Joe Sinnott 91, 92, 94–96 (Thor)
Don Heck 98–100 (Thor)

Originally a 1950s horror and science fiction comic, *Journey into Mystery* became the birthplace for Thor the Thunder God in 1962. Created by Stan Lee and Jack Kirby, the origin story was scripted by Stan's brother, Larry Lieber. Lieber and Robert Bernstein scripted Thor for the first year, until Lee took over the writing chores in 1963.

In addition to Thor, early issues (#s 83–96) contained science fiction stories, usually by Larry Lieber and Steve Ditko. By late 1963, the science fiction stories were replaced by the long-running "Tales of Asgard" feature by Jack Kirby.

The comic was officially retitled *Thor* in 1966 with issue #126.

JUDOMASTER

Charlton Comics

	Issue #s
Published 5/66–12/67	89–98
Silver Age 5/66–12/67	89–98

Major Characters
Judomaster 89–98
Thunderbolt 90
Sarge Steel 91–98

Significant Issues
Note: Judomaster first appears in *Special War Series* #4 November 1965.

Iron Man #8 © 1968 *Marvel Entertainment Group, Inc.* George Tuska, Frank Giacoia.

Judomaster #90 ©1966 *Charlton Comics*. Frank McLaughlin.

Justice League of America #3 ©1961 DC Comics, Inc. Murphy Anderson.

93—Introduction of Tiger, Judomaster's sidekick.

Artists
Frank McLaughlin 89–98 (Judomaster)
Pete Morisi 90 (Thunderbolt)
Dick Giordano 91–98 (Sarge Steel)

The first martial-arts superhero, Judomaster was originally Sgt. Rip Jagger, a World War II army sergeant. Trapped on a Japanese-held island, Jagger is rescued by guerilla fighters and taught the secrets of a Sensei warrior—karate, judo, and Jiu-Jitsu. He devises a costume and spends the rest of his World War II career fighting the Japanese as Judomaster. To perhaps defuse criticism of using Japanese as the principal enemies, Judomaster was given a Japanese-American boy, Tiger, as his sidekick. Tiger came from a Japanese-American relocation camp in Wyoming—an unusual revelation of a World War II social issue in a 1960s comic book.

Created, drawn, and written by artist Frank McLaughlin (with a scripting assist from veteran Charlton writer Joe Gill on the origin story), *Judomaster* was ahead of its time, coming several years before the Bruce Lee/Kung Fu martial arts entertainment boom of the late 1960s and early 1970s.

JUSTICE LEAGUE OF AMERICA

DC Comics

		Issue #s
Published	10/60–4/87	1–261
Silver Age	10/60–12/69	1–77

Major Characters
Justice League of America 1–77

Significant Issues
4—Green Arrow joins the JLA.
9—Origin of the JLA.
14—Atom joins the JLA.
21, 22—First Justice Society of America (JSA) team-up with the JLA. First 1960s appearance of Dr. Fate, Hourman, and Black Canary.
24—Adam Strange appears.
29, 30—JSA and JLA second team-up. First 1960s appearance of Starman.
31—Hawkman joins the JLA.
37, 38—JSA and JLA third team-up. First 1960s appearance of Mr. Terrific.
39—Reprints JLA stories from *Brave and the Bold* 28, 29 and *Justice League of America* 5.
41, 43, 52, 53—Hawkgirl appears.
42—Metamorpho appears.
46, 47—JSA and JLA fourth team-up. First 1960s appearance of the Sandman.
48—Reprints JLA stories from *Brave and the Bold* 29 and *Justice League of America* 2, 3.
51—Elongated Man appears.
55, 56—JSA and JLA fifth team-up.
58—Reprints.
64—First appearance of Red Tornado.
64, 65—JSA and JLA sixth team-up.
67—Reprints.
69—Wonder Woman leaves JLA.
70—Creeper appears.
71—Martian Manhunter leaves JLA.
72, 73—JSA and JLA seventh team-up.
74—Black Canary joins the JLA.
76—Reprints.

Artists
Mike Sekowsky 1–63, 67, 76
Dick Dillin 64–66, 68–75, 77

Within three months after its succcesful tryout in *Brave and the Bold*, the Justice League of America received its own book in 1960. Although many of the stories were formula-ridden in order to accommodate the large lineup of heroes, the book was immensely popular with readers who enjoyed seeing all their favorite characters in one title.

Gardner Fox wrote the first 65 issues and Denny O'Neil wrote the remaining 1960s issues. Both writers relied heavily upon science fiction elements to shape their stories, but O'Neil's scripts, particularly beginning with issue #71, brought a new depth of characterization to the title along with some dramatic changes in the JLA membership.

LAUGH COMICS

Archie Comics

		Issue #s
Published	Fall 1946–1987	20–400
Silver Age	11/61–3/63	127–144

Major Characters
Jaguar 127, 130, 131, 133, 135, 140, 141, 142, 144
The Fly 128, 129, 132, 134, 136, 137, 138, 139, 143

Significant Issues
136, 137, 139, 143—Fly Girl appears.

Artists
John Giunta 127–136, 138–143 (Jaguar, Fly)

John Rosenberger 137, 144 (Fly, Jaguar)

Laugh Comics featured stories of those lovable teenagers, Archie Andrews, Jughead Jones, Betty Cooper, and Veronica Lodge, all through the 1940s, 1950s, and 1960s. The Archie teens also shared *Laugh Comics* with Katy Keene, a clothes model who wore reader-designed fashions in her stories.

In the early 1960s, the Jaguar and the Fly were added to the comic to build their popularity. Robert Bernstein wrote most of the stories.

MARVEL SUPER-HEROES

Marvel Comics

	Issue #s
Published 12/67–1/82	12–105
Silver Age 12/67–5/69	12–20

Major Characters
Captain Marvel 12, 13
Spider-Man 14
Medusa 15
Phantom Eagle 16
Black Knight 17
Guardians of the Galaxy 18
Ka-Zar 19
Dr. Doom 20

Significant Issues
12—Origin and first appearance of Captain Marvel.
14—Spider-Man story.
20—Reprints *Young Men Comics* #24 (December 1953) which contains the first 1950s appearances of Captain America, Human Torch, and Sub-Mariner.

Artists
Gene Colan 12, 13, 15, 18 (Captain Marvel, Medusa, Guardians of Galaxy)
Ross Andru 14 (Spider-Man)
Herb Trimpe 16 (Phantom Eagle)
Howard Purcell 17 (Black Knight)
George Tuska 19 (Ka-Zar)
Larry Lieber 20 (Dr. Doom)
Tom Palmer 23 (The Watcher)

Marvel Super-Heroes was the replacement title for a reprint comic book, *Fantasy Masterpieces*. It began its numbering with issue #12 and featured new stories and characters in its first nine issues. With issue #21, the title changed over to reprinting stories of the Sub-Mariner, Hulk, Daredevil, Iron Man, etc.

METAL MEN

DC Comics

	Issue #s
Published 4/63–2/78	1–56
Silver Age 4/63–12/69	1–41

Major Characters
Metal Men 1–41

Significant Issues
Note: Origin and first appearance of Metal Men in *Showcase* #37.
13—First appearance of Nameless, Tin's girlfriend.
14, 25—Chemo, the Chemical Menace, appears.
27—Origin of Metal Men retold.

Artists
Ross Andru 1–29
Gil Kane 30, 31
Mike Sekowsky 32–41

Dr. Will Magnus created a team of robots, each out of a specific metal: gold, iron, lead, mercury, tin, and platinum. These Metal Men (plus one woman) had built-in "responsometers" which made them behave almost like humans. The Metal Men were more than robots made out of different metals, however. They could alter and change their bodies and use their unique metallic properties to fight all types of evil-doers, under the scientific leadership of Dr. Magnus.

Editor and writer Robert Kanigher created the Metal Men and gave each of them a distinct personality. "Gold was the most difficult—he's a noble metal. How do you handle nobility without making him Mr. Clean? Lead was easy. I made him like William Bendix, the actor, except not as intelligent. I had him speak with 'uh-uh, dese, dose, and dems.' Iron was the strong man of metals, Mercury the most ill-tempered. Tin the lowliest, who knew it, hence his inferiority complex and stammer. Out of Platinum, I made Tina. She didn't believe she was a robot. She fell in love with Doc Magnus. Gave him a lot of trouble. Delicious. The kind that men fantasize about."

The art team of Ross Andru and Mike Esposito drew the Metal Men for its first four years. Esposito remembered that "the strip was really before its time. The characters were so well drawn . . . every personality came through in the writing and design. There was a realness in them, but with a light touch."

Marvel Super-Heroes #20 ©1969 Marvel Entertainment Group, Inc. Larry Lieber, Vince Colleta.

Metal Men #23 ©1966 DC Comics, Inc. Ross Andru, Mike Esposito.

Metamorpho #3 ©1965 DC Comics, Inc. Ramona Fradon.

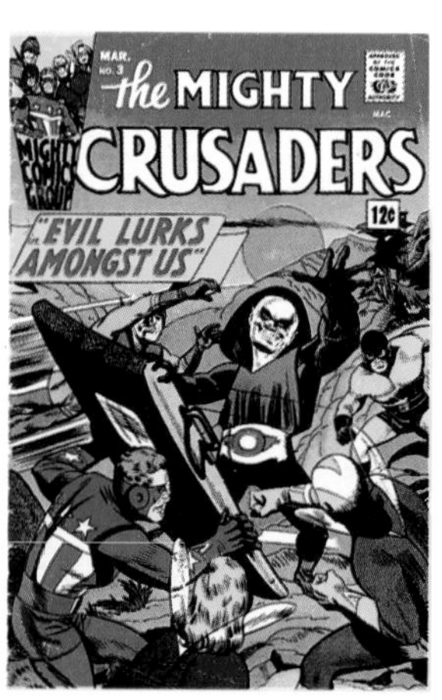

Mighty Crusaders #3, ©1966 Archie Comics. Paul Reinman.

METAMORPHO

DC Comics

	Issue #s
Published 7/65–3/68	1–17
Silver Age 7/65–3/68	1–17

Major Characters
Metamorpho 1–17

Significant Issues
Note: Metamorpho first appears in *Brave and Bold* #57.
10—Origin and first appearance of Element Girl.
13–15, 17—Element Girl appears.

Artists
Ramona Fradon 1–4
Joe Orlando 5–9
Sal Trapani 10–16
Jack Sparling 17

Rex Mason, soldier of fortune, is hired by wealthy scientist Simon Stagg to retrieve the "Orb of Ra" from a pyramid. While in the pyramid, Mason is bathed in a meteorite's rays. He discovers he can change his body into any chemical element and assume any shape. He can become a giant marble statue, a hard carbon drill, fire-smothering foam—anything. He is Metamorpho, the Element Man.

Unfortunately, he is also a freak. The process which turned him into Metamorpho also bleached and mummified his face, changed one leg to mud and the other one bright silver, and covered his torso with orange scales. Still, Metamorpho managed an admirably active love life with Sapphire Stagg, the boss's daughter.

Created by writer Bob Haney and initially drawn by Ramona Fradon, Metamorpho tried to be the hippest of all the 1960s DC superheroes: "Easy, baby," he tells his ardent girlfriend. "Uncle Sam needs me, I guess—so old Metamorpho better do his bit for Mr. Whiskers! I'll be okay—and when I get back, it'll be love and kisses for breakfast, lunch, and dinner!"

Readers also picked up a few chemistry facts while reading about the Element Man. In order to sink a submarine in one adventure, Metamorpho turns himself into a lightweight "*magnesium* torpedo with a tail of pure *sodium,* which reacts *violently* with *water.*"

MIGHTY COMICS

Archie Comics

	Issue #s
Published 11/66–10/67	40–50
Silver Age 11/66–10/67	40–50

Major Characters
The Web 40, 43, 45, 46
The Shield 41, 43–45, 48
Black Hood 41–44, 46, 47, 50
Steel Sterling 44, 46, 49
Hangman 45, 46, 48
Mr. Justice 47
The Fox 49

Significant Issues
45—Origin of Web retold.
48—Wizard appears.
49—Black Hood and Steel Sterling team up.
50—Inferno appears.

Artists
Paul Reinman 40–50 (Web, Shield, Black Hood, Steel Sterling, Hangman, Mr. Justice, Fox)

This title was the offspring of the recently defunct *Mighty Crusaders* and *Fly Man. Mighty Comics* featured stories about the various superheroes who made up the Mighty Crusaders.

The creative team of writer Jerry Siegel and artist Paul Reinman continued its work from the previous Archie superhero comics.

MIGHTY CRUSADERS

Archie Comics

	Issue #s
Published 11/65–10/66	1–7
Silver Age 11/65–10/66	1–7

Major Characters
Mighty Crusaders 1–7
The Shield 1
Steel Sterling 7
Comet 2
Fly Man 3, 7

Significant Issues
1—Origin of the Shield retold.
2—Origin of the Comet retold.
3—Origin of Fly Man retold.
4—Fireball, Inferno, Web, Fox, Blackjack, Bob Phantom, Zambini, Kardak, Mr. Justice, Steel Sterling, Captain Flag, Yank, Dusty, Roy the Mighty Boy, Wizard, Hangman,

and Jaguar appear in "Too Many Super Heroes!"
5—Fox, Web, and Captain Flag appear. First appearance of the Terrific Three (Mr. Justice, Steel Sterling, and Jaguar).
7—Origin of Fly Girl retold.

Artists
Paul Reinman 1–7 (Mighty Crusaders, Shield, Comet, Fly Man)
Mike Sekowsky 2, 7 (Mighty Crusaders, Steel Sterling)

The Mighty Crusaders consisted of the Fly Man, Fly Girl, the Shield, the Black Hood, and the Comet. These heroes had first appeared in *Fly Man* comics earlier in 1965. Now Archie Comics was following the lead of Marvel (*Avengers*) and DC Comics (*Justice League of America*) by putting its most popular superheroes together on a team.

The series was written by veteran superhero author Jerry Siegel.

MY GREATEST ADVENTURE

DC Comics

	Issue #s
Published 1/55–2/64	1–85
Silver Age 6/63–2/64	80–85

Major Characters
Doom Patrol 80–85

Significant Issues
80—Origin and first appearance of the Doom Patrol (Elasti-Girl, Robotman, Negative Man, and the Chief).

Artists
Bruno Premiani 80–85

The first 79 issues of *My Greatest Adventure* featured first-person accounts of unlikely and ridiculous things that suddenly happened to people minding their own business, like "I Fought a Live Volcano," "I Battled the Abominable Snowman," "I Hunted a Flying Saucer," and "I Became a Merman."

By 1963, writer Arnold Drake recalled, "*My Greatest Adventure* was in trouble, and Murray Boltinoff (the editor) wanted a feature that might get it out of trouble. So I started working on a notion. . . ."

For issue #80, Drake and writer Bob Haney, along with artist Bruno Premiani, created one of the world's strangest teams of superheroes—the Doom Patrol. The series appeared in the next five issues of the comic until the title was offically changed over to the *Doom Patrol* with issue #86.

MYSTERIES OF UNEXPLORED WORLDS

Charlton Comics

	Issue #s
Published 8/56–9/65	1–48
Silver Age 5/65–9/65	46–48

Major Characters
Son of Vulcan 46–48

Significant Issues
46—Origin and first appearance, Son of Vulcan.

Artists
Bill Fraccio 46–48

The first 45 issues of *Mysteries of Unexplored Worlds* featured stories of people falling into other dimensions while on their way to buy groceries, or discovering their next-door neighbor is an alien spy. Occasional stories by Steve Ditko in the late 1950s were the book's standouts.

In 1965, editor Patrick Masulli created a Thor-inspired superhero called Son of Vulcan for the comic book. Johnny Mann, a newspaper reporter with a lame leg, is granted superpowers by the Roman god Vulcan. He is given a shield and sword forged in Olympian fires and the ability to follow radio waves and throw fireballs.

A mixture of mythological nonsense and misplaced angst, the stories usually featured Mars the War God attacking the Son of Vulcan in order to take him down a notch—a sort of god one-upmanship. "I have called upon Vulcan to lend me a weapon to fight this foe . . . but he has failed me. I stand naked against his wrath!"

MYSTERIOUS SUSPENSE

Charlton Comics

	Issue #s
Published 10/68	1
Silver Age 10/68	1

Major Characters
The Question 1

Significant Issues
Note: The Question first appears in *Blue Beetle* #1 (1967).

Artists
Steve Ditko 1

My Greatest Adventure #80 ©1963 DC Comics, Inc. Bruno Premiani.

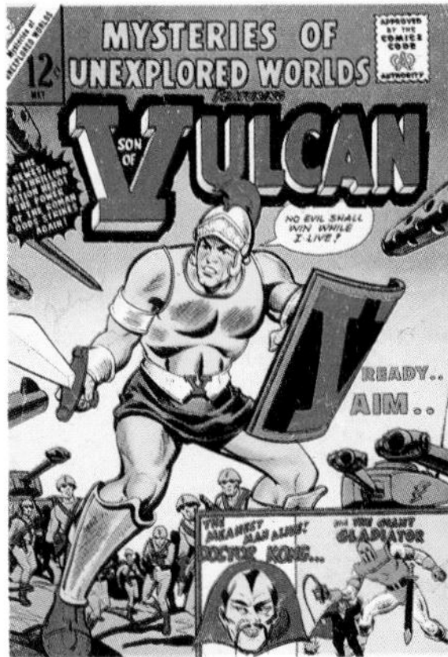

Mysteries of Unexplored Worlds #46 ©1965 Charlton Comics. Dick Giordano.

Mysterious Suspense #1 ©1968 Charlton Comics. Steve Ditko.

Mystery In Space #86 ©1963 DC Comics, Inc. Carmine Infantino, Murphy Anderson.

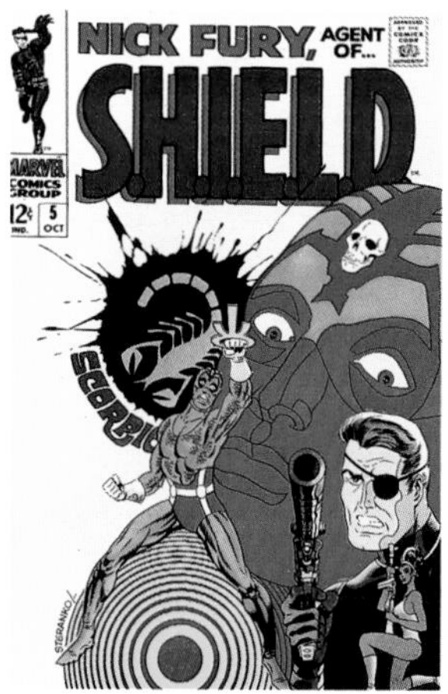

Nick Fury Agent of SHIELD ©1968 Marvel Entertainment Group, Inc. Jim Steranko.

Vic Sage, an investigative reporter, assumes his secret identity as The Question to fight corruption and crime. To become The Question, Sage blots out his face with a transparent mask and releases a special gas which changes his business suit into a light blue costume. The Question was a hard-edged ethician, ready to serve up bare-knuckled justice.

"The greatest battle a person must constantly fight is to uphold proper principles, known truths, against everyone he deals with! A truth cannot be defeated! But when a man refuses to know what is right or deliberately accepts, or does, what he knows is wrong . . . he defeats himself! The truth remains unbeaten!"

Created and drawn by Steve Ditko, The Question was a colorful sounding board for Ditko's own objectivist philosophy.

MYSTERY IN SPACE

DC Comics

	Issue #s
Published 4/51–9/66	1–110
Silver Age 8/59–11/65	53–103

Major Characters
Adam Strange 53–100, 102
Hawkman 87–90
Space Ranger 92–99, 103

Significant Issues
75—Justice League of America appears.
87—Hawkman series begins; ends #90.
90—Adam Strange and Hawkman team up.
94, 98—Adam Strange and Space Ranger team up.

Artists
Carmine Infantino 53–91 (Adam Strange)
Murphy Anderson 87–90 (Hawkman)
Lee Elias 92–100, 102 (Adam Strange)
Phil Kelsey 92–95 (Space Ranger)
Howard Purcell 96–99, 103 (Space Ranger)

An early DC science fiction title, *Mystery in Space* featured stories by Julius Schwartz's stable of artists (Murphy Anderson, Gil Kane, Carmine Infantino) and writers (Gardner Fox, John Broome). There were early series, such as Space Cabbie and Interplanetary Insurance, but no superhero character appeared until Adam Strange in 1959.

Archaeologist Adam Strange, while exploring Incan ruins, is suddenly transported by a "Zeta-beam" across 25 trillion miles of space to the planet Rann. There he meets the exotically beautiful Alanna and helps her repel an alien invasion. Just as Alanna and Adam are getting cozy, the Zeta-beam wears off and he is transported back to Earth. Fortunately, he is able to discern where and when the Zeta-beam will strike again so he is able to return sporadically to Rann and his new girlfriend. Adam and Alanna's biplanetary relationship, coupled with the slick futuristic artwork of Carmine Infantino and Murphy Anderson, kept readers coming back for more.

In 1963, Hawkman joined Adam Strange as a cofeature in the comic. Gardner Fox wrote both the Adam Strange stories and the Hawkman series. After the book changed editorial hands in 1964, Space Ranger moved over from *Tales of the Unexpected* to share the comic with Adam Strange.

NEUTRO

Dell Comics

	Issue #s
Published 1/67	1
Silver Age 1/67	1

Major Characters
Neutro 1

Significant Issues
1—Origin and only appearance of Neutro.

Artists
Jack Sparling 1

A thousand years ago, a flying saucer flies over Midwestern America and discards crates of disassembled machine parts—space junk.

In 1967, two scientists discover the crates in a burial mound. Putting all the parts together, they create a giant 12-foot, blue-steel robot—Neutro.

Neutro appeared to be the ideal superhero: "He can bend steel like paper . . . catch whales with a single hand." As the scientists lamented, however, "His only failing is, Neutro has no brain!"

Being brainless, Neutro is also amoral. Since "Neutro does not know the difference between right and wrong," who could control the robot could control the world. After all, here was a guy who"if an atomic bomb exploded in his presence it would be as if a mere balloon had burst!"

Nevertheless, Neutro lasted but one issue.

NICK FURY, AGENT OF SHIELD

Marvel Comics

	Issue #s
Published 6/68–3/71	1–18
Silver Age 6/68–11/69	1–15

Major Characters
Nick Fury 1–15

Significant Issues
4—Origin retold.
Note: First appearance of SHIELD series in *Strange Tales* #135.

Artists
Jim Steranko 1–3, 5
Frank Springer 4, 6–11
Barry Smith 12
Herb Trimpe 13–15

World War II is long over. Nick Fury and two of his Howling Commando army buddies, Gabriel Jones and Dum-Dum Dugan, are looking for government work. A new organization needs seasoned war veterans like them who can think on their feet and shoot on the run. An organization called SHIELD—Supreme Headquarters International Espionage Law-enforcement Division—hires Fury and his men as special agents.

SHIELD is like the FBI, the CIA, and the United Nations Peace Forces all rolled into one and with a trillion-dollar budget. SHIELD is everywhere; it has gadgets, airplanes, cars, and weapons that make James Bond look like Mad Magazine's "Spy vs. Spy." SHIELD is the *Man from UNCLE* on steroids. It's an immensely powerful superspy organization, and Fury is its chief operative.

As an agent of SHIELD, Fury and his men fight an international group called HYDRA, a well-bankrolled organization of international terrorists who wore green-hooded costumes and held strange Klan-like rituals. There were so many of them and they all looked alike—interchangeable, ubiquitous bad guys: "Hail Hydra! Immortal Hydra! We shall never be destroyed! Cut off a limb and two more shall take its place!"

NOMAN

Tower Comics

	Issue #s
Published 11/66–3/67	1, 2
Silver Age 11/66–3/67	1, 2

Major Characters
NoMan 1, 2
Lightning 1, 2

Significant Issues
1, 2—Dynamo appears.

Artists
Gil Kane 1 (NoMan)
John Giunta 1 (NoMan)
Chic Stone 1, 2 (Lightning)
Ogden Whitney 1, 2 (NoMan)

Doctor Dunn is a dying scientist. He has invented a corps of identical blue-skinned androids with blank brains. Before he dies, he transfers his "entire mental makeup to electronic impulses . . . and into the brains of the androids." Dr. Dunn's consciousness now exists in the body of one of the androids. Even better, the doctor discovers: "I can transfer my consciousness into any of the androids I choose!"

In his android body, Dr. Dunn is almost invincible. If he should be threatened, he can simply transfer his consciousness to another android body. He truly has no single body—he is "NoMan. . . . Not an individual, not even a human being, but several android bodies with one identity."

He is also an ideal candidate for the THUNDER Agent team of superheroes. As a THUNDER Agent, NoMan acquires an "invisibility cloak" which he can turn on and off. Part of NoMan's appeal was that he had no fear for his physical body. He would volunteer for suicide missions, launch himself into airless space, enter a machine gun barrage, and then—at the last moment—teleport his consciousness to another, safely hidden android body.

After appearing in the first issue of THUNDER Agents, NoMan received his own comic book a year later. The character was created by Wally Wood, and writers included Steve Skeates and Bill Pearson.

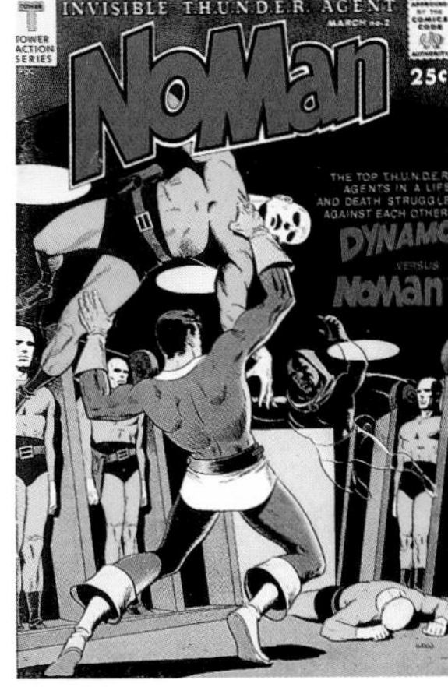

NoMan #2 ©1967 Tower Comics. Wally Wood.

Nukla #2 ©1966 Dell Comics. Dick Giordano, Sal Trapani.

NUKLA

Dell Comics

	Issue #s
Published 10/65–9/66	1–4
Silver Age 10/65–9/66	1–4

Major Characters
Nukla 1–4

Significant Issues
1—Origin and first appearance of Nukla.

Artists
Sal Trapani 1
Dick Giordano 2, 3
Steve Ditko 4

Matthew Gibbs, a U-2 air force spy pilot, is on a special mission over Red China. Suddenly, his plane is hit by a heat-seeking missile.

Owl #2 ©*1968 Western Publishing Co.* Tom Gill.

Peacemaker #5 ©*1967 Charlton Comics.* Pat Boyette.

"In a sudden, obliterating flash of pure energy and blazing light, Matthew Gibbs 'dies'! Not crushed or demolished in an ordinary way, but vaporized! Turned into an unrelated mass of atoms, neutrons, protons . . ."

Gibbs is changed into a superpowered being, Nukla, who can materialize or dematerialize at will and direct atomic power through his fingertips. He also has the power to reconstitute his demolished U-2 plane so he can patrol the world in his new superhero identity.

"Yes, Matthew Gibbs, as Nukla, is up there now, patrolling the world from the edge of space, seeking evil wherever it exists, sometimes in a form man can see, but more often silent and invisible . . . moving amongst us, alert for any danger to the world he has sworn to preserve!"

THE OWL

Gold Key

	Issue #s
Published 4/67–4/68	1, 2
Silver Age 4/67–4/68	1, 2

Major Characters
The Owl 1, 2

Significant Issues
1—Origin of 1960s Owl.

Artists
Tom Gill 1, 2

Nick Terry, special investigator for the Yorkstown police department, has to operate outside of the law to see that justice is done. Inspired by a creature of the night, he becomes the Owl. He devises a flying Owlmobile, complete with Owlbombs, an Owlgun, and a black-light ray. His fiancé, Laura Holt, becomes his companion, Owl Girl. Together, they fight criminals in their lavender-colored jumpsuits and owl-beaked hoods.

The Owl was originally conceived by Frank Thomas for *Crackajack Funnies* in 1940, almost exactly one year after Batman's debut. The character disappeared by the early 1940s, and was brought back over 20 years later in a new comic from Gold Key. Superman cocreator Jerry Siegel wrote both issues with hip-1960s dialogue: "Ha-ha! Look at the Owl and Owl Girl freaking out! Guess they don't dig our fab collection of way-out weapons!"

PEACEMAKER

Charlton Comics

	Issue #s
Published 3/67–11/67	1–5
Silver Age 3/67–11/67	1–5

Major Characters
The Peacemaker 1–5

Significant Issues
4—Origin retold.
Note: The Peacemaker first appeared in *The Fightin' Five* (#40, 41).

Artists
Pat Boyette 1–5

The ultimate diplomat, Christopher Smith is a U.S. peace envoy who travels the world to lobby for nuclear disarmament and human rights. When his diplomatic methods fail, Smith straps on his special weapons and climbs into his Peacemaker costume to wage all-out "peace."

Created by writer Joe Gill and artist Pat Boyette, the Peacemaker was a taciturn, cool-headed, war-hating weapons expert. "This is a man who detests war, violence and the dreadful waste of human life in senseless conflicts between nations—a man who loves peace so much, he is willing to fight for it!"

PEP COMICS

Archie Comics

	Issue #s
Published 1/40–1987	1–411
Silver Age 10/61–1/63	150–160

Major Characters
Jaguar 150, 152, 157, 159
The Fly 151, 154, 160
Fly Girl 153, 155, 156, 158

Significant Issues
157—Jaguar's foe Kree-Nal, the Sea Circe from Space, appears.

Artists
John Giunta 150–156, 158, 159 (Jaguar, Fly, Fly Girl)
John Rosenberger 157, 160 (Jaguar, Fly)

Originally a superhero comic (the Shield first appeared in issue #1), *Pep Comics* introduced Archie, Jughead, and Betty in its December 1941 issue. Within five years, the teenagers would oust the superheroes entirely.

After 15 years, superheroes like the Jaguar, the Fly, and Fly Girl returned to *Pep Comics* briefly as a secondary feature (primarily written by Robert Bernstein). Archie, Betty, and Veronica, however, still reigned supreme, and the superheroes were shortly replaced with "Jughead's Joke" pages and Li'l Jinx stories.

PLASTIC MAN

DC Comics

	Issue #s
Published 11/66–10/77	1–20
Silver Age 11/66–5/68	1–10

Major Characters
Plastic Man 1–10

Significant Issues
2—Origin retold in three different versions.
7—Origin of Plastic Man.
Note: Plastic Man also appeared in *House of Mystery* #160, *Brave and Bold* #76, and *Inferior Five* #2.

Artists
Gil Kane 1
Win Mortimer 2–7
Jack Sparling 8–10

Plastic Man was one of few 1940s superheroes to survive into the mid-1950s. Much of Plastic Man's success was due to his tongue-in-cheek style and self-reflective humor.

DC Comics acquired the rights to the character from its original publisher, Quality Comics, and revived the character in 1966. Editor Murray Bolitinoff (who handled a stack of DC humor comics, like *Jerry Lewis, Bob Hope,* and *Fox and Crow*) put Arnold Drake in charge of updating Plastic Man for a new generation of readers. Unfortunately, the new Plastic Man was more silly than funny and failed to find an appreciative readership. The character vanished in 1968, underwent a resurrection in 1976 and again in 1988.

Plastic Man #2 ©1967 DC Comics, Inc. Bob Oksner.

RIP HUNTER . . . TIME MASTER

DC Comics

	Issue #s
Published 3/61–11/65	1–29
Silver Age 3/61–11/65	1–29

Major Characters
Rip Hunter 1–29

Significant Issues
Note: Rip Hunter first appeared in *Showcase* (#s 20, 21, 25, 26).

Artists
Ross Andru 1–3
Nick Cardy 4, 5
Alex Toth 6, 7
Bill Ely 8–29

Rip Hunter and his team of explorers—Corky, Bonnie, and Jeff—travel through time in a bathysphere-shaped "Time Sphere." The four time travelers have adventures in every historical era, encountering 8th-century Baghdad magicians, Olympian centaurs, and one million-year-BC dinosaurs.

The stories, mostly written by Jack Miller, often centered on the time travelers straightening out some recently discovered historical inaccuracy: "We're headed for a town called New Windsor, in New York. The mission is to find out if George Washington was really a—a traitor to his country!"

Rip Hunter. . . Time Master #4 ©1961 DC Comics, Inc. Nick Cardy.

SEA DEVILS

DC Comics

	Issue #s
Published 9/61–5/67	1–35
Silver Age 9/61–5/67	1–35

Major Characters
Sea Devils 1–35

Significant Issues
Note: The Sea Devils first appeared in *Showcase* (#s 27–29).

Artists
Russ Heath 1–10
Irv Novick 11, 12, 14, 15
Joe Kubert 13
Gene Colan 13
Ross Andru 13
Jack Abel 14
Bruno Premiani 16
Howard Purcell 16–33, 35
Chic Stone 34

The Sea Devils are four undersea divers: Dane (the brain), Judy (the beauty), Biff (the beast), and teenager Nicky (the brat). Together, they battle such menaces as giant Coral Creatures, water-breathing gorillas, and King Neptune himself.

Created by Robert Kanigher, the *Sea Devils*

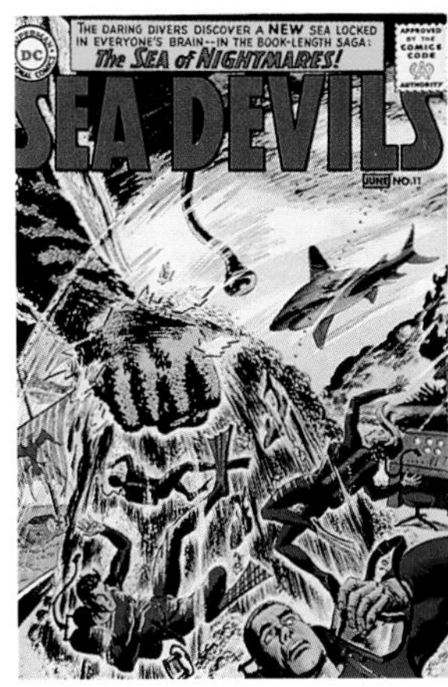

Sea Devils #11 ©1963 DC Comics, Inc. Irv Novick, Jerry Serpe.

Secret Six #4 ©1968 DC Comics, Inc. Jack Sparling.

Shadow #5, ©1965 Archie Comics. Paul Reinman.

were a heroic foursome in the tradition of *Challengers of the Unknown* and the *Fantastic Four.* Kanigher wrote many of the 1960–64 issues; other writers included Bob Haney and Ed Herron.

Russ Heath, who drew the first ten issues, said the *Sea Devils* was a challenging assignment with its underwater scenes. The problem was, according to Heath, there were too many main characters in the comic. "The more people you have in a strip the less reader identification there is with any of them. You've got four people in every panel. It just waters the whole thing down."

SECRET SIX

DC Comics

	Issue #s
Published 4/68–4/69	1–7
Silver Age 4/68–4/69	1–7

Major Characters
Secret Six 1–7

Significant Issues
1—Origin and first appearance of Secret Six.

Artists
Frank Springer 1, 2
Jack Sparling 3–7

According to E. Nelson Birdwell, who created the *Secret Six* along with Carmine Infantino, the comic was about "a group of heroes with a leader who was secretly one of them—but no one knew which. He had saved the life of each, but he also had other holds on them, so they dared not disobey him."

Birdwell took Infantino's basic concept "and added an idea of my own—Mockingbird, a character who not only stopped criminals, but held them up to ridicule. Carmine got together with the original artist, Frank Springer, to work out what the six looked like. One character, King Savage, was based on Frank himself—and this was Carmine's idea! Nothing else I have written in comics had the originality, maturity and daring to try new fields that *Secret Six* possessed."

SHADOW, THE

Archie Comics

	Issue #s
Published 8/64–11/65	1–8
Silver Age 8/64–11/65	1–8

Major Characters
The Shadow 1–8

Significant Issues
1—Origin of Shadow.
3—New costume.

Artists
John Rosenberger 1, 2
Paul Reinman 2–8

The first two issues of *The Shadow* were loosely based upon Walter B. Gibson's popular pulp and radio hero, and were written by Robert Bernstein. By the third issue, Jerry Siegel, cocreator of Superman, was writing the comic and turned the Shadow into a superhero, complete with costume and gimmicky weapons.

The comic book was a curious mixture of 1930s pulp mythology and 1960s spy movies. The Shadow fought old foes like Shiwan Khan, but also used gadgets like his airjet-powered boots and a sonic whistle.

"I feel great! Now that I've had my morning danger tonic, I'll switch back to my Lamont Cranston identity . . . join my secretary, Margo Lane, and get on with the necessary chore of managing my vast enterprises!"

SHOWCASE

DC Comics

	Issue #s
Published 3/56–9/78	1–104
Silver Age 10/56–12/69	4–87

Major Characters
Flash 4, 8, 13, 14; Lois Lane 9, 10; Challengers 6, 7, 11, 12; Space Ranger 15, 16, Adam Strange 17–19; Rip Hunter 20, 21, 25, 26; Green Lantern 22–24; Sea Devils 27–29; Aquaman 30–33; Atom 34–36; Metal Men 37–40; Dr. Fate and Hourman 55, 56; Teen Titans 59; The Spectre 60, 61, 64; Inferior Five 62, 63, 65; The Creeper 73; Hawk and Dove 75; Nightmaster 82–84

Significant Issues
4—Origin and first appearance of 1950s/1960s Flash.
6—Origin and first appearance of Challengers of the Unknown.
9—First Lois Lane comic book.
15—First appearance of Space Ranger.
17—First appearance of Adam Strange.
20—First appearance of Rip Hunter, Time Master.
22—Origin and first appearance of 1960s Green Lantern.

27—Origin and first appearance of Sea Devils.
30—Origin of 1960s Aquaman.
34—Origin and first appearance of 1960s Atom.
37—Origin and first appearance of Metal Men.
60—First appearance of 1960s Spectre.
62—Origin and first appearance of Inferior Five.
73—Origin and first appearance of the Creeper.
75—Origin and first appearance of the Hawk and Dove.
79—Reprints Aqualad's origin.

Artists
Carmine Infantino 4, 8, 13, 14 (Flash)
Ruben Moreira 9 (Lois Lane) 20 (Rip Hunter)
Wayne Boring 10 (Lois Lane)
Jack Kirby 11, 12 (Challengers)
Bob Brown 15, 16 (Space Ranger)
Mike Sekowsky 17–19 (Adam Strange) 21 (Rip Hunter) 65(Inferior Five)
Gil Kane 22–24 (Green Lantern) 34–36 (Atom)
Joe Kubert 25, 26 (Rip Hunter)
Russ Heath 27–29 (Sea Devils)
Ross Andru 28 (Sea Devils) 37–40 (Metal Men)
Ramon Fradon 30 (Aquaman)
Nick Cardy 31–33 (Aquaman) 59 (Teen Titans)
Murphy Anderson 55, 56 (Dr. Fate & Hourman) 60, 61, 64 (Spectre)
Joe Orlando 62, 63 (Inferior Five)
Steve Ditko 73 (The Creeper) 75 (Hawk and Dove)
Jerry Grandenetti 82 (Nightmaster)
Berni Wrightson 83, 84 (Nightmaster)

The first three issues of *Showcase* spotlighted the heroic exploits of firemen, frogmen, and dogs. With the first appearance of Flash in issue #4, the book began evolving into a true showcase for DC Comics' new superheroes.

The comic book provided a testing ground for new heroes like Green Lantern, Atom, Metal Men, and Aquaman. If the *Showcase* issues sold well, the characters were given their own books. If sales were disappointing, the new characters might return for another tryout or quietly vanish.

The track record of *Showcase* was impressive: Out of the seventeen superheroes who first appeared in the comic from 1956 to 1969, thirteen later received their own comic books.

SILVER SURFER

Marvel Comics

	Issue #s
Published 8/68–9/70	1–18
Silver Age 8/68–12/69	1–11

Major Characters
Silver Surfer 1–11
The Watcher 1–7

Significant Issues
1—Origin of the Silver Surfer retold. Hulk and Dr. Doom appear.
4—Thor appears.
5—Fantastic Four appear.

Artists
John Buscema 1–11 (Silver Surfer)
Gene Colan 1–3 (The Watcher)
Howard Purcell 4, 5, 7 (The Watcher)
Syd Shores 6 (The Watcher)

After appearing in a dozen issues of the *Fantastic Four,* the Silver Surfer started his own series in a big way. The first seven issues were 64 pages long, including a 40-page Surfer story. Stan Lee wrote the stories.

The first seven issues of the comic featured a backup story of the Watcher. The series was dropped by the eighth issue when the page count went down to a normal 32 pages and the price was dropped from 25 cents to 15 cents.

SON OF VULCAN

Charlton Comics

	Issue #s
Published 11/65–1/66	49, 50
Silver Age 11/65–1/66	49, 50

Major Characters
Son of Vulcan 49, 50

Significant Issues
Note: Son of Vulcan first appears in *Mysteries of Unexplored Worlds* (#s 46–48).

Artists
Bill Fraccio 49, 50

The Son of Vulcan hero from *Mysteries of Unexplored Worlds* took over the title with issue #49. Joe Gill wrote the first issue. The second (and last) issue marked the professional writing debut of future Marvel Comics writer and editor Roy Thomas. Thomas won the Charlton's amateur writing contest with his first story, "The Second Trojan War."

Showcase #55 ©1965 DC Comics, Inc. Murphy Anderson.

Silver Surfer #1 ©1968 Marvel Entertainment Group, Inc. John Buscema.

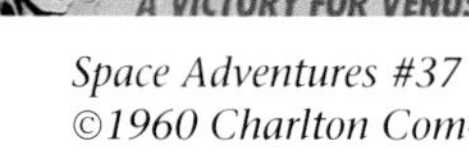

Space Adventures #37 ©1960 Charlton Comics. Steve Ditko.

Spectacular Spider-Man #2, ©1968 Marvel Entertainment Group, Inc. John Romita.

Spectre #2 ©1968 DC Comics, Inc. Neal Adams.

SPACE ADVENTURES

Charlton Comics

	Issue #s
Published 7/52–7/69	1–60, 2–8
Silver Age 3/60–10/61	33–42

Major Characters
Captain Atom 33–40, 42

Significant Issues
33—Origin and first appearance of Captain Atom.

Artists
Steve Ditko 33–40, 42
Rocke Mastroserio 42

Captain Adam of the U.S. Air Force is making last-minute adjustments on the nuclear warhead of an Atlas missile. He drops a screwdriver, tries to retrieve it, and is prematurely launched into outer space.

The missle explodes, with Captain Adam on board, and then . . ."At the instant of fission, Captain Adam was not flesh, bone and blood at all! The dessicated molecular skeleton was intact but a change, never known to man, had taken place!"

He is transformed into Captain Atom, a nuclear-powered superhero with powers of superstrength, invisibility, and invulnerability. Captain Atom was quickly commissioned by President Kennedy to fight the growing communist menace in outer space and behind the Iron Curtain.

Joe Gill wrote the scripts. Steve Ditko designed and drew Captain Atom over two years before he helped create Spider-Man.

Captain Atom was one of the first truly new superheroes of the 1960s, being neither a revival nor a continuation of a 1940s character.

SPECTACULAR SPIDER-MAN

Marvel Comics

	Issue #s
Published 7/68–11/68	1, 2
Silver Age 7/68–11/68	1, 2

Major Characters
Spider-Man 1, 2

Significant Issues
1—Origin retold.
2—Green Goblin appears.

Artists
John Romita 1, 2
Larry Lieber 1

This magazine-sized *Spider-Man* comic book was an interesting experiment by Marvel to take advantage of its new distribution system in 1968 which gave it greater newsstand exposure. The first issue was printed in black-and-white; the second issue was in color. The 35-cent price tag (at a time when regular Spider-Man comics sold for 12 cents) and its unusual size (for a comic) prevented the title from becoming a success.

SPECTRE

DC Comics

	Issue #s
Published 11/67–5/69	1–10
Silver Age 11/67–5/69	1–10

Major Characters
Spectre 1–10
Hourman 7

Significant Issues
3—Wildcat appears.

Artists
Murphy Anderson 1 (Spectre)
Neal Adams 2–5 (Spectre)
Jerry Grandenetti 6–10 (Spectre)
Dick Dillin 7 (Hourman)
Berni Wrightson 9 (Spectre)
Jack Sparling 9, 10 (Spectre)
José Delbo 10 (Spectre)

Detective Captain Jim Corrigan has the spirit of the Spectre, a ghostly all-powerful being, locked within his body. When his psyche divides into two personalities, the Spectre is able to emerge and fight criminals.

Created by Jerry Siegel in 1940, the Spectre faded away before the end of the decade. The character was revived in 1966 by writer Gardner Fox and artist Murphy Anderson for a series of appearances in *Showcase*. The following year, the Spectre had his own comic book, the only member of the original Justice Society of America to do so in the 1960s.

Gardner Fox labored mightily in his scripts to come up with interesting opponents for the all-powerful cosmic hero.

Murphy Anderson, who illustrated Fox's scripts, sympathized: "The Spectre was one of the few characters that I couldn't see any way of handling, unless you watered down his powers. The Spectre is virtually God, and who can fight God? Just the devil. So we were faced with doing virtually the same story over and over unless we watered down his powers. It was a real problem . . . trying to find a believable menace for someone with the powers of God."

THE SPIRIT

Harvey Comics

	Issue #s
Published 10/66–3/67	1, 2
Silver Age 10/66–3/67	1, 2

Major Characters
The Spirit 1, 2

Significant Issues
1—New retelling of the Spirit's origin.

Artists
Will Eisner 1, 2

The Spirit was created by Will Eisner in 1940 as a hero for a seven-page, full-color newspaper supplement. Eisner wrote and drew the adventures of the Spirit until the early 1950s.

Seven stories from the late 1940s were collected and reprinted in each of these giant-sized comics published in 1966 and 1967. Eisner also wrote and drew a new story for each issue.

The Spirit (who is actually a back-from-the-dead criminologist, Denny Colt) was a wry, adult comic book hero. The cinematic look of the stories made them as fresh and gripping in the 1960s as when they were first published.

SPYMAN

Harvey Comics

	Issue #s
Published 9/66–2/67	1–3
Silver Age 9/66–2/67	1–3

Major Characters
Spyman 1–3
Robolink 2

Significant Issues
1—Origin and first appearance of Spyman.

Artists
George Tuska 1 (Spyman)
Dick Ayers 2 (Spyman)
Carl Pfeufer 2 (Robolink)
Bill Draut 3 (Spyman)

Johnny Chance, an American superspy, burns his hand off while removing a radioactive core from an enemy bomb. Government scientists replace his hand with a cybernetic glove, chock-full of explosive devices, black-light rays, and atomic blasters. His gunbelt comes complete with extra screw-in finger weapons for his robotic hand.

Spyman cruises for villains in his helicopter-jet, the Flying Hand. "We must never rest until our shores are safe from those who would seek to enslave free men!" This superspy guy was created by Jim Steranko and written by Otto Binder and Ed Herron.

STRANGE ADVENTURES

DC Comics

	Issue #s
Published 8/50–10/73	1–244
Silver Age 6/65–1/69	177–216

Major Characters
Immortal Man 177, 185, 190, 198
Animal Man 180, 184, 190, 195, 201
The Enchantress 187, 191, 200
Split Man 203
Deadman 205–216

Significant Issues
177—Origin and first appearance of Immortal Man.
180—Origin and first appearance of Animal Man.
205—Origin and first appearance of Deadman.

Artists
Jack Sparling 177, 185, 190, 195, 198, 201, 203 (Immortal Man, Animal Man, Split Man)
Carmine Infantino 180, 190, 205 (Animal Man, Deadman)
Gil Kane 184 (Animal Man)
Howard Purcell 187, 200 (Enchantress)
Jay Scott Pike 191 (Enchantress)
Neal Adams 206–216 (Deadman)

Strange Adventures was the first DC science fiction comic book. In addition to the alien invasion and giant flying saucer stories, there were also science fiction series like Captain Comet, Star Rovers, and the Atomic Knights.

Beginning in 1965, superheroes like Immortal Man and Animal Man began replacing the straight science fiction stories. Animal Man was originally Buddy Baker, a motion picture stuntman who was bathed in radiation from an exploding alien spaceship. Afterwards, whenever he is within

Spirit #2 ©1967 Will Eisner. Will Eisner.

Strange Adventures #190 ©1966 DC Comics, Inc. Carmine Infantino, Murphy Anderson.

Strange Suspense Stories #75 ©*1965 Charlton Comics*. Steve Ditko.

Strange Tales #115 ©*1963 Marvel Entertainment Group, Inc.* Steve Ditko, Dick Ayers.

30 yards of an animal he assumes that creature's powers.

Immortal Man died at least twice in each story. Each time, his spirit would reincarnate in another living being. No matter what body he happened to be in, Immortal Man possessed superstrength, supervision, and hypnotic powers. Even with all his body swapping, Immortal Man kept a steady girlfriend whom he dated in several lives.

Another off-beat superhero was Deadman. Boston Brand, a circus aerialist, is murdered after he discovers one of the circus people is selling opium. A sentient "spirit of the universe," Rama Kushna, sends the dead Brand back to Earth to avenge his death, as well as the wrongdoings of others. Still wearing his acrobat costume, Brand becomes Deadman and has the power to enter the bodies of the living.

STRANGE SUSPENSE STORIES

Charlton Comics

	Issue #s
Published 1/54–9/69	16–77, 1–9
Silver Age 6/65–10/65	75–77

Major Characters
Captain Atom 75–77

Significant Issues
75—Origin of Captain Atom reprinted from *Space Adventures* #33.

Artists
Steve Ditko 75–77 reprints

Strange Suspense Stories began as a comic book with stories about people who suffer from Egyptian curses or discover miniature space ships in their backyards.

In 1965, Charlton Comics used the comic to test the waters for a new line of superhero comics. It reprinted three issues of Captain Atom stories from the early 1960s *Space Adventures*. Satisfied with the response, it turned the title into a new *Captain Atom* comic with issue #78.

STRANGE TALES

Marvel Comics

	Issue #s
Published 6/51–11/76	1–188
Silver Age 10/62–5/68	101–168
	Annual 2

Major Characters
Human Torch 101–122 Annual 2
The Thing and The Human Torch 123–134
Dr. Strange 110, 111, 114–168
Nick Fury 135–168

Significant Issues
101—Human Torch begins.
107—Human Torch versus the Sub-Mariner.
110—First appearance of Dr. Strange.
114—Appearance of villain dressed as Captain America.
115—Origin of Dr. Strange.
116—Human Torch versus The Thing.
120—X-Men appear.
123—Thor appears.
125—Sub-Mariner appears.
135—Origin of Nick Fury, Agent of SHIELD.
156—Daredevil appears.
159–162—Captain America appears.
Annual 2—Spider-Man appears.

Artists
Jack Kirby 101–105, 108, 109, 114, 120, 135, 141, 142 Annual 2 (Human Torch, Nick Fury)
Dick Ayers 106, 107, 110–113, 115–119, 121, 122, 124–129 (Human Torch, The Thing, and Human Torch)
Steve Ditko 110, 111, 114–147
Carl Burgos 123 (The Thing and Human Torch)
Bob Powell 130–134 (The Thing and Human Torch)
John Severin 136–138 (Nick Fury)
Joe Sinnott 139 (Nick Fury)
Don Heck 140, 145–148 (Nick Fury)
Howard Purcell 143, 144 (Nick Fury)
Bill Everett 148–152 (Dr. Strange)
Ogden Whitney 149 (Nick Fury)
John Buscema 150 (Nick Fury)
Marie Severin 153–160 (Dr. Strange)
Jim Steranko 151–167 (Nick Fury)
Dan Adkins 161–165, 167, 168 (Dr. Strange)
George Tuska 166 (Dr. Strange)

At the beginning of the Marvel superhero age in 1962, Stan Lee recalled, "*Strange Tales*, like many other Marvel titles, contained various short stories of mystery and fantasy, but no main characters who continued from issue to issue." In an attempt, as Lee put it, "to tie the whole Marvel line more closely together," he introduced the Human Torch as a solo star in the first half of the *Strange Tales* comic.

Lee recalled that "the idea seemed to catch on. Sales increased by leaps and bounds—or perhaps I should say flight and flame. But the Torch's sales accounted for only half the magazine . . . I figure if one superhero could make a mag successful, think of what two might do. See what I mean?"

The second superhero was the master of the mystic arts, Dr. Strange, as drawn by Spider-Man artist Steve Ditko. Ditko had a major influence on the strip, and often both plotted and drew the transdimensional adventures.

Later, The Thing was added to the Human Torch series, making it the "Odd Couple" of the *Fantastic Four*. Stan Lee wrote most of the Human Torch stories, except for a period in 1963 when Robert Bernstein (R. Berns), Larry Lieber, and Ernie Hart (H. Huntley) contributed scripts.

When James Bond movies and the *Man from UNCLE* television series started the superspy craze, a new Lee and Jack Kirby series, *Nick Fury, Agent of SHIELD*, replaced The Thing and the Torch.

SUB-MARINER

Marvel Comics

	Issue #s
Published 5/68–9/74	1–72
Silver Age 5/68–12/69	1–20

Major Characters
Sub-Mariner 1–20

Significant Issues
1—Origin of Sub-Mariner retold. Storyline continues from *Iron Man and Sub-Mariner* #1.
2—Inhumans appear.
8—The Thing (from Fantastic Four) appears.
14—Sub-Mariner versus Toro, sidekick of 1940s Human Torch.
20—Dr. Doom appears.

Artists
John Buscema 1–8, 20
Marie Severin 9, 12–19
Gene Colan 10, 11

After appearing in *Tales to Astonish* for nearly 17 months, the Sub-Mariner received his own book in 1968. The Sub-Mariner mythos was greatly elaborated, with old and new villains and a developing love relationship. Roy Thomas wrote all the issues published in the 1960s.

SUPER HEROES

Dell Publishing

	Issue #s
Published 1/67–6/67	1–4
Silver Age 1/67–6/67	1–4

Major Characters
Fab Four 1–4

Significant Issues
1—Origin and first appearance of the Fab Four.

Artists
Sal Trapani 1–4

While visiting the "Hall of Heroes" wax museum, four teenagers discover the bodies of four superpowered androids. As the teens stand gasping at the inanimate (but fully operational) "superheroic androids," an atomic power feedback surges through the room. Suddenly, their minds are transferred into the bodies of the androids!

The four kids—Tom, Don, Reb, and Polly—now control the bodies of the android superheroes. "El," the first android, has laser powers. "Hy" can shoot hypersonic blasts. "Crispy" can freeze things immediately. "Polymer Poly" is a heat-resistant, flying "female" android. The teens discover that their minds can enter and leave the android bodies at will, allowing them to become superheroes whenever danger threatens. They leave the android bodies in an abandoned opera house and return whenever they need to perform their mind swap.

As the four superpowered androids, they are known as the Fab Four. During their career, they encountered villains like Mr. Mod, Mr. Nutt, Johnny Boom-Boom, and the Clown.

SUPERBOY

DC Comics

	Issue #s
Published 3/49–12/79	1–258
Silver Age 10/58–12/69	68–161

Major Characters
Superboy 68–161
Legion of Super-Heroes 147

Significant Issues
68—Origin and first appearance of original Bizarro.

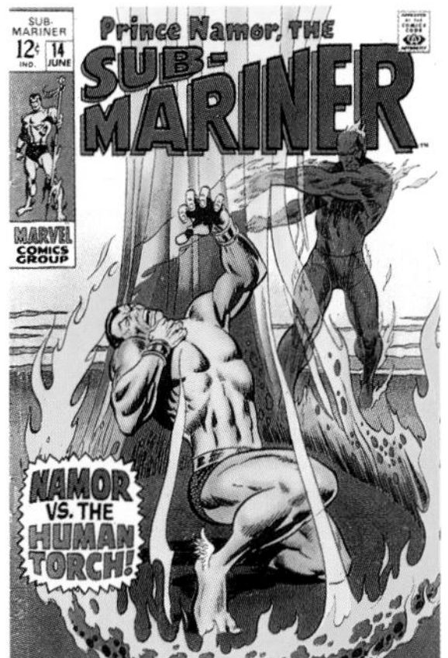

Sub-Mariner #14 ©1969 *Marvel Entertainment Group, Inc.* Marie Severin, Frank Giacoia.

Super Heroes #1 ©1967 *Dell Publishing*. Sal Trapani.

Superboy #68 ©1958 *DC Comics, Inc.* Curt Swan, Stan Kaye.

Superman #149 ©1961 *DC Comics, Inc.* Curt Swan, Shelly Moldoff.

Superman's Girlfriend Lois Lane #16 ©1960 *DC Comics, Inc.* Curt Swan, Stan Kaye.

76—Origin of Super-Monkey.
78—Origin of Mr. Mxyzptlk; origin of Superboy's costume.
80—Supergirl appears.
85, 86, 92, 96, 131, 135, 161—Lex Luthor appears.
86—Introduction of Pete Ross, Superboy's friend.
86, 93, 98, 100, 117, 125, 147—Legion of Super-Heroes appears.
89—First appearance of Mon-el
98—First appearance of Ultra-Boy.
100—Anniversary Issue; map of Krypton.
104—Origin of Phantom Zone.
124—Origin and first appearance of Insect Queen (Lana Lang).
126—Origin retold of Krypto, the Super Dog.
129, 138, 147, 156—Contain reprints; 80-page, giant-sized issues.
131, 132, 136—Krypto appears in Space Canine Patrol.
145—Superboy's parents take youth serum.
147—Origin of the Legion of Super-Heroes.

Artists
George Papp 68–73, 75–79, 81, 83–97, 99–102, 104–146, 148, 156
Johnny Sikela 69–72, 74–80, 82, 129, 138, 142, 146
Creig Flessel 72, 149
Curt Swan 73, 80, 89, 91, 98, 100, 103–107, 112, 117, 118, 121, 123, 126, 132, 136, 147, 148, 156
Al Plastino 79, 81, 83, 86, 88, 90, 93, 96, 98, 102, 105, 107, 108, 110, 114, 116, 125, 128, 133, 137, 140, 143, 149
Pete Costanza 147 (Legion)
Bob Brown 150–155, 157–161

As he had done with the *Superman* comic book, editor Mort Weisinger introduced new characters, storylines, and gimmicks into the *Superboy* comic book in the late 1950s.

A "Bizarro-Superboy" appeared in 1958. Mon-El, Superboy's superfriend, followed a year later. The Legion of Super-Heroes made many appearances in *Superboy*. Other new elements added to the Superboy legend included a basement trophy room (an early version of the Fortress of Solitude), a closetful of Superboy robots, and new revelations about Superboy's Kryptonian past.

Even Lana Lang, Superboy's would-be girlfriend, got a new look. Thanks to a Bio-Genetic ring, she became Insect Queen and could change into any insectlike creature.

Writers included Otto Binder (1954–68), Jerry Siegel (1959–66), Bill Finger (1961–64), and Leo Dorfman (1962–69). George Papp, Al Plastino, and Curt Swan drew most of the Boy of Steel's adventures in the late 1950s and 1960s.

SUPERMAN

DC Comics

		Issue #s
Published	Summer 1939–9/86	1–423
Silver Age	8/58–12/69	123–222

Major Characters
Superman 123–222

Significant Issues
123—Pre-Supergirl tryout story, "The Girl of Steel."
127, 138, 142, 147—Titano, the Super Ape appears.
129—First appearance and origin of Lori Lemaris, Superman's mermaid girlfriend.
131, 136, 144, 146—Superboy appears.
134, 140, 142, 144, 150, 152, 154, 156, 157, 161, 176, 199—Supergirl appears.
140—First Blue Kryptonite.
140, 144, 147, 149, 164, 167, 168, 170, 173, 175, 194, 213—Lex Luthor appears.
141—First appearance of Lyla Lerrol.
142, 156—Batman appears.
146—Superman's life story.
147, 149, 152, 155, 156, 162, 172, 173—Legion of Super-Heroes appears.
152—Superbaby appears.
158—First appearance of Flamebird and Nightwing.
162—Story of Superman-Red and Superman-Blue.
183, 187, 193, 197, 202, 207, 212, 217, 222—80-page giants; contain reprints.
199—Superman and Flash have a race. Justice League of America appears.

Artists
Dick Sprang 123
Al Plastino 124, 125, 129–131, 133, 135, 136, 138, 139, 144–147, 150–153, 157, 160, 161, 163–165, 169–174, 178–180, 183, 184, 186, 188, 191, 193, 194, 196, 198, 201, 203–207, 212–214, 217, 218, 222
Kurt Schaffenberger 124–126, 128, 131, 142, 150
Wayne Boring 124–130, 132–136, 138–143, 155, 183, 187, 189, 190, 195–197, 200, 202, 207, 208, 215, 217
Curt Swan 127, 130, 137, 139, 147–182, 186, 187, 192–195, 197–199, 201, 207–215, 218–222

John Forte 143, 153, 202
George Papp 152, 173, 177, 212
Pete Costanza 185, 203
Jim Mooney 185
Ross Andru 204, 211, 216

Superman was already an American institution by the late 1950s. No other superhero had been so well received or so overexposed. After twenty years of appearing in comic books, as well as in movies, TV, newspapers, and radio, the Man of Steel was ready for an overhaul in 1958. Editor Mort Weisinger and writer Otto Binder began fashioning new stories and new characters to revitalize the Superman legend.

Superman's life in the late 1950s and 1960s would be irrevocably changed by new storylines which introduced gold and red kryptonite, a world full of Bizarro-Supermen, superpowered visitors from the Bottle City of Kandor, Phantom Zone fugitives, and a mermaid girlfriend, Lori Lemaris. Outrageous plots and covers were dreamed up in hopes of capturing the attention of ten-year-olds.

The *Superman* comics of the 1960s became so riddled with gimmicky plots, trick endings, imaginary stories, robot doubles, and alien impersonators that the covers had to promise skeptical readers that the story inside the comic was "Not A Hoax! Not An Imaginary Tale—But *Real*!!!"

Wayne Boring, Al Plastino, and Curt Swan drew over 90% of all the *Superman* stories from 1958 to 1969. Writers included Otto Binder, Edmond Hamilton, Jerry Siegel, Leo Dorfman, Bill Finger, and Jim Shooter.

SUPERMAN'S GIRLFRIEND LOIS LANE

DC Comics

	Issue #s
Published 3/58–9/74	1–137
Silver Age 3/58–11/69	1–97

Major Characters
Lois Lane 1–97

Significant Issues
7, 10, 12, 17, 21, 22, 26, 31–33, 36, 38, 40, 41, 43, 44, 50–54, 56, 57, 59, 60, 63, 66, 69, 71, 76, 77, 79—Lana Lang (Lois's rival) appears.
9—Pat Boone appears.
12—Aquaman appears.
14, 20, 35, 38, 39, 55—Supergirl appears.
19, 20, 23, 25, 39, 60—"Mr. and Mrs. Clark Kent" series appears.
23, 28, 34, 46, 64, 65, 69—Lex Luthor appears.
29—Batman, Green Arrow, and Aquaman appear.
47—Legion of Super-Heroes appears.
59, 70, 71, 89—Batman appears.
68, 77, 86, 95—Reprints; 80-page giants.
70—First 1960s appearance of Catwoman. Penguin appears.
71—Catwoman appears.
93—Wonder Woman appears.

Artists
Kurt Schaffenberger 1–28, 30–81, 84–88, 94, 95, 97
Wayne Boring 2, 4, 6–8, 10, 13, 77, 78
Al Plastino 5, 12, 18, 20
John Forte 9, 24, 25, 28, 29, 31, 50, 57
Curt Swan 17, 27, 29, 32, 33, 35–39, 41, 45, 54, 59, 68, 72, 86, 89, 91, 92, 94, 96
Irv Novick 82–85, 87, 88, 90, 93, 96, 97

"My lips were begging for Superman's kiss . . . sob! . . . and he took off with just a cool goodbye! Oh how I wish I had never met him!" It was a tough job being Superman's girlfriend, even for a savvy and scheming newspaper reporter like Lois Lane.

The popularity of the Superman TV show prompted DC to try Lois Lane out for a series on her own. After appearing in two 1957 issues of *Showcase*, she got her own comic book in 1958.

The Lois Lane comic book captured readers with its attractive artwork by Kurt Schaffenberger and the whacky stories by writers Otto Binder, Jerry Siegel, Edmond Hamilton, Robert Bernstein, Leo Dorfman, Bill Finger, and Dave Wood.

No situation was too humiliating for Lois to endure in her shameless quest to discover Superman's secret identity or ensnare him in marriage. She fakes her own death, makes a pact with the devil, and even exposes herself to deadly rays in an effort to become Mrs. Superman.

A popular feature of the *Lois Lane* comic book were the "Imaginary Stories," which showed what might happen if Lois and Superman ever wed. Even in the "imaginary stories," Lois is frustrated: "Great! While I stay at home, minding babies, cleaning house, Lana Lang steals my job and now she's after my husband Superman! This means war!"

SUPERMAN'S PAL JIMMY OLSEN

DC Comics

	Issue #s
Published 9/54–2/74	1–163
Silver Age 9/58–12/69	31–125

Major Characters
Jimmy Olsen 31–125

Superman's Pal Jimmy Olsen #68 ©1963 DC Comics, Inc. Curt Swan, George Klein.

Tales of Suspense #58 ©1964 Marvel Entertainment Group, Inc. Jack Kirby, Chic Stone.

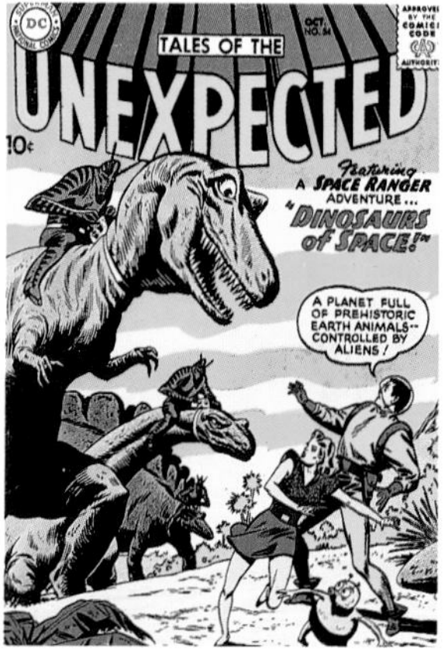

Tales of the Unexpected #54 ©1960 DC Comics, Inc. Bob Brown.

Significant Issues
31—Origin and first appearance of Jimmy Olsen as Elastic Lad.
36—First appearance of Lucy Lane (Lois's sister and Jimmy's sometimes girlfriend).
37, 46, 54, 99, 101—Elastic Lad appears.
40, 45, 46, 51, 57, 63, 70, 75, 94, 101, 102, 117—Supergirl appears.
49—Jimmy becomes Congorilla.
55—Aquaman appears.
58, 92, 117—Batman appears.
62, 72, 76, 85, 106, 117—Legion of Super-Heroes appears. Jimmy also appears as Elastic Lad.
69—Flamebird (Jimmy Olsen) and Nightwing (Superman) story.
70—Silver Kryptonite story.
74, 87, 109, 118—Lex Luthor appears.
80—First appearance of Bizarro-Jimmy Olsen.
115—Aquaman appears.

Artists
Curt Swan 31–55, 57–72, 74–79, 81–91, 95, 104, 106–114, 116, 119, 121–123, 125
Al Plastino 50, 55, 56, 60, 64, 73, 76, 78, 87
John Forte 56, 58, 59, 61–77, 80, 81, 83–85, 87, 88
Kurt Schaffenberger 56, 66, 81, 89, 117
George Papp 79, 80, 82, 84, 86, 88, 90, 94
Pete Costanza 91–94, 96–103, 105–107, 109, 111, 112, 114–121, 123–125
Jim Mooney 92

Superman's Pal, Jimmy Olsen was published in 1954 during the popularity of the Superman TV show. Readers may have bought the new comic for Superman the first time, but they returned to it again and again for the "zany" adventures of cub reporter Jimmy Olsen.

Although Superman regularly appeared in every story (usually in summons to Jimmy's signal watch—zee! zee! zee!), Jimmy took center stage. In some adventures he uses his disguise collection to dress up for such adventures as "Jimmy Olsen, Juvenile Delinquent" or "Miss Jimmy Olsen" ("Wow! My female impersonation worked! Big Monte likes me—his girlfriend is burning up!").

His time is also occupied by Lucy Lane, Lois Lane's sister ("What a doll! I'll impress her—I'm Superman's pal, you know! Why he hardly goes anywhere without taking me!"). Jimmy also has two superhero identities as Elastic Lad and Flamebird.

Otto Binder wrote the first 30 issues, and many of the later ones as well. Other writers included Jerry Siegel, Edmond Hamilton, Robert Bernstein, Leo Dorfman, Bill Finger, and Dave Wood.

TALES OF SUSPENSE

Marvel Comics

	Issue #s
Published 1/59–3/68	1–99
Silver Age 3/63–3/68	39–99

Major Characters
Iron Man 39–99
The Watcher 49–58
Captain America 59–99

Significant Issues
39—Origin and first appearance of Iron Man.
40, 48—New Iron Man costume.
49—X-Men appear.
52—Origin and first appearance of the Black Widow.
53—Origin of the Watcher.
57—Origin and first appearance of Hawkeye.
58—Iron Man versus Captain America.
63—Origin of Captain America.
65—First appearance of the Red Skull (old Captain America villain) in 1960s comic.
66—Origin of Red Skull.
67, 68, 72, 79–81, 89–91—Red Skull appears.
97–99—Black Panther appears.

Artists
Don Heck 39, 42, 44–46, 50–72 (Ironman)
Jack Kirby 40, 41, 43 (Ironman) 59–70, 72–74, 78–86, 92–99 (Captain America)
Steve Ditko 47–49 (Ironman)
Larry Lieber 49–57 (Watcher)
George Tuska 58 (Watcher) 71 (Captain America)
Gene Colan 73–99 (Ironman)
Dick Ayers 75 (Captain America)
John Romita 76, 77 (Captain America)
Jack Sparling 87 (Captain America)
Gil Kane 88–91 (Captain America)

The 1959–62 issues of *Tales of Suspense* usually featured monster and supernatural stories by Jack Kirby, Steve Ditko, and Don Heck. In 1963, these same artists would be working on a new superhero series for the comic: Iron Man. Larry Lieber wrote the first story, based on Stan Lee's plot, and Jack Kirby created the costume. Don Heck, Kirby, and Steve Ditko drew Iron Man during its first three years.

After several issues written by Robert Bernstein, Stan Lee took over the writing chores on

Iron Man for the rest of the *Tales of Suspense* issues.

In early 1964, a series featuring the Watcher, Marvel's cosmic do-nothing peeping Tom ("As for my task, it is only to observe and record, for I am . . . the Watcher!"), ran as a secondary feature with the Iron Man stories for nearly a year.

Captain America replaced the Watcher in issue #59, and soon became the comic's most popular feature. Jack Kirby, cocreator of Captain America, drew the majority of the stories. Stan Lee scripted the series.

Both Captain America and Iron Man were popular enough to rate their own books by 1968. Iron Man left the comic and got his own comic while Captain America took over the title with issue #100.

TALES OF THE UNEXPECTED

DC Comics

	Issue #s
Published 2/56–12/67	1–104
Silver Age 8/59–10/66	40–97

Major Characters

Space Ranger 40–82
Automan 91, 94, 97

Significant Issues

Note: Space Ranger first appears in *Showcase* 15 and 16.
40—Space Ranger series begins; ends #82.
91, 94, 97—Automan series.

Artists

Jim Mooney 40–46, 49 (Space Ranger)
Bob Brown 47, 48, 50–77 (Space Ranger)
Phil Kelsey 78–82 (Space Ranger)
Lee Elias 91 (Automan)
Bill Ely 94 (Automan)
Jay Pike 97 (Automan)

Rick Starr is the Space Ranger, an interplanetary adventurer who fights crime throughout the solar system. Starr has an asteroid hideout where he keeps his Space Ranger uniform and weapons like thermoblaze blasters and electron displacer rayguns.

The guardian of his hideout is Cryll, a bubble-gum-pink and basketball-shaped alien from Pluto. Space Ranger once rescued the Plutonian and thus earned his eternal loyalty. Cyrll has the ability to change into any interplanetary animal ("Don't tell anyone—I've changed into a Neptunian electric eel and can absorb electricity as a sponge absorbs water!").

The Space Ranger's girl Friday is Myra Mason. As he leaves on another dangerous mission, he tells Myra to remain behind and check in at "the Martian Moon Hotel." She pouts, "I never get in on the fun!"

Space Ranger first appeared in 1958 after editor Jack Schiff discussed the idea for the character with writer Arnold Drake. Drake and artist Bob Brown created the Space Ranger for a two-issue tryout in *Showcase*. The character was successful enough to land a five-year series in 1959 in *Tales of the Unexpected*, a science fiction comic which had no regular feature or characters until that time.

Automan, a mechanical superhero and "star graduate of Professor Sterling's Robot Tech," appeared from 1965 to 1966 in a three-issue series written by Bob Haney.

TALES TO ASTONISH

Marvel Comics

	Issue #s
Published 1/59–3/68	1–101
Silver Age 1/62, 9/62–3/68	27, 35–101

Major Characters

Ant-Man 27, 35–48
Giant-Man 49–69
The Wasp 51–58
Incredible Hulk 60–101
Sub-Mariner 70–101

Significant Issues

27—First appearance of Henry Pym, who later becomes Ant-Man.
35—Origin of Ant-Man.
44—Origin and first appearance of Wasp.
49—Ant-Man becomes Giant-Man.
52—Origin and first appearance of Black Knight.
57—Spider-Man appears.
59—Giant-Man versus the Hulk.
60—Incredible Hulk series begins.
69—Giant-Man series ends.
70—Sub-Mariner series begins.
82—Iron Man appears.
92, 93—Silver Surfer appears.
100—Hulk versus the Sub-Mariner.

Artists

Jack Kirby 27, 35–40, 44 (Ant-Man) 49–51 (Giant-Man) 68–70 (Incredible Hulk) 83 (Sub-Mariner)
Don Heck 41–43, 45–48 (Ant-Man) 54 (Giant-Man)
Dick Ayers 52, 53, 55–60 (Giant-Man)

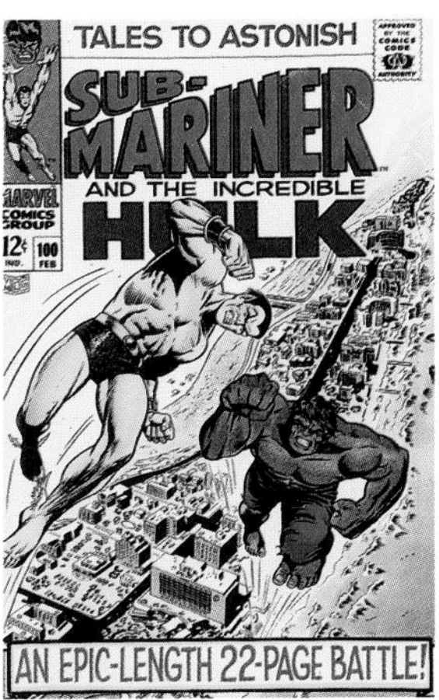

Tales to Astonish #100 ©1968 Marvel Entertainment Group, Inc. Marie Severin, Dan Adkins.

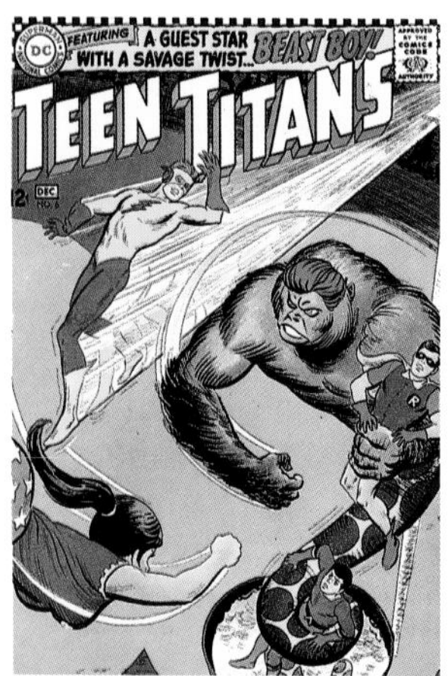

Teen Titans #6 ©1966 DC Comics, Inc. Nick Cardy.

Thor #156, ©1968 Marvel Entertainment Group, Inc. Jack Kirby, Vince Colletta.

Steve Ditko 61 (Giant-Man)
Carl Burgos 62–64 (Giant-Man)
Bob Powell 65, 68, 69 (Giant-Man) 73, 74 (Incredible Hulk)
John Romita 66, 67 (Giant-Man) 77 (Incredible Hulk)
Larry Lieber 51–58 (The Wasp)
Steve Ditko 60–67 (Incredible Hulk)
Mike Esposito 71, 72, 75 (Incredible Hulk)
Gil Kane 76, 88–91 (Incredible Hulk)
Bill Everett 78–84 (Incredible Hulk) 87–91, 94–96 (Sub-Mariner)
John Buscema 85–87 (Incredible Hulk)
Marie Severin 92–101 (Incredible Hulk) 100 (Sub-Mariner)
Gene Colan 70–82, 84, 85, 101 (Sub-Mariner)
Jerry Grandenetti 86 (Sub-Mariner)
Dan Adkins 92, 93, 99 (Sub-Mariner)
Werner Roth 97, 98 (Sub-Mariner)

Before there were Marvel superheroes, there were monster stories with mad scientists, alien invaders, giant insects, and unspeakable creatures. *Tales to Astonish* featured stories like "I Found the Abominable Snowman" and "The Man in The Anthill."

This last story introduced Henry Pym, a scientist who would return a few months later as a superhero called the Ant-Man. Ant-Man became a regular feature in the comic and later acquired a partner, the Wasp.

After discovering a growth gas, Henry Pym changed from Ant-Man to Giant-Man. The Giant-Man series, along with a backup feature called "Tales of the Wasp," would make up most of the 1964 issues.

The Incredible Hulk (who had not had a regular comic book series since 1963) shared the pages of *Tales to Astonish* with Giant-Man and the Wasp beginning in late 1964. The Hulk series, drawn most notably by Steve Ditko and Marie Severin, continued for the rest of the title's run.

The Sub-Mariner replaced Giant-Man in *Tales to Astonish* in 1965. He shared the comic with the Hulk for its last three years.

After the Sub-Mariner received his book in 1968, the Hulk took over *Tales to Astonish* with issue #102.

TEEN TITANS

DC Comics

		Issue #s
Published	1/66–2/78	1–53
Silver Age	1/66–11/69	1–24

Major Characters
Teen Titans 1–24

Significant Issues
Note: Teen Titans first appear in *Brave and the Bold* #54. Also see *Brave and the Bold* #s 60, 83 and *Showcase* #59.
1—Batman, Flash, Wonder Woman, and Aquaman appear.
3—Batman appears.
4—First appearance of Speedy in Teen Titans title.
6—Doom Patrol and Beast Boy appear.
11—Speedy appears.
18—First appearance of Starfire.
19—Aqualad leaves the Titans and Speedy joins.
21—Hawk and Dove appear.
22—Origin of Wonder Girl. Wonder Woman appears.

Artists
Nick Cardy 1–7, 13, 14, 16, 17
Irv Novick 8–12
Lee Elias 15
Bill Draut 18
Gil Kane 19, 22–24
Neal Adams 20–22

The Teen Titans consisted of Kid Flash, Aqualad, Robin, and Wonder Girl, and (later) Speedy. The teens were DC Comics' junior sidekicks of the Flash, Aquaman, Batman, Wonder Woman, and Green Arrow. After a successful tryout in both *Brave and Bold* and *Showcase*, the Teen Titans got their own comic book in 1966.

The teenage superheroes have a secret headquarters ("Titan Lair") and hold meetings, reminiscent of an adolescent Justice League of America. They take on cases that their adult mentors are too "old" to deal with, like teen runaways, crooked rock and roll musicians, and juvenile delinquent monsters.

Unfortunately, the teens sometimes tried a little too hard to be hip and cool—even for a 1960s comic. Everything was a "groovy, freaky kind of scene or happening." Wonder Girl was usually called Wonder Chick or Wonder Doll by her yet-to-be liberated male counterparts.

Bob Haney, who created the Teen Titans, wrote all of their stories for the first two years. Other writers included Len Wein, Marv Wolfman, Mike Friedrich, and Neal Adams.

THOR

Marvel Comics

		Issue #s
Published	3/66–	126–
Silver Age	3/66–12/69	126–171 Annual 2

Major Characters
Thor 126–171
Tales of Asgard 126–145
The Inhumans 146–152

Significant Issues
126, 128–131—Hercules appears.
136—Thor loses Jane Foster as girlfriend.
137—Lady Sif, Thor's new love, appears.
146, 147—Origin of the Inhumans.
158, 159—Thor origin reprinted and true origin of Dr. Blake revealed.
165, 166—Adam Warlock appears as "Him."

Artists
Jack Kirby 126–171 Annual 2 (Thor, Tales of Asgard, The Inhumans)

Formerly published as *Journey Into Mystery* until issue #125, *Thor* became one of Marvel's main titles in the mid-1960s.

Kirby ended his epic "Tales of Asgard" series in 1967 and began a new series called "The Inhumans," based on characters that he created earlier for the *Fantastic Four*.

Stan Lee wrote and Jack Kirby drew all the 1960s issues. Vince Colletta, continuing his long inking stint on Thor from *Journey Into Mystery*, also inked all the 1960s issues except the last four.

THRILL-O-RAMA

Harvey Comics

	Issue #s
Published 10/65–12/66	1–3
Silver Age 10/65–12/66	1–3

Major Characters
Man in Black 1–3
Pirana 2, 3
Clawfang 2

Significant Issues
2—Origin and first appearance of Pirana.

Artists
Bob Powell 1 (Man in Black)
Jack Sparling 2, 3 (Pirana, Man in Black)
Al Williamson 2 (Clawfang)

Ed Yates is an oceanographer who is experimenting with better ways for divers to breath underwater. His experiment backfires when he receives an electric shock which alters his metabolism. Now he must always breathe underwater and live in the ocean, like a fish.

"H–how will I survive? I'll just be a little 'fish' among monsters in the sea! Unless I'm as strong as my pet piranha, pound for pound, I'm sunk," he moans. But then an idea, "Of course—That's it!" Yates decides to become a human piranha, and he equips himself with jet-propelled flippers and underwater weaponry. He soon acquires a pair of pet barracudas called, of course, Bara and Cuda. He fights baddies like Murderina Mermaid, Chief Ooz, and Brainstorm.

Otto Binder, the author of several Aquaman stories some eight years earlier, also wrote the underwater adventures of Pirana.

Thrill-O-Rama #3
©1966 Harvey Comics.
Jack Sparling.

THUNDER AGENTS

Tower Comics

	Issue #s
Published 11/65–11/69	1–20
Silver Age 11/65–11/69	1–20

Major Characters
THUNDER Agents 1–14, 16, 17, 20
Dynamo 1–20
NoMan 1–20
Menthor 1–7, 18
Lightning 5–16, 19
Raven 8–12, 14

Significant Issues
1—Origin and first appearance of Dynamo, NoMan, Menthor, and the THUNDER Squad.
4—Origin and first appearance of Lightning.
7—Menthor dies.
8—Origin and first appearance of Raven.
20—Dynamo origin; rest reprints.

Artists
Wally Wood 1–8, 10, 15, 17, 20 (THUNDER Agents, Dynamo)
Reed Crandall 1, 4, 5, 18, 20 (NoMan, Dynamo)
Gil Kane 1, 5, 14, 16 (Menthor, NoMan, Raven)
Mike Sekowsky 1–12, 19 (THUNDER Agents, Menthor, NoMan, Lightning)
Dick Ayers 2 (NoMan)
John Giunta 3–9, 11, 12, 14, 20 (NoMan, Menthor, THUNDER Agents)
Steve Ditko 6, 7, 12, 14, 16, 18 (NoMan, Menthor, Dynamo)
George Tuska 7, 8, 10, 13–17, 19 (THUNDER Agents, Raven, Dynamo)
Dan Adkins 8, 9, 11, 13, 16, 19 (THUNDER Agents, Dynamo)
Ogden Whitney 9, 10, 13, 15, 17, 18

THUNDER Agents #2
©1966 Tower Comics.
Wally Wood.

Thunderbolt #1 ©1966 *Charlton Comics.* Pete Morisi.

Tiger Girl #1 ©1968 *Western Publishing Co.* Jack Sparling.

(THUNDER Agents, NoMan)
Manny Stallman 9–12 (Raven)
Chic Stone 11, 13–18, 20 (THUNDER Agents, Lightning, Dynamo)
Paul Reinman 19 (Dynamo, NoMan)

They were The Higher United Nations Defense Enforcement Reserves. They were THUNDER—THUNDER Agents, superheroes recruited to battle any menace which might threaten earth.

They were Dynamo, NoMan, Menthor, Raven, and Lightning, supersecret agents with powers ranging from invincibility to invisibility. There was also the THUNDER Squad, a trained band of operatives and highly skilled specialists who, with the THUNDER Agents, engaged in international skirmishes with aliens, zombie armies, and crazed dictators.

The comic book came out at the height of the superhero boom. Designed and packaged for the newly created Tower Comics by Wally Wood, the title contained some of the nicest artwork of the time. "I was not only Tower's top artist," Wood once said, "I created the characters, and wrote most of the THUNDER scripts. I functioned as a free-lance editor and did as much of the art as I could."

The title was successful enough to launch two spin-off titles, *Dynamo* and *No-Man.* Writers included Wood, Len Brown, Larry Ivie, Bill Pearson, Steve Skeates, Gil Kane, Russ Jones, and Roger Brand.

THUNDERBOLT

Charlton Comics

	Issue #s
Published 1/66–11/67	1, 51–60
Silver Age 1/66–11/67	1, 51–60

Major Characters
Thunderbolt 1, 51–60
Judomaster 52
Captain Atom 53
The Sentinels 54–59
The Prankster 60

Significant Issues
1—Origin and first appearance of Thunderbolt.
(Note: For other Thunderbolt appearances, see *Judomaster.*)

Artists
Pete Morisi 1, 51–56, 58 (Thunderbolt)
Pat Boyette 57, 59, 60 (Thunderbolt)
Frank McLaughlin 52, 53 (Judomaster, Captain Atom)
Sam Grainger 54–59 (The Sentinels)
Jim Aparo 60 (The Prankster)

Peter Cannon, orphaned son of American missionaries in Tibet, is raised in a Himalayan monastery by lamas who train him in the mystic ways of the East. He returns to America as Thunderbolt with his Tibetan companion Tabu, where he fights the Hooded One, Evila (a demummified Egyptian sorceress), and Tong, master of an Oriental crime empire.

Written and drawn by Pete A. Morisi ("PAM") for all but three issues, Thunderbolt was a strict 1960s pacifist who hated fighting and being away from his monastic retreat in the Himalayas. "I don't want any part of a civilization that fosters its own evil, through greed, hate, and violence! Tranquility, brotherhood, peace amongst men . . . these are the things that matter! Must there always be war, crime, and violence? Will men never learn the futility of chaos, and the fallacy of power?"

TIGER GIRL

Gold Key

	Issue #s
Published 9/68	1
Silver Age 9/68	1

Major Characters
Tiger Girl 1

Significant Issues
1—First and only appearance of Tiger Girl.

Artists
Jack Sparling 1

"As beautiful as Venus . . . and as fierce as a creature of the jungle . . . is that mysterious, masked crusading chick famed the world over as Tiger Girl! Through the city streets prowls this amazing doll, stalking the most evil criminals on this planet . . . tracking them to their lairs . . . battling them with the ferocity of a Bengal tiger! You'll dig this Terrific Pussycat as heartily as arch-villains despise her!"

In her secret identity as "a shapely aerialist" for the Dingaling and South Circus, Lily Taylor uses her acrobatic skills when she becomes Tiger Girl. She is accompanied by a circus tiger called Kitten, with whom she maintains an ESP link.

Jerry Siegel was the writer and creator of Tiger Girl, one of the few new 1960s superheroines. Despite Siegel's references to her as an "amazing doll" and "terrific pussycat," Tiger Girl was an early attempt to recognize women as equal to men, at least in the superhero department. When a secret agent tells her that crime fighting is for guys like him, and "You should be home scrambling eggs over a hot stove," Tiger Girl responds: "It's conceited apes like you who keep women from achieving equal rights!" To which the guy still thinks, "What a sizzle-tempered cutie!"

UNEARTHLY SPECTACULARS

Harvey Comics

	Issue #s
Published 10/65–3/67	1–3
Silver Age 10/65–3/67	1–3

Major Characters
Tiger Boy 1, 2
Jack Quick Frost 2, 3
Miracles, Inc. 2, 3

Significant Issues
1—Origin and first appearance of Tiger Boy.
2—Origin and first appearance of Jack Frost.

Artists
Doug Wildey 1 (Tiger Boy)
Gil Kane 2 (Tiger Boy)
Jack Sparling 2 (Jack Frost)
Wally Wood 2 (Miracles, Inc., Earthman)
Bill Draut 3 (Jack Frost)
Joe Orlando 3 (Miracles, Inc.)

Unearthly Spectaculars was a combination of science fiction and superhero stories from Harvey Comics, the publishers of Richie Rich, Baby Huey, and Little Dot.

James Flynn, an agent of the U.S. "International Counterintelligence Agency," is tossed into Arctic waters by enemy agents and freezes solid. After an atomic blast thaws him out, he discovers he can freeze anything with his breath and shoot icicles from his fingertips. He rejoins the Agency as a superhero, Jack Quick Frost. Unfortunately, Jack has to refreeze himself every half hour and live in a giant air conditioning unit. These cool adventures were written by Ed Herron.

The other hero in the comic was Tiger Boy, who in reality is Paul Canfield, a high school student whose parents are from the planet Jupiter. As a native Jovian, Paul has the ability to change into any shape (like a tiger!), teleport, levitate, and transmute elements. He discovers his secret powers and alien ancestry while in his living room one day: "Look, Dad! Mom! I'm making the furniture fly around the room! The chairs are dancing, the table does cartwheels . . . as I ordered 'em to!"

WEREWOLF

Dell Comics

	Issue #s
Published 12/66–4/67	1–3
Silver Age 12/66–4/67	1–3

Major Characters
Werewolf 1–3

Significant Issues
1—Origin and first appearance of Werewolf.

Artists
Tony Tallarico 1–3

USAF flier Major Wiley Wolf crashes in the Arctic and suffers from amnesia. Living with a wolf pack, he is finally rescued by the CIA. They turn him into a superagent (code name: Werewolf) and hypnotize him so he learns how to alter his face anyway he wants. He also gets a one-molecule-thick costume which protects him from gas and bullets and allows him to survive underwater as well. "This belt which fits inside my costume," Werewolf reveals to his readers, "has a number of devices, some unfortunately still classified so I can't tell you about them, but all quite deadly and effective. Smoke bombs, acid pills, high energy capsules, radio pills . . . quite a few."

Werewolf's constant companion is Thor, one of the wolves he lived with in the Arctic. The CIA conveniently installed radio implants in Thor's head and Werewolf's throat so they could talk to each other directly. They also gave him a secret hideout—Wolf's Lair. "It's quite a place, completely secluded and accessible only by swimming under the lake to the far end out the mountain and into another smaller lake. Elaborate, but very necessary for my identity is tantamount."

WONDER WOMAN

DC Comics

	Issue #s
Published Summer 1942–2/86	1–329
Silver Age 5/58–11/69	98–185

Major Characters
Wonder Woman 98–185
Wonder Girl 105–107, 109, 111, 113–117, 119, 134, 144, 151–153
Wonder Tot 126, 130

Significant Issues
98—New origin and new art begins.

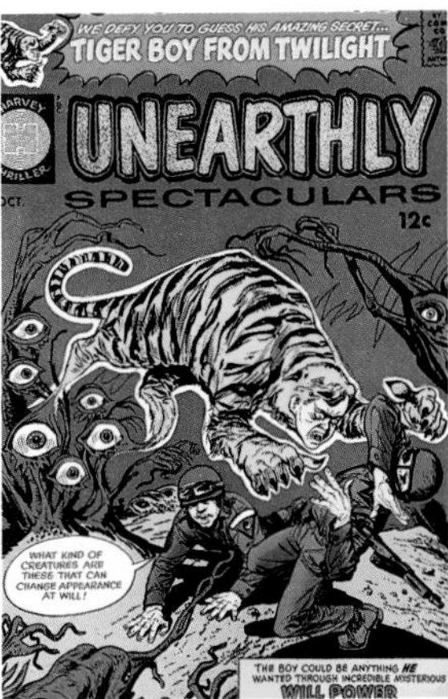

Unearthly Spectaculars #1 ©1965 Harvey Comics. Jack Sparling.

Werewolf #1 ©1966 Dell Comics. Tony Tallarico.

Wonder Woman #113 ©1960 DC Comics, Inc. Ross Andru, Mike Esposito.

World's Finest #114
©1960 DC Comics, Inc.
Curt Swan, Stan Kaye.

105—Wonder Woman's "secret origin." Wonder Woman appears as Wonder Girl.
106—Gains new power to "ride the air currents."
106, 107, 109, 111–117, 119, 133, 134, 135, 140, 144, 151–153—Wonder Girl appears.
107—First appearance of Merboy (later known as Merman), Wonder Girl's boyfriend.
122—First appearance of Wonder Tot.
124—Appearance of Wonder Family (Wonder Woman, Wonder Girl, and Wonder Tot).
126, 130, 133, 135, 140—Wonder Tot appears.
128—Origin retold of Wonder Woman's invisible airplane.
152, 159—Origin retold.
156, 159–164—Reprise of Golden Age (1940s) art and stories.
178—"Mod" look begins.
177—Supergirl appears.
179—Wonder Woman loses her powers and becomes a plainclothes adventuress.
180—Steve Trevor, Wonder Woman's boyfriend, dies.

Artists
Ross Andru 98–171
Irv Novick 172–175
Ric Estrada 176
Win Mortimer 177
Mike Sekowsky 178–185

Like all long-running DC superheroes, Wonder Woman has undergone several stages since her first appearance in 1941. A major change occurred in 1958 when editor and writer Robert Kanigher introduced a new art team and origin for Wonder Woman.

The late 1950s and early 1960s Wonder Woman stories were slanted for young girls. Such characters as Wonder Girl and Wonder Tot were added to make a Wonder Family. There were cute romance stories and mild adventure stories, with Wonder Woman fighting robot dinosaurs ("Suffering Sappho!") or evil doubles of herself ("Help me Hera!").

By 1966, Kanigher decided to go for the growing superhero audience by making Wonder Woman a replica of a 1940s comic book. He filled the stories with 1940s fashions and villains. The experiment failed, however, and in 1968 a new creative team took over the title.

In 1969, Wonder Woman loses her superpowers, becomes an independent businesswoman, and practices an Oriental discipline. As the 1960s end, her longtime boyfriend Steve Trevor is murdered. Mike Sekowsky, artist for the death issue, voiced the feelings of many readers: "Steve Trevor was dull and boring and I didn't like him much, so I disposed of him."

WORLD'S FINEST

DC Comics

	Issue #s
Published Summer 1941–1/86	2–323
Silver Age 5/58–12/69	94–190

Major Characters
Superman and Batman 94–190
Green Arrow 94–134, 136, 138, 140, 143, 145, 154, 159, 187
Aquaman 125–133, 135, 137, 139, 144, 147

Significant Issues
94—Origin of Superman-Batman team.
94, 100, 104, 117, 126, 129, 137, 148, 153, 172, 177, 183, 189, 190—Lex Luthor appears.
113, 123—Bat-mite and Mr. Mxyzptik appear.
113—First appearance of Miss Arrowette in Green Arrow.
99, 117, 139, 154, 157—Batwoman appears.
129, 156, 159, 166, 177—Joker appears.
133—Early "Aqua-girl" tryout.
141—New look begins with editor (Mort Weisinger) and artist (Curt Swan).
142—Legion of Super-Heroes appears.
161, 170, 179, 188—Contain reprints; 80-page, giant-sized issues.
167, 182—Supergirl appears.
168, 172—Legion of Super-Heroes members appear as adults.
169, 176—Supergirl and Batgirl appear together.
187—Origin of Green Arrow reprinted (1950s).

Artists
Dick Sprang 94–108, 110–115, 118, 119, 123, 131, 135, 161, 170, 179, 188 (Superman and Batman)
Curt Swan 109, 116, 117, 124, 141–160, 162–164, 166–169, 171–173, 177, 178, 184 (Superman and Batman)
Jim Mooney 120–122, 125–130, 132–134, 136–140, 188 (Superman and Batman)
Al Plastino 165 (Superman and Batman)
Pete Costanza 174 (Superman and Batman)
Neal Adams 175, 176 (Superman and Batman)
Ross Andru 180–183, 185–187, 189, 190 (Superman and Batman)
George Papp 94, 95 (Green Arrow)
Jack Kirby 96–99, 187 (Green Arrow)

Lee Elias 100–134, 136, 138, 140, 143, 145, 154, 159 (Green Arrow)
Nick Cardy 125, 126 (Aquaman)
Ramona Fradon 127–133, 135, 137, 139, 144, 147 (Aquaman)

DC Comics had so many successful superheroes in the 1940s that it often featured them in other comic books. Superman and Batman, each already starring in two books each of his own, were made the stars of *World's Finest* in 1941. Besides Superman and Batman, this extra-large-sized comic book (96 pages for 15 cents!) featured a string of secondary heroes all through the 1940s: Green Arrow, the Boy Commandoes, Tomahawk, etc.

By the 1950s, the (now 68 pages) 15-cent comic book could not compete with the 10-cent comics on the newsstands. DC editor Jack Schiff turned *World's Finest* into a regular length comic. Instead of dropping characters, however, when the page count declined, he put Superman and Batman together in one story in 1954. The experiment proved enormously successful and *World's Finest* became the regular meeting ground for Superman, Batman, and Robin, as well as an anthology title for other heroes like Aquaman and Tommy Tomorrow.

By 1965, Superman editor Mort Weisinger took over the title, and the Aquaman, Green Arrow, and Tommy Tomorrow strips were dropped in favor of book-length Superman and Batman stories.

X-MEN

Marvel Comics

	Issue #s
Published 9/63–	1–
Silver Age 9/63–12/69	1–63

Major Characters
X-Men 1–63
Cyclops 38–43
Ice Man 44–47
The Beast 48–53
The Angel 54–56
Marvel Girl 57

Significant Issues
1—Origin and first appearance of X-Men. First appearance of Magneto.
4—First appearance of Quicksilver and Scarlet Witch and the Brotherhood of Evil Mutants.
4–7, 11, 17, 18, 43–45, 50–52, 62, 63—Magneto appears.
6—Sub-Mariner appears.
9—Avengers appear.
10—First appearance of 1960s Ka-Zar.
12—Origin of Professor X.
13—Human Torch appears.
15—Origin of the Beast.
19—First appearance of the Mimic.
27—Spider-Man appears briefly.
27—Mimic joins X-Men.
28—First appearance of Banshee.
29—Mimic leaves X-Men.
35—Spider-Man appears.
39—New costumes.
49—First appearance of Polaris.
56—First appearance of Havoc.
62–63—Ka-Zar appears.

Artists
Jack Kirby 1–11
Alex Toth 12
Werner Roth 13–29, 31–33, 35, 42–57
Jack Sparling 30
Dan Adkins 34
Ross Andru 36, 37
Don Heck 38–42
George Tuska 43–47
Jim Steranko 50, 51
Barry Smith 53
Neal Adams 56–63

The original X-Men, a team of teenage mutants, consisted of Cyclops, Ice Man, the Beast, Angel, and Marvel Girl. The origins of the characters were revealed slowly over the series. From 1968 to 1969, each character was spotlighted in a miniseries that ran in back of the comic.

Jack Kirby drew the first 11 issues and did the layouts on the next half dozen. Stan Lee wrote the scripts for the first 19 issues, and then Roy Thomas took over. Other 1960s writers included Gary Freidrich and Arnold Drake.

The title was suspended in March 1970, and revived later that year with only reprints. In 1975 the new X-Men appeared in issue #94 and soon made it the most popular comic book of the late 1970s and 1980s.

X-Men #6 ©1964 Marvel Entertainment Group, Inc. Jack Kirby, Chic Stone.

CHRONOLOGY

SUPERHERO COMIC BOOKS, 1953-1970

1953

Superman television show premieres. Fawcett Publishing ceases publication of *Captain Marvel,* the most popular superhero of the 1940s (November).

Marvel Comics revives the Human Torch, Captain America, and Sub-Mariner (from the 1940s) for *Young Men,* an adventure/war comic.

Jack Kirby and Steve Ditko draw *Captain 3-D,* the first "three-dimensional" superhero comic magazine, for Harvey Comics. The first new superhero created since the 1940s.

Young Men #24 (December)
Captain 3-D #1 (December)

1954

Marvel Comics gives the Human Torch, Captain America, and Sub-Mariner their own comics (continuing the numbering from their 1940s series). The three heroes are also featured in *Men's Adventures.*

Joe Simon and Jack Kirby create the first new superhero comic book series of the 1950s, *Fighting American.*

DC Comics launches its first new superhero title of the 1950s, *Superman's Pal, Jimmy Olsen.*

Farrell Publications revives several 1940s superheroes created by the S.M. Iger comic book shop *(Phantom Lady, Flame).*

Charlton Comics reprints 1940s Blue Beetle stories in *Space Adventures* #13 and #14.

Sterling Publishing begins a four-issue run of the second new 1950s superhero, *Captain Flash.*

Sub-Mariner #33 (April)
Human Torch #36 (April)
Fighting American #1 (April)
Captain America #76 (May)
Men's Adventures #27 (May)
Superman's Pal, Jimmy Olsen #1 (September)
Space Adventures #13 (October)
Black Cobra #1 (October)
Captain Flash #1 (November)
The Flame #5 (December)
Phantom Lady #5 (December)

The Comics Code, a set of self-regulatory guidelines for comic books, takes effect in October.

1955

Three comic book publishers (Charlton, ME, and Farrell) try their hand at old *(Blue Beetle)* and new *(Avenger)* superheroes, but none lasts beyond the year.

DC Comics introduces an alien superhero—J'Onn J'Onzz, Manhunter from Mars—in *Detective Comics*.

The Avenger #1 (January)
Strongman #1 (February)
Blue Beetle #18 (February)
Samson #12 (April)
Wonder Boy #17 (May)
Detective Comics #225 (November)

1956

DC Comics revives an old 1940s superhero for its new tryout title, *Showcase*. With a new costume, identity, and origin, the Flash eventually becomes the most successful superhero to be introduced in the 1950s.

Charlton Comics continues to test the superhero market with *Nature Boy* and *Mr. Muscles*. Neither would last beyond a year.

Plastic Man, the only non-DC superhero from the 1940s to survive into the mid-1950s, disappears when Quality Comics ceases publication (November).

Showcase #4 (February)
Mr. Muscles #22 (March)
Nature Boy #3 (March)

1957

DC Comics introduces the Challengers of the Unknown, a heroic group of adventurers as drawn by Jack Kirby in *Showcase* #6.

After the success of the Superman TV show, DC Comics features Lois Lane in two issues of *Showcase* (#s 9 and 10).

With the Superman TV show ending production, story editor Mort Weisinger returns to his full-time duties as editor of the Superman line of comic books.

Showcase #6 (February)
Showcase #9 (August)

1958

DC Comics introduces the Legion of Super-Heroes, a group of 30th-century super teenagers, in *Adventure Comics*.

Jack Kirby draws the first several issues of the new *Challengers of the Unknown* title for DC Comics.

Superman's Girlfriend Lois Lane #1 (April)
Adventure Comics #247 (April)
Challengers of the Unknown #1 (April)
Strange Worlds #1 (December)

Kirby leaves DC Comics and begins drawing science fiction stories for Marvel Comics. The first new title featuring his work is called *Strange Worlds*.

1959

Marvel Comics launches *Tales to Astonish* and *Tales of Suspense*, two titles which will eventually become home for its 1960s superheroes.

After several appearances in *Showcase*, DC Comics gives the Flash his own comic book.

Editor and writer Robert Kanigher begins a new era in *Wonder Woman* with new origin and art team.

Supergirl first appears in *Action Comics*.

Joe Simon and Jack Kirby create two superheroes, the Fly and the Shield *(Double Life of Private Strong)*, for Archie Comics.

DC Comics revives a second 1940s superhero, the Green Lantern, for *Showcase* comics.

Tales to Astonish #1 (January)
Tales of Suspense #1 (January)
Flash #105 (March)
Wonder Woman #98 (April)
Action Comics #252 (May)
Double Life of Private Strong #1 (June)
Adventures of the Fly #1 (August)
Showcase #22 (October)

1960

DC Comics introduces the Justice League of America in *Brave and the Bold*.

Charlton Comics publishes the first adventures of Captain Atom by Steve Ditko in *Space Adventures*.

Green Lantern and the Justice League of America both receive their own books.

Brave and the Bold #28 (February)
Space Adventures #30 (March)
Green Lantern #1 (July)
Justice League of America #1 (October)

1961

DC Comics revives Hawkman *(Brave and the Bold)* and the Atom (*Showcase* #34). Aquaman appears in *Showcase* #30 to test the waters for his own comic.

DC brings back the Flash of the 1940s (*Flash* #123) as a prelude to resurrecting more Golden Age heroes.

Archie Comics begins the *Adventures of the Jaguar*.

Showcase #30 (January)
Brave and the Bold #34 (February)
Showcase #34 (September)
Adventures of the Jaguar #1 (September)
Flash #123 (September)
Fantastic Four #1 (November)

Marvel Comics publishes its first superhero comic book of the 1960s, the *Fantastic Four.*

Last year that comics cost 10 cents.

1962

DC Comics introduces the Metal Men (*Showcase* #37) and gives the Legion of Super-Heroes its own series (*Adventure Comics* #300). *Aquaman* and *Atom* receive their own titles.

Marvel Comics introduces the *Hulk*, Spider-Man (*Amazing Fantasy* #15), Thor (*Journey Into Mystery* #83), and Ant-Man (*Tales to Astonish* #35). The Sub-Mariner is revived (*Fantastic Four* #4), and the Human Torch is given his own series (*Strange Tales* #101).

Dell Comics publishes its first superhero comic book, *Brain Boy.*

Gold Key publishes its first superhero comic book, *Dr. Solar.*

Harvey Comics test the superhero market with reprints of its 1940s superheroine, the *Black Cat.*

Aquaman #1 (January)
Showcase #37 (April)
Brain Boy #1330 (April)
Incredible Hulk #1 (May)
Fantastic Four #4 (May)
Atom #1 (June)
Amazing Fantasy #15 (August)
Journey Into Mystery #83 (August)
Tales to Astonish #35 (September)
Adventure Comics #300 (September)
Strange Tales #101 (October)
Dr. Solar #1 (October)
Black Cat #63 (October)

1963

Marvel gives Spider-Man his own comic, and introduces Dr. Strange (*Strange Tales* #110) and Iron Man (*Tales of Suspense* #39). It also publishes two new team titles, *Avengers* and *X-Men.*

DC Comics introduces the Doom Patrol in *My Greatest Adventure* #80. The *Metal Men* also receive their own book.

Amazing Spider-Man #1 (March)
Tales of Suspense #39 (March)
Metal Men (May)
My Greatest Adventure #80 (June)
Strange Tales #110 (July)
Avengers #1 (September)
X-Men #1 (September)

1964

Marvel Comics revives Captain America in the *Avengers* and also premieres its last major new 1960s superhero, *Daredevil.*

DC Comics revamps Batman with a "New Look" (*Detective Comics* #327). The *Doom Patrol* and *Hawkman* receive their own books.

Charlton Comics brings back a 1940s/50s superhero, the *Blue Beetle.*

Archie Comics launches the *Shadow*, a superhero adaptation of the 1930s pulp character.

Avengers #4 (March)
Doom Patrol #86 (March)
Hawkman #1 (April)
Daredevil #1 (April)
Detective Comics #327 (May)
Blue Beetle #1 (June)
Shadow #1 (August)

1965

ACG premieres two new superheroes, Magicman and Nemesis, in *Forbidden Worlds* and *Adventures into the Unknown*, respectively.

Dell Comics introduces *Nukla*.

Tower Comics launches a new line of superhero comics with *THUNDER Agents*.

Archie Comics adds the *Mighty Crusaders* to its superhero lineup.

Charlton Comics brings back a second superhero, *Captain Atom*.

Forbidden Worlds #125 (January)
Adventures into the Unknown #154 (February)
Metamorpho #1 (July)
Nukla #1 (October)
THUNDER Agents #1 (November)
Mighty Crusaders #1 (November)
Captain Atom #78 (December)

1966

Batman TV show premieres (January).

Harvey Comics becomes the seventh publisher to enter the 1960s superhero market with *Spyman, Fighting American*, and other titles.

Tower Comics adds *Dynamo* and *NoMan* to its titles.

Charlton Comics brings out *Thunderbolt* and *Judomaster*.

MF Enterprises publishes its first superhero title *Captain Marvel.*

DC Comics revives *Plastic Man* and gives the *Teen Titans* their own comic.

Marvel Comics give *Thor* his own title.

Teen Titans #1 (January)
Thunderbolt #1 (January)
Thor #126 (March)
Captain Marvel #1 (April)
Judomaster 89 (May)
Dynamo #1 (August)
Spyman #1 (September)
Fighting American #1 (October)
The Spirit #1 (October)
NoMan #1 (November)
Plastic Man #1 (November)

1967

A new comic book company, Milson Publishing, debuts with *Fatman the Human Flying Saucer* but folds the same year.

Charlton Comics launches its last new 1960s superhero title, *Peacemaker.*

Gold Key publishes another new superhero character, the Owl.

DC Comics publishes its last major new superhero title of the 1960s, the *Spectre.*

Archie Comics, Dell Comics, Harvey Comics, and MF Enterprises cease publishing superhero comics.

Peacemaker #1 (March)
Fatman the Human Flying Saucer #1 (April)
The Owl #1 (April)
Spectre #1 (November)

Heath, Russ. Interview. *Comics Journal* #117 September (1987).

Heck, Don. Interview. *Comics Feature* #21 November (1982).

Horn, Maurice, ed. *World Encyclopedia of Comics*. New York: Chelsea House Publishers, 1976.

Jacobs, Will, and Gerard Jones. *The Comic Book Heroes*. New York: Crown Publishers, 1985.

Kane, Gil. Interview. *Comics Journal* #64 July (1981).

Kane, Gil, and Howard Chaykin. Interview. *Comics Journal* #91 July (1984).

Kanigher, Robert. Interview. *Comics Journal* #s 85 & 86, October/November (1983).

Kanigher, Robert. "Detour! . . . Danger Trail." *Robin Snyder's History of Comics*. Vol 1 #4 April (1990).

Kirby, Jack. Interview. *Golden Age of Comics* #6 November (1983).

Kirby, Jack. Interview. *Comics Feature* #44 May (1986).

Kirby, Jack. Interview. *Comics Interview* #41 (1986).

Kirby, Jack. Interview. *Comics Journal* #134 February (1990).

Lee, Stan. *Origins of Marvel Comics*. New York: Simon and Schuster, 1974.

Lee, Stan. *Son of Origins of Marvel Comics*. New York: Simon and Schuster, 1975.

Lee, Stan. Interview. *FOOM* #17 March (1977).

Lee, Stan. Interview. *Comics Journal* #42 October (1978).

Lee, Stan. Interview. *Comics Interview* #5 July (1983).

Lee, Stan. Interview. *Comics Feature* #44 May (1986).

Lillian III, Guy H. "Mort Weisinger: The Man Who Would Be Superman." *Amazing World of DC Comics* #7 July/August (1975).

Lillian III, Guy H. "Strange Schwartz Stories." *Amazing World of DC Comics* #3 November (1974).

Maronie, Sam. "Joe Sinnott." *Comics Scene* #2 March (1982).

Mougin, Lou. "The Back-Seat Super-Heroes" (5-part series). *The Comics Reader* #s 197–201, December–May (1981–1982).

Murray, Will. "Project: Captain America." *Comics Scene* #14 August (1990).

O'Neil, Dennis, ed. *Secret Origins of the Super DC Heroes*. New York: Crown Publishers, 1976.

Overstreet, Robert M. *Overstreet Comic Book Price Guide*. Cleveland, Tennessee: Overstreet Publications, 1990.

Romita, John. Interview. *FOOM* #18 June (1977):.

Rovin, Jeff. *The Encyclopedia of Superheroes*. New York: Facts on File Publications, 1985.

Rozarkis, Bob, and Jack C. Harris. "The Incredible Infantino." *Amazing World of DC Comics* #18 September (1975).

Schiff, Jack. "Reminiscences of a Comic Book Editor." *Overstreet Comic Book Price Guide.* (1983).

Schwartz, Julius. Interview *Amazing World of DC Comics*. #14 March (1977).

Schwartz, Julius. Interview. *Comics Feature* #30 July (1984).

Schwartz, Julius. Interview. *Comics Interview* #88 (1990).

Severin, Marie. Interview. *FOOM* #16 December (1976).

Shooter, Jim. "Marvel and Me."
Overstreet Comic Book Price Guide #16 (1986).

Simon, Joe. "Memoirs of a Comic Book Maker."
Comics Scene #15 October (1990).

Smith, Barry.
Comic Art Convention Program Guide. (1975).

Sprang, Dick and Charles Paris. Interview.
Amazing Heroes #167 June 15 (1989).

Steranko, Jim.
The Steranko History of Comics, I & II.
Reading, PA.: Supergraphics, 1970, 1972.

Stewart, Bob. "Memories of Wally Wood."
Comics Journal #70 January (1982).

Swan, Curt. "An Interview with Superman's Main Artist." *Comics Journal* #73 July (1982).

Thomas, Roy. Interview.
Comics Feature #44 May (1986).

Toth, Alex. Interview.
Comics Journal #98 May (1985).

Van Hise, James.
The Art of Al Williamson. San Diego: Blue Dolphin Enterprises, 1983.

Weston, James K.
The Schwartz Index. : James K. Weston, 1965.

Wrightson, Berni. Interview.
Comics Journal #100 July (1985).

INDEX

T

U

V

W

X

Y

Z